DATE DUE

NOV 5 1986			
JUN 1 9 1992			

The Jews of Palestine

M. AVI-YONAH

The Jews of Palestine
A Political History
from the Bar Kokhba War
to the Arab Conquest

Schocken Books · New York

First Schocken edition 1976

© in this translation Basil Blackwell 1976

Library of Congress Cataloging in Publication Data

Avi-Yonah, Michael, 1904–1974.
  The Jews of Palestine.

  Translation of author's Bi-yeme Roma u-Bizantiyon.
  Bibliography: p.
  Includes index.
  1. Jews in Palestine—History.   2. Jews—History—
70–1789. 3. Palestine—History—70–638.   1. Title.
DS123.5.A943   956.94′02   74–26912
ISBN 0–8052–3580–9

This volume is translated and adapted
by the author from M. Avi-Yonah:
Geschichte der Juden im Zeitalter des Talmud
Hebrew editions 1946, 1952, 1962, 1969
German edition published by Walter de Gruyter & Co.,
Berlin, 1962

Printed in Great Britain

Contents

Illustrations   ix

Abbreviations   x

Preface to the English Edition   xii

Publisher's Note   xvi

From the Preface to the Hebrew Edition   xvii

Introduction   1

I The Era of Reconstruction   15
   1. *The Demographic and Economic Situation*   15
   2. *Repairing the Damage of a Lost War*   25

II A Political Compromise:
The Jewish Problem from the Roman Point of View   35
   1. *The Background*   35
   2. *The Emperors and Judaism; 'Antoninus' the Friend of
     the Patriarch Judah I*   39
   3. *The Roman Governors and the Jews*   42
   4. *The Roman Policy of Appeasement*   44

III The Compromise between the Jews and Rome
from the Jewish Point of View   54
   1. *The Renewal of the National Establishment. The Patriarchate* 54
   2. *Roman Rule in Jewish Eyes*   64
   3. *The Jews and Greek Culture*   71
   4. *The Age of Revolts Comes to an End*   76

v

5. *The Limits of the Compromise : Jerusalem and the Proselytes*   79
6. *Conclusion*   83

IV Palestine Jewry and the Crisis of the Empire
in the Third Century   89
1. *The Crisis and its Causes*   89
2. *Aspects of the Political Crisis in Palestine*   91
3. *The Economic Results of the Political Crisis : Conscription,*
   Forced Labour, New Taxes   93
4. *The Collection of the New Taxes and its Abuses*   98
5. *The Inflation*   102
6. *The Social Results of the Economic Crisis*   104
7. *The Counteraction of the Patriarchate*   108

V The Political Results of the Crisis   115
1. *Introduction*   115
2. *The Dissension between the Patriarch and the Scholars*   116
3. *The Functions of the Patriarchate Limited* de facto
   and de jure   121
4. *The Decline in the Status of Palestinian Jewry*   123
5. *The Relations with the Roman Government in the Times*
   of Crisis. Palmyrene Domination   125
6. *The People Changes its Attitude to Roman Rule. The*
   Revival of the Messianic Hopes   127
7. *Summary of the Effects of the Crisis*   132

VI Judaism and Christianity
to the Accession of the Emperor Constantine   137
1. *Introduction*   137
2. *Palestine Jewry and the Judaeo-Christians. The 'Minim'*   138
3. *Christianity and its Relation to Judaism till the End of*
   the Second Century   145
4. *The Relaxation of Tension and Cessation of Disputes in*
   the Third Century   149
5. *Origen and Eusebius on Judaism and the Jews*   150
6. *Christian-Jewish Relations on the Eve of the Christian*
   Empire   152
7. *Summary*   154

VII The Beginnings of Christian Rule in Palestine   158
PART I: THE REIGN OF CONSTANTINE I (324–337)   158
1. *Christian Rule and its Immediate Consequences*   158
2. *The Character and Policy of Constantine ; his Laws*
   concerning the Jews   161
3. *The Jewish Reaction to Constantine's Policy*   166

PART II: THE REIGN OF CONSTANTIUS II (337–361)　174
    4. *New Anti-Jewish Legislation*　174
    5. *The Revolt against Gallus Caesar*　176

VIII　The Emperor Julian and the Jews　185
    1. *The Rise of Julian and his Political Principles*　185
    2. *Julian's Relation to Judaism in Theory and Practice*　187
    3. *Julian's Meeting with a Jewish Deputation at Antioch.*
       His Decision to Return Jerusalem to the Jews　191
    4. *Jewish Reactions to Julian's Proclamation*　193
    5. *The Beginnings of the Restoration of the Temple. The*
       Work Interrupted. Julian's End　198

IX　The Great Assault on the Jews
and Judaism, 363–439　208
    1. *The Division of the Period*　208
    2. *The Period of Transition*　209
    3. *The Rise of Theodosius I, the Orthodox Emperor*　210
    4. *The New Legislation concerning the Jews*　213
    5. *The Christians Become the Majority in Palestine*　220
    6. *The Jewish Share in the Material Prosperity of the*
       Byzantine Period　221
    7. *The Spiritual Situation of Palestine Jewry. The*
       Messianic Hopes　223
    8. *The End of the Patriarchate*　225

X　Division in the Christian Camp: Two Generations
of Peace and Strengthening for the Jews　232
    1. *The Division in the Christian Camp*　232
    2. *The Influence of the Ecclesiastical Divisions on*
       Byzantine Policy　234
    3. *The Influence of the Byzantine Divisions on Palestine*
       Jewry　236
    4. *The Situation of the Jews in Palestine towards the End*
       of Byzantine Rule　237
    5. *The Jews and the Samaritan Revolts*　241

XI　The Emperor Justinian and the Jews　246
    1. *Renewal of the Anti-Jewish Legislation*　246
    2. *The Conflict between Byzantines and Jews in the Red Sea*　251
    3. *The Successors of Justinian*　253

XII　The Persian Invasion
and the End of Byzantine Rule　257
    1. *The Last War between Persia and Rome*　257
    2. *The Persian Invasion and the Jews*　259

3. *The Persians Conquer Palestine with Jewish Aid*   261
4. *Jewish Rule in Jerusalem*   265
5. *The Change of Persian Policy. Expulsion of the Jews from Jerusalem*   268
6. *The Restoration of Byzantine Rule in Palestine. The Revenge of Heraclius*   270
7. *The Arab Conquest*   272
8. *Conclusion*   275

Index   279

Illustrations

Map 1 Palestine after 135   17

Diagram showing the Number of Known Jewish Settlements   20

Map 2 The Revolt against Gallus Caesar   177

Diagram of the Temple Mount in the Time of Julian   202

Map 3 The Persian Invasion, 614   264

Abbreviations

Ant.   Josephus, *Antiquities of the Jews*

BJ   Josephus, *Bellum Judaicum*

b   *Babylonian Talmud*

CAH   *Cambridge Ancient History*

CIJ   J. B. Frey, *Corpus inscriptionum judaicarum* Vols. I–II, Rome 1947, 1952

CIL   *Corpus inscriptionum latinarum*

CJC   *Corpus juris civilis* ed. Mommsen, Krüger, Schöll, Kroll, Berlin, 1929

CSCO (SS)   *Corpus scriptorum christianum orientalium* (*Scriptores syrii*)

C Th   *Codex Theodosianus*

EJ   *Encyclopaedia Judaica*, A–L, Berlin 1928–1934

GCS   *Griechisch-christliche Schriftsteller* (ed. Berlin Academy)

IEJ   *Israel Exploration Journal*

j   '*Jerusalem*' *Palestinian Talmud*

JQR   *Jewish Quarterly Review*

M   *Mishnah*

PG   *Patrologia graeca* ed. J. B. Migne

PJB   *Palästinajahrbuch*

PL   *Patrologia latina* ed. J. B. Migne

PO   *Patrologia orientalis*

QDAP   *Quarterly of the Department of Antiquities in Palestine*

R   *Midrash Rabbah*

RB   *Revue biblique*

REJ   *Revue des études juives*

ROC   *Revue de l'Orient chrétien*

SEG *Supplementum epigraphicum graecum*
SHA *Scriptores Historiae augustae*
  T *Tosefta*
ZDPV *Zeitschrift des deutschen Palästina-Vereins*

Preface to the English Edition

The present work was written in the years 1944–46; it was published in Hebrew under the rather romantic title: *Bi-yimey Roma u-Vizantion* ('In the Days of Rome and Byzantium'), the publisher considering the matter-of-fact title proposed by the author: *Political History of the Jews of Palestine from the Bar Kokhba War to the Arab Conquest* to be unattractive, in fact only good enough for a sub-title. For whatever reason the Hebrew edition found sufficient favour in the eyes of the reading public to justify a reprint in 1952; a third edition, corrected and enlarged, was issued in 1962; and reprinted in 1969. A German edition was published in 1962 by W. Gruyter & Co., Berlin, as Volume II of their series, 'Studia Judaica'; the editor then chose the, in our opinion, still more misleading title *Geschichte der Juden im Zeitalter des Talmud*.

The original Hebrew text was written for a public well versed in Jewish history but less familiar with the general course of events in the Roman or Byzantine empires. This historical background needed, therefore, a somewhat more elaborate treatment than seemed necessary for educated English or American readers. In preparing the German (and now the English text) various passages could be omitted as redundant. Moreover, several paragraphs which no longer reflected the author's opinion, or which contained statements disproved by later discoveries, have been either deleted or modified. Other passages have been added, reflecting recent work in the appropriate fields. Two longer descriptions of the art and archaeology of the Jews in the Roman and Byzantine period have also been added (pp. 74–6; 238–40 of this edition).

In this edition various mistakes pointed out by reviewers have been corrected; in this respect the author is especially grateful to P. L. Ligiér,

S.J., L. Prijs and E. Demougeot. As regards the many fundamental objections to the point of view from which this book was written, the reviewers are entitled to their own views; but the author claims the same right for himself.

Our basic views have not changed; the reader will find them on pp. xix–xx reproduced from the preface to the original Hebrew edition.

We would like to add a few words on the Talmudic sources, which have served as a basis for a large part of this work. These sources consist of two entirely different kinds of material. One kind is concerned with the interpretation of the law of the Pentateuch, the so-called 'Written Law'. The discussions, as reported, lead to definite legal decisions, which were henceforth regarded as 'the Oral Law' (not having been originally written down), the presumption being that the later refinements were, so to speak, already contained in the bud in the Mosaic law. This kind of material is known as the *Halakah*. The second part of the Talmudic material consists of passages of homiletic or legendary nature meant to instruct or to edify morally; it is known as the *Haggadah*. The most ancient part of the Talmud is the *Mishnah*, a compilation of *halakot* edited by the patriarch Judah I (late second to early third century AD). The Mishnah is divided into 63 tractates, the result of the work of the scholarly scribes and the learned men from the time of Ezra onwards. Those scholars who contributed to the Mishnah are known as the *Tannaim* (singular: *Tanna*). They are grouped into five generations, of which only the three last are of interest here: the third (*c.* 130–160), the fourth (160–200), and the fifth (200–220). The Mishnah is composed almost entirely of halakic (juristic) material. Matters which for one reason or another found no place in the Mishnah, were collected separately into the *Tosefta* ('Addendum') which is arranged on the same principle as the Mishnah.

After the completion of the Mishnah, the further elaboration of the Oral Law was continued on parallel lines in Palestine and Babylonia. The scholars who were engaged on this task are known as the *Amoraim* (sing. *Amora*). They too are divided into five generations: first (220–250), second (250–280), third (280–320), fourth (320–360) and fifth (360–400). About 400 their work ended in Palestine with the final editing of the *Palestinian Gemara*; this, together with the Mishnah, forms what is commonly (but wrongly) called the *Jerusalem Talmud* (here abbreviated j). The parallel labours of the Babylonian scholars continued till about 525; they formed, again together with the Mishnah, the *Babylonian Talmud* (abbreviated b). In both cases the Gemara did not embrace the whole of e Mishthnah.

In both Talmuds the Gemara is composed of a mixture of halakic and haggadic elements; it represents a kind of record of proceedings of a discussion which lasted for centuries. The various opinions recorded reflect the currents of opinion in the Judaism of that time, but they can no more be regarded as representing Judaism in general than would the records of Parliament or Congress represent public consensus in England or the United States. Only the final resolution, the *halakah*, was regarded as binding, the rest being only records of various scholarly opinions. If in our text a 'legal' decision is mentioned this refers to the various *halakot* which were regarded by the Jews of Roman Palestine of their own free will as legally binding.

The third group of rabbinical sources are the *Midrashim* (sing.: *Midrash*). These are a collection of commentaries on the various books of the Bible, and are of a purely haggadic character. They are called partly by the names of the biblical books they comment upon, and partly by various more or less fanciful appellations, such as *Sifre*, *Sifra*, *Mekilta*, *Shoher Tob*, *Tanhuma*, *Pesiqta* etc. The most important is the *Midrash Rabbah* the ('Great Midrash'), which is quoted by the name of the biblical book commented upon with the addition of an *R*, e.g. Genesis *R*, Song of Songs *R*, Lamentations *R*, etc.

The Mishnah (M) and Tosefta (T) are quoted by tractate, chapter and halakah, e.g. M Abodah Zarah 4,5 = Mishnah tractate Abodah Zarah chapter 4, halakah 5). The Babylonian Talmud is quoted by tractate and the leaf of the standardized editions, each leaf having two pages (*a* and *b*), thus b Yebamot 47b stands for page b of leaf 47 of the tractate Yebamot. The 'Jerusalem' Talmud is quoted by tractate, chapter and halakah with the prefix j; in addition the leaf of the *editio princeps* (Venice 1523) and one of its four columns of text (a–d) is usually added, e.g. j Bikkurim 1,4–64a means chapter 1, halakah 4 of the tractate Bikkurim, first column of leaf 64.

The tractates of the Mishnah are grouped into six *Sedarim* ('Orders') as follows:

   I. *Zeraim* ('Seeds') with the tractates Berakot, Peah, Demai, Kilaim, Shebiit, Terumot, Maaserot, Maaser Sheni, Hallah, Orlah, Bikkurim.

  II. *Moed* ('Festivals'): Shabbat, Erubbin, Pesahim, Shekalim, Yoma, Sukkah, Beitsah, Rosh ha-Shanah, Taanit, Megillah, Moed Katan, Hagigah.

 III. *Nashim* ('Women'): Yebamot, Ketubot, Nedarim, Nazir, Sotah, Gittin, Kiddushin.

 IV. *Neziqin* ('Torts'): Baba Kamma, Baba Metsia, Baba Batra, Sanhedrin, Makkot, Shebuot, Eduyyot, Abodah Zarah, Abot, Horayot.

  V. *Qodashim* ('Holy Things'): Zebahim, Menahot, Hullin, Bekorot, Arakin, Temurah, Keritot, Meilah, Tamid, Middot, Kinnim.

 VI. *Toharot* ('Purifications'): Kelim, Ohalot, Negaim, Parah, Toharot, Miqwaot, Niddah, Makshirin, Zabim, Tebul Yom, Yadayim, Uktsim.

The standard English translation of the Mishnah is by H. Danby, Oxford 1933; that of the Babylonian Talmud the Soncino edition edited by I. Epstein, London 1948–52. A few Midrashim have been translated (Midrash Rabba ed. H. Freedman and M. Simon, London 1939 and Psalms (*Shoher Tob*) by W. G. Brande, New Haven 1959, the *Mekilta* by J. Z. Lauterbach, Philadelphia 1933–35.

The patriarchs of the House of Hillel have been mentioned so often in the following pages that a table of the whole dynasty might prove useful:

Hillel I ('the Elder')—time of King Herod
Gamliel I (teacher of the apostle Paul)
Simeon I (at the time of the First Roman War 66–74)
Gamliel II (at Yabneh, third generation of Tannaim)
Simeon II (elected at Ushah, fourth generation of Tannaim)
Judah I ('Rabbi')—fifth generation of Tannaim
Gamliel III (first generation of Amoraim)
Judah II (second generation of Amoraim)
Gamliel IV (third generation of Amoraim)
Judah III⎫
Hillel II ⎬ (fourth generation of Amoraim)
Gamliel V ⎫
Judah IV ⎬ (fifth generation of Amoraim)
Gamliel VI (400–*c.* 425).

In the transliteration of the Hebrew and Aramaic words and names into Latin characters, we have used a simple system designed to be intelligible to the reader who does not know those languages. The exceptions to this rule are the proper names which appear in the Old and New Testaments; here the common spelling has been adopted. The Greek, Roman and Byzantine words and names appear in their Latin form.

The proper appellation for the scholarly class which dominated Jewish society in the period here dealt with, and whose labours resulted in the talmudic literature, is a matter of special difficulty. We have chosen to call them rabbis (corresponding to the Hebrew terms *hakam* (literally 'sage'), or *zaken* (literally 'elder'). The reader must remember that in this context 'rabbi' does not have its modern sense, i.e. a minister of a Jewish congregation. The scholars who formed the 'rabbinate' were the products of the great schools attached to the sanhedrin, or the pupils of single scholars; they were 'ordained', i.e. received the *semikah* and could henceforth themselves teach or decide on points of religious law. However, the *semikah* was by no means equivalent to appointment to a salaried post. Only the 'ordained' scholars could take part in the discussions of the sanhedrin. On the whole their position resembled that of the doctors promoted by the great medieval universities.

One more term which has not been used in its usual sense is that of 'Hellenes' to describe the adherents to the old religion in the late Roman Empire; the common term 'pagan', which literally means 'backwoodsmen', is unnecessarily abusive; besides the term 'Hellenes' was in common use in the late Roman period for just this purpose.

In conclusion I would express my deepest gratitude to those who have laboured to improve the contents and language of my text: Dr. Oswyn Murray, Tutor in Classics and Fellow of Balliol College, Oxford in the first place; he was also the *spiritus movens* of the English edition; next Miss Susan Williams, former reader of the publishers, and Mr. J. K. D. Feather of the same firm. Mr. Feather has been a staunch friend in need throughout the long labours which preceded publication.

Hebrew University, Jerusalem
February 1973

Publisher's Note

Professor Avi-Yonah himself wrote this English version of *Geschichte der Juden im Zeitalter des Talmud*, basing it on both the German and the Hebrew editions. We regret that he died before the manuscript was sent to the printer and was unable to see the book through the press. The publisher's grateful thanks are due to those who assisted in this task. Mr. C. T. R. Hayward of Worcester College, Oxford, read and checked the manuscript and Mrs. Tessa Rajak of Reading University read the proofs. Miss Hannah Katzenstein, formerly of the Israel Department of Antiquities, Jerusalem, also corrected the proofs, supplied missing references and prepared the index, which is based on the German.

From the Preface
to the Hebrew Edition

Lytton Strachey has defined the qualities that make a historian as three: a capacity for absorbing facts, a capacity for stating them, and a point of view. My learned colleagues will decide whether I have been able to fulfil the first condition, and the readers can judge the second. It seems worthwhile, however, to state briefly the point of view from which this work was written.

As the Jews of Palestine of a certain period, and their history, are the subject of this book, the events are described with reference to this; but as they did not live on a desert island, and because their political fate depended on forces which were active outside Judaism and outside Palestine, exterior events had to be described as far as necessary.

The book has been written by a Jew about Jews. I have endeavoured, however not to regard everyone who acted against our nation in the past as a criminal or a rogue. In all generations people have acted from motives of their own and have often come into conflict with Jewish interests. This fact does not by itself make them moral delinquents. Polemics with enemies of our people are right and proper in the present, but a historian should approach the past *sine ira et studio*.

We are dealing here with political history, that is with the complex of facts, problems and tendencies, which we are used to calling 'politics' and which are focused upon the life of an organized community. This is not always the case; recent history has shown that a political will can serve as a substitute for a state. In the period dealt with here the Jews of Palestine had no state, but they still kept their political will; the book ends at the moment when that will became temporarily extinct. Economic and spiritual matters have been dealt with only as far as they affected political

xvii

history. We are of course aware that this period was one of an enormous spiritual activity and saw the final edition of the Mishnah and the compilation of the Gemara, which were of vital importance for many centuries of Jewish history.

This work is based upon the assumption that the Jewish nation as such and not any metaphysical force, has been the main factor in shaping Jewish history in all periods, from the time of Moses to the present day. National consciousness is like a pulse—sometimes it beats strong and clear, and sometimes it is difficult to catch—but there is no life without it. The national strivings of Israel, the manifestations of which have varied from time to time, existed at all times throughout Jewish history.

The author remembers with gratitude the late G. Allon, who gave him valuable advice and help. Prof. B. Mazar and Prof. W. Z. Hirschberg have both helped, each in his own sphere of learning; they deserve our thanks.

Introduction

The thousand years of Jewish history from Alexander's conquest to the Arab invasion (332 BC to AD 640) are characterized by the struggle of Judaism with its Greco-Roman and Byzantine environment, the culture of of which throughout these centuries was based on Greek foundations. Judaism was then threatened by two diametrically opposed dangers. The physical existence of the Jewish nation in its homeland had to be secured; as a relatively small nation it was in constant danger of destruction. The second danger, that of peaceful dissolution in the Greek environment, was even greater. In both cases the continuity of Jewish existence would be in jeopardy; but the second peril, that of peaceful assimilation, was more dangerous, just because it was not a material one. Even if the physical existence of the nation, or of the individuals composing it, could be secured in such a case, it would lose its vitality rooted in the Law. Jewish nomocracy was created in the period between the end of the Babylonian exile and the beginning of the Hellenistic age; it remained for centuries the foundation of Judaism. The Law replaced for a long time the independent commonwealth of the Davidic dynasty; the high priest, priests and the Temple now stood for the king, nobles and court who were no more.

The Persian Period: The Priestly Rule and the Atrophy of Political Life

The early years after the return from the Babylonian exile—roughly till the dedication of the Second Temple in 519 BC—were a kind of continuation of the history of the kingdom of Judah before the destruction of

I

Jerusalem. A scion of David (at first Sheshbazzar, later on Zerubbabel)
administered the country under the suzerainty of the Persian king and his
satrap, more or less as did the last king of Judah under the Babylonians.
The attempts of Zerubbabel to obtain independence,[1]* recall similar efforts
of Hezekiah, Josiah and Zedekiah. With the failure of these separatist
trends the Davidic dynasty disappeared finally from the political scene.
The rule over Judah remained in the hands of the high priests and of the
nobles who advised them. The period of priestly rule over Judah is
characterized by a deliberate attempt to make the people lose all interest
in politics. The aim of the new régime, the establishment of a nomocracy,
could be achieved only in a period of political calm. The only notable
development in the fifth and fourth centuries BC was the tightening of the
rule of the priests and of their allies, scribes (*soferim*). The nomocratic
theory of the state became the only valid one, as the potentially hostile
elements lost their power. Because of the endeavours of the priestly
administration to keep the country quiet at all costs, this period of political
atrophy and loss of will was a time of economic and demographic con-
solidation.

The Hellenistic Period: Cultural Division and Religious Persecution

The conquest of Alexander, and even more the rule of the Ptolemies
(312–198 BC) and of the Seleucids which followed, brought politics to life
again. The mere fact that Judaea was now situated geographically on the
border between two rival dynasties (Egypt in the south and Syria in the
north) caused a certain degree of polarization. A considerable section of
the Jewish population refused to abstain from sharing in the increasing
economic activity of the Hellenistic period; they wanted to have their part
in the material advantages of this process. Nor can one disregard the
attraction of Greek cultural life, both its literature and its visual arts; the
pleasant Greek way of living also had its allurements.

The conflicts between these tendencies and the traditional form of
Jewish life created a division among the Jews both on the ideological and
the personal plane. The high priests from the house of Onias were by
their function representatives of the traditional party; their rivals, the
house of Tobias, favoured assimilation to the ruling culture. The Tobiads
did indeed lose their power in the troubled times which followed the
Seleucid conquest of Palestine; but at the same time the conservative
priestly caste split asunder. Many priests, and especially the younger ones
who lived in Jerusalem, and who were expected to become the future
rulers, began to adopt Greek ways of life. At the beginning such imitation

* All notes are to be found at the end of the chapter to which they refer.

of Greek ways was modest enough; it remained a matter of dress and sports. However, anyone familiar with the close connection of Greek athletics and Greek religion could foresee much danger to the traditional ways of Judaism in these apparent trifles. The reformers were opposed by the league of the Hasidim (i.e. 'The Pious Ones') whose strength lay in the country outside Jerusalem. The conservative elements in Judaea could appeal to the 'charter' of Antiochus III, granted in 198 BC.[2] In this document the king recognized the right of the Jews to live according to the laws of their ancestors; the high priests still had to be confirmed by the king, but he was limited in his choice by dynastic and ritual considerations. When Antiochus IV (175–164 BC) deposed a high priest, he did what the Persian king had done before him,[3] and thus remained within the bounds of the charter; but when he appointed a certain Menelaus, whose qualifications were at least dubious,[4] he infringed the charter of his father and Jewish law at the same time. This arbitrary act was the result of his complete misjudgement of the real state of opinion in Judaea. Antiochus and his advisers seem to have believed the assertions of the radical Jewish Hellenizers, who assured them that the majority of the Jewish nation was ready to abandon the religion of its ancestors and to adopt not only Greek culture, but even Greek religion. The Hellenizers seem to have imagined a kind of syncretism of Judaism and Greek religion, such as was common at that time. Most of the oriental nations living under Hellenistic rule—or at least their upper classes—had adopted Greek ways of life, including a syncretistic faith. Even the local dynasts, who opposed the Hellenistic monarchies on the political plane, appreciated Greek culture.[5] Such Hellenization seemed to the Greeks a natural process, because in their eyes the orientals were barbarians without cultural values of their own. Starting from these mistaken premises, Antiochus IV tried to establish Greek culture and religion in Judaea by force. Jerusalem was occupied by the royal army; under its protection a new quarter was built side by side with the old city, and the fortress Acra was built in its centre. The Temple was re-dedicated to Dionysus Sabazius, whose name had some similarity with that of the Lord Sabaoth; another temple, probably dedicated to the Olympian Zeus, Antiochus' favourite deity, was at least begun. The opposition which these radical measures evoked seemed senseless to the king and his advisers, and they decided to break it by terror. The exercise of the Jewish religion was forbidden and those transgressing the prohibition were threatened with death. It was the first religious persecution known in history.

The Maccabaean Revolt

The Maccabaean revolution, which broke out in reply to this terrorization from above, was basically conservative. The Hasidim, who were a majority in the army of Judas Maccabaeus, fought to restore the legal position which had existed under the charter of Antiochus III, i.e. they wished for religious freedom under Seleucid suzerainty. Only a minority of the rebels strove from the beginning for complete political independence; it is true of course that this minority included the leaders of the revolt and their adherents: they believed that the tolerance which had characterized Persian rule could not be expected from a Hellenistic monarchy. Judas Maccabaeus and his brothers assumed that spiritual freedom for Judaism could be assured only in a state of political independence. In spite of this divergence of aims the two groups (Hasidim and Maccabaeans) worked and fought together in the first stage of the revolt, at least till the restoration of worship in the Temple. As soon as the successors of Antiochus IV began to appreciate the position realistically and appointed a high priest Eliakim (Alcimus) whose credentials were unimpeachable, the Maccabaean forces were split. The majority of the Hasidim, who desired only religious freedom, accepted the new high priest. Judas and his adherents had to leave Jerusalem and retreated into the mountains of Gophna.

Soon, however, it became clear that Eliakim could not or would not give up his Hellenizing ways. On the contrary, he seems to have supported religious assimilation, for instance by breaking down the balustrade which prevented Gentiles from entering the Inner Temple. When the local Greek commander, Nicanor, openly threatened the Temple and its priests, even the Hasidim had to admit that the original conception of Judas Maccabaeus was correct and that there could be no sure hope of religious freedom under foreign rule. This was the moment when the Jewish nation opted mentally for political freedom. Although the battle continued for many years, the decision to seek freedom was taken once and for all and could not be reversed. The objective causes of the success of the Hasmonaeans were the weaknesses of the Seleucid state, and in particular the struggle for succession within the dynasty between the descendants (or those who pretended to be such) of Seleucus IV and those of his brother Antiochus IV. The appointment of Jonathan the son of Mattathias the Hasmonaean as governor of Judaea *and* as high priest (for the Hasmonaeans, luckily, were of priestly descent) made him a royal official in theory, but an independent ruler in practice. It marked the breakthrough of the trend for complete national independence. The whole nation enthusiastically supported the new régime, except for a dwindling group of partisans of the Zadokite priestly family (i.e. the house of Onias, who lived in exile in Egypt, having built their own temple at Leontopolis) and of course apart from the extreme Hellenizers. The remaining adherents of Hellenism who survived in the country outside their fortress (the Acra of Jerusalem) were persecuted by Jonathan (they are called 'the impious' in the contemporary sources).[6] With the fall of the Acra in 141 BC—during the reign of Simeon, Jonathan's brother and successor— Hellenism had apparently ceased to exist in Jewish lands.

The Hasmonaean State and its Problems

The victory of the Hasmonaeans—at first in Judaea and then in the whole of Palestine, and the restoration of the Davidic kingdom to almost its whole extent, seemed at first a final and complete solution to the problems of the Jewish nation. A sovereign Jewish state could assure its citizens a way of life according to the Law. The enlargement of the nation's territory and in particular access to the sea (both of which Judaea had lacked in the Persian and the Hellenistic periods) appeared to ensure the nation's future in the material sense also.

However, it was precisely the completeness of their victory which endangered the Hasmonaeans. The new rulers soon became aware that in the second century BC a state could not survive if it followed a way of life which was planned for a Persian province four centuries earlier. Judaea was still surrounded by enemies on all sides. These included both the refugees from the conquered Greek cities, who had fled to their compatriots in the neighbouring countries, and other oriental nations such as the Nabataeans and the Ituraeans. In the beginning of the Maccabaean revolt these had been the natural allies of the Jewish rebels, but in the course of time the former friends had fallen out over the division of the spoils. The Jewish state could only survive if it adopted the technical achievements of the Hellenistic world, especially in matters of administration, warfare, technology and economics. The problem was how to limit the effect of these vital but alien factors, and prevent them from 'contaminating' all parts of public life. As a result of the needs of the state we observe a paradoxical situation. The Hasmonaeans (especially those of the third and fourth generation) at one and the same time carried on a war of destruction against the Greek colonies in their vicinity, and fought the Seleucid kings, while adopting a great deal of the way of life of their enemies. Finally the great popular party of Pharisees (the 'separated ones') —descendants in the direct line of the Hasidim from the early days of the revolt—turned against the dynasty and its Sadducean adherents. The great mass of the people supported the Pharisees. The political and military necessities of the state were not as clear to them as to the kings, who had gained practical experience in the difficulties of administration and warfare. In principle the opponents of the Hasmonaeans were ready to leave the political affairs to them (even if some were opposed to the assumption of the royal title by Alexander Jannaeus, 103–76 BC, and his

successors; for in their eyes only the descendants of David were entitled
to the title of king). In any case, all demanded the separation of political
and religious leadership, that is to say they required the Hasmonaeans to
give up the high priesthood. The Pharisees did not consider the difficulties
which this dyarchy would be likely to cause. They were also on the whole
opposed to the policy of conquest of the Hasmonaeans and the political
and military steps which this policy involved. They were joined in their
opposition by various extremist sects, including the Community of the
Covenant (the so-called Dead Sea Sect). This latter was bitterly opposed
to the Pharisees on the religious plane. The first signs of a split in the
nation appeared in the reign of John I Hyrcanus. Under Alexander
Jannaeus, his son, and his grandsons Judah II Aristobulus and John II
Hyrcanus, the disunion erupted into a civil war. Jannaeus hired foreign
mercenaries to keep his people in check and persecuted his opponents
with barbaric cruelty; on one occasion he executed hundreds of them.
The Pharisees on the other hand did not hesitate to engage in open treason
and to ally themselves with the enemies of the state. They appealed for
help to the Seleucids, the Nabataeans and finally also to the Romans.

The Roman Conquest

Although the Roman general Pompey appeared with his legions before the
walls of Jerusalem only in 63 BC, the influence of Rome in the affairs of
the East had been felt a long time before. One can even venture to state
that the whole Hasmonaean period of Jewish history was dominated by
the great events which resulted in Roman dominion over the eastern basin
of the Mediterranean. Already in the time of Antiochus III the Romans
had dealt the Seleucid empire a deadly blow at Magnesia (189 BC). After
that they followed a consistent policy aimed at the dismemberment of the
Seleucid state. Their policy caused the counter-attempt by Antiochus IV
to unite his kingdom through a policy of rapid Hellenization, and thus led
indirectly to the Hasmonaean revolt. The Roman government supported
the Hasmonaean revolt in its beginnings. In fact Roman intervention in the
East had become almost inevitable after Magnesia, in view of the decay of
the Seleucid monarchy. Unfortunately it occurred in Judaea at the worst
possible moment, when the country was in the throes of a fratricidal
struggle. As a result the conditions of the final capitulation were especially
hard. The Jews lost more by Pompey's arrangement than all their neighbours. They lost access to the sea. Their territory was split up into two
parts situated at some distance from each other: Galilee in the north and
Judaea proper (with Idumaea and Peraea beyond the Jordan) in the south.
In spite of all this, the Jews had kept a good deal of the Hasmonaean con-

quests, in particular the territories in which the Hasmonaeans had settled Jews, or had forced the inhabitants to adopt Judaism. The religious policy of the Hasmonaeans was thus retroactively vindicated in Jewish eyes, for all its odiousness. In the end Julius Caesar returned to the Jews Jaffa and the 'great plain' (the Valley of Jezreel). Regaining access to the sea was especially important at a time when the Jewish Diaspora began to play an ever increasing role in Jewish life.

The Roman conquest had two additional consequences: Hellenism was strengthened throughout the Orient, and the Hasmonaean dynasty perished in the conflict with Rome. The Roman decision to save Greek culture in the East was deeply rooted in the influence Greek culture had gained at Rome from the third century onwards, which was especially strong among the powerful aristocracy. Once in power in the East, the Romans restrained all the elements which had fought Greek culture and which, by the middle of the first century, had almost annulled the effects of Alexander's conquests. As the power of Rome was infinitely superior to that of the declining Hellenistic monarchies, most of the opponents of Greek culture gave up the struggle, at least openly. The Nabataeans and Ituraeans made their peace with Rome and with Hellenism. The Parthians did indeed continue the struggle, but they were soon confined to the areas east of the Euphrates. The Arabs of the desert were outside the reach of Roman power, but they were commercially dependent on Rome. Only the Jews continued the apparently hopeless battle. Their country was geographically part of the Mediterranean area and thus belonged, in Roman eyes, to the Roman sphere of interest. Consequently they were now exposed to the full pressure of Roman power and of the Roman army. They continued nevertheless stubbornly to resist Graeco-Roman culture. The way they clung to their traditions and their struggle against alien culture is astonishing, if one remembers that the culture they were fighting against was a world civilization dominating (at least on the surface) all the countries in their vicinity. Although the last Hasmonaeans were unable to carry on the struggle with success, and although the Herodian dynasty, which followed the Hasmonaeans, aimed at a compromise and did not in any circumstances plan to turn against its Roman benefactors, the Jewish resistance against Graeco-Roman culture did not weaken. It became stronger year after year.

The Messianic Movement in the Time of Herod

The ideological cause of this paradoxical situation was the rise of the Messianic movement. The fall of the Hasmonaean state and the loss of national independence led to a deep spiritual crisis amongst the Jews. In the time of the First Temple the prophets had pointed out that the people were guilty of idolatry and that their sins would be punished. When the kings of Assyria and Babylonia did carry out the punishment, they appeared only as scourges in the hands of a wrathful God. The sins of the people were thus atoned for and the nation regained its mental balance.

In contrast with the times of their forefathers the Jewish people in the first century BC did not feel guilty of sinning against their ancestral God. Idolatry had been thoroughly rooted out by the first Hasmonaeans. Apart from a few eccentric sects the nation felt like Job; it was being unjustly persecuted. If the tribulations from which it suffered were not a result of its sins, certainly the Messianic age was drawing near. The suffering and shame could only be forerunners of the Day of Judgement. The Messianic belief became for the first time in history a political factor of great importance. Most of the Jews began to believe that the existing order of things could not last much longer.

Herod and his successor were continuously aware of this dangerous mood. The bloodshed accompanying the rise of Herod and the rule of terror which had served to strengthen his throne had created a deep chasm between the dynasty of the 'Edomite slave' and the majority of his subjects. Part of the Pharisees and the Essene sect, as well as the Babylonians whom Herod had settled beyond the Jordan were ready to support Herod's rule, or at worst to tolerate it, even if they did regard him as a 'punishment from heaven'. Herod's policy was directed towards keeping this base of his power among the Jews, and he succeeded on the whole throughout his reign in avoiding crises which would have shaken his throne.

Herod's dynasty lasted eighty years. Throughout this time the Jewish nation was divided politically into five parties. Their relation to the reigning dynasty and to Graeco-Roman culture served as the criterion of each group. Two of the parties affirmed the dominant culture, two denied it. For many years the undecided middle held the balance. The elements approving of Greek culture and of Roman domination were the Herodian court and its partisans, the 'Herodians'.[7] In their opinion a compromise with the environment was a vital necessity, even if they understood that it could only be achieved gradually. The people had to be weaned out of their isolation, and to learn to appreciate Greek cultural values. In the meantime the rulers would avoid carefully any political or religious commotion, and in particular any conflict with the Romans. Such a collision would of necessity cause the destruction of the Jewish state, and with it, as the Herodians believed, of the Jewish nation. One cannot deny the logic of their approach, even if events gave the lie to their opinions. The tendency to cultural compromise even had a certain success in the field of art and ideology; in the course of time the attitude of the Jews to Hellenic culture did change.[8] We can follow this process best in the fields of art, numismatics and epigraphy. It is enough to compare the coins of Herod I and those of his grandson Agrippa I.[9] The grandfather had to introduce a few pagan symbols on the sly, and had to refrain from all images of man and beast. Agrippa I, although regarded as a much better Jew than the 'Edomite slave' who was one of his ancestors, could allow himself to represent on his coins not only the emperor, but even himself and his son. People forgave the grandson what they would not have tolerated from the grandfather. The efforts of the Herodians to create a bridge between the Jews and Graeco-Roman culture were not quite vain, if we disregard political relations. Here the time at their disposal was not enough for the achievement of lasting results.

Allied with the Herodians was the Neo-Sadducean party. They had hardly more than the name in common with the old Sadduceans, the state party of the Hasmonaean period. The new aristocracy was composed of families, partly of Idumaean, Egyptian or Babylonian origin, who had crystallized around the high priestly clans favoured by the king. These families formed a close-knit oligarchy, administering the 'king's land' (*chōra*), i.e. the half of the kingdom which was not shared out between the semi-autonomous Greek cities, and which was inhabited by the great mass of Jews. The social position and the estates of this new aristocracy (for the old one had perished with the Hasmonaeans) were entirely dependent on the continuation of the Temple services and in general on the stability of the existing social order. A destruction of the Temple would make the high priestly families redundant both socially and economically. Naturally the high priests and their party were interested in a compromise with Rome. However, as they were the official guardians of the religion in Israel, they could not go as far on the way of assimilation as the Herodians.

The opponents of Rome included the remnants of the old Sadducee party, who had managed to survive the many attempts at revolt in the time of Hyrcanus II and the blood-bath of Herod after the fall of Jerusalem. These 'Sadducees' had in Hasmonaean times supported the dynasty in its national policy; now that the king and people went different ways they kept faith with the people and not with the king. They were joined by a group recruited mainly from the separatists and some of the Pharisees. Those were the people to whom the fall of the Hasmonaean monarchy had caused a deep psychic shock, and who were daily expecting the Last Judgement. This group wished to repeat the heroic exploits of the first Maccabees. They were the nucleus of the 'zealots' or 'sicarii', the implacable enemies of Rome. For a long time they could only carry on guerilla warfare. In the end the majority of the Pharisees were converted to their Messianic ideal. However, this process took a long time, during which the

mass of the people followed the moderate Pharisees and vacillated from
one point of view to another.

The Roman government employed all kinds of devices to keep Judaea
loyal. The importance of this small province was due to its geographical
position. It was the land-link between the two centres of Roman power in
the East, Syria and Egypt. In the second place its importance lay in the
number of Jewish communities dispersed through Egypt, Asia Minor and
even Italy. The Jews living in the Diaspora kept up strong religious and
emotional ties with Jerusalem, and were accordingly most sensitive to
what was happening there. The Roman government was interested—
within limits—in gaining the goodwill of the Jews both in Judaea and in
the Diaspora and went a long way to meet their demands. Jewish privileges
included the right to an autonomous community organization, the right to
live according to their traditional laws, and freedom from military service
in the *auxilia*. In some cases Jews were entitled to become full citizens of
the Greek cities in the East. However, as the taking up of such rights
involved worship of the local Gods, religious Jews could not do so.[10] In
Judaea the Romans made additional concessions: for instance, the
legionary ensigns, which were decorated with images of gods, were
carried round Judaea while the legions themselves marched through it,
but infringement of the sanctity of the Temple was punishable with death,
even if the culprit was a legionary.

In order to keep Judaea quiet, the imperial government for a time tried
indirect rule. A native dynasty was left in possession, first the Hasmonaean
Hyrcanus II, and then Herod and his dynasty. However, this particular
experiment miscarried, as it did in most of the other provinces. When the
failure of the Herodian epigoni made direct Roman administration a
necessity, the imperial government did not select its representatives well.
The officials left in charge were of a low rank: they were procurators,
i.e. fiscal officials.

The deepest shock was caused to the Jews by the insane decision of the
emperor Caligula to have his statue put up in the Temple at Jerusalem. On
that occasion the Jewish people as a whole lost the last remnants of its
trust in the restraint and tolerance of the Roman rulers. Although the
experiment itself miscarried, a second Caligula could any day follow the
first. Under these circumstances the opinion became almost general that
in order to safeguard its future the Jewish nation should now do as it had
done in the days of the Maccabees, even if this meant taking up arms
against Rome. This view began to prevail about the middle of the first
century AD. The Pharisees, who formed the majority of the nation, now
split into two groups. A minority, led by Yohanan ben Zakkai, was ready
to continue to carry the burden of Roman rule; but the majority joined the
Zealots. The inhabitants of the great Jewish centres in Galilee, the cities

or Sepphoris and Tiberias, were also interested in keeping the peace, mainly for material reasons. Smaller groups, including the nascent Christian community in Jerusalem, took the road to peace. It seems, however, that the Essenes (including the 'Dead Sea Sect') supported the Zealots. Under these circumstances began what may be called (from the Jewish point of view) the First Roman War or (from the Roman) the First Revolt. It lasted from 66 to 74.

The First Roman War

The war began as a popular rising under the zealot Menahem. Soon after its outbreak it changed its character. Part of the high priestly aristocracy joined the revolt. These circles were well versed in the affairs of the Roman empire, and believed that the revolt could succeed. They counted on the general dissatisfaction with the emperor Nero, both in Rome and in the provinces. A war between Rome and Parthia, which seemed to loom just over the horizon, was another source of hope. In such cases the Parthians would evidently support the Jewish rebels, as the Romans had supported the Hasmonaeans against the Seleucids. Other revolts could break out among the provincials under Roman rule. Moreover, the Jews abroad, especially those of Egypt (numbering about a million) and those of Babylonia (who lived under Parthia and were free from Roman rule) were likely to assist the rebels.

These calculations were not without a solid foundation. It was owing to them that a Jewish defeat was put off for four long years. Nevertheless, the aristocrats now in charge at Jerusalem miscalculated the time factor. The revolt against Nero took place two years after the outbreak of the Jewish revolt. It could only slow down the Roman campaign, but could not avert the final disaster. Moreover, the aristocratic way of conducting the war was mistaken from the start. Against all reason they attempted to create a Jewish field force which could meet the Roman legions face to face. As they could not under the circumstances raise within a very short time an army equivalent to that of Rome, they took refuge in the fortresses of Judaea and Galilee. Giving the efficient siege methods of the Romans, the fall of such strongholds was only a matter of time. The high priestly generals were loth to carry on guerilla warfare in the open, as was demanded by the Zealots. The despair which grew among the people as one defeat followed another resulted in a series of inner revolts within the revolt. In such inner struggles the remnants of Jewish power were destroyed. The slow, cautious, systematic but implacable process of Roman strategy, which was executed by Vespasian with consummate mastery, ended with the destruction of the Jewish state and of its great symbol, the Second Temple. However, even after the disaster the bulk of the Jewish population remained settled on its land. A temporary leadership was constituted at Jamnia (Yabneh); it consisted of a patriarch from the House of Hillel and of a revived Sanhedrin.

The Period of Transition (74–132)

The Roman government could hope that with the destruction of the Zealots and the burning of the Temple, the carriers and focus of the Messianic movement respectively, spirits would calm down. The two generations between the First and Second Roman Wars were a period of transition, in which no significant changes occurred till the very end. Jerusalem remained in ruins and the Tenth Legion camped on its remains; but Jews were allowed to live in the Holy City. The lost war did not mark the end of the Zealots so much as of the 'Herodians' and the high priestly party. These groups which had advocated compromise with Rome lost their whole standing. Their power bases, the Temple and the royal court, were no more. The chasm between Judaism and Graeco-Roman culture had become deeper than ever. The moderate Pharisees, who were the one surviving peace party, were now the real rulers of the nation. Even the Zealots had not entirely disappeared. When the people were told that the Emperor Hadrian had decided to turn the Holy City into a Roman colony, almost the whole nation, and the majority of its leaders, were ready to begin a new war.

The Second Roman War and the Hadrianic Persecution

The history of the Second Roman War (the so-called Second Revolt or revolt of Bar Kokhba) proved that the Jews had learnt from the mistakes of the first. This time everything was carefully prepared and the leaders did not have to improvise, as had happened in 66. Arms were accumulated, fortifications prepared in the field, funds were collected. The revolt broke out in 132 as soon as all preparations were completed and as soon as the emperor Hadrian was safely out of the country. The leadership of the revolt remained constant throughout its course, and it was remarkably united. Rabbi Akiba, the spiritual leader of the generation, headed the Sanhedrin, the 'Prince' (*nasi*) Simeon bar Kozziba (called Bar Kokhba— 'Son of a Star') commanded the army and was in charge of the administration till the end. The objective conditions for the revolt were now much worse than in the time of Nero. The rule of Hadrian was generally acknowledged, the Parthians lived in peace with Rome, after Hadrian had given back to them the conquests of his predecessor Trajan. The Jewish Diaspora was still suffering from the consequences of the two great revolts in Egypt and Cyprus under Trajan. Nevertheless Bar Kokhba succeeded in carrying on with the war for over three years (132–135). The fight was carried out in the open field, in which the Romans suffered heavy losses and some defeats. The rebels forced the Roman garrison of Jerusalem to leave. A whole legion, the XXII Deiotariana, disappeared in the course of the war. Bar Kokhba established his government in Jerusalem and probably resumed the Temple ritual as far as possible. We lack a Josephus to give us a just appreciation of the Bar Kokhba war. The few documents recovered from the Judaean desert are no substitute for a connected narrative.[11]

This second Jewish revolt caused the Roman government to attempt a radical solution of the 'Jewish Question'. They decided to expel those Jews who still survived in and around Jerusalem, and to suppress systematically such Jewish religious practices as were regarded as the root of the evil afflicting the province. The Hadrianic persecution lasted two or three years: circumcision, the teaching of the Law and ordination of Rabbis were punishable with death. However, as it was not carried out systematically, it failed in its purposes. The chief sufferers were the Jews of Galilee, who in the main had kept away from the revolt. The communities of the Diaspora, whether big or small, were not molested. Even had the government of Hadrian decided to extend the persecutory legislation over the whole of the empire, the Jewish communities of Babylonia would still have been beyond its reach. The Hadrianic persecution can therefore be regarded more as an expression of the hatred of Jews and all things Jewish which inspired the inhabitants of the Roman Orient, a hatred due to the fright which Jewish successes during the Bar Kokhba war had given to the Gentiles. In any case, Hadrian was dead barely two years after the suppression of the revolt. His successor, Antoninus Pius, made a vain effort to continue the same policy, but soon afterwards changed his opinion and chose the way of tolerance.

If we regard Jewish history as a whole, we cannot deny that in a certain sense the Zealots were successful in their struggle. The destruction of the Temple and the elimination of Jewish statehood widened an already existing gulf between Judaism and its environment to such a degree that no conciliation in the fields of art and literature could bridge it. Judaism secluded itself within its own boundaries. It succeeded in detaching itself more or less completely from the common fate of the ancient world. If Israel has kept its national identity to this day, the only nation of antiquity to do so, and has survived the decline and fall of the ancient world, this is due in no small measure to the warriors of its two lost wars against Rome. From the point of view of Jewish nationality their desperate undertakings thus appear in a positive light, however much one can regret the amount of suffering caused to the community and to individuals.

At the end of the Hadrianic persecution the leaders of the Jewish nation had no time to devote themselves to such considerations. They faced the practical task of restoring, so far as was possible, national life in the land of Israel. With the assembly held by the survivors in Usha about 140 we begin the story of the five centuries following the last wars fought by the Jews as a nation at least until our own times.

Notes to Introduction

1. Haggai 2, 23.
2. Josephus, *Ant.* XII, 145–6.
3. Ibid., XI, 298.
4. In 2 Macc. 4, 23 Menelaus is called the brother of Simeon, a 'Benjaminite' (ibid., 3, 4); the suggested emendation to 'Minjaminite' seems probable; for the family of priests called Minjamin see 2 Chron. 31, 15.
5. Plutarch, *Crassus* 33.
6. 1 Macc. 9, 73.
7. Matthew 22, 16.
8. See below, pp. 71–6.
9. G. Hill, *British Museum Catalogue of Greek Coins: Palestine*, London, 1914, pp. 220–7, 237.
10. V. Tcherikover, A. Fuks, *Corpus Papyrorum Iudaicarum* I, Cambridge, Mass., 1950, pp. 39–41.
11. P. Benoit, J. T. Milik, R. de Vaux, *Les grottes de Murabba'at*, Oxford, 1961, Nos. 24, 25, 29, 42, 43–8; Y. Yadin, *IEJ*, 11 (1961), pp. 40–52; B. Lifshitz, *Aegyptus*, 42 (1962), pp. 240–56; Y. Yadin, *Bar-Kokhba*, London, 1971, pp. 172–83.

I

***

The Era of Reconstruction

***

1. *The Demographic and Economic Situation*

Early in the reign of the emperor Antoninus Pius (137–161) the repressive edicts of Hadrian were repealed. The leaders of the Jewish nation were at last able to take counsel together; they met for this purpose in the small Galilean town of Usha. It was a sombre meeting at a sombre hour. All present had undergone many hardships. Some, like Rabbis Meir, Yose bar Halafta and Yohanan the sandal-maker had fled abroad, and only now were able to return. Others, Rabbis Simeon bar Yohai and Eliezer ben Yose the Galilean had been hiding within the country and had been saved in a miraculous manner. They came to the meeting full of memories of the days of the persecution, and well aware of the seriousness of the situation.

At the time the meeting at Usha was convened, the Jews of Palestine had passed through the three-and-a-half years of Bar Kokhba's war, followed by five or six years of savage persecution. Tens of thousands had perished, myriads had been sold into slavery in the neighbouring countries or had been carried into bondage over the seas. Multitudes had fled the country; refugees from Judaea crowded into the ports of the Mediterranean.[1] A great part of the national wealth had been destroyed, or had passed into alien hands. The time had now come to count the losses and to consider how best to restore the country and the nation.

Much of the damage was indeed irreparable. The most serious was the total destruction of Jewish settlement in Judaea proper. Since the days of the Maccabees the Jews had been settled in two big compact areas: one was formed by Judaea, their ancient homeland, which now included the adjacent regions called Idumaea and Peraea; the other area was Galilee.

In the war of Bar Kokhba most of the fighting took place in Judaea, and especially in the hilly region known as 'The King's Mountain' (*Har ha-Melekh*; called in Greek *Oreine*), in the area between Bethel in the north, Kefar Lekitaya and the Emmaus—Beth Gubrin-Hebron road in the south-west and south.[2] In the third year of the war the Jewish forces were finally cooped up in this area and all the localities within it were wiped out in the fighting.[3] After the fall of Bar Kokhba's last fortress, Beth-Ter (Bethar), Hadrian ordered the expulsion of the remaining Jews from Judaea. The Jews of the districts of Oreine, Gophna, Herodium[4] and Akraba[5] were affected. Before Bar Kokhba's war we know the names of seventy-five settlements in Judaea inhabited by Jews; after the fall of Beth-Ter there is no evidence of Jews continuing to live in even a single one of them.[6] What made matters worse from the Jewish point of view was that the Roman government proceeded systematically to re-settle Judaea with Gentiles, mainly Syrians and Arabs.[7] There could be always hope of returning to a deserted countryside; there could be little expectation of re-establishing the lost towns and villages once they had been occupied by others under the protection of the Roman government.[8]

Some Jewish villages managed to cling to the fringes of the Judaean hills. They were concentrated in three areas: in the Jordan valley, on the desert fringe to the south and in the coastal plain in the west.

From the time of Herod and his dynasty extensive plantations had been established in the southern part of the Jordan valley; their main products were dates and balsam. After the extinction of the house of Herod these plantations became the property of the Roman treasury. The new rulers had to continue to employ Jews, because only they understood how to tend the profitable plants. When Rabbi Yose mentioned the Jews who worked as 'harvesters of balsam from Engedi to Haramatha',[9] he referred to these villages extending from the western shore of the Dead Sea to the plain east of the Jordan. There remained about a dozen villages in the Jordan valley. The settlements south of the Dead Sea, such as Zoar and its dependencies, belong to the same category.

The so-called *Darom* ('South') was another area still inhabited by Jews after 135. The surviving settlements here formed a belt of territory stretching from Engedi on the Dead Sea in the east[10] to the district of Gerar in the west.[11] Somehow this area managed to remain unaffected by the destruction wrought by Bar Kokhba's war. Seven Jewish villages continued to exist there. Living as they did on the border of the desert and the town, the population was concentrated for defence in a few big villages: Thella, En Rimmon, Carmel etc.

The districts of Lydda, Jamnia and Azotus had become Jewish in the early days of Hasmonaean rule. After the destruction of Jerusalem, the Patriarch and the Sanhedrin had settled at Jamnia (Yabneh). These areas

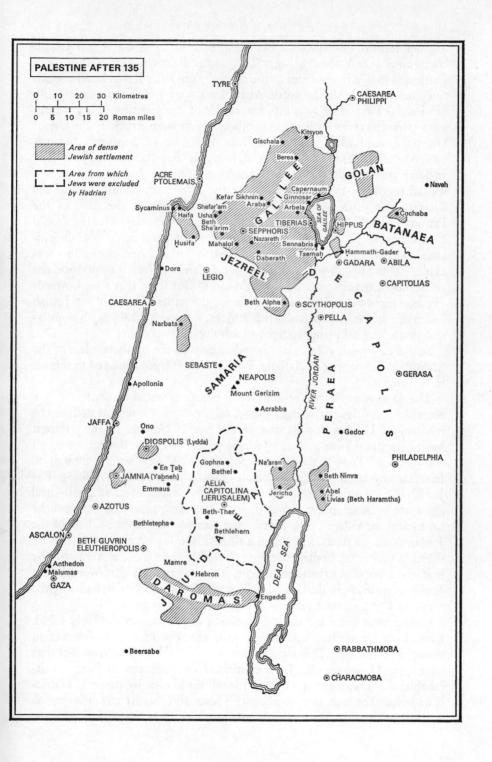

PALESTINE AFTER 135

| 0 | 10 | 20 | 30 | Kilometres |

| 0 | 5 | 10 | 15 | 20 | Roman miles |

Area of dense
Jewish settlement

Area from which
Jews were excluded
by Hadrian

TYRE

CAESAREA
PHILIPPI

Kitsyon

Gischala

GOLAN

Naveh

Berea

GALILEE

ACRE
PTOLEMAIS

Capernaum

Kefar Sikhnin
Ginnosar

Sycaminus

Shefar'am
Araba
Arbela

BATANAEA

Haifa
Usha

SEA OF GALILEE

Cochaba

Beth
She'arim
SEPPHORIS

TIBERIAS

HIPPUS

Husifa

Nazareth

Sennabris

Mahalol

Daberath

Tsemah

Hammath-Gader

JEZREEL

GADARA
ABILA

Dora

LEGIO

D
E
C
A
P
O
L
I
S

CAPITOLIAS

CAESAREA

Beth Alpha
SCYTHOPOLIS

Narbata

PELLA

SEBASTE

SAMARIA

NEAPOLIS

RIVER JORDAN

Apollonia

Mount Gerizim

PERAEA

GERASA

Acrabba

JAFFA

Ono

Gedor

DIOSPOLIS (Lydda)

Gophna

Na'aran

PHILADELPHIA

'En Ṭab

Bethel

JAMNIA (Yabneh)

Beth Nimra

Emmaus

AELIA
CAPITOLINA
(JERUSALEM)

Jericho

Abel
Livias (Beth Haramtha)

AZOTUS

Beth-Ther

ASCALON

Bethletepha

Bethlehem

J
U
D
A
E
A

DEAD SEA

BETH GUVRIN
ELEUTHEROPOLIS

Mamre

Anthedon

Hebron

Maiumas

GAZA

D A R O M A S

Engeddi

Beersabe

RABBATHMOBA

CHARACMOBA

did not remain unscathed in Bar Kokhba's war, but the urban Jewish communities and some villages had escaped destruction. Other Jews continued to live in the cities of the coastal plain from Raphia in the south to Ptolemais (Acre) in the north. At Lydda the control of the municipality did indeed for a time pass into the hands of the Gentiles. This we can learn from the coins with pagan symbols which were struck by the city of Diospolis, as Lydda was called from the time of Septimus Severus onwards (208–209).[12] Many Jews did, however, stay there and at Jamnia.[13] In later generations efforts were made to keep for Judaea at least one special privilege, the proclamation of the intercalary month and of the dates of the main holy days.[14] However, as early as the days of the Patriarch Gamliel II it had to be admitted that 'intercalary months should be declared in Judaea, but if the declaration has been made in Galilee, it should stand'.[15] In the time of the Patriarch Judah I one more effort was made. Rabbi Hiyyah was sent down to En Tab near Lydda to perform the ceremony of proclaiming the New Moon.[16] But from that time onwards circumstances proved too strong even for the natural desire of the Jewish leadership not to lose contact with Judaea. Evidently, the Jewish population of the coastal plain managed to survive, but only just.

Scattered Jewish villages continued to exist in the northern plain of the Sharon, in the district of Narbata. Five Jewish villages managed to remain in this region.[17]

The Decapolis (league of ten Greek cities) tolerated on its territory a score or so of Jewish villages. Most of these were concentrated in the territory of Hippus-Susitha east of the Sea of Galilee. In the adjacent territories (the Golan and the Bashan) which had been the patrimony of the house of Herod, the Jewish population proved strong enough to frustrate any attempts of the Roman government to establish cities. The Jewish communities in that region were of the same half-urban, half-rural character as those in the coastal plain. There the proportion between the towns and the villages with Jewish communities was 14 to 25. East of the Jordan it was 14 to 20. More than a third of the Jewish communities were urban in character. Considering that the urban communities were, unit by unit, more populous than the villages, it seems probable that over half the Jewish population in the coastal plain and beyond the Jordan had adopted a way of living characteristic of the Jews of the Diaspora.[18]

Galilee thus remained the main bastion of Judaism in the Holy Land. Even this province had not escaped quite unscathed from the destruction wrought by the war. The names of seven villages disappear from our lists after 135. However, the Jews continued to form the majority of its inhabitants. The number of Jewish localities known by name in Galilee is 63 before the war, and 56 after it. There were hardly any non-Jewish settlements in this area. The two main cities, Tiberias and Sepphoris, remained Jewish towns. After the fall of Bar Kokhba the Roman government indeed made an effort to set up Gentile municipalities in these towns, but this attempt failed within a very short time for lack of popular support.[19] Galilee also contained a number of Jewish townlets big enough to accommodate the patriarch and the Sanhedrin (Shefaram, Beth Shearim), or to serve as the headquarters of regional authorities (Dabberat, Mahalol, Arabah[20] etc.). However, the Jewish population of Galilee was not crowded into a few cities or townlets. In the main it was a population of peasants living in the countryside. Of the 56 Jewish settlements known after the war of Bar Kokhba, no less than 52 were villages or semi-rural communities. Obviously Galilean Jewry remained, both actually and potentially, the most weighty Jewish factor in the political events in Palestine. At the same time it became the principal target for the enemies of Israel.

It is very difficult to arrive at a reliable estimate of the numbers of Jews and Gentiles living in Palestine at that period. We can only compare the number of places where Jews were known to live with the total number of localities. Of course very many settlements have disappeared without leaving a name. In Palestine west of the Jordan we know of over 2,000 ruins of the Roman period, whereas all the place-names quoted in ancient sources do not exceed 500: three-quarters of the places inhabited in antiquity have left no mark in ancient literature. Another objection to the counting of place-names only is that in this way a big city and a tiny village are counted as units of equal value.

It is only after stating these reservations that we may venture to place before the reader the following estimate of the number of Jews and Gentiles in Palestine after 135. It seems that after the defeat of Bar Kokhba the Jews formed about three-quarters of the population of Galilee and about one-quarter of the population of the coastal plain and the lands east of the Jordan.[21] The whole population of Palestine on both sides of the Jordan has been estimated for this period as about two and a half million. In comparing the rates of density of settlement in the various parts of the country, we arrive at an estimate of the total Jewish population of Palestine before the war of Bar Kokhba as 1,300,000. After the fall of Beth-Ter there were left only between seven and eight hundred thousand, of which between three and four hundred thousand were concentrated in Galilee.[22] These rough estimates indicate the full extent of the disaster which befell Jewry in the Bar Kokhba war: but it also goes to show that the survivors and especially the Jews of Galilee formed a numerical factor of sufficient importance to be taken into account by the Roman government.

The strength of Palestine Jewry lay not only in its numbers, but also in the solid basis of its economy. Here too we lack precise statistical data. A review of the available sources, especially of the Mishnah, shows that the Jews of Palestine were still a nation of peasants, with the addition of a considerable number of craftsmen and a smaller number of merchants. As an economic entity they were almost self-sufficient, except as regards a few luxury imports.

The Number of Known Jewish Settlements 135–640

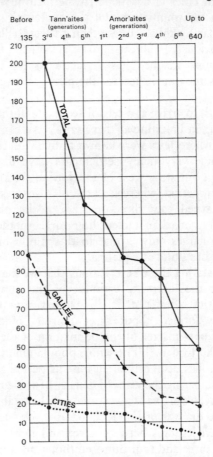

The function of agriculture as the economic basis emerges from an analysis of the thirty-nine kinds of work forbidden on the Sabbath as listed by the Mishnah.[23] Farming and food processing account for 18 of these, the production of garments (including weaving and spinning) for 13, building 2 and all other crafts and trades only 6. This impression of a predominantly rural economy is reinforced by a study of the thousands of rules, collected mainly in the first part of the Mishnah, which regulate farming and farm produce.[24] That agriculture was regarded as the foundation of national existence is evident from such sayings as that recorded of Rabbi Judah: 'If a man seeks after money and owns no land—what does it profit him?'[25] The peasants (in the terminology of the Mishnah 'the house owners'—*baale batim*) were the most esteemed of all classes of society.

Farming was performed in Galilee in a socially healthy manner by a multitude of small peasant owners. The emperor owned big estates in the Jordan valley and in the other plains, and there were some well-connected Jewish families (including the patriarchal house of Hillel) who were big land-owners; there were also rich individual land-owners, such as Rabbi Tarfon. Big estates were, however, exceptional. The great estates were situated outside the area of dense Jewish settlement. Some of these lati-fundia were in the coastal plain, where Jewish agriculture had dis-integrated under the stress of war. Other estates were in the regions beyond the Jordan (the Golan, Bashan etc.) colonized first by the Herods. Colonizing development had been always in the hands of the great land-owners, whether public or private; they had the capital and enterprise necessary for large-scale undertakings.[26] In Galilee, on the other hand, most of the land-owners worked their land themselves, with the help of their families and a few hired labourers. Slave labour seems to have been quite exceptional in Jewish farming. A typical estate is that attributed to Rabbi Hiyya ben Abba: 'a field, a vineyard and an olive grove', a property which could be comfortably managed by one family. The estates of Rabbi Tarfon—'one hundred vineyards, one hundred fields' etc.—are obviously legendary in character.[27]

Jewish farming in Palestine was already progressive in the days of the Second Temple. This is evidenced by the experiments with many foreign plants, which were successfully acclimatized. Beans, mustards and gourds came from Egypt; other plants from Greece and Cilicia. All these appear in the Mishnah as home-grown products, distinguished only by their foreign names. Cattle-breeders showed similar care for improving their stock: bulls were brought from Egypt[28] and asses from Lycaonia. The variety of fruit-trees mentioned in the Mishnah points to scientific farming, as well as the many expressions used to describe the various kinds of soil. Rabbi Jonathan ben Eleazar said that farmers in the land of Israel were able to state: 'This land is good for olives . . . that for grapes . . . this for figs.'[29] Good farmers were of course as knowledgeable regarding the weather. Rabbi Aha said: 'There were old men in Sepphoris who smelt the soil after the first rain and could predict the rainfall for the whole year.'[30] The variety of crops freed the farmer from excessive dependence on a single crop. It also made the Galilean economy as a whole almost independent of food imports from abroad in normal years.

The efforts of the farmers as producers of food were complemented by the hunters and the fishermen. The latter especially supplied considerable quantities of nutriment. The fishermen of Acre and Tiberias are frequently mentioned in our sources. Pools for breeding fish (*vivaria*) were in existence in the vicinity of Tiberias. They are another proof of the progressive character of the Palestinian economy at the time.

The abundance of agricultural produce is also evidenced by the strict observation of the rules for keeping the earth fallow in the Sabbatical year. Only a community with well stocked granaries could allow itself such a luxury. It required the economic crisis in the third century to reverse this trend.[31]

Among manufacturing industries, textiles easily took first place, together with subsidiary crafts, such as sheep-rearing, flax-growing, dyeing and sewing.[32] The great demand for the raw materials for weaving caused a growth in sheep-rearing, which in its turn caused conflicts between the crop-farmers and sheep-rearers. At least this dispute proves the importance of the textile industry itself.[33] Sheep-breeding was mostly concentrated in the regions of the big estates, the vicinity of Lydda, Jaffa and Jamnia, as well as in the lands beyond the Jordan, the districts of Machaerus and of Capitolias (Beth-Resha). Obviously the raising of sheep required a considerable investment and large grazing areas; only the great land-owners possessed these.

The weaving industry made at least as much technical advance as scientific farming. In the days of the Second Temple the finest linen, that used for the robes worn by the High Priest on the Day of Atonement, came from India by way of Pelusium in Egypt. In the third and fourth centuries, however, the finest linen of all was woven at Beth-Shean, Usha, Beth Mehoza and Arbel. In Galilee (and in particular at Giscala) silk was spun, the raw material coming probably from the Far East by way of the Red Sea and Elath. The finished products were sent to the trade fairs of Tyre.[34] Dyeing, which was always closely connected with the textile industry, developed especially at Beth-Shean and Lydda, the great centres of the textile industry. The needs of the common people were supplied by the weavers of rough cloth at Tiberias and the mat-makers of Usha and Tiberias.

Food-producing, the production of wearing-apparel and the trade connected therewith furnished the means of subsistence to the great majority of the Jews in Palestine. We read of 180 thousand (!) hawkers of food at Sepphoris. Even if we disregard such Haggadic exaggerations, a similar story is told by an unimpeachable source, the tombstones of the Jaffa Jews, dating from the third and fourth centuries. These texts mention two bakers, one hawker, one dyer and one common labourer.[35] In Caesarea were found epitaphs of a Jewish cobbler and a mechanic specializing in water-works.[36] The great necropolis of Beth Shearim, which was grouped round the mausoleum of the patriarch Judah I, was on the other hand used by the upper classes: teachers of the Law, officials, physicians, bankers etc. Obviously a burial in this central necropolis was costly. A Galilean Jew wishing to be buried there had to compete with Jews from distant places—Himyar in Arabia and Palmyra in the Syrian desert. An analysis of the trades and crafts by which the various rabbis made their living shows a cross-section of society on the level of the Jaffa community. Rabbi Yose bar Halafta was a tanner, Rabbi Meir a scribe, Rabbi Isaac a smith, Rabbi Simeon a weaver, Rabbi Nehemiah a potter, Rabbi Judah a baker, Rabbi Yohanan a cobbler and so on.[37] Similar trades and crafts are mentioned in the well-known story of how the renegade Elisha ben Abuyah entered a rabbinical school during the Hadrianic persecution and chased the pupils away, telling each to choose a craft: 'Be thou a mason, thou a carpenter, thou a painter, thou a tailor!'[38]

Jewish commerce in Palestine was mostly in retail. We hear of the peddlers of Kefar Hanania in Galilee who spent the whole week hawking their wares in the various villages and who returned home only for the Sabbath.[39] We may therefore assume that Jewish trade, like Jewish farming and Jewish industry, was of the type normal in oriental countries. The production and distribution of the various commodities were in the hands of a multitude of small producers and merchants. The characteristics of a typical oriental economy are further evidenced by the fact that the crafts-men and merchants of the same trade were already concentrated in particular streets or bazaars.

Against this background of small craftsmen and peasants there appear here and there signs of large-scale economic activity, usually connected with certain definite types of goods. The largest of these undertakings, which required much initiative and much capital, was the export of olive oil. Jewish Galilee was famous for the large quantity of oil produced there, for the quality of the product and last but not least for its ritual purity. According to Josephus[40] plenty of oil was produced in Galilee already in the days of the Second Temple. In the war of Bar Kokhba the groves suffered damage. 'At first olive-trees were common' said Rabbi Simeon bar Yakim (an Amora of the third generation, *c.* 250–280) 'but since then the wicked Hadrian came and ruined the whole land'. He added: 'But now olive trees are plentiful again.'[41] It appears therefore that the fer-tility of the groves was restored within a few generations. The Haggadah is full of stories, mostly legendary, about the enormous quantity of oil produced in Galilee. In the time of the patriarch Judah I, Rabbi Eleazar ben Simeon contrasted the riches of Galilee with the poverty of the rest of the Holy Land, saying 'it is easier for a man to rear a legion on the olives of Galilee than one infant in the rest of the Land of Israel'.[42] As an oil producer Galilee had a special advantage over many of the other countries of the Orient. In Babylonia the inhabitants were forced to use sesame oil, in Media oil from nuts, in Egypt oil from radishes and in Cappadocia mineral oil.[43] The ritual purity of Galilean oil constituted its principal advantage in the eyes of the Jewish consumers abroad. The supply and distribution of the quantities of oil required abroad involved a well-developed commercial organization and a considerable outlay of capital. The oil trade was therefore always concentrated in the hands of rich men who were able to undertake large-scale operations.

Another exception to the general prevalence of small crafts was the glass industry, in which Jews played a large part from the time of the Second Temple onwards.[44] Common pottery, however, followed the general rule; it was produced by many small craftsmen. Families of potters were concentrated in certain villages (such as Kefar Soganeh, Kefar Hanania or Kefar Shihin in Galilee)[45] because of the clay available in the vicinity. These potteries were engaged in supplying local needs. Since the invention of glass-blowing in the time of Augustus, glass-making had been developed in certain well defined centres, one of which was the coast of Northern Palestine and Phoenicia. The production of glass required technical skills much above those of an ordinary potter; it also demanded larger investments in kilns and tools, and the import of raw materials from some distance. Glass kilns are mentioned in the Mishnah;[46] the glass makers of Tiberias were especially well known.[47] Indeed the ruling that glass vessels were susceptible of uncleanness was clearly designed to protect Jewish glass-making, since it made the wares of Gentile competitors suspect to the orthodox Jews.

Another export product was *oxygarum* (fish sauce); it was produced at Taricheae (Migdal) on the Sea of Galilee and at Migdal Maliha on the shore of the Mediterranean. It is probable that a few big undertakers bought up the catches of the fisheries, and exported the finished product to Greece, Italy and Gaul.

Industrial potential has been always an important factor in the struggles of nations. It should be noted therefore that the Jews in Palestine possessed not only a potential industrial capacity, but were actually making weapons. Dio Cassius states that before the war of Bar Kokhba large-scale orders were given to Jewish armourers by the Roman government and that the arms produced were afterwards used by the Jews against the Romans. But even after the disastrous end of the war some weapons remained in Jewish hands. The Mishnah expressly forbids an orthodox Jew to go about on a Sabbath with a sword, a bow, a shield, a spear or a javelin.[48]

We have seen that the social composition of Galilean Jewry was that of a large class of well-to-do people and only a few exceptionally rich individuals. The extant inscriptions on the synagogues and in the necropolis of Beth Shearim, and the fines imposed by the rabbinical courts all confirm this view. At Beth Shearim, for example, hardly a single family among the upper classes could afford to buy a whole burial hall. Usually many shared one catacomb. In the synagogues too many shared the cost of the building: one individual donated a column, another a porch, a third a staircase, a fourth a lintel and so on. The cost of a whole synagogue was apparently beyond the means of a single person.[49]

The survey of the economic position of Jewry after the war of Bar Kokhba shows that even after the disastrous outcome of the war and the Hadrianic persecution, the Jews of Palestine were still formidable in their numbers and their economic and military potential.

2. *Repairing the Damage of a Lost War*

Before this potential strength could be applied to the solution of the various political problems which faced the Jewish nation from 140 onwards, various emergency measures had to be taken against some of the temporary ills resulting from the Bar Kokhba war and its aftermath.

The first danger which threatened Jewry was emigration. The Hadrianic persecution had led to the exodus of many of the nation's foremost leaders; several of these, such as Rabbis Judah ben Bathyra and Mattithiah ben Heresh, did not return; even a nephew of the patriarch Simeon II stayed on in Asia Minor.[50] There must have been of course many more less prominent exiles. This movement, if allowed to continue, would in the course of time have dispersed the remnant of the people left in the country. Counter-action was accordingly undertaken by the Jewish leaders to prevent Jews from leaving the Holy Land. Two lines of action were followed: one legal, the other religious or moral. The first included a series of regulations intended to encourage immigration. It was decided, for instance, that a husband and a wife could immigrate even against the will of one spouse. Considering the dominant status of the husband under Jewish law, this was a revolutionary decision in the case of the wife. 'If he (the husband) intends to go to the Land of Israel and she (the wife) refuses, she may be compelled to go; if she wants to go and he refuses, he may be compelled.'[51] The same rules, but the other way round, held in cases of intended emigration. It was also enacted that 'whoever vowed to buy a house . . . or to buy land (in the Land of Israel) he is not to be compelled to do so at once'; he could prolong his stay in Palestine, and possibly even decide to remain there.[52] Preference was also given to the local currency in the payment of dowries or alimony.[53]

Many of the emigrants went to Syria, in particular to the parts of it nearest Palestine. They evidently hoped in this way to be released from the special obligations (Sabbatical year, tithes etc.) which were attached to the soil of the Holy Land. To counter this it was decided that 'a Jew buying a field in Syria is to be considered as if he had bought it in the suburbs of Jerusalem'.[54]

Babylonia attracted still more emigrants. Life was very cheap there, food and clothing costing little; and there was the added attraction of a numerous Jewish community, free of Roman rule, which would give a stranger from the Holy Land (especially if he were a scholar) a great welcome. It was therefore decided that 'no person may leave Palestine unless wheat costs two seah for one *sela*' (four denarii).[55] Rabbi Simeon bar Yohai, the zealot, extended this prohibition to anyone who could afford to buy wheat in Palestine, whatever the price.[56]

The rabbis were especially severe in the matter of emigration with regard to two classes of people: priests and students. The continued residence of the priests on the soil of the Holy Land was regarded in some way as a continuation of their Temple service, or at least as a sign of readiness to resume that service at any moment. Even the patriarch Judah I, who as a rule was most lenient in his views,[57] was upset when he met the son of a priest settled at Ptolemais (Acre),[58] a city which was considered outside the ritual boundary of the Holy Land.[59] Once he found out that the father of the young man had transgressed by marrying a woman forbidden to a priest, and had thereby deprived his son of his priesthood, the patriarch calmed down.

As regards the other class affected, rabbinical students, an effort was made to use the right to formal ordination as a mark of distinction between the Holy Land and Babylonia; even the scholars of the latter country could be ordained in Palestine only.[60] This conclusion was derived by Rabbi Levi from the verse: 'the house of Israel dwelt in their own land' (Ezekiel 36, 17)—all 'dwelling' (i.e. the right to teach) could be only in your own land (i.e. the Land of Israel).[61] Such formal provisions were further strengthened by the condescension felt by the Palestinian scholars towards their Babylonian colleagues. The latter were generally scared of 'laughter in the West'—the derision of the scholars of the Holy Land. Rabbi Simeon ben Lakish for example made a general distinction between those Babylonians who had stayed at home (and whom he disliked) and those who went to Palestine (such as Rabbi Hiyya and his sons),[62] and had thereby redeemed themselves in his eyes. His colleague, Rabbi Yohanan, was of the same opinion. The young students who were required to stay were very poor at that time—we read that six of them had to cover themselves at night with one cloak.[63]

Parallel to the legal enactments, all kinds of moral pressures were exercised. Preachers stressed the sanctity of the Holy Land. 'There are ten degrees of holiness and Erets Israel is holier than all other countries.'[64] Residence in Palestine was 'equivalent to the observance of all the (other) prescriptions of the Law taken together';[65] 'whoever lives in the Land of Israel is free of sin'.[66] The Zealot Rabbi Simeon bar Yohai was the most prominent among the advocates of residence in the Holy Land in the first generation after the Bar Kokhba war. He said: 'The Holy One measured all the lands but found none worthy of Israel but the Land of Israel';[67] 'all Israel should live on its own land'.[68] Even his moderate contemporary Meir was loud in his praises of the Holy Land: 'Whoever lives in the Land . . . may be sure that he will be worthy of entering Paradise';[69] 'a man should always live in the Land of Israel . . . for whoever lives in the Land of Israel is like one who worships the true God . . . and whoever lives abroad is like one who worships false gods.'[70] Jews were required to stick to Palestine even in the hardest of times: 'A man should live in the Land of Israel even in a city with a Gentile majority; and he should not live abroad even in a place inhabited by Jews only.'[71] Not only residence but even a temporary stay in the Land of Israel was regarded as highly meritorious. 'Whoever walks four cubits in the Land of Israel gains Paradise'[72] said Jeremiah bar Abba in the name of Rabbi Yohanan. Merit was also acquired even by being buried in Palestine: 'Whoever is buried in the Land of Israel is as if he was buried under the altar (of the Temple).'[73] Rabbi Meir, who died in Asia, ordered his coffin to be set out on the shore, because the Mediterranean Sea also washed the sacred shores of the Holy Land.[74] We can understand now why so many Jews from the Diaspora let themselves be buried at Beth Shearim and why this small town became the central necropolis of Jewry in the third and fourth centuries.

Another means of impressing on the mind of every Jew the importance of living in Palestine was to stress the value of the Holy Land among those living abroad. 'Whoever stands abroad should direct his heart towards the Land of Israel'.[75] The sites in Palestine traditionally associated with the great events of Jewish history were sanctified. It was decided that everyone beholding certain sites and monuments should say a special benediction. These sites included 'The fords of the Jordan, the descent of Beth-Horon, the stone which Og King of Bashan intended to throw on Israel and the stone on which Moses sat while Joshua fought with Amalek, and Lot's wife and the wall of Jericho which was swallowed up by the earth.'[76] In this way arose gradually the local traditions which centred around the sacred sites in the Holy Land. They grew gradually stronger, passed beyond the confines of Judaism and finally had a decisive importance for the history of the country.

In consequence of this kind of moral persuasion we find that many scholars who intended to leave Palestine tore their garments when they reached the boundary and decided to stay. Such decisions are highly praised in our sources; the many others who decided to go on are passed over in silence. Yet we may well believe that by precept and example, by law and moral persuasion, any who were wavering were persuaded to stay; each of them strengthened numerically the remnants of Judaism in Palestine.

It was not enough, however, to forbid emigration; those willing to stay had to be provided with a living. As we have seen, the basic economic structure of the nation was sound.[77] The Roman authorities did not place too many difficulties in the way of the Jews, as we shall see in the next two chapters.[78] There were however many temporary difficulties, both moral and physical, caused by defeat in war and the period of persecution. These had to be dealt with by legislative measures.

One of these liabilities, though not perhaps the most onerous, was the decree of the Roman government which devalued the coins issued by the revolutionary authorities under Bar Kokhba, the so-called 'Kozebite' or 'Jerusalem' coins.[79] In theory this was a great economic loss; however in the conditions prevailing in antiquity, when all the coins were of metal, they kept their value as such. This was especially true of the Bar Kokhba coins, as many of them were Roman denarii or tetradrachms re-struck. Those still holding them could recast them without difficulty.

The greatest danger to Jewish economy came, however, not from external factors, but from inside the community. As usual after the great social upheaval caused by defeat in war, all kinds of dubious elements and hangers-on came to the fore. There were only too willing to exploit public distress for their private benefit. Legislative action of an energetic character had to be taken to curb their activities.

Heavy losses were caused to the Jewish economy in Palestine by short-sighted persons who were out for quick returns and who began to raise herds of sheep and goats ('small cattle' in the Talmudic language) in areas once cultivated but now temporarily abandoned. Such enterprises were apparently very profitable, due to the quick expansion of the textile industry. Rabbi Yohanan was recorded as saying: 'Whoever wishes to become rich, should raise small cattle'.[80] The rapid increase in the number of sheep and goats was bound in the end to ruin the crops and wooded areas; it was therefore decided that 'small cattle may not be raised in the Land of Israel, but only in Syria and in the deserts of the Land of Israel'.[81] The Jewish authorities undertook to protect the trees of their country; their point of view was expressed thus: 'Because of four things daylight is extinguished . . . because people cut down good trees and raise small cattle'.[82] On this point they could appeal to Biblical authority: 'for the tree of the field is a man's life'.[83]

Another prohibition of the same kind concerned the export of foodstuffs, an act which endangered local supplies. 'Products (of the field) may not be exported from the Land of Israel, nor whatever is necessary for human sustenance, such as wine, oil and wheat.'[84] This regulation probably caused losses to merchants and exporters, but was essential to the national economy in a time of emergency, when economic productivity had declined after the war.

More delicate and more complicated problems arose out of the necessity to protect and to defend Jewish landed property. As usual in times of war, the safety of private property was in danger. The Roman authorities had confiscated the properties of the 'rebels' and handed them over to others, veterans, soldiers, strangers, or Jewish supporters of the Roman government. The new settlers are called in Jewish sources 'robbers', 'persecutors' or 'oppressors'[85] who had 'seized the Land of Israel and from whom it was more difficult to get a penny than to extract water from a stone'.[86] Many people had perished in the war, had become enslaved, or had disappeared; their properties were often seized by others by guile or by force.[87] 'Violent men who by force got hold of the vineyard of a Jew'—are mentioned in the Mishnah.[88] The resulting instability of economic relations was fought by the Jewish authorities with a series of emergency rulings. Later on these rulings survived their utility and led to fresh difficulties. They then had to be amended in a hurry.[89]

We can best follow this development in the laws concerning the sicarii (*sikarikun*). This term is applied to a series of regulations concerning the acquisition of immovable property not from its rightful owners, but by *de facto* seizure, or from the Roman government who auctioned off (*sub hasta*) confiscated properties.[90] Many Jews were willing to purchase these lands from the new owners, and the Jewish authorities found it necessary to regulate the matter by a special law. At first it was held that anyone purchasing land under the *sikarikun* law had first to obtain the consent of the legal owners, before he could carry out the transaction with the actual, but unlawful, possessor. If he failed to obtain this consent, the purchase was invalid. This rule continued to be applied in Galilee ('Galilee is for ever subject to *sikarikun*').[91] It seems that Jewish landed property was much safer in Galilee and could be protected by emergency legislation. In Judaea, however, matters were different. Here the law had to be gradually adapted to a changing situation. Apparently more and more lands passed from their original proprietors to the *sikarikun* owners and from the latter to Jewish purchasers. The new owners had to be recognized, lest worse befall. After the turmoil of war the original owners could not be traced in many cases. If the law was enforced, the lands could not be acquired by Jews and would fall into Gentile hands. It was decided therefore that the lands of Judaeans known to have perished in the war were to be exempted from the provisions of the *sikarikun* law. In the case of other property, the lawful owners were given the right of pre-emption from the *sikarikun* owners. If they were unable to effect the purchase, they had to be satisfied with a compensation equal to one-quarter of the purchase money. Finally the patriarch Judah I limited the option of the original owners to twelve months, after which their rights were regarded as lapsed. This gradual adaptation of the law to changing circumstances reflects the deep anxiety of the Jewish authorities as regards the future of landed property, the basis of Jewish national existence.

After the Bar Kokhba war several other regulations were made with the same intent. Thus Rabbi Meir decided: 'No houses may be let to them (the Gentiles) in the Land of Israel and *a fortiori* no fields'.[92] The duty to conserve the land of Israel prevailed even over the sanctity of the Sabbath. The rabbis allowed Jews to write out purchase agreements concerning houses even on the Sabbath, if Jewish property could be saved in this way.[93] Such transactions could be registered with the Roman authorities ('the archives') because 'he (the Jew) saves it (the land) from their hands (the Gentiles)'. Rabbi Yohanan decided that 'the sages fine whoever leases land from the Gentiles, but not him who leases it from a Jew'.[94] This was to force the lessee of a Gentile to prefer outright purchase of the land to the continuation of a lease. At the same time the value of the Gentile's land was lowered, so that lessees would be more difficult to find for it and outright sale would be preferable.

As time went on, the wounds left by the war were gradually healed. The restrictions imposed by the emergency regulations became more and more galling to businessmen. Attempts were therefore made to suit them to the needs of another age. The law regulating the sale of moveables may serve as an example of such adaptation. In the time of economic scarcity which followed the war and its aftermath, there was no assurance that agreements for sale would be honoured, even if the purchase-price had already been paid. It was decided therefore that 'goods acquire money but money does not acquire goods; this is the rule: all goods acquire each other'.[95] In order to safeguard the interests of the purchaser and to prevent fraud or prevarication, all objects sold would remain the property of the seller till the transaction was completed by their delivery, or till they were exchanged for other goods. When the situation changed for the better, it was found under the changed conditions that this rule gave opportunities to dishonest people to evade their legal obligations. The old regulation was left in force, but a solemn curse was pronounced on people who did not stand by their undertaking. 'HE who gave their deserts to the generation before the Flood and to the generation of the Separation (i.e. Korah), HE will punish those who do not stand by their word.'[96] It should be noted that the emergency regulations outlined above were valid only in the transactions between Jews. As regards the Gentiles, the law remained that once the money was paid over the purchase became valid, even if the goods had not yet been delivered.

During the course of this chapter we have seen how the Jewish nation, even after defeat in the field, knew how to hold fast to its soil; how it strove to mitigate, as far as possible, the harmful results of a lost war, to keep its manpower intact and to adapt its laws to the needs of the time. A defeated people thus became again a political factor in its land and began to gather its forces as if for a third struggle against foreign rule. And yet nothing of the kind happened. The two hundred years after the end of the Bar Kokhba war were the most peaceful in the whole history of Roman Palestine. Our next chapters are devoted to the analysis of the causes of this remarkable and unexpected development.

Notes to Chapter I

1. As, for example, the Tryphon with whom Justin Martyr disputed; he fled to Corinth: Justin, *Dialogus cum Tryphone* (*PG* 6, *c.* 473). Jewish slaves were sold even on the shores of the Black Sea; Hieronymus, *In Abdiam* 20 (*PL* 25, *c.* 1115).

2. This area is defined in *Lamentations R* 1, 16 (ed. Buber, p. 416). The military importance of the Beth Gubrin-Hebron road was recognized by A. Alt, *PJB*, 1931, p. 18.

3. The last survivors of the revolt hid in the caves of the Judaean desert.

4. j *Nedarim* 38a, l. 13f.

5. j *Yebamot* 9d, l. 14.

6. *Sefer ha-Yishub*, ed. S. Klein, *Jerusalem*, 1939.

7. Justin, *Dial. c. Tryph.* 16 (*PG* 6, *c.* 509); Origen, *Homil. in. Jos.* XVII, I (*GCS* 30, p. 401); Eusebius, *Dem. evang.* VII, 1, 79 (*GCS* 23, p. 312), 91 (p. 314f.), VIII, 3, 10–12 (ibid., p. 393); Jerome, in *Isa.* I, 7 (*PL* 24, *c.* 30).

8. H. Mattingly and E. A. Sydenham, *Roman Imperial Coinage*, Vol. II, London, 1926; pp. 327, 448, Pl. XVI, 322; H. Mattingly, *Coins of the Roman Empire in the British Museum*, London, 1936, pp. 493–4.

9. b *Shabbat* 26a.

10. For the survival of Jewish villages in that area in the fourth century see Eusebius, *Onomasticon*, ed. Klostermann (*GCS* 11, i), pp. 26, 86, 88, 92, 98, 108.

11. Beyer, *ZDPV*, 1931, p. 246f.

12. Hill, *British Museum Catalogue of Greek Coins, Palestine*, London, 1914, p. xxiii.

13. b *Rosh ha-Shanah* 31b.

14. b *Rosh ha-Shanah* 25a.

15. T *Sanhedrin* 2, 13, p. 417, l. 32 (Zuckermann ed.).

16. See above, n. 14.

17. 1 Macc. 5, 23.

18. All such calculations are based on the enumeration of Jewish settlements in the *Sefer ha-Yishub*, I, 2, ed. S. Klein; see also the maps 1–4 and the diagram, Fig. 9; on the economic results of Bar Kokhba's War see A. Büchler, *The Economic Conditions of Judaea*, London, 1912, pp. 28–9, 66.

19. See below, pp. 46–7.

20. Klein, *EJ*, I, col. 1190.

21. This calculation is based on the total number of settlements known to us (cf. M. Avi-Yonah, *Map of Roman Palestine*, 2nd ed. Oxford 1940, index) and those settled by Jews, for which see the *Sefer ha-Yishub*.

22. The estimate is based on the population in 1947, as later changes have entirely altered the picture.

23. M *Shabbat* 7, 2.

24. M *Zeraim*, passim.

25. *Ecclesiastes R* 5, 8, Par. 1.

26. S. Klein in *Bulletin of the Jewish Palestine Exploration Society*, I, pp. 3–9; ibid. III, pp. 109–116; as regards the development of the territories of the Herodians, see P. Le Bas—W. H. Waddington: *Voyage archéologique en Grèce* etc., Paris, 1847–, inscriptions, No. 2329.

27. *Leviticus R* 30, 1; b *Shabbat* 25b, end.

28. b *Sukkah* 21b.

29. b *Shabbat* 85a.

30. j *Taanit* 65b, l. 13.

31. See below, pp. 108–9.

32. M. Avi-Yonah, *Trade, Industry and Crafts in Palestine in Antiquity* (*Library of Palestinology* IX–X) Jerusalem, 1937, pp. 94–8; F. Heichelheim: *Economic Survey of the Roman Empire* (ed. T. Frank), Vol. IV, Baltimore, 1938.

33. See below, p. 28.

34. *Ecclesiastes R* 2, 8, 2.

35. Sepphoris: see b *Baba Batra* 75b; Jaffa; see Frey, *CIJ*, II, Nos. 902, 929, 937, 940.

36. M. Schwabe, *IEJ*, 1 (1950–1), pp. 49–53; *SEG*, VIII, No. 138a.

37. For the crafts of the rabbis see the biographical items in M. Margaliouth, *Encyclopaedia of the Talmudic Sages and the Gaonim*, Jerusalem, 1946, *ad loc.*, and the various items in the *Encyclopaedia Judaica*, Jerusalem, 1971.

38. j *Maaserot* 2, 3–49d.

39. j *Hagigah* 2, 1–77b, l. 13.

40. *BJ*, II, 592; *Vita* 74–5.

41. j *Peah* 20a, l. 17.

42. *Genesis R* 20, 6, p. 190.

43. b *Shabbat* 26a.

44. P. P. Kahane, *Antiquity and Survival*, 2 (1957), p. 224. Raw materials and waste of a glass factory from the period of the Second Temple have been found by N. Avigad in the excavations of the Jewish quarter of the Old City: see N. Avigad, *IEJ*, 22 (1972), pp. 199–200.

45. M *Kelim* 5, 4; *Genesis R* 86 (p. 1058); T *Baba Metsia* 6, 3 (p. 383).

46. M *Kelim* 8, 9.

47. The usual editions of the Mishnah have the version *bor* ('well') which has to be corrected to *kor* ('oven'); for the *ilissis* (ὑαλῶσις—'glass factory') at Tiberias see *Genesis R* 96 (p. 1240).

48. M *Shabbat* 6, 4.

49. B. Mazar, *Beth Shearim*, I, Jerusalem, 1957, p. 27f.; Frey, *CIJ*, II, passim.

50. b *Sotah* 49b.

51. T *Ketubot* 13, 2.

52. T *Baba Kamma* 8, 16.

53. M *Ketubot* 13, 11.

54. T *Terumot* 2, 10.

55. T *Abodah Zarah* 4(5), 4.

56. Ibid.

57. See below, p. 105.

58. j. *Gittin* 1, 2–43c, l. 39.

59. T *Shebiit* 4, 11.

60. b *Ketubot* 112a.

61. j *Bikkurim* 65d, end.

62. b *Sanhedrin* 17b; b *Sukkah* 20a.

63. b *Sanhedrin* 20a.

64. M *Kelim* 1, 6.

65. T *Abodah Zarah* 4(5), 3.

66. b *Ketubot* 111a.

67. *Leviticus R* 13, 2.

68. T *Abodah Zarah* 4(5), 4.

69. j *Shekalim* 3–47 c., l. 1 bottom.

70. b *Ketubot* 110b.

71. T *Abodah Zarah* 4(5), 3.

72. b *Ketubot* 111a.

73. T *Abodah Zarah* 4(5), 3.

74. j *Kilaim* 32c, l. 12 bottom.

75. b *Berakot* 30a.

76. Ibid. 54a.
77. See above pp. 19–25.
78. See below, pp. 44ff.
79. b *Baba Kamma* 97b.
80. b *Hullin* 84b.
81. M *Baba Kamma* 7, 7.
82. T *Sukkah* 2, 5.
83. *Deuteronomy* 20, 19.
84. b *Baba Bathra* 90b, end.
85. T *Sanhedrin* 5, 5.
86. Sifre, *Deuter.* 317.
87. M *Sotah* 9, 15.
88. M *Kilaim* 7, 6.
89. H. Klein, *JQR* (NS), 23 (1932–3), pp. 21ff.
90. A. Gulak, *Tarbiz*, 5 (1933–4), pp. 23–7.
91. j *Gittin* 5, 6–47b, l. 17.
92. M *Abodah Zarah* 1, 8.
93. b *Baba Kamma* 80b.
94. j *Demai* 25b, l. 23.
95. M *Baba Metsia* 4, 1.
96. Ibid. 4, 2.

II

A Political Compromise: the Jewish Problem
from the Roman Point of View

1. *The Background*

At the time of the assembly at Usha (*c.* 140), over two hundred years had
passed since Pompey had brought Judaea under Roman rule. In the
course of this period of nearly seven generations, the relations between the
rulers and the ruled had been almost uniformly bad. The Roman government tried indirect rule in Judaea by a dynasty of submissive native
princes (the House of Herod); direct rule by procurators combined with
internal autonomy, the high priests and the Sanhedrin; rule by governors
for the whole of the Jewish area; splitting up the region into a number of
autonomous territories. The whole arsenal of political devices known to
the Romans was tried and found wanting. The one step which would
settle the problem once and for all, viz. Roman evacuation of Judaea,
could not possibly be entertained by the Roman government for many
reasons: the importance of the country as a land bridge connecting the
two centres of Roman rule in the East (Alexandria in Egypt and Antioch
in Syria); the necessity of keeping a firm hold on the whole of the Mediterranean sea-shore; the responsibility of the Romans for the survival of
Hellenistic culture in the East in general—and of the Greek cities in
particular; and last but not least, reasons of Roman prestige. Till the days
of the Emperor Hadrian the Roman frontiers had never receded at any
point.

The Jews on their side had tried twice to throw off the Roman yoke by
open warfare, and had twice failed. It was now obvious to anyone in his
senses that where the great commanders of the past, Simeon Bar Giora,
John of Gischala and Simeon Bar Kokhba, had failed (and, moreover,

failed at a time when the Jewish nation was strong and numerous) no one could hope to succeed unless by a miracle. The Romans could hope that after two defeats in war their Jewish adversaries would be ready to accept a compromise suited to the needs of the emipre.

The Roman reasons for accepting a compromise solution were obvious. They, and the other Gentile nations who took their cue from them, had by now learnt to appreciate the strength of the Jewish nation as a political and religious entity. The fantastic misrepresentations, invented by the Hellenistic anti-Semitic propagandists about the alleged secrecy and grotesque character of the Jewish cult, and the general Gentile feeling of contempt for the peculiar Jewish customs and manners—all these came to an end with the war of Bar Kokhba. While the fighting was in progress (and even during the earlier Jewish revolts under Trajan, which had ravaged Egypt and Cyrenaica) a wave of anti-Jewish hatred and fear rose in the Roman East. The Greek historian Appian tells how he was forced to flee for his life before the Jewish bands in Egypt. Apollonius of Tyana, the itinerant preacher and miracle-worker, refused even to put his foot on the soil of Judaea, lest he be polluted by mere contact with the despised race. After the war there was, however, a marked change of temper. A note of respect for the defeated nation creeps into the pronouncements of the victors. After all, the Roman losses in the war had been so heavy that the Emperor Hadrian had refrained from using the time-honoured formula: 'I am well and my army is well' in his victory dispatch to the Senate. As we learn from Fronto,[1] the heavy losses of the Second Jewish war were not forgotten fifty years after the event.

The healthy respect for the military prowess of the Jews continued. This martial quality did not disappear entirely, even after all the blood-letting of the Bar Kokhba war; it was merely transferred from an actual threat to a potential one. A very practical mark of such respect was the permanent posting of another legion to Palestine. The garrison of the province was increased from one legion to two already before the Bar Kokhba war. The newcomers, Legio VI Ferrata (the 'Ironsides'), were encamped at Kefar Otnay near Megiddo. Its camp and the city surrounding it became known as Legio, preserved till this day in a slightly different form as the Arabic Lajjun. The new camp was placed at a strategic cross-roads; newly-made roads converged on it from four directions, Galilee and Caesarea, and from Ptolemais and Beth-Shean (Scythopolis). At Legio the Roman troops stood between Caesarea, their capital in Palestine, and Galilee with its potential threat of a new Jewish revolt. Early in the reign of Hadrian a road was made straight from Legio to Sepphoris, one of the main cities in Galilee and an important Jewish centre. The Sixth Legion would thus be able in an emergency to advance into the heart of Galilee with all speed and comparative ease.[2] A military diploma dated

139 indicates that 'Syria Palaestina' was then still garrisoned heavily.[3]

The doubling of the Roman garrison in Palestine had another important consequence: the province rose automatically in rank from a praetorian to a consular one. Henceforward its Roman governors were drawn from the highest class of senatorial officials, those who had served as consuls.[4] The concentration of one-fifteenth of their whole available military force in such a small country (and not even a frontier province, where a garrison could do double duty against internal and external enemies) was most inconvenient for the Roman command, always hard pressed for a mobile reserve. This military burden was therefore an additional incentive for the Emperor Antoninus Pius and his government to choose the path of a compromise and to try appeasing the unruly Jews. The change of policy, once effected, produced the desired result. Soon after the revocation of the Hadrianic edicts, a detachment of the Sixth Legion could be safely sent to Numidia, where it appeared in 145 and helped to suppress a local revolt.[5]

The trend favourable to the Jews was not, however, caused solely by the potential power of Palestinian Jewry as political or military trouble-makers. There were other, more imponderable reasons. Although most of the Gentile inhabitants of the Greek cities bordering on Judea and Galilee, and many Gentiles in other provinces, felt bitter hatred for the Jews, not a few Gentiles were attracted by the Jewish religion. Although most of them did not feel able to shoulder the whole burden of the Law, they sympathized with Judaism. This numerous class is called 'the God-fearing' (*sebomenoi*) in inscriptions and texts;[6] in the Jewish sources they are often described as 'proselytes of the gate'. They were to be found in the provinces as well as in Italy, even at Rome. The Christian patriarch Cyril of Alexandria recalls that the 'God-fearing' could be found even in Palestine and Phoenicia, where one would expect them the least. As they often belonged to the upper classes, their mere presence added in the eyes of the authorities to the weight of Jewish influence in general, and of Palestinian Jewry in particular.

Another cause for the caution with which the Roman government addressed itself to the Jewish problem was the close ties of the Jews living within the empire with those who lived outside the boundaries. The Roman government was always especially sensitive in dealing with nations half in and half out of the empire. It usually attempted as far as possible to bring both halves entirely under its rule. For instance, the close relations between the Celts of subject Gaul and free Britain were one of the reasons which prompted the conquest of the latter by Claudius. The Roman emperors had tried several times to conquer Babylonia, home of the majority of Jews outside the empire. Their aim was to forestall the Parthian danger threatening Syria from the East. It is at least possible that Trajan dreamt of reviving the empire of Alexander. Roman expansionism clashed here head on with the hardly less powerful drive of the Parthians, who wished to restore to its full extent the rule of their Persian forefathers over the Eastern coasts of the Mediterranean. These conflicting aims led to a series of Parthian and Persian wars, which continued from the time of Pompey right down to the last days of Roman (or Byzantine) rule in the East.[7] In all they lasted seven hundred years, one of the longest conflicts in the history of mankind and one which had the least effect.

The fact that the Jews formed a very considerable percentage of the population just in the westernmost provinces of the Parthian empire, i.e. in those which lay across the path of the Roman army advancing eastwards, was of considerable political and military importance. Their obstinate resistance to the army led by Trajan during the siege of Nisibis undoubtedly delayed the Roman advance and upset its timetable. The Jews of Babylonia and Mesopotamia were, at all times, closely linked with their Palestinian brethren. When the latter were being persecuted, fast days were proclaimed in Babylonia. Deputies from beyond the Roman frontiers visited the Holy Land from time to time, to study on the spot the situation of the local Jewry. The exclusive right of the patriarchs residing in Palestine to fix the dates of the feasts and to proclaim leap-years was respected for centuries in Babylonia. Equally uncontested was their right to ordain and to appoint judges for the Babylonian communities. Communities of Babylonian Jews lived at Tiberias, Sepphoris and Jaffa, where they had their own synagogues.[8] The Palestine Jews were also in constant touch with almost every corner of the empire; their links with the communities in southern Asia Minor were especially close. At Tiberias there was a synagogue of Tarsians (Tarsus was the home city of the apostle Paul). The Jews of Cappadocia had one at Sepphoris; Cappadocian Jews also lived at Jaffa. So close were the ties between Cappadocia and Palestine that the Mishnah quotes that country as the standard example of a Diaspora community. An *archisynagogus* from Pamphylia appears in an inscription from Beth Shearim. He was either a native of Caesarea in Cappadocia or lived in Caesarea in Palestine. The community of Jaffa was in close contact with that of Alexandria and with Egyptian Jewry in general.[9] The Jews, with the patriarch at their head, formed therefore a kind of 'State within the State' inside the Roman empire, and this secondary state maintained its own foreign relations. Palestine and Babylonian Jewries formed in fact one national body separated by an artificial political boundary.

The power of Judaism in the third century was also felt in another, more intangible way. From the end of the second century onwards the whole spiritual atmosphere in the empire became more favourable for Judaism. From the days of Hadrian the Roman, i.e. the western traditions began to weaken. For the first time since the victory at the battle of Actium (31 BC) of the West under Augustus over the East under Antony and Cleopatra, the Eastern half of the empire began to make headway. The East might of course still be inferior from the military point of view; but it had always been superior in its economic and cultural weight. The comparative peace and tranquillity under the later Antonine emperors brought a change in the relative balance between the military West and the productive East. The rise of the East was also expressed in a re-assessment of spiritual and religious values. The decline of traditional Graeco-Roman religion, which dated back at least to the days of Augustus, now reduced the Olympian gods to mere figments. The intellectuals of the period either sought refuge in complete scepticism (of which Lucian of Samosata was the wittiest representative), or they sought salvation in one of the many oriental religions. These now competed in offering solace to the frustrated metaphysical longing of the times. All the gods of the East were 'Gods that listened to prayer' (*theoi epēkooi*), who promise individual salvation and eternal bliss in the afterlife. The principal gainers from the bankruptcy of the old religions were Christianity and Mithraism, and, in a lesser degree, various Syrian and Egyptian cults.

This spiritual trend led also to some extent to the revaluation of the traditional attitude to Judaism. Of course the difference between Judaism and the other oriental religions went deep into matters of principle, both of metaphysics and way of life. The demands of the latter effectively prevented a mass conversion of Gentiles to Judaism. Nevertheless there were many individuals, such as the 'God-fearing' souls already mentioned, who found their way to the austere national religion of Israel. The scorn and abuse heaped upon the Jews from the time of Augustus to that of Trajan, and the blind hatred in the days of Trajan and Hadrian, were now replaced by a quite different emotion. It is important to note that this change of attitudes was especially marked in the circles that really mattered, the official aristocracy, not excluding the emperors themselves. In the reign of the Stoics Antoninus Pius and Marcus Aurelius this changed attitude was based more on a feeling of justice and duty and on political and military calculations. Marcus, at least, despised personally all Orientals in general, and the Jews in particular.[10] However, all this was changed with the accession of Septimius Severus and his dynasty of Libyans and Syrians. There appears a note of personal warmth towards Judaism, quite different from the utilitarian calculations of their predecessors.

2. The Emperors and Judaism: 'Antoninus' the Friend of the Patriarch Judah I

In 192 Commodus, the son and successor of Marcus Aurelius, was assassinated and the rule of the so-called Antonine dynasty came to an end. It had ensured peace in the Roman empire for almost a century. After a short period of civil war and anarchy Septimius Severus defeated all his rivals and reigned supreme. The new emperor was born at Lepcis Magna in Libya, originally a Phoenician colony. He was the first Roman emperor of non-Roman descent. His family still spoke Punic, and the new emperor was a fanatical admirer of Hannibal, Rome's arch-enemy. As a result of his origins Severus was very far from the common Roman contempt for all other peoples.[11] He ruled with the support of the army and was a friend of the common soldier. He hated the senatorial aristo-cracy, a feeling heartily reciprocated. He was married to Julia Domna, a lady of a noble Syrian family. Because of the origins of the imperial pair oriental peoples could hope for more understanding from Severus and his family (including his successor Caracalla) than from the Italo-Spanish Antonines.

The story of the relations between Severus' son and successor, Marcus Aurelius Antoninus, known as Caracalla (206–217), and the Jews is con-nected with the well-known problem of the identity of an emperor 'Antoninus', the friend of the patriarch Judah I, an emperor who plays a considerable part in rabbinical legends.[12]

On re-examining the whole material found in our sources, we find that it can be classified under four heads: (1) historically possible facts, (2) legends, (3) a collection of witty sayings, and (4) the fragments of a philosophical treatise.[13] In the first category, which is the only one of interest to us, we note the following items: (a) a consultation between 'Rabbi' (i.e. Judah I) and the emperor 'Antoninus' as regards the chances of a revolt in Egypt; (b) the decision of 'Antoninus' to make Tiberias a Roman colony; (c) grants of land in the Gaulanitis to the patriarch and his house; (d) the superior breeding of the patriarchal cattle, which served to improve the inferior herds owned by the emperor, (e) the form of letters which passed between the emperor and the patriarch, and (f) a gold candlestick, suitably inscribed, presented by 'Antoninus' to 'Rabbi'.

It is upon these facts that we must decide which one of the emperors called Antoninus can be best fitted to them. Six Roman emperors in all were called Antoninus. Of these we may at once eliminate Antoninus Pius and Commodus, because neither of them to our knowledge ever visited Palestine. They could not therefore have met Judah I at Caesarea, as we are told in our sources. Of the remaining four, we may at once discard Antoninus the son of Macrinus, who was a mere child during the reign of his father. Heliogabalus (officially styled Marcus Aurelius Antoninus) reigned too late. It is also uncertain if he ever visited Palestine, even if he did pass the first winter of his reign (217–218) in its vicinity. We are thus left with only two possibilities: the philosopher Marcus Aurelius and Severus Antoninus, the son of Septimius Severus, known as Caracalla.

The former's openly declared contempt for the Jews[14] hardly fits him for the role of the friend and protector of the patriarch. Moreover, he was entirely unconnected with anyone called 'Severus', as is the Antoninus of our sources. We are therefore forced to conclude that if the 'Antoninus' of the Talmud did ever exist, he must be identical with Caracalla. If we examine the history of this emperor we may note some facts which correspond remarkably well to the historical items detailed above.

(a) The favours shown by Severus and Caracalla to the Jews in general have been mentioned in several non-Jewish sources. Thus we are told that when Caracalla was still a boy, he saw one of his playmates beaten by his father because he inclined to Judaism. Caracalla is reported to have been angry with the father for a long time afterwards. Jerome states briefly that 'Severus and his son Antoninus greatly favoured the Jews'.[15] Caracalla visited Palestine at least twice: once in 199, in the company of his father, and once in 215 when on his way from Antioch to Alexandria. This latter visit would be the most suitable occasion for the consultation with the patriarch concerning the affairs of Egypt which we find mentioned in our sources; for just at that time Egypt had revolted against the emperor. The patriarch, who was the head of all Jewry, that of Egypt included, was of course particularly well informed as to the state of affairs in that country; for the Jews were still a large percentage of the population of Egypt. Such a meeting would make the patriarch out to have been very long-lived; but on this point there is some supporting evidence.[16] We could even assume that the meeting took place in 199, because Caracalla was already co-regent with his father Severus then. According to Malalas both even then had many enemies in Egypt.[17]

(b) The alleged intention of Antoninus to make Tiberias a Roman colony reflects the many foundations of cities or grants of colonial rights in the time of Severus (in Palestine e.g. to Diospolis-Lydda and Eleutheropolis-Beth Gubrin). We know also that Caracalla is reported to have intervened with his father on behalf of the cities which had fought for Niger and against Severus, in particular Byzantium.[18] It is therefore quite possible that the change in Severus' attitude towards several of the Palestinian cities (especially Neapolis), which he deprived of their rights in 194 and pardoned in 199, might also be due to the intervention of Caracalla. We might connect this hypothesis with the definite statement, even if one from a late source, that 'Antoninus was a friend of the Samaritans' who were, as is well known, the majority of the inhabitants of Neapolis.[19]

The facts quoted under (c)–(e) are probably historical, although we have no external evidence to support them.

(f) The story of the dedication of a golden candlestick in a synagogue agrees well with what we already know about the many synagogues built in Galilee under the rule of Severus and his house. It recalls in particular the inscription from Kitsyon, in which this emperor and his family are honoured by the local Jewish community.[20]

All this leads to the conclusion that of all the emperors named Antoninus, Caracalla is the one who best fits the Talmudic traditions. The Roman sources in which Caracalla is described as a cruel and depraved tyrant have biased the judgement of many later historians. It is likely enough that the same ruler might be judged quite differently by the senatorial party and its historians, and by the provincials. Tiberius is one example of such historical dichotomy. The Antoninus of the Jewish sources is called in some manuscripts a proselyte; but this tradition is negatived in the better copies.[21] The fragments of the philosophical dialogue which are interwoven with our story have rendered the equation of the 'philosopher' Antoninus with the rough and soldierly Caracalla unlikely, to say the least. However, if we restrict ourselves to the historical part of the tradition only, we do not have to attribute to Antoninus any of the philosophic qualities required of a Stoic philosopher or the moral ones of a proselyte.

The positive attitude towards Jews and Judaism did not change throughout the reign of the Severan dynasty. The sick fancies of Heliogabalus, who dreamt of a religion to unite all religions (the Jewish included) in the worship of his Syrian god had no practical consequences. Curiously enough Heliogabalus was, as a Syrian priest, perhaps the only emperor who was circumcised and who abstained from eating pork. The many stories of the favours shown to the Jews by Severus Alexander are unhistorical. It has been proved conclusively that the 'Life of Alexander' included in the *Historia Augusta* is a historical novel composed in the reign of the emperor Julian. On the other hand, even a novelist would not attribute such inclinations to Severus Alexander, if they did not have some substratum of fact.[22] With the death of Severus Alexander (225) there begins the long period of anarchy, which lasted till the accession of Diocletian (284). For two generations the Roman empire lacked a stable government, and we should not therefore look for any consistent political line in its relations with the Jews. The only period during which the conditions were more or less stable was the rule of Odenatus and Zenobia, the rulers of Palmyra who had extended their rule over the whole of the Roman East and defended it against all comers. The particular problems of this period will be discussed below.[23]

3. *The Roman Governors and the Jews*[24]

It is obvious that the governors, who administered 'Syria Palaestina' from the days of Antoninus Pius onwards must have followed the general political line of the emperors. As we have already seen, the addition of a second legion to the garrison of Palestine at once raised the province from praetorian to consular rank. The days when Judaea was governed by incompetent and corrupt officials, like Gessius Florus, or by freedmen like Felix, were now definitely past. The Romans had learned from bitter experience that the pacification of Palestine and its good government required an administrative capacity of the very first order. In consequence the governors who were appointed after the revolt of Bar Kokhba were prominent personalities, the very best ones available in the circumstances. Several of them were by origin or upbringing particularly well fitted for the rule of oriental nations. For example, Publius Calpurnius Attilianus, *consul ordinarius* in 135 and governor of Syria Palaestina in 139, was the descendant of a Syrian priestly family.

At the beginning of the reign of Marcus Aurelius the governor of Palestine was Gaius Julius Severus. He had served in Syria in 132 as an officer of the Fourth Legion. At that time his father was acting governor of Syria, while the governor himself had gone southwards with part of his troops to assist in the fighting against Bar Kokhba. Julius Severus the son later on served at Rome as *praetor urbanus*, and commanded the Thirtieth Legion. He became *consul ordinarius* in 155, and was later on appointed governor of Syria Palaestina. It is an instructive fact that the governors of this supposedly troublesome province were chosen from among the more select *consules ordinarii*, in preference to the less prominent *consules suffecti*. Julius Severus had therefore had some experience of oriental affairs from the time of his Syrian service in the days of Bar Kokhba. He was also related to one of the last descendants of Herod, king of the Jews. This family connection was an inheritance from his father, also called Gaius Julius Severus. The latter was half Greek and half Galatian. He was related to one of the senatorial families of Asia Minor, probably descended from the Herodians and the kings of Commagene; of course they had long ago abandoned any connections with Judaism.

Another governor of Palestine, perhaps the one who directly succeeded Gaius Julius Severus, was Julius Commodus Orfitianus, former governor of Thrace. He had been consul in 158, and director of public works (*curator operum publicorum*) at Rome; from this post he passed *c.* 161 to the governorship of Palestine. Amongst the governors who succeeded Orfitianus was Flavius Boethus, a native of Ptolemais (Acre). He was a distinguished follower of Plato, a student of natural history and medicine. He was a close friend of the famous physician Galen, who composed 27 treatises at the request of his friend Boethus. The governor in 173 was Gaius Erucius Clarus, son of a consul, who was appointed to the governorship of Palestine immediately after his own term of office as consul, without the usual period of waiting.

These distinguished public servants, and others, whose names are unknown to us, but whose deeds are mentioned in the sources, treated the people of the province in a quite different manner from the brutal and savage ways of the low-born governors under the early empire. The Talmudic sources praise in several instances the correct behaviour of the Roman governors. Thus we are told that Rabbi Yohanan was once sitting in front of a synagogue of the Babylonians at Sepphoris, as the Roman governor happened to pass by. The rabbi was deeply sunk in his thoughts and forgot to rise in honour of the legate. The governor, however, did not reproach him, but sent him gently on his way.[25] Rabbi Hanina ben Hama and Rabbi Joshua ben Levi, two of the teachers of Rabbi Yohanan, were treated with equal consideration by a former proconsul. Rabbi Abbahu, who lived in the fourth century, was received with much honour in the governor's palace at Caesarea; his welcome is described with legendary embellishment in the Talmud.[26]

4. *The Roman Policy of Appeasement*

If we want to go to the root of the Roman policy towards the Jews of Palestine, we must remember that with all their sympathy and readiness to compromise as described above, both the emperors and the governors, even the most friendly among them, remained Romans first and foremost. They were above all concerned with the welfare of the empire they were administering. Thus the new policy, even if it marked a big change from the former terror and repression, represented at the best only a kind of *modus vivendi* between Rome and the Jews, based on a compromise by both sides. Each party, as is usual in such cases, kept in principle to its point of view, but consented to meet the other side as far as was necessary to prevent the outbreak of another struggle.

As regards Roman policy, we have to distinguish between concessions in theory, as embodied formally in laws, and concessions made in practice. The latter meant in effect the toleration *de facto* by the Roman government of Jewish practices which were in themselves illegal. It involved also a softening in practice of the anti-Jewish measures still on the statute-book from the past era of conflict. All the concessions made on the Roman side were only meant to restore the *status quo* before the war of Bar Kokhba. The Romans did not even consider the possibility of a return to the state of affairs before the First Jewish War, that is the re-establishment of a Jewish state, even as a vassal of Rome, or the restoration of the Temple. The *fait accompli* of Aelia Capitolina, the pagan city which stood on the ruins of Jerusalem, was to be permanent. The Roman concessions offered after 140 were purely practical and were meant as a palliative. The failure of the Hadrianic policy of repression was now obvious; therefore the Romans were ready to allow the Jews to live in Palestine in peace, provided the *pax Romana* remained undisturbed.

The main step in this direction was, of course, the restoration of freedom of religious worship, with all that it implied: freedom of assembly, freedom of teaching, the recognition of the corporate rights of Jewish communities, and the release of Jews from civil duties such as emperor-worship or military service, which involved taking part in idolatrous practices. In the language of the Mishnah these included[27] 'the Kalendae and the Saturnalia and the day of *Kratesis* (the accession of the Kings)'.[28] Judaism now reverted to its former status as a lawful creed (*religio licita*).

On one point only did the Romans refuse to go back to the *status quo ante bellum*. They were ready to recognize Judaism as a lawful religion, but insisted on the cessation of Jewish proselytising activities. This demand was the logical consequence of one of the basic conceptions of antiquity, the co-existence of national religions. In contrast to the Middle Ages, the peoples of antiquity were ready to tolerate the beliefs of each other. Ultimately all these were taken to be the manifestations of the same deity or deities with different names. No ancient religion demanded for itself the privileged status regarded as a matter of course by each of the three monotheistic faiths. In antiquity the right of every nation to its own gods was never questioned by the authorities; there was no other way to ensure a peaceful co-existence for the thousands of ancient deities.

The right of the Jewish nation to its own belief was fully admitted, on the same principle, but with the corollary that this religion should remain within its proper national pale. By the edict of Antoninus Pius, which abolished the oppressive decrees of Hadrian, the Jews were allowed to circumcise only their own children. Every attempt to extend the practice to Gentiles was considered by the law to be an attempt at castration, and as such punished according to the criminal code of Sulla (*lex Cornelia de veneficiis*) by exile to a desert island and confiscation of property. Contrary to the usual Roman practice, under which slaves were considered objects only, this provision was extended to protect them. This was in accordance with the humane trend of imperial legislation, which limited the absolute rights of the masters by forbidding the killing and the maiming of even their own slaves.

As we shall see below, the Jews refused to obey this imperial rescript and continued to receive Gentiles into the bosom of Abraham. The continuation of the practice of proselytism is attested by the edicts of just those emperors who are known to have been particularly favourable towards the Jews, Severus and his son Caracalla. They made the law more severe; the old penalty of exile and confiscation was left in force as regards the upper classes only (the *honestiores*), while the common people (*humiliores*) who had contravened the law were henceforward to be put to death. There can be no doubt that most of those convicted of proselytising were in the latter category. The death penalty was also to be applied to physicians who performed the operation and to every Jew who had his slave circumcised.[29]

In all other matters there was a distinct tendency to restore the Jews to their former status and to equalize their rights with those of the rest of the population. In civil status the Jews remained as before, tribute-paying provincials without Roman citizenship; however, in case of doubt they were put as far as possible on the same footing as all the other subjects of Rome. This tendency conformed to the generally egalitarian policy of the later emperors. For example, Severus and Caracalla admitted Jews to all the rights and duties of lawful trustees and guardians, provided the assumption of these functions did not involve doing anything contrary to their religious beliefs.[30]

The whole problem was put on a new basis with the famous edict of Caracalla, which accorded Roman citizenship to all free inhabitants of the empire (the *Constitutio Antoniana*, AD 212). Between this date and the restrictive legislation of the Christian emperors[31] all Jews were as individuals equal to all other Roman citizens, having in addition the special privileges accorded to them as Jews.[32]

In public matters concerning the Jewish nation as a whole, and not the individual alone, the same trend towards a restoration of the former status is evident. In this field, however, this policy is expressed less by legal enactments than by the extension of Jewish rights in practice. This change of policy is evident especially in two most important matters, the restoration of the Jewish municipalities and the re-establishment of an autonomous Jewish jurisdiction.

One of the measures of Hadrian directed against the Jews was the abolition of their municipal self-government. This matter was of great importance in antiquity, because the cities were the basic administrative units in such matters as taxation. The handing over of the municipality to a Gentile minority was a matter of serious import to every Jew, whether living in a town or a village; for the villages were apportioned amongst the city territories. The Hadrianic decree affected in particular Galilean Sepphoris and Tiberias. In Sepphoris, for instance, we notice that pagan symbols are conspicuously absent on the coins of the city struck under Vespasian or Trajan, but that from the time of Antoninus onwards, the emblems include a temple with the image of Zeus, as befitted a city officially called Dio-Caesarea.

There is more evidence of a Jewish municipality restored to power in Tiberias after Hadrian. We know that a great temple, to be called the Hadrianeum, was planned at Tiberias. A similar building was erected in

Caesarea, where it stood for centuries. In the days of Constantine we find that the Hadrianeum was still uncompleted. Apparently the Jewish majority in the municipal council refused to continue with the construction of a building associated with the hated memory of a persecutor.[33] A still more striking piece of evidence comes from another source: in the middle of the third century Rabbi Yohanan ordered the destruction of the statues of the Greek gods in the public baths, and this order was duly carried out.[34] In the days of the patriarch Judah I not only the municipal council (*boulē*) was composed of Jews, but the heads of the city, the *stratēgoi*, were also Jewish, for both bodies asked the patriarch to arbitrate between them in a tax dispute.[35] In the fourth generation of the Amoraim, in the days of Rabbi Abbahu, there still stood in Tiberias a special synagogue for the members of the muncipality called the synagogue of the *boulē*.[36]

In Sepphoris the restoration of municipal rights came somewhat later, but not very much later than at Tiberias. Rabbi Yose bar Halafta, a Tanna of the first generation after the war of Bar Kokhba, mentioned the 'old régime (*arche*) of Sepphoris' and therefore indicated by implication that in his time there was a new municipal authority, most probably a Gentile one. Since, however, Severus and Antoninus (Caracalla) recognized by edict the right of the Jews to serve on the municipal councils, with all the privileges and obligations arising therefrom, we may assume that at least in their time, if not before, the municipality had again become Jewish. We have evidence for Jewish municipal councillors from the days of the patriarch Judah I, for *bouleutai* (municipal councillors) are mentioned expressly among the crowd which thronged his antechamber every morning. By the beginning of the fourth century both Sepphoris and Tiberias were purely Jewish, to such an extent that Christianity could gain no foothold there except by direct intervention of the emperor.[37]

It seems, however, that in Jaffa and Lydda the municipal rights of the Jews were not restored to the same extent, for there the pagan coinage continued to the end. This difference in the fate of the Jewish municipalities of Galilee and of Judaea is in accordance with what we know of the decline of Jewish population on the coastal plain.[38]

The restoration of Jewish municipal rights involved in itself the reestablishment to a certain extent of Jewish courts. Under Roman law the municipalities had a limited amount of jurisdiction. However, the Jewish autonomous courts were not limited to the narrow boundaries of municipal status. Gentile courts and land registries were indeed set up in Palestine after the defeat of Bar Kokhba. They were part of the general policy of Hadrian to crush the remnant of Jewry. As we have seen, Jews were allowed by their authorities to have recourse to these institutions in order to protect Jewish landed property from being sold to Gentiles.[39] We may

C

therefore understand by implication that as a rule they were forbidden to resort to them. General Jewish jurisdiction seems to have been anulled by Hadrian. This we may learn from the Talmudic statement that 'in the days of Rabbi Simeon bar Yohai civil jurisdiction in money matters was taken away from Israel'.[40] However, with the re-establishment of the Sanhedrin and the patriarchate,[41] the need for Jewish autonomous tribunals became once more urgent. Roman law did in fact allow a loophole for the establishment of such courts, by allowing the parties to a civil suit to choose arbitrators. If they decided to go to the local Jewish judges it was their affair. Gradually the Jewish courts obtained fuller recognition from the Roman authorities. In Jewish law the rules relating to religious matters are so closely bound up with those affecting civil affairs and fines, that no clean cut could be made between the two. As the Roman courts could not in any case decide upon Jewish religious problems such as those concerning the purity of ritual food or the validity of a marriage, they had to allow the existence of Jewish religious courts as soon as they admitted Judaism to be a lawful religion at all. Naturally the Jews strove, and undoubtedly also succeeded, to enlarge the authority of their courts in civil matters. We can prove from our sources that Jewish tribunals of three or five members were actually sitting in every generation from the time of Rabbi Simeon bar Yohai (second century) to the completion of the Jerusalem Talmud (fifth century). In the third generation of Tannaim Rabbi Jonathan was deciding cases of land-law. In the fourth generation, disputes concerning inheritances were brought before Rabbi Ishmael ben Yose, and money matters before Rabbi Hama, the father of Bar Kappara, and before Rabbi Hosheyahu. The story told of Rabbi Bannah, who belonged to the same generation, is of special interest. He gave judgement in a matter of inheritance. The losing party appealed to the Roman authorities on the grounds that judgement was given without hearing the witnesses and in general on insufficient evidence. Thus the *existence* of the Jewish court was taken for granted by the Romans, and the only point in dispute was whether the judges had conformed to the rules of evidence required for a fair trial. In the first generation of the Amoraim Rabbi Joshua ben Levi was giving judgements. In the third generation there occured the well-known incident of the woman named Tamar. She was condemned by a court composed of Rabbis Hiyya, Assi and Ammi, and lodged a complaint against them before the Roman governor at Caesarea. The governor appointed a commission of three 'rhetors' (probably meaning lawyers) to investigate the case, but the timely intervention of Rabbi Abbahu led to a *nolle prosequi*.[42]

Most of the cases referred to above concerned money matters. Jewish civil law is, however, closely connected with a system of fines. It was impossible to stop Jewish courts from imposing penalties for the infringement of religious obligations. Besides, the patriarch and his courts dispensed some very efficient penal measures, besides fines, for example excommunication in various degrees of severity. Such measures were not recognized by the Romans, but they were not less dreaded because of this and probably led to a more prompt compliance than the fines and other penalties which could be imposed by Gentile courts.

When Roman authority was at its weakest, in the middle of the third century, the patriarchs apparently succeeded in extending their *de facto* jurisdiction into the domain of criminal law proper. According to a letter of the Christian scholar Origen to his friend Africanus (*c.* 240) the Sanhedrin sitting at the patriarchal court pronounced sentences of death, which were executed promptly.[43] This course of action was in flagrant disregard of Roman law; however the short-lived emperors reigning at that time of general confusion dared not join open conflict with the patriarchate. The political organization of Palestinian Jewry, which had already formed a kind of 'State within a State', aimed naturally at recovering the full attributes of national sovereignty, including that of imposing the death penalty. Such cases were, however, exceptional and the consequence of a temporary state of affairs. Normally the Jewish courts restricted themselves to civil matters, and were subject to the supervision of the Roman governors.[44] The tolerant attitude of the Roman government even allowed for execution of the judgements delivered by the Jewish courts through its own officials. This is already in evidence in the Mishnah.[45] There we are told that an order to divorce was enforced by the Romans. They inflicted corporal punishment on the condemned party, forcing him 'to do as ordered by Israel'.[46]

After the restoration of Jewish municipalities and Jewish courts, there remained three special matters in which the Jews were discriminated against; but even in these there was a certain mitigation, if not in law, at least in practice.

From the days of Vespasian all male Jews in the Empire were subject to a special annual tax of two drachmae or dinars to Capitoline Jupiter. In theory this payment represented the former Temple dues of half a shekel, which were paid by all Jews while the Temple was still standing. Of course, the name of Jupiter Capitolinus was a mere pretence and the tax was actually collected for the imperial treasury by a special department known as the *fiscus iudaicus*. Its chief was the Supervisor of the Jewish Registry (*procurator ad capitularia Iudaeorum*.[47]) This tax was still collected in the middle of the third century. In the letter of Origen to Africanus quoted above we find the following passage: 'and till this day the Romans are keeping them (i.e. the Jews) in subjection and the Jews pay the tax of two drachmae'[48] (this was written *c.* 240). The imperial treasury was naturally most unwilling to give up any part of its revenue, especially in times of financial crisis. However, as the tax was a fixed sum of two drachmae, it must have shrunk to practically nothing in the inflation of the third century. Probably even the poorest Jew could afford it easily. Our sources, which are full of complaints about the ruinously high taxation and the evils of tax-gathering, are almost entirely silent as regards the *fiscus iudaicus*.

The matter of the poll-tax was somewhat different. As a collective punishment for the rising under Bar Kokhba, the Emperor Hadrian had raised the rate of the poll-tax paid by the Jews of Palestine. From a comparison with conditions in Syria we learn that this so-called poll-tax was really a tax on landed property. It was assessed at a certain percentage of the value of such property. We do not know exactly the percentage collected from the Jewish landed proprietors, but we know that they were discriminated against, as compared with the other land-owners of the same province.[49]

The third and most resented of the special laws against the Jews concerned Jerusalem. The status of the Holy City and of the Temple remained the greatest obstacle in the way of reconciliation between Jews and Romans. Hadrian's reconstruction of Jerusalem as a pagan city led to the outbreak of the Bar Kokhba war. The founding of Aelia Capitolina and the expulsion of the Jews from its vicinity were the abiding results of that bitter struggle. From the imperial point of view the Roman government could not give up this symbol of its victory in war. Neither could it abandon the great number of Gentiles settled at Aelia by its invitation and continuing to live there under its protection. On the other hand the eternal hope of seeing the 'Great and Holy House' rise again in Jerusalem was for ever anchored in the Jewish consciousness. Every Jew repeated it three times daily in his prayers. On this point there could be neither compromise nor a mutual give and take.

Therefore the edict of Hadrian barring the Jews from access to their ancient capital remained on the statute book. This edict is very frequently mentioned by Christian writers in their polemics against the Jews. They understood it to be evidence of the fulfilment of the prophecies of destruction uttered by Jesus and of Jewish guilt. The decree is prominent in the collection of 'Testimonies against the Jews', which was compiled by the Christians in the second century in support of their missionary activities. Parts of this collection were copied by Church Fathers from Justin of Neapolis and Tertullian down to Eusebius of Caesarea. From these fragments the wording of the original edicts can be reconstructed with tolerable certainty. It seems that it was couched in the form of a *senatus consultum*, a resolution adopted by the Senate, of course upon imperial recommendation. It was decreed 'that it is forbidden to all circumcised persons to enter and to stay within the territory of Aelia Capitolina; any person contravening this prohibition shall be put to death'.[50]

The edict thus applied to all circumcised persons, not just to the Jews. In consequence it affected also the Judaeo-Christian community, which had to give up its residence in Jerusalem. The bishop of Jerusalem was replaced by one of Gentile stock. As the prohibition extended over the whole municipal territory of Aelia Capitolina, and not just the city itself, it included the three districts of Oreine or Har-ha-Melek ('Royal Mountain'), Gophna to the north and Herodium (which included Bethlehem) to the south.[51] Christian authors laid special stress on the fact that the Jews were forbidden henceforward even to look at Jerusalem from afar. Tertullian also confirms that in his days (the end of the second century) no more Jews were left in Bethlehem.[52] But as in the case of the injunction against proselytism the Jews refused to obey the imperial order, so they did also in the present case.[53] After a certain lapse of time the Roman authorities connived at the increasingly numerous contraventions.[54]

Notes to Chapter II

1. Appian XXIV in fine (*Arabicus liber*)—*Fragm. histor. graec.* V, p. lxv; Philostratus, *Vita Apollonii* V, 27 ed. C. L. Kayser, Leipzig, 1870–1; Dio Cassius lxix, 14 (ap. Xiphil.) ed. L. Dindorf and I. Melber, Leipzig, 1890; Fronto, *De bello parthico*, p. 218 (ed. Naber).

2. The road from Sepphoris to Legio was built in the time of Hadrian, before the Bar Kokhba war. M. Avi-Yonah, *QDAP*, 12 (1945), pp. 96–7, 101–2.

3. Heron de Villefosse, *RB*, 1897, p. 599.

4. See below, pp. 42–4.

5. *CIL*, VIII, 10230.

6. Acts of Apostles 13, 50, Frey, *CIJ*, I, 748.

7. See below, pp. 257ff.

8. Babylonians in Tiberias—j *Yoma* 7, 1–44b top; at Sepphoris—j *Shabbat* 6, 1–8a, centre; at Jaffa—Frey, *CIJ*, I, 902.

9. Alexandrians at Jaffa—*ib.* II, Nos. 918, 928, 930, 934; Cappadocians at Sepphoris—j *Shebiit* 9, 5–39a; at Jaffa—Frey, *CIJ*, II, 910, 931; Tarsians—ibid., No. 925; synagogue of the Tarsians at Tiberias—j *Shekalim* 2, 7–47a; archisynagogus of Pamphylia—M. Schwabe and B. Lifshitz, *Beth Shearim*, II, Jerusalem, 1967, No. 203.

10. Ammianus Marcellinus, XXII, 5, 5 (ed. G. U. Clark *et al.*, Berlin, 1910).

11. Fluss, 'Severus', *PWRE*, II A, IV, c. 1980–1, 2000–2; Rostovtzeff, *Soc. & Econ. History of the Roman Empire*, Oxford, 1926, p. 351ff.; *CAH*, XII, p. 24.

12. The sources have been collected by S. Krauss in his *Antoninus und Rabbi*, Wien, 1910.

13. Wallach, *JQR*, 31 (1940–1), pp. 259–86.

14. See above, n. 10.

15. Jerome, *In Dn.* xi, 27 (*PL* 25, *c.* 570); *SHA* Caracalla 1, 6 (i, p. 183). The identification of Antoninus with Caracalla has been already proposed by Just and others, see S. Marmorstein, *EJ*, II, *c.* 1116.

16. See below, p. 103.

17. Malalas (ed. Bonn), p. 293.

18. *SHA* Caracalla, 1, 7; ibid., Severus, 14, 6.

19. See the Samaritan sources *ap.* J. A. Montgomery, *The Samaritans*, Philadelphia, 1907, p. 93, n. 40. (Montgomery gives a different interpretation of the texts.)

20. Frey, *CIJ*, II, pp. 157–9, No. 972.

21. S. Lieberman, *Greek in Jewish Palestine*, New York, 1942, pp. 78–81 on j *Megillah* 3, 2–74a.

22. Heliogabalus and Judaism—*SHA* Heliogabalus 3, 4–5, 7, 2; 28, 4; Severus Alexander—ibid., Alex., 22, 4; 28, 7; 51, 7; on the evidential value of the life of Alexander Severus see N. Baynes, *The Historia Augusta, its Date and Purpose*, Oxford, 1926. [The author was aware of more recent work on the *HA*, and would not have allowed this characterization to stand; for other views, see e.g. A. Momigliano, *Secondo Contributo alla Storia degli Studi Classici*, Rome, 1960, pp. 105–44; R. Syme, *Emperors and Biography. Studies in the Historia Augusta*, Oxford, 1971; ibid., *The Historia Augusta*, Bonn, 1971 (Ed.).]

23. See below, pp. 125–7.

24. For a list of the governors of Palestine see R. E. Brünnow and A. Domaszewski, *Die Provincia Arabia*, Strassburg, 1909, III, pp. 300–2; P. V. Rohden, *De Palaestina et Arabia provinciis Romanis*, Berlin, 1885. The lives of the various governors mentioned are described in *PWRE* under Calpurnius (III, *c.* 1366, No. 20; also Krauss, *REJ*, 80, p. 121); Julius (*PWRE* X, *c.* 811–822); Erucius (ibid., VI, *c.* 522, No. 4); Boethius (III, *c.* 604, No. 10); Julius Commodus (X, *c.* 569, No. 793); cf. also Krauss, loc. cit., pp. 113ff.

25. j *Berakot* 1, 4a, l. 27.

26. b *Ketubot* 17a.

27. M *Abodah Zarah* 1, 3.

28. E. E. Urbach, *IEJ*, 9 (1959), p. 240.

29. *Digest* 48, 8, 3, 5; Paulus, *Sententiae* 5, 22, 3; *SHA* Severus 17, I.

30. *Digest* 27, 1, 15, 6.

31. See below, pp. 174, 213–40.

32. J. Juster, *Les Juifs dans l'empire romain*, I, Paris, 1914, p. 213f.

33. Epiphanius, *Panarion* 30, 12, 1 (*GCS* 25, p. 347).

34. G. Allon, *Tarbiz* 14 (1942), pp. 145–55.

35. j *Abodah Zarah* 4, 4–43d.

36. j *Shekalim* 7, 4–50c.

37. The 'old *archê* of Sepphoris' is mentioned Num. R. 9, 7; the edict of Severus and Antoninus: *Digest* 50, 2, 3, 3; the counsellors attending on Rabbi j *Shabbat* 12, 3–13c end; Sepphoris as a Jewish town in the 4th century—Epiphanius, *Panarion* 30, 10, 10 (*GCS* 25, p. 347); in the 5th: Theodoretus, *Hist. eccl.* IV, 22, 35 (*GCS* 19, p. 260).

38. See above, p. 18.

39. See above, p. 30.

40. j *Sanhedrin* 14, 2–24b.

41. See below, pp. 54ff.

42. Jonathan—j *Baba Batra* 2, 14–13c; Ishmael ben Yose b *Sanhedrin* 29b; Hama and Hosheyahu—j *Shebuot* 6, 2–37a; Banaah—b *Baba Batra* 58a; Joshua ben Levi—j *Gittin* 4, 4–45d; the affair of Tamar—j *Megillah* 3, 2–74a.

43. Origen, *Ep. ad Africanum* 14 (*PG* 11, *c.* 84).

44. See above, p. 48.

45. M *Gittin* 9, 8.

46. See also T *Yebamot* 12, 13 (p. 256) j *Gittin* 9, 10d, l. 19.

47. *CIL*, VI, 8604.

48. Origen, op. cit. (*PG* 11, *c.* 81).

49. Appian, *Syriaca* VIII, 50 (Reinach, *Textes d'auteurs grecs et romains relatifs au judaisme*, Paris 1895, p. 152); see also the commentary of Heichelheim ap. T. Frank, *Economic Survey of the Roman Empire*, IV, Baltimore, 1938, p. 231.

50. J. Rendel Harris, 'Hadrian's decree of expulsion of the Jews from Jerusalem', *Harvard Theological Review*, 19 (1926), pp. 199–206.)

51. See Map 1, p. 17.

52. Eusebius, *Hist. eccl.* IV, 6, 3 (*CGS* 9, p. 308); Tertullian, *Adv. Judaeos* 13 (*PL* 2, *c.* 673).

53. See below, pp. 79ff.

54. Ibid.

III

The Compromise between the Jews and Rome from the Jewish Point of View

1. The Renewal of the National Establishment. The Patriarchate

Before peaceful relations between the Jews and Rome could even be thought of, an organization had to be created capable of negotiating on behalf of the Jewish nation and of enforcing any agreement. Without such an authority there could be no hope of joint national action; in its absence the Jews of Palestine would degenerate into an amorphous agglomeration of individuals, an inanimate mass without a will of its own and at the mercy of every external pressure.

In this matter everything had to begin from scratch. The authorities of the old Jewish state had perished with the destruction of the Temple. The provisional organization created after 70, which had existed precariously between the two wars, had been set aside by the revolutionary government of Bar Kokhba; and this in its turn had been buried under the ruins of Beth-Ter. While the Hadrianic persecution lasted, the nation could be likened to a drowning man, clutching at every straw and only anxious to prolong its existence for a few moments more, hoping for some unexpected salvation. There was at that perilous time neither opportunity nor leisure to begin the work of national organization afresh. After 140, with the pacification of the country and the re-assembling of the leaders at Usha, the moment had come.

Apart from achieving bare physical survival, and the latent possibilities of a sound economic structure, the Jews of Palestine had kept throughout the wars and persecutions the invaluable spiritual heritage of an unbroken and universally acknowledged chain of tradition. The survival of this spiritual authority was due to the heroic self-sacrifice of Rabbi Judah ben

54

Baba, who had ordained five of Rabbi Akiba's pupils at a time when the Roman authorities punished both those ordinating and those receiving ordination with death.[1]

This matter of ordination (*semikah*) is sufficiently important to deserve detailed consideration. In later times the term *semikah* meant no more than the appointment to a rabbinical office,[2] as the rabbinical ordination and the appointment usually coincided. In the Jerusalem Talmud the expression 'ordained' is often used in the sense 'appointed'; this was the meaning of the term *somek* in the later period.[3] However in the first three generations of Tannaites (that is to say up to about 160) the meaning of the term was both wider and less precise. While the Sanhedrin was sitting at Yabneh each rabbi ordained his pupils as he pleased. Even at that time the ordination implied not only permission to teach, but established the recipient as a link in the chain of tradition set out in the 'Sayings of the Fathers' (*Pirke Abot*, a tractate of the Mishnah) which began with Moses at Mount Sinai and continued through Joshua and the Elders, the Prophets and the Men of the Great Assembly and the 'Pairs' of scholars down to the present. The laying-on of hands was regarded among scholars as the right to share in the spiritual authority derived from Moses.

The continuation of this practice was therefore absolutely essential for the legitimate transmission of national authority from one generation to another; its interruption would—in the eyes of that generation—deprive all future authorities of their legitimacy. The Roman persecutors, guided by such renegade scholars as Aher, were perfectly aware what the *semikah* meant to Israel. They would hardly have punished with death the mere appointment to a rabbinical office, nor would Judah ben Baba have laid down his life in defence of such right. Both parties understood perfectly the significance of his act and its far-reaching consequences.

The pupils of Rabbi Akiba thus ordained constituted—together with the surviving members of the old Sanhedrin—the legitimate successors of the assembly which had sat at Yabneh. When they met at Usha they performed as of right the various religious and political functions reserved for a properly constituted Sanhedrin, such as the proclamation of the intercalary month and of the dates of the feasts, as well as the enacting of various regulations for the reform of public and private life. An assembly of several dozen scholars could however only deliberate; it could not function as a national executive. The most important act of the Sanhedrin at Usha was therefore the creation of such an executive organ by reviving the patriarchate.

In fact—although perhaps not formally—the revived patriarchal authority was quite different from that which had existed at Yabneh. There Rabban Gamliel II had fulfilled a function which was without precedent in Jewish history: that of a head of the nation who was neither a king nor a high priest. His title (*nasi*) had indeed been used already by the prophet Ezekiel as the equivalent of that of king[4] and it might have served also as the Hebrew term for 'ethnarch', one of the titles of the Hasmonaeans before they assumed the royal title. It was used by Bar Kokhba (who was called '*nasi* of Israel'), probably as a reminiscence of Hasmonaean times, which left open the question of the Messianic king. Now at Yabneh Rabban Gamliel II had inherited only the prescriptive right to the presidency of the Sanhedrin, which had been held *de facto* by the leaders of the Pharisees even at the time when the nominal president was the Sadducee high priest. Of course Rabban Gamliel had enjoyed the prestige of having among his forefathers four generations of the House of Hillel, each in his time president of the Sanhedrin. This tradition had perforce been interrupted in his childhood, when after the death of his father Simeon I (who probably perished with the fall of Jerusalem) Rabban Yohanan ben Zakkai had for a time assumed the presidency of the Sanhedrin at Yabneh, although not himself a Hillelite. When Rabban Gamliel II arrived at his majority Rabban Yohanan resigned and retired to Beror Hayil; whereupon Rabban Gamliel II resumed his hereditary position as head of the Sanhedrin. During his patriarchate Rabban Gamliel had stressed the need for a strong central authority. The rival claimants for national leadership, the high priests, had vanished with the destruction of the Temple; but he met with strong resistance from the members of the Sanhedrin. There were frequent conflicts between the patriarch and the majority of the assembly and on one occasion his opponents even succeeded in deposing him for a short period. The struggle between patriarch and Sanhedrin went on till both were pushed aside by the revolutionary and military dictatorship of Bar Kokhba. When the fall of Beth-Ter ended the period of military rule, the Hadrianic persecution made any attempt at reconstituting the patriarchate illusory. Now, with the return of tranquillity, all eyes were turned towards Rabban Simeon II, the son of Rabban Gamliel II and the legitimate heir of the house of Hillel.

Rabban Simeon himself did not take part in the deliberations at Usha. During the Hadrianic persecution he had succeeded in escaping imprisonment through the connivance of a friendly Roman official, although the order for his arrest had been given.[5] We do not know how and where he had lived during the reign of terror and the period immediately following it. It is possible that he did not wish to appear at Usha as a simple member of the assembly until his authority was acknowledged; in any case he knew how to bide his time. He was soon satisfied. When the other Jewish authorities were restored at Usha, his election as patriarch was generally acclaimed. Yet his authority was not undisputed; two leading members of the Sanhedrin were invested with functions which encroached on the authority of the patriarch: Rabbi Meir became *Hakam* (chairman of the Sanhedrin *vice* the patriarch) and Rabbi Nathan *Ab Bet Din* (President of the Rabbinical High Court). Obviously the members of the Sanhedrin intended to prevent the concentration of too much power in one hand; some of them may have remembered the conflicts which had occurred at Yabneh. However in the course of time Rabban Simeon succeeded, slowly and almost imperceptibly, in establishing what amounted to monarchical rule. Not for nothing did he call himself (in contrast with his son and successor Rabban Judah I) 'more fox than lion'.

The competence of the patriarch was gradually enlarged; in particular the right to appoint to the various communal offices in Palestine and abroad was concentrated in his hand, and the concurrent authority of the Sanhedrin was gradually reduced. 'A court (Sanhedrin) which makes an appointment without consulting the patriarch—its appointment is invalid; a patriarch who appoints without consulting the court—his appointment is valid.'[6] The monarchic character of Rabban Simeon's rule found its expression even in matters of protocol. His father, Rabban Gamliel II, used in his official correspondence the formula: 'By me and my colleagues'—his son, however, wrote 'By me' only.[7] The superior position of the patriarch was marked by an elaborate ceremony at the meeting of the Sanhedrin: 'When the patriarch enters the hall, everybody must stand till he asks them to sit down' whereas the *Hakam* and the *Ab Bet Din* received graduated but lesser honours.[8] These innovations stirred up opposition; but times had changed since the days when Rabban Gamliel had been deposed. Then the majority of the Sanhedrin had been opposed to the patriarch; but now, even if the leaders of the opposition were the two greatest scholars of the age, Rabbis Meir and Nathan, the majority of the assembly saw the need for a strong ruler in times of crisis. They supported the patriarch even while he was encroaching upon their privileges. Rabban Simeon II thus paved the way for the absolute rule of his son, Judah I (called 'Rabbi' *par excellence*).

In the days of the latter, the patriarchate did indeed reach its apogee, in its power over Jewish life in Palestine and the Diaspora, its riches and external honours, and its intellectual ability. Later generations regarded these times with nostalgia as days of unparalleled glory. The patriarch had an almost royal status. The public prayed for his welfare; after his death he was mourned ceremonially. Public mourning was observed for a whole year and huge quantities of incense were burnt at the funeral (this usage is recorded already in the time of Rabban Gamliel).[9] For the day of his funeral 'priesthood was abolished'—priests were allowed to enter the cemetery in spite of the prohibition to do so in normal times.[10]

In the time of Judah I the daily ceremony of the morning salutation of the patriarch by the public was introduced, modelled on a similar pageant at the imperial court. We hear of it for the first time in the days of his grandson Judah II, but it could hardly have originated during the stormy reign of the latter. The heads of the families who had to see the patriarch daily assembled in his antechamber and were arranged according to their rank; they saluted the patriarch by order of their precedence in the official hierarchy.

Various fragments of the Haggadah illustrate the ways in which the adherents of the patriarch tried to impress the people with his charismatic status. The alleged descent of Hillel from the House of David was apparently stressed, especially in connection with such Biblical passages as Ezekiel 34, 23 'And I will set over them . . . my servant David' and 37, 25 'David my servant shall be their prince for ever'. Some of the courtiers, such as Rabbis Hiyya Rabba and Ishmael ben Yose, applied to Judah I such extravagant designations as 'the Lord's anointed'. The Davidic descent received Messianic undertones. In popular homiletics the verse (Genesis 25, 23) 'Two nations are in thy womb' was understood as meaning 'Two proud ones (*geyyim* for *goyyim*) are in thy womb' viz. Antoninus and Rabbi (Judah).[11] The patriarch, as the head of Israel, was on a level with the emperor, the head of 'Edom' (the Roman empire). In later times, the sages of Babylonia recalled the days of the patriarch Judah I and his house as times of legendary glamour; this reflected the veneration with which 'Rabbi' (the patriarch) had been regarded during his lifetime. Rabbi Samuel bar Abba (one of the pupils of Judah I) claimed that the Lord had set up the House of Hillel as he had set up Daniel and his companions in the days of Nebuchadnezzar, Mordecai and Esther in the days of Haman, or Simeon the Just and the Maccabees in the days of the Greek oppressors.[12] Rabbi Simeon ben Judah Menasya summed up the excellences of Rabbi Judah and his house thus: 'Grace and power and wisdom and wealth and long life and honour and splendour and sons who are just men'.[13] Raba the Babylonian expressed the opinion of succeeding generations when he said: 'From the days of Moses till the days of Rabbi (divine) wisdom and (worldly) greatness were not found together'.[14]

Opposition did not cease entirely even in the days of Rabbi. The sons of Rabbi Hiyya, for instance, are recorded as saying that the son of David (the Messiah) would not come until two dynasties, the House of Hillel (the patriarchs) and that of the exilarch in Babylonia,[15] became extinct. Possibly the mysterious statement of the Christian writer Theodoret, according to which the patriarchal family was descended from King Herod, originated in the whisperings of the Jewish scholars who were deriding in secret the 'Davidic' descent of Hillel.[16] In any case such views were, during the lifetime of Rabbi, only those of isolated individuals. Their importance lies in the fact that they form a connecting link between the opposition to the patriarchate in the days of Rabban Gamliel II and his son Simeon II, and that active in the days of the Patriarch Judah II, the grandson of Rabbi.

The power of the patriarch was not based exclusively on external honours. It had a solid economic basis. Our sources contain many details concerning the wealth of the patriarchal dynasty. The House of Hillel had been prominent for many generations and could hardly have failed to acquire landed property. Its moderate political attitude preserved its property from confiscation by the Roman government. Already in the days of Rabban Gamliel II the patriarch owned many olive groves and vineyards in the vicinity of Lydda. In the time of Judah I vast areas in the Valley of Jezreel and in the Golan were leased to the patriarch by imperial favour. He seems to have possessed also part of the rich balsam groves of the Jordan Valley, as the 'balsam of the patriarch' is mentioned together with that of the emperor.[17] In addition to foodstuffs such as wheat, oil and wine the patriarchal estates produced raw materials for industries; balsam for perfumes and medicaments and linen and wool for weaving.[18] They had fishing fleets which produced the fish for the *oxygarum* (fish sauce). The patriarchs had their own ships which carried the produce of their estates to lands beyond the sea.[19]

The income derived from all these sources served to augment the magnificence of the patriarchal court, to maintain his numerous slaves and servants, his mules and his stables. In the various legendary sources this splendour is described in detail, down to the golden candlesticks and the golden keys of the House of Rabbi. Popular imagination found some consolation for the lost glories of Jerusalem in contemplating the greatness of the foremost Jew of his time.

The friendly relations which existed between the Roman authorities and the patriarch[20] left their mark on the patriarchal court. In the days of Rabban Gamliel III, the son of Judah I, and in later times, there appear among the court personnel Gothic and German bodyguards. These were prisoners of war, who had been imperial slaves and were presented by the emperor or the governor to the patriarch. Such bodyguards placed physical force at the disposal of the patriarch and he occasionally used it.[21] The patriarch, however, possessed other and subtler means of enforcing his will. The tenants who lived on his estates were many. Every morning they crowded to the palace gates to greet their lord. The patriarch, who was himself one of the richest men of his generation, felt bound to identify himself with men of his class. We are told that on certain occasions Judah I called out, when the crowd at a reception was too great: 'Make room for this owner of 100 minae, for that owner of 200!'[22] His basic attitude led occasionally to a certain harshness towards the poor. None the less the patriarch Judah I, who was one of the great landowners of the country, took care to alleviate the lot of the farmers. Although he himself subjected his estates to the full rigour of the Law as regards tithes, the sabbatical year etc., he was always ready to relax the rulings as far as possible for the benefit of the poorer peasants.[23]

The duties of the patriarch were manifold: in Palestine and the Diaspora he represented the Jewish nation in its external relations with the Roman authorities,[24] and in all internal matters he exercised the triple powers of legislator, judge and administrator.

The patriarch presided over the Sanhedrin, which was the supreme legislative authority of Palestine Jewry; and as such he had a great and often decisive influence on its decisions, although he was not entitled to issue edicts on his own authority. When Judah I learned that a Babylonian judge had decided a controversial matter with a verdict opposed to his, he shrugged the matter off by saying: 'He is a scholar, and I am a scholar'.[25] He was far less tolerant towards his own disciples, advising his son Gamliel III on his death-bed: 'Keep the (rabbinical) students well in hand'[26] and acting on this principle during his lifetime.[27] In the days of Judah I the concentration of powers in the hands of the patriarch was greater than before or after. Apparently the posts both of deputy-chairman of the Sanhedrin (*Hakam*) and of the President of the High Court (*Ab Bet Din*)[28] remained vacant between the time of Rabbi Meir (a contemporary of Judah's father Simeon II) and of R. Judah's I son Simeon. Quite possibly these functions were therefore temporarily concentrated in the hands of the patriarch.

In his judicial capacity the patriarch was assisted by the president of his 'small tribunal', a kind of Privy Council, a body nominated by the patriarch and dependent on his goodwill. This council dealt mostly with such matters as the calendar and the dates of the feasts. Rabbi Judah (a namesake of the patriarch), who was *morina* (jurisconsult) of the patriarchal court,[29] seems to have been connected with it. This tribunal extended its competence step by step, with the connivance of the Roman authorities.[30] Both in Palestine and Babylonia the right of the patriarch to annul a decree of excommunication (*nidduy*) by a local court was fully recognized, in cases where the excommunicating authorities were unable to do so themselves.[31]

The most important functions of the patriarch were, however, undoubtedly executive. He supervised the local authorities and appointed local officials. The relations of the central with the local Jewish authorities in Palestine in the second and third centuries have so far not been clarified. It is known, however, that the patriarch had a list (*pitkah*, i.e. a slip of paper)[32] in which he noted the candidates for ordination, and the appointment to a post which usually followed ordination. Judah I was very circumspect in making such appointments—not more than two in a year, and even then he reserved the right to annul the nomination. Only on his death-bed did he advise his son Gamliel III to nominate a greater number at once. Local protests could influence such a nomination.[33] A decision made at the same time established that a student could not give legal decisions unless authorised by his teacher: and as we have seen the right to give such authorisations was concentrated in the hands of the patriarch. We may learn from the case of the townlet of Simonias (Khirbat Samuniya in Galilee, near Beth Shearim), that the patriarch appointed scholars to act as judges and teachers in the small community.[34] The patriarchal appointees automatically became leaders of their respective communities. They naturally supported the central authority which had put them in their offices.

In the larger cities there was a 'city council' (*heber ha-ir*), the 'good men of the city', the council of the *decemprimi* in the Roman municipal administration. This board was either elected or appointed by the Roman governor; but the patriarch (or his representative) had the right to appoint scholars as 'welfare commissioners' (*parnasim*). Their main duties were to supervise ritual matters, charities and education, and to decide cases requiring rabbinical learning. The city council dealt with all other communal matters, in particular with the distribution of the tax-burden.[35] A clear-cut division of competences was probably never attained. As the powers of the scholarly class went on increasing[36] the influence of their local representatives, the *parnasim*, grew, and with it the authority of the patriarch who had appointed them. The patriarch visited the various communities in person, for instance Lydda.[37] To remote districts, such as the *Darom* (South),[38] he sent his commissions of enquiry.[39] The territorial divisions of the Holy Land, as set out in the Mishnah[40] are a rudimentary sketch of the Jewish administrative divisions of this period. We find for example three districts in Galilee: 'the Plain', which can be identified with the municipal territory of Tiberias; 'the Mountain'—in Roman administrative terms the Tetracomia, i.e. Upper Galilee,[41] and the 'Highlands' (the territory of Sepphoris), which completed the rest of Galilee.

The political duties of the patriarch did not end with the management of the internal affairs of local Jewry and with representing it before the Roman authorities. The patriarch was also the recognized head of all the Jews living under Roman jurisdiction. He appointed commissioners ('apostles' *apostoloi*) who travelled in the Diaspora from one community to another. They collected the various taxes due to the patriarch, the 'crown tax' and the *apostolé*, and transferred them to Palestine. They were also charged with the supervision of the chiefs of the local synagogues. In emergencies they were even empowered to depose the local chiefs and to appoint others in their stead.[42] A patriarchal ordination was valid not only in Palestine, but throughout the empire and even in Babylonia beyond its boundaries.[43] Scholars leaving Palestine had to ask for the permission of the patriarch before they could act abroad as teachers and judges, especially in matters of ritual law. The deep respect for the patriarch felt by Jews abroad is evidenced *inter alia* by the inscription found in the ruins of the synagogue of Stobi in Macedonia. Offenders are there threatened with a fine of a quarter-million denarii, to be paid to the patriarch.[44] The right to appoint (or at least to confirm) the heads of the synagogues throughout the Diaspora gave the patriarchate much power; for such rabbinical officials were permanent, while the heads of the communities (archons) were elected for a fixed time only and thus changed frequently. His influence over the Jews of the Empire naturally gave the patriarch much importance in the eyes of the Roman government. Even after the bloody suppression of the revolts in the reign of Trajan and after the war of Bar Kokhba the Jews of the empire constituted a considerable percentage of its population.

One of the most important privileges of the patriarch was the declaration of the dates of feasts. As there was no calendar accessible to the public, an observant Jew could only comply with the Law if he accepted patriarchal authority—and the days proclaimed by it. Otherwise he could unwittingly sin heavily by going to work on a day on which work was forbidden. The right to fix the dates of the feasts was essential for the authority of the patriarch and the rabbis, as well as for national unity.[45] This explains why all attempts by Babylonian scholars to fix these dates in their own country were opposed with great obstinacy by the patriarch and his commissioners.[46]

For all its powers, rights and privileges, the patriarchate was burdened by the hereditary principle. From the days of Judah I hereditary descent of this dignity in the House of Hillel was unchallenged. Before his death Judah I divided the various functions between his sons and dependants. The patriarchate in particular he willed to his second son as if it were a piece of personal property. 'Simeon my son shall be *Hakam*, Gamliel my son shall be patriarch; Hanina ben Hama shall preside (in the court of Law?)'.[47] By passing over his first-born, the dying patriarch showed his sharp understanding. Nevertheless the hereditary transmission of the patriarchate was but the first step on the road to its decline in the future.

We have discussed the various aspects of the patriarchate in detail, because of its overwhelming importance in the history of Palestine Jewry in the period to follow. Without strong authority at the centre the nation would very soon disintegrate into an agglomeration of local communities, without either the will or the power to take political action. In the new organization, which turned a people without a capital or national independence into a politically active body, the patriarchate was the kingpin of the whole.

Once the central authority had been set up, it had to make itself obeyed.

While the Temple and the state were still in existence, the legal Jewish authorities possessed ample means to enforce their will by physical force. Now the physical and moral factors in government had been separated. The Roman government exercised alone the power of the sword. The Jewish authorities had at first to rely solely on moral persuasion. The time when the two came to a close understanding had not yet arrived. Later the emperors and governors supported the patriarchate at any cost. Occasionally police action by the bodyguards of the later patriarchs could be anticipated by voluntary activities of rabbinical students. The pupils of Rabbi Meir once suggested that they should bring before him a man who had given offence and give the offender a sound beating.[48] Such sporadic acts could not serve to maintain a stable authority. It was necessary to bring about a more or less voluntary submission to the newly constituted authorities, using persuasion and not force. This process has been recorded in our sources as a conflict between the 'scholars' (*talmide hakamim*) and the 'common people' (*am ha-arets*). Its origin and course need not be discussed here in detail,[49] but only as far as it concerns the problem before us.

It is well known that already in the days of the Second Temple there existed an organization of Pharisees comprising all those who had pledged themselves to a strict observance of the ritual law both written and oral. Members of this organization were each called the 'associate' (*haber*) or 'reliable' (*neeman*). All those outside the organization were called 'common people' or 'people of the land' (*am ha-arets*). After the destruction of the Temple and the abolition of the old authorities who derived their title from their priestly descent, the 'associates' became the only extant cadre for an autonomous national organization. The nucleus of the new order therefore arose from their midst—first at Yabneh and then at Usha. They now undertook to impose the authority of the Sanhedrin on the masses. The action towards the people followed two lines. As soon as Jewish tribunals were allowed to function,[50] the 'associates' became the judges, because they were learned in the Law. From the bench they could use the precedent-making power of the courts to establish the rule of the rabbinical class. At the same time they used all the means at their disposal of influencing the people, by sermons and the like. In spite of these two powerful instruments of law and propaganda, popular opposition to rabbinical leadership continued for a long time. Both parties expressed their mutual distaste with much verbal violence; of course such expressions have come down to us in greater quantity from the more vocal rabbinical class. The discussion on this matter continued from the days of Rabbi Yohanan ben Zakkai to those of Judah I the Patriarch.[51] One of the principal reasons for the discussions between the scholars and the people was that the rabbis were exempted from taxation, and the communities of the towns in which they lived were bound to supply their needs. This controversy lasted till the great economic crisis in the middle of the third century.[52] Only then did new lines of social cleavage obliterate the old divisions. Only a few of the more tradition-bound scholars continued to treat their old adversaries with their former scorn; one of them was the consistent traditionalist Rabbi Eleazar ben Pedath. On the whole, however, the danger of a national split on the lines scholars vs. people was averted, even if for some time it had seemed that the Jewish nation would be divided into two entities between whom there would be neither *commercium* nor *conubium*.[53] The opposition to the rabbinical class came not only from the poorer *amme ha-arets*; in fact the more prosperous among them showed the greater daring.

Before the war of Bar Kokhba some of the scholars were also opposed to rabbinical rule in the municipalities. Rabbi Akiba himself is reported to have once advised his son: 'Do not dwell in a city, at the head of which are scholars'.[54] Possibly, however, he remembered the strictures of his youth, when he himself had been an *am ha-arets*. In the end, however, the rabbis prevailed. They succeeded in establishing themselves as the leading class in the surviving fragment of the Jewish nation. In the Babylonian Talmud we find an enumeration of the various groups of top people.[55] Scholars head the list, followed by 'the great men of the generation' (presumably non-scholars), the heads of the synagogues, heads of communities etc. Of course this saying, like most of the others recorded, was composed by the scholars and is in consequence biased in their favour. There can, however, be no doubt that rabbinical opinions in the end penetrated all classes, the *amme ha-arets* included; and in consequence, the supreme authority of the patriarch and the Sanhedrin, who were themselves at the head of the ruling class, was generally acknowledged throughout the nation.[56] The resulting rule of the rabbis has continued since then in Judaism almost down to the present generation. The crowd of people of all classes who thronged the antechamber of the patriarch was symbolic of the creation of a new national focus.

2. *Roman Rule in Jewish Eyes*

From the earliest days of their subjection to Roman government the Jews of Palestine evolved four different attitudes towards foreign rule: one positive, one moderate, one neutral and one hostile.[57]

Those who approved Roman rule outright were always a small minority among the Jews. They derived their importance from their superior social standing and from the fact that their Roman friends had confided to them the reins of government. This group included the House of Herod and its followers, and many of the high priestly families. In the days of war this party was the first object of popular fury. In the days of the uneasy peace that followed the destruction of the Temple its natural tendency was to assimilate with the Graeco-Roman aristocracy and to leave Judaism altogether. In consequence of this process of attrition at both ends, we find that by the middle of the third century this class had almost disappeared. Its descendants had intermarried with the Roman senatorial aristocracy and the client dynasties of the Romans. After the destruction of the Jewish state they had lost interest in Judaism, because their training and abilities were for administration, and without a state they could not make use of them. Their last traces disappear with the war of Bar Kokhba. The Jewish leaders of the succeeding generations, even the most moderate among them, remained true to Judaism at all times.

In the period under consideration here only three parties were left among the Jews as far as the attitude towards Rome was concerned. Their various points of view were admirably summed up in the celebrated discussion reported in the Babylonian Gemara[58] between three scholars, the leaders of the third generation of the Tannaim, the generation which followed the war of Bar Kokhba. Rabbi Judah ben Ilai, the moderate, Rabbi Yose ben Halafta, the neutral, and Rabbi Simeon bar Yohai, the zealot. 'Rabbi Judah began and said: "How beautiful are the deeds of that nation (the Romans). They set up market places, build bridges, construct baths." Rabbi Yose kept silent. Rabbi Simeon replied: "Everything they do for their own good. They set up market places to place there their harlots; baths for their pleasures, bridges to levy tolls." ' The three trends outlined above continued to co-exist, as we see, even after the disaster of Beth-Ter. The only thing changed was their relative strength.

The fateful decision whether the Jews should acquiesce in Roman rule or whether they should continue to try to shake off its yoke depended mainly on the attitude of the neutral or middle party. This was due both to its middle stance between two extremes, and also because it included the mass of the common people, which kept away from politics and was almost exclusively interested in worshiping in freedom and making a living. After the destruction of the Temple this majority swung to the moderate and supported their leader, Rabban Yohanan ben Zakkai. The strong and enthusiastic personality of Rabbi Akiba and the influence of the Pharisee organization (the *heber*) led by him gradually swung the masses of the people to the party of revolt. In the course of the war of Bar Kokhba most of the zealots lost their lives, and the others were sobered up. From the time when political reconstruction became at all possible, that is from the abolition of the edicts of Hadrian, the people again placed its trust in the leaders of the moderate party. They continued to do so right down the centuries, to the Persian invasion of the seventh century.

The zealot minority did not, of course, disappear. Rabbi Simeon bar Yohai remained for a whole generation the guardian of the anti-Roman tradition. He lived in hiding for twelve years, pursued all the time by the agents of the government. On one occasion he formulated the hopes and expectations of his party in one sentence: 'When you see a Persian horse tethered in the Holy Land—prepare for the coming of the Messiah'.[59] He and his party hoped for the help of the Parthians, the inveterate foes of the Romans in the East. His extremist opinions explain his constant complaints against the denunciations (*delatio*) 'which were more than the world could put up with'.[60]

In the succeeding generations, from the last quarter of the second century to the great crisis in the middle of the third, zealot influence was on the wane. Hatred of Rome did indeed continue to burn in many breasts, especially among the popular preachers and orators, the Haggadists. These were always comparing 'the wicked kingdom (i.e. Rome) with a serpent; they fervently hoped for the day in which Israel would be able to say to the Gentiles: 'Where are now your *hypatikoi* (consuls) and your *hēgemones* (governors)?'[61] From these circles we hear all the time complaints about the police spies and informers, of the 'evil tongue' (*leshon ha-ra*). Some scholars stuck to the traditions of the zealots of former days. One of them was Rabbi Nahum ben Simai, who was called 'Nahum the Holy', because throughout his life he steadfastly refused to look upon a coin with the unlawful image of the emperor struck on it.[62] The zealots were especially bitter enemies of the moderates, particularly those who collaborated with the Romans. Rabbi Joshua ben Karhah did not hesitate to abuse the son of Rabbi Simeon bar Yohai himself, because he had abandoned the extremist views of his father. Thus the hidden fire of zealotry continued to glimmer throughout the period of appeasement, till the economic and political upheavals of the third century furnished it with fresh fuel and it burst alight again.

Parallel with the rise of the zealots in the first Tannaitic generation came the decline of the moderate party; in fact the fortunes of the two parties were naturally balanced. After Rabban Yohanan ben Zakkai, Rabbi Joshua ben Hanania was the leader of this party; he still possessed considerable influence. However Rabbi Yose ben Kisma, the moderate leader of the next generation, was practically isolated. When Rabbi Akiba called the nation to revolt and pointed to Bar Kokhba as the hoped-for Messiah, only one scholar dared to oppose him. This was Rabbi Yohanan ben Turta, an almost unknown personality, who was suspected of being a proselyte, and was bereft of all political influence.

It was only after the disastrous defeat of the revolt that the people turned again to the House of Hillel, the acknowledged leaders of the moderate party. Of course the terms 'moderate' and 'zealot' are to a certain extent misleading. We need only to compare the views of the so-called moderates with those of the out-and-out Romanizers in order to see that the gulf dividing the moderates from the activists was one of practice, not of theory. Even the moderates turned scornfully away from such supporters of the Roman rule as the dynasty of Herod or 'that other one' (i.e. Aher, the renegade Elisha ben Abuyah). During the Hadrianic persecution some leaders were indeed ready to submit. Thus Rabbi Yose ben Kisma was angry with Rabbi Hanina ben Teradion, who held meetings and taught the Law although the Roman government had forbidden it.[63]

The leaders of the first generation after the fall of Bar Kokhba, Rabban Simeon II ben Gamliel, the patriarch and Rabbi Meir, were opposed to each other in matters of internal policy, but united in their moderation as regards relations with government. Both nevertheless felt very acutely the harsh circumstances under which Israel had to live in the Holy Land. Rabban Simeon is recorded as saying: 'If we had to write (all our sufferings) we would never finish'.[64] In Rabbi Meir's copies of the Book of Isaiah the words 'the burden of Dumah' (Isa. 21, 11) were found changed to 'the burden of Rome'.[65] Rabban Judah I, the patriarch, the friend of the emperor Antoninus, was found sighing deeply when he remembered the wrong done to Israel by the Roman oppressors. When he remembered the fall of Beth-Ter he used to interpret the verse, 'The voice is Jacob's voice but the hands are the hands of Esau' (Gen. 27, 22), as follows—Jacob was lamenting at the wrong done at Beth-Ter by the hands of Esau (=Rome).[66] When, reciting the 'Lamentations', he read the verse 'and cast down from heaven to earth the glory of Israel' (Lamentations 2, 1), he let the book fall and repeated 'from a very high tower unto the deepest pit'.[67] When he went to Caesarea to meet the Emperor, his companions would compare the Roman soldiers garrisoning the capital to the flies which were soiling the baskets of figs and grapes heaped up in the market.[68] This tradition of deep mistrust towards the government was also felt by Rabban Gamliel III, his son. He warned his hearers against 'the rulers who never favoured a man but for their own ends'.[69] This pessimistic view of the Roman authority was repeated after many generations by another leading scholar, one who had much experience in pleading the Jewish cause at the governor's court. This was Rabbi Abbahu of Caesarea, who, although he was honoured by the Roman rulers, is nevertheless reported as saying: 'This government is full of deceit and lies, fraud and false pretences and bribery.'[70]

The leaders of the nation had to admit, however, that, relatively speaking, the situation of Israel was not as desperate as it might be. Rabban Simeon II ben Gamliel and Rabbi Yannai, a contemporary of Rabban Judah I, both remarked that although 'we do not enjoy the pleasures of the wicked' (who are going to expiate their sins in hell) 'yet we do not suffer the sufferings of the just' (who are going to enjoy paradise).[71]

In everyday practice the patriarchs and their followers were therefore ready to recognize the existing situation and to assist the government in pacifying the country. Such practical considerations gained additional weight from the fact that their own position within the Jewish community was to a large extent dependent on keeping up good relations with the Roman government. It is known that before the patriarch could exercise his functions he needed the formal confirmation of the Roman governor.[72] When the governor of Palestine went to Syria to consult with his colleague there, the patriarch had to follow in his wake from Acre to Tyre, from Tyre to Sidon, and even beyond, to Berytus and Antioch.[73] In case of need the patriarch himself, or a delegation of scholars from his court, went to Rome to propitiate the emperor in person; they could hardly do so if they were on bad terms with the government.

The patriarchs of the House of Hillel were also not likely to forget that in times of revolt against Rome the authority of their fathers and fore-fathers had twice been set aside in favour of an insurrectionary govern-ment. They had clearly a personal interest in keeping the peace. After two centuries of incessant strife and two wars, their own needs coincided with those of the entire nation.

The moderate party tried by all means to influence the masses in favour of peace. As they could hardly come out openly in support of Roman rule, they represented it as a dispensation of providence which it would be impious to oppose. They tried to tone down as far as possible all expecta-tions of immediate redemption, because the Messianic movement, the mainspring of rebellion, fed on such hopes. One of the first to praise peace was the patriarch Rabban Simeon II ben Gamliel. His contem-porary, Rabbi Yose bar Halafta, described a message of God to Esau (=Rome) in these terms: 'If you see Jacob your brother throwing off the yoke of the Law—punish him and rule over him'.[74] Roman rule was supposed to avenge offences against the Law and therefore to be regarded as sent from heaven; this scholar was in fact continuing the line of argu-ment of the pacifist prophets who saw in Assyria and Babylonia the 'scourge of the Lord'. In the generation of Rabban Judah I there is much evidence of cordial relations between the patriarch and the government, as we have seen. Even when the patriarch exchanged gifts with the Parthian king Artabanus he did not go beyond expressions of vague sym-pathy. Pro-Roman views continued to be voiced in the following genera-tion. Rabbi Simeon ben Halafta said 'The Holy One, blessed be He, did not find a greater instrument of benediction for Israel than peace'.[75] A whole 'Chapter on Peace' in the *Derekh Erets Zuta* (the supplement to the Talmud dealing with ethical matters) is devoted to this subject. We find there a confused anthology on the praise of peace of every kind: domestic peace, peace between neighbours, peace between one man and another, and peace between nations.

Parallel with the exhortations on peace came the insistence on the power of the government. The last Tannaim taught: 'Moses honoured the authorities . . . as God ordered him to do . . . so Joseph, so Hanania, so Mishael and Azariah'.[76] In the first generation of Amoraim we find Rabbi Yannai saying: 'The fear of the government should be always upon you'[77] adding, 'and how can mere mortals escape its powers?'[78] In the second generation Rabbi Yose ben Hanina said that God 'was entreating Israel not to rebel—and if they revolted nevertheless, their blood would be spilt like that of deer' (i.e. they would be hunted like beasts).[79] Even during the political and economic crisis of the third century, which strained to the utmost relations with the Roman government,[80] some solitary voices were still justifying the ways of the government. Rabbi Simeon bar Lakish— who indeed changed his mind later on—once said: '"It was very good" (Gen. 1, 12)—these are the ways of kingship on earth . . . which demands justice (*dikion*, from the Greek *dike*) amongst the people'.[81] The last scholar to hold such views was Rabbi Abba bar Kahana, who, while he compares the Roman government to a snake, adds: 'Just as a snake does not bite a man except when ordered to do so from on high . . . so the government does not persecute one unless ordered to so do (by Providence)'.[82]

Together with the stress laid upon the power of the government and on its function as the agent of Providence, the people were warned against dreamers and visionaries, who were forever calculating the coming of the Day of Judgement and who were expecting daily the arrival of the Messiah. The Messianic hope had already served as mainspring of the two revolts with their disastrous results. This is indubitable as regards the war of Bar Kokhba. In his history of the First War, Josephus did his best to cover up the Messianic tendency, because it would make the defeated Jews appear still dangerous to the eyes of the Romans; nevertheless its existence is evident. In latter generations the Messianic expectation remained the most sublime manifestation of Judaism. Whoever lost his belief in the coming of the Messiah was considered not to be a Jew. It was a fact that those who despaired of the future usually ended by opting out of the oppressed and persecuted nation. Yet the expectation of *immediate* salvation appeared to the leaders of the generations following the Bar Kokhba revolt as no less dangerous than the opposite; Messianism was an instrument of the zealots, and suspect as such. The official line was that the arrival of the Messiah was a matter which concerned only God. No mere mortal could foretell the end of Roman rule and thereby infringe the prerogative of divine Providence.

The earliest evidence for the moderate point of view is furnished by Rabbi Yose ben Halafta in the first generation after the fall of Beth-Ter. He is reported as saying: 'Whoever calculates (lit. gives) the end (i.e. the Messianic coming) . . . has no share in the world to come'.[83] In the next generation Rabbi Simeon ben Eliezer warned against youthful enthusiasm: 'If children tell you: "Go, build the Temple"—do not listen to them'.[84] In the last Tannaite generation Hiyya Rabba stressed the slow coming of the redemption: 'The redemption of Israel will come step by step'.[85] An anonymous Tannaitic Baraita mentions among the seven mysteries hidden from the eye of man 'the time of the fall of the kingdom of Edom (i.e. of Rome)'.[86] In the first generation of Ammoraim Rabbi Jonathan ben Eleazar solemnly cursed 'those calculating the end'.[87] His contemporary Hanina ben Hama did indeed make such a calculation himself, but he assumed the coming of the Messiah four centuries after the destruction of the Temple (i.e. for the year 470);[88] since he himself lived in the third century he was not likely to have to verify his arithmetic. In the second and third generation of the Amoraim, when expectations of immediate salvation were rising amongst the commons because of the bad times, similar voices of warning could still be heard. Rabbi Yohanan ben Napaha compares Israel to a man who makes his way in darkness. 'He made a light and it went out, he made another and it went out again; so he said: "How long must I tire myself out and struggle with this lamp; it would be better to wait for sunrise". So Israel was oppressed in Egypt and Moses came and delivered them; and again in Babylonia . . . in Elam . . . in Persia and Media . . . by the Greeks . . . and finally by wicked Edom. And now Israel has said: "We are tired of being oppressed and saved again and again (by mortals). Now we shall not ask for flesh and blood to deliver us, but we shall wait for the Holy One himself to light our way".'[89] In another place a saying of his is recorded that the end of the Second Exile—in contrast with the Babylonian captivity—was not to be foreseen. 'The first exiles, whose guilt was evident, knew also when their exile was going to end; the later, whose guilt was hidden, have the end hidden from them too.'[90] His contemporary, Rabbi Simeon ben Lakish, represents God as saying: 'The time of the salvation I have made known to my heart alone and not even the ministering angels know it'.[91] He said also: 'The deep (Gen. 1, 2)—this stands for the wicked rule (of Rome). As the deep cannot be plumbed, so the wicked rule has no known termination.'[92]

Some attempts were even made to attenuate the memory of the past disasters in popular memory. Those killed by the Romans were not to be mourned. Brides might again pass through the city in an *apiryon* (probably a kind of *lectica* or sedan-chair), although this had formerly been forbidden as a sign of national mourning.[93] Judah I the patriarch is reported as having contemplated a plan 'to abolish the (fast of the)

Ninth of Ab'; he gave this idea up because of the opposition of the Sages.[94]

Judah I even advised collaboration with the Romans not only politically but fiscally. He recommended his sons to be honest in paying custom duties[95] and was always ready to help settle taxation disputes as far as it was possible.[96]

A few members of the moderate or appeasing party were prepared to go further and to collaborate actively with the Roman authorities in ferreting out the activist zealots. It is characteristic of this generation of appeasement that amongst them were not only Rabbi Ishmael the son of Rabbi Yose ben Halafta, the leader of the neutral party, but even Rabbi Eleazar ben Simeon, the son of Rabbi Simeon bar Yohai, the leader of the zealots of the preceding generation. In answer to the reproaches of his father's old associates Rabbi Eleazar told them: 'I am merely weeding out the thistles (criminals) from the vineyard (Israel)', but in the eyes of the opposite faction, led by Rabbi Joshua ben Karhah, he was called 'Vinegar, the son of Wine', because he was delivering God's people to slaughter.[97] We are also told that the prophet Elijah appeared in his wrath to Rabbi Ishmael bar Yose, because he did not escape to Laodicea from the authorities (as his father had fled to Asia before him), but stayed at home and obeyed the Emperor's orders.[98] Rabbi Ezechiel (bar Abba, an Amora of the first generation) justified this point of view: 'One is allowed to inform against those who divide the people'.[99] The true reasons for this collaborationist attitude of some of the scholars are to be found in the circumstances by which Rabbi Joshua ben Levi of the first generation of Amoraim justified his action in handing over the rebel Ulla to the authorities after the latter had fled to Lydda: 'It is better that this one man should perish than that the whole community should suffer because of him'.[100] This problem is also discussed in the Palestinian Gemara.[101] 'A band of Jews was going its way and met a band of Gentiles. They said: "give us one of you that we may kill him; if not we shall kill all of you". Even should they all die, they may not deliver one soul of Israel. But if the enemies look for a definite person, such as Sheba the son of Bichri (2 Sam. 20), they may give him up and escape death.' Rabbi Yohanan said: 'Even if he did not deserve the death of Sheba'—that is even if the person sought for by the authorities was innocent under Jewish law.

3. *The Jews and Greek Culture*

The reaction of the various Jewish groups to the Hellenistic language and culture may also serve to elucidate their approach to the political problems of the time. Knowledge of Greek was absolutely essential to anyone either obliged or willing to get in touch with the Gentiles and their rulers. By implication it furthered the cause of the *modus vivendi* which was the aim of the moderates among the Jewish leaders.

Opposition to Greek culture was therefore strongest among the popular preachers or Haggadists, who were the mainstay of the zealot party. In their eyes knowledge of Greek was the first step to perdition, to the complete assimilation of Israel amongst the nations. They pointed to the fact that most of the known apostates had begun their career of betrayal by meeting Gentiles and reading their books, especially the works of the Greek philosophers.[102] The saying was current in these circles: 'All liquids mix except water and oil; so Israel does not mix with the Gentiles.[103] They recalled the former attempts at assimilation, which had borne no fruit: 'After Joseph's death the Jews said: "Let us live like the Egyptians". And in the days of Ezekiel they wanted to live like all the other nations.' These preachers opposed assimilation in all its forms including assumption of Gentile names by Jews. Rabbi Eleazar ha-Kappar said that 'Israel was delivered out of Egypt because of the merit they had acquired by not changing either their names or their speech'.[104]

On this point even the moderates agreed to a certain extent with the extremists. They too were interested in the survival of the traditional way of life. But because they had always shunned radical courses, they could not refuse all contact with the outer world. As such contact required of necessity a knowledge of Greek, they were ready to accept a good deal of compromise. This extended to a measure of tolerance towards various manifestations of pagan faith which abounded in everyday life in all non-Jewish cities in Palestine and abroad.

The patriarchal house was of necessity in this matter on the side of the compromisers. Rabban Gamliel ben Simeon drew a fine distinction between the statues of gods made for the purpose of decoration only and statues which were cult objects proper.[105] We are told that he once went and bathed in the Bath of Aphrodite at Ptolemais-Acre, although it contained an image of the goddess. When his attention was drawn to the statue, he is reported to have replied 'I did not come into her precincts, but she came into mine. One does not say that the bath was made to adorn Aphrodite, but that Aphrodite was made to adorn the bath.'[106] His son, Rabban Simeon II, remembered that in the house of his father there were 'five hundred' boys studying the Law and 'five hundred' others who studied 'Greek wisdom'.[107] Because of its contacts with the Roman government, which were a national necessity, much was condoned in the patriarchal court which was forbidden elsewhere. According to Rabbi Hanina ben Gamliel a human likeness (*prosopon*) was engraved on the patriarchal seals.[108] Negotiators who acted on behalf of the patriarch were allowed to dress their hair in the Greek fashion, although in general this was 'in the ways of the Amorites and contrary to the biblical prohibition of "marring the edges of the beard" ' (Lev. 19, 27).[109]

Political necessities also coloured the attitude of the patriarchs towards Greek. They preferred, of course, Hebrew, the holy language; but Hebrew was in their time no longer spoken by the majority of Jews, who were using Aramaic in their daily speech. The patriarchs preferred Greek to Aramaic, in speech and in writing. Rabban Simeon ben Gamliel did not allow any but Greek and Hebrew books.[110] Rabban Judah I spoke scornfully of the current Judaeo-Aramaic dialect. 'Rabbi has said: "In the Land of Israel, why this clipped Syrian talk? (a pun on *Suri*—'Syrian' and *sursi* 'castrated')—either the Holy Tongue or Greek".'[111]

In spite of all these efforts life went its own way. The Judaeo-Aramaic language had struck deep roots amongst the people and could not be eradicated from above. The influence of Greek declined with the decline of the patriarchal house after the death of Rabban Judah I. In the first generation of Amoraim Rabbi Joshua ben Levi decided that boys could be taught Greek only in those hours which were neither of the day nor of the night, i.e. practically never.[112] In the next generation Rabbi Yohanan did indeed appreciate Greek culture to some extent. He taught that because both Shem and Japheth had honoured their father Noah 'Shem was found worthy of the prayer shawl (*talit*) and Japheth of the *pallium* (philosopher's mantle).'[113] Nevertheless he allowed only girls to be taught Greek 'because Greek is an adornment for them'.[114] As relations with the Gentile government worsened in the course of the third century, Rabbi Yohanan renewed the ban on the study of Greek by the boys 'for fear of delation'.

Ultimately, the problem of assimilation in the Greek world bore the same stamp of compromise as so many other aspects of the period. The Jewish authorities opposed assimilation in theory and asked their people to remain spiritually independent. In practice, however, they had to give way in many matters, in order to enable the individual Jews to keep good relations with their neighbours and the authorities and to maintain themselves in a hostile world.

The Jewish inscriptions from Palestine, and especially the tombstones, supply us with an objective yardstick with which to assess the extent of Greek influence. From them we may learn that Hellenization had progressed much farther than would appear from the literary sources, or from rabbinical law. We already find lists of Greek and Latin names used by Jews in the Midrash.[115] As usual in such cases the Hebrew names were translated sometimes by sound and sometimes by sense. Isaac became Gelasios 'the laughing one', Menahem—Paregorios 'the consoling one'. On the other hand Esther became Astreia, Reuben—Rufus, Joseph—Justus and so on. The epitaphs from the Jaffa cemetery prove the extent to which Greek names had penetrated even among the poorer classes, usually much more conservative and inimical to change than their social 'betters'. In the necropolis of Beth Shearim, where the buried were of well-to-do families, the percentage of Greek names reaches 80 and more.[116] It must be remembered of course that Beth Shearim served at that time as the central burial place for the Jews from the whole East, and that it is therefore not quite representative of Palestine Jewry, but rather reflects conditions abroad. In any case it is abundantly clear that the Greek language permeated deeply into all social strata of Jewry. This fact was not without its political significance. The knowledge of the language of the ruling culture contributed undoubtedly towards a more moderate attitude. At the end of the period under consideration here the Helleniz-ing tendency reached a new height. Rabbi Levi ben Hittah went to Caesarea and there heard the *Shema* prayed *hellenistin* (i.e. in Greek).[117] The text of the Jerusalem (i.e. Palestinian) Talmud bears ample evidence of Greek influence both in vocabulary and syntax. It shows that the Greek language had penetrated even into the rabbinical circles, the very fastness of the old traditions and of the observance of the Law.

We may therefore sum up the extent to which Greek spread among the Jews in Palestine as follows:[118] the locally born scholars, especially those of the fourth century, who lived in the great cities, show great familiarity with Greek legal precepts and parables, including Greek literature and law. Those who had come from Babylonia knew hardly any Greek at all. Those living in provincial towns and the middle classes in towns and cities alike knew but little Greek. The *am ha-arets* (common people), especially the peasants, knew either no Greek at all or just enough to sell their produce in the cities. The lower class Jews in the towns spoke fluently the vulgar Greek jargon of their pagan neighbours.

In the Hellenized Orient Greek art was even more important than Greek literature. The latter demanded a thorough knowledge of the Greek language, whereas the former was accessible to everyone with a feeling for form and eyes to see. The synagogues built in Galilee in the second to fourth centuries and the ornaments of the Jewish tombs and sarcophagi at Beth Shearim make it possible to assess the degree of penetration of Greek visual elements into Jewish popular consciousness.

As we have already seen,[119] the synagogues had been built by the contributions from many individuals; the choice of the architect was prob-ably decided upon by the leaders of the community. We have epigraphical proof that the builder of a synagogue in Galilee was also busy in the Bashan region.[120] This was no individual case. The style of the Galilean synagogues of the early type is undoubtedly influenced by the Syrian architecture of the Roman period.[121] The architects merely followed the style fashionable in their time, which was also agreeable to their clients. The details of architectural ornament were chosen—as is evident from their selection—by the architect and conformed to late Hellenistic patterns. The execution, on the other hand, was carried out by the local stonemasons who adapted the Greek patterns to their own orientalizing traditions.[122]

As regards the planning of the synagogues, the Jewish architects faced the challenge of a new creation. Pagan temples were supposed to serve as the dwelling place of the god. Their interior was hidden from profane eyes in a mysterious darkness and only priests could enter; the mass of worshippers assembled in the court around the altar of sacrifices. The Jewish cult as established after the destruction of the Temple required a quite different architectural approach. A hall had to be created in which the whole community could assemble; and which had enough light to make the reading of the Law possible. Moreover, the interior of the synagogues had to be plain, so as not to distract the attention of the worshippers from the spoken word. The main ornamentation of these synagogues was therefore placed on the outside.

The solution to these requirements was an adaptation of the type of the Greek *bouleuterion*. The hall was almost square, with three aisles around a central space. The roof rested on two rows of columns lengthwise and one crosswise. It is possible that there was a special gallery for women. In the hall benches were placed along three of the walls. A special seat of honour, the so-called 'Seat of Moses' (Matth. 23, 2) was decorated more richly than the rest. The early synagogues had no special fixed receptacle for the scrolls of the Law. These were kept in a wooden ark, which was brought forward from a side-room at the hours of prayer. The synagogue hall was paved with flagstones.

The main architectural ornaments (portals, façade and column capitals) followed the fashion of the time; the façade turned towards Jerusalem was especially richly decorated. It had a main door and two side doors. It seems likely, however, that the worshippers entered by one of the side doors and then turned towards the main portal to pray. Above it was a big arched window, a sign of remembrance of the Eternal City and orientation towards it (Daniel 6, 10).

The ornaments of the synagogue are especially instructive for the liberal tendency of contemporary Judaism. Besides the common Greek plant ornament and the accepted symbols of Jewish religion (the seven-branched candlestick or *menorah* and the Ark of the Law)—which are not especially prominent—the ornaments used included the fertility symbols of the Holy Land (palm tree, vine). We also find old oriental magical symbols, such as the pentagram and the hexagram (called in later times 'Seal of Solomon' and 'Shield of David'). Most interesting is a whole group of symbols borrowed from Syro-Roman syncretism: the sun-eagle, the wreath held by two winged Victories, fabulous animals such as the griffon and sea monsters, also lions and bulls in pairs facing each other.[123] Occasionally rabbinical tolerance went very far. At Chorazin for instance we find Greek mythological elements (Heracles, Medusa, Centaur), or representations of village scenes (such as a vintage) which included images of human beings.[124] It should be noted that this liberal interpretation of the Second Commandment (Exodus 20, 4) only extended to reliefs; apart from two free-standing statues of symbolical lions, no three-dimensional sculpture was allowed.

The same liberal tendency in visual art can be observed at Beth Shearim.[125] Subjects which were formerly entirely forbidden are allowed. The frieze of a mausoleum found above catacomb 11 had representations of the sun-eagle, flanked by groups of wolves fighting each other on one side, and a peaceful procession of animals on the other. In the same mausoleum stood a (reused) sarcophagus, with the representation of Greek myths, Achilles on Scyrus, Meleager (?) and Leda and the Swan. The latter subject is treated with a remarkable degree of sensuality.[126] The entrance to catacomb 11 below the mausoleum was decorated with a mosaic pavement on which dolphins are represented.[127]

One could possibly argue that this mausoleum represented the liberal taste of the Diaspora Jewry, as most of those buried at Beth Shearim were brought there from outside Palestine. This argument cannot, however, be valid for catacomb 20, a huge hall with side rooms which included coffins of rabbis described as 'holy', and of members of the patriarchal family. Here too were found coffins ornamented with representations of men and beasts, made locally, together with many fragments of imported marble sarcophagi with amazonamachies and other mythological scenes.[128]

This liberal attitude to visual arts has left its traces in rabbinical literature of the third century.[129] It can be explained only partly by economic reasons (the Jewish craftsmen in the mixed cities had to compete with pagan workmen who had no inhibitions as regards Greek mythology), but mainly by the general decline of the Olympic religion and the consequent decrease of the danger of idolatry. This liberal attitude is the more remarkable because it contrasts strongly with the continued prohibition concerning the cult of the emperors. The same rabbis who allowed representations of the Olympian gods and myths were absolutely inflexible about statues of the emperors and of still active pagan cults, such as that of Isis.

4. *The Age of Revolts Comes to an End*

The common view of Jewish history in Palestine held hitherto and still occasionally entertained, is that the period we are considering now was a series of revolts and of savage Roman reprisals. Before, however, setting out the contrary view and, as we believe, the true one, we should like to survey the sources for the alleged 'revolts'.

In the *Historia Augusta* (Life of Antoninus Pius 5, 4) we find the following statement: 'he suppressed through his governors and legates many peoples, including the rebellious Jews'.[130] We must remember that it was precisely in the reign of Pius that the edicts of Hadrian were rescinded, and the rights of the Jews to religious and communal autonomy admitted, and the patriarchate and the Sanhedrin were restored to their former powers.[131] Obviously this passage refers to the first three years of this emperor, when the edicts were still in force and the Jews continued to struggle against them.

Next we come to Eusebius, the bishop of Caesarea, who composed in the fourth century a *Chronicle* from the days of Abraham to his own times. The Greek original of this chronicle is lost and we possess only the Latin and Armenian versions, the former being the work of Jerome who lived at Bethlehem in the early fifth century. In this chronicle of Eusebius-Jerome we find the following entry under the year 197: 'Jewish and Samaritan war'.[132] Eusebius' chronicles served as a source book for most of the early Christian historians. These writers understood this passage in two diametrically opposed senses. Some thought it to mean 'War of the Romans *against* the Jews and Samaritans', who presumably had revolted together. Others read it 'War *between* the Jews *and* the Samaritans'. To the former group belong Sulpicius Severus (fourth century), Orosius (fifth century) and Michael the Syrian (twelfth century); to the second, Dionysius of Tell Mahra (ninth century) and Bar Hebraeus (Abu el Faraj, thirteenth century).[133] There are several good reasons why we should for once accept the later tradition. Septimius Severus was friendly to the Jews both by reason of his upbringing and his origins.[134] For this we have epigraphical evidence in the Greek inscription found in the ruins of the synagogue at Kitsyon (near Safed) in Galilee.[135] It reads: 'For the welfare of our lords, the emperors Lucius Septimius Severus (the empress Julia Domna), Marcus Aurelius Antoninus ("Caracalla") and Lucius Septimius Geta, his sons, a dedication *ex voto* of the Jews'. It should be noted that this is the only known inscription dedicated by Palestinian Jews to any Roman emperor. One can hardly assume that all the others had disappeared, when there are scores of extant dedicatory inscriptions from non-Jewish sources. It cannot be that all of the Jewish and hardly any non-Jewish inscriptions should have been lost. Moreover there is no mention of the alleged revolt of the year 197 in Talmudic sources, whereas all the other risings against the Romans down to and including that against Gallus Caesar in 351[136] have been recorded in more or less detail.

In the course of a civil war Severus also conquered Palestine from his rival Pescennius Niger, the governor of Syria. As usual many of the cities and legions of the empire saw in the civil war an excellent opportunity to pursue private feuds and to settle old scores. At that time Laodicea fought with Antioch, Tyre with Berytus and so on. Such hostilities between close neighbours were nothing unusual at the time. We learn from a Midrash[137] that there was a deep enmity between Halamish and Naveh, Castra and Haifa, Susitha (Hippus) and Tiberias, Jericho and Naaran, Lydda and Ono, all of them pairs of neighbours. In Palestine the Sixth Legion, camping at Legio in the Plain of Jezreel, took the side of Severus, and fought the legions which had sided with Niger. This state of anarchy in the empire explains the cryptic statement of Eusebius.

We learn from the *Historia Augusta* that Severus deprived the city of Neapolis of its municipal rights, because 'its citizens had fought for a long time on the side of Niger'.[138] Severus did not restore these rights until his second visit to Palestine in 199. The expression 'for a long time' to describe the losing fight of the Samaritans of Neapolis explains why the relevant item appears in the *Chronicle* of Eusebius in the year 197, although Niger had been already defeated in 194. It seems that the Samaritans continued the struggle for some time. The inhabitants of Byzantium had also kept faith with Niger till 197 and had resisted for three whole years the army of Severus which besieged them. Eusebius noted both events for that year, when resistance to Severus had ended everywhere.

The notice in the *Chronicle* of Eusebius seems therefore to indicate that there was enmity between the Jews and the Samaritans. The rival parties profited from the general anarchy of the civil war to start fighting. The alliance of the two peoples in the time of Bar Kokhba, and their renewed cooperation under the Christian emperor, need not preclude an intermediate period of hostility. After their common defeat in Bar Kokhba's war the relations between the former allies may well have taken a turn for the worse, as often happens in such cases. Luckily for themselves, the Jews chose the winning side, the Samaritans the losing one. The Jews were able thenceforward to bask in imperial favour. We have seen that the laws promulgated by Severus were far from hostile to the Jews. As he was notorious for severity towards his opponents, the fact that he took no revenge on the Jews is proof in itself that they did not revolt against him.

The Roman historian Dio Cassius (third century) relates the story of a robber named Claudius, who was active for a long time in Judaea and Syria. Dio Cassius does not state that Claudius was a Jew. There were very few Jews left in Judaea in the time of this Claudius. But even if we accept for argument's sake that Claudius was a Jew, he might quite well have been a member of the dwindling minority of zealots whose influence was hardly perceptible and who were denounced by the majority.[139] If we accept this theory, the area most likely to have been the centre of his activities might have been the region of Emmaus. This district was already the centre of Jewish zealotism in the time of the expedition of Varus (4 BC). The revolt was then led by a shepherd, Athronges. As late as the sixth century the security of the district was threatened by one Cyriacus, nicknamed 'the wolf', in whose band there were both Samaritans and Jews.[140]

In the 'Life of Severus' quoted above we also read[141] that the emperor allowed his son Caracalla a triumph, 'for the senate had decreed to him a triumph over Judaea because of the successes achieved by Severus in Syria' (Loeb ed. trsl. O'Brien-Moore: but the Latin reads: 'cui senatus Iudaicum triumphum decreverat, idcirco quod et in Syria res bene gestae fuerant a Severo'. According to Eusebius' Chronicle Caracalla triumphed over the Parthians in 202, after the victories of Severus there. The two notices cannot be connected, as the alleged defeat of the Jews must have taken place in 197. The 'Iudaicus triumphus' might well mean 'triumph over the Jews' and not 'over Judaea', then known as Syria Palaestina. In the time of Severus, and even more so in the period in which the *Historia Augusta* was composed, the distinction between Syria and Palestine was well established and a mistake unlikely. It seems that we should connect the triumph of Caracalla with the Parthian war. There was then a great deal of fighting in Adiabene, a kingdom with a considerable Jewish population since the days of the proselyte dynasty of Queen Helena (before 70). Adiabene might have been considered part of Syria; still more likely the text might have been corrupted to 'Syria' from 'Assyria'; Adiabene (the region round Mosul) most certainly belonged to the latter.

In short—there is no evidence whatsoever for Jewish revolts between 135 and 351, and none seem to have happened in fact.

5. *The Limits of the Compromise: Jerusalem and the Proselytes*

For all their interest in appeasement, even the Jewish moderates could not accept the edict which excluded them from Jerusalem and its territory.[142] The original decree, indeed, remained in force; but, as in the case of similar prohibitions which went against strong popular sentiment, it could not be enforced in full and for ever. We cannot *prima facie* assume that no Jew visited Jerusalem for 190 years, especially in a period of growing anarchy and administrative disorder in the Roman empire. The guard kept by the Romans around Jerusalem at such times would of necessity become less strict.

These assumptions are amply borne out by our sources. There is much evidence that pilgrimages to Jerusalem continued after the fall of Beth-Ter. In examining the evidence we should not, of course, put too much weight on legal decisions, because the codifiers of the Mishnah and Gemara

D

continued to decide on legal matters of purely theoretical importance, including points concerning Jerusalem. They deemed such decisions to be matters of significance in the eternal hope of a restoration of Temple and State. Decisions of this kind include the treatises of the Mishnah (*Middot, Tamid*) dealing with the structure and the sacrifices in the Temple; and the decisions concerning the purchase of cattle in Jerusalem and its transport to the Holy City.[143] The story about Elisha ben Abuyah (Aher—'the other one') who rode past the Holy of Holies on the Day of Atonement does not prove anything, for this faithful servant of the Romans was probably exempt from all restrictions upon the Jews.[144] The stories concerning the pilgrimages of Rabbi Yose ben Halafta, his meeting with the prophet Elijah in Jerusalem and how he heard the *Shekinah* (Divine Spirit) bewail the lost Temple,[145] are obviously legendary. The tale told by Rabbi Isaac in the next generation of how fruits were brought from Ginnosar to Jerusalem is clearly anachronistic.

Only in the fifth generation of Tannaim (first half of the third century) is there more and more evidence of a genuinely historical character. The first Jews who ventured into Jerusalem were of lowly station, and thus more likely to escape undetected. The first one to be mentioned was Simeon Kamtra, a donkey-driver, who was a contemporary of Rabbi Hiyya bar Abba (probably the earlier of the two scholars of that name). This Simeon enquired from the rabbis concerning the rules governing pilgrimage to Jerusalem. He was passing the city frequently in the course of his business and wanted to know whether he would have on every such occasion to rend his garments as prescribed for those beholding the desolation of the sanctuary. In the first generation of the Amoraim we have good evidence that the Rabbis Hanina, Jonathan and Joshua ben Levi visited Jerusalem.[146] Non-Jewish sources, such as Origen, support the Talmudic evidence.[147] With the continued disintegration of Roman authority in the second half of the third century, the prohibition on entering Jerusalem was set aside in practice. Rabbi Yohanan, the foremost scholar of the second generation of the Amoraim, said openly with reference to earthly Jerusalem (in contrast with the heavenly city): 'Anyone who wants to go up there, can go'.[148]

For a short time in the era of the 'thaw' between Rome and the Jews in the early days of the Severan dynasty, the prohibition was so far relaxed as to allow a group of pupils of Rabbi Meir to settle in Jerusalem. They founded a 'Holy Community' (*kehillah* or *edah kedoshah*), the decisions of which are quoted by the Patriarch Judah and his contemporaries. None of the five or six members of the community are well known and most of them are quoted only once or twice in the Talmudic sources. The decision of Rabbi Meir that the stones of the wall of Jerusalem were 'sacred' and no profit should be made from them, might indicate some building activity in this same connection. In any case the 'community' lasted only one generation and left no traces after the balmy period of Rabbi Judah I.[149]

But even if Jews were allowed to visit Jerusalem, the Holy City still remained an alien colony. When they reached Mount Scopus and beheld the ruins of the Temple, they had to rend their clothes. They saw the Sanctuary desolate, a Temple of Jupiter and two statues of Hadrian standing upon its esplanade. The one was an equestrian statue, the other represented the Emperor raising up the province kneeling before him.[150] No facilities for pilgrimages to Jerusalem could obliterate the stark fact that the Jewish nation was deprived of its freedom and independence, and that the ruins of the Temple, once the proud symbol of its state, were in alien hands.

Proselytism was the second matter on which the Jews refused to accept the restrictions imposed upon them. They continued to disregard them deliberately. As we have already seen the Romans allowed religious liberty to the Jews within the *status quo*; but they forbade under heavy penalties any extension of the privilege by adding converts to their number. On this point there was some disagreement between the rabbinic legislators themselves. Some advocated the admission of Gentiles, others denounced it. The final outcome was that on this point the party ready to appease Rome remained a minority (contrary to the trend in other matters). The majority simply refused to obey the Roman order. This decision, however, was arrived at only after many vacillations.

The second generation of Tannaim, the one that preceded the war of Bar Kokhba, was on the whole against the conversion of Gentiles. Rabbi Hanania ben Gamliel attacked with much acrimony converts who refused to follow all the religious precepts. Rabbi Eleazar ben Hyrcanos regarded circumcision as a necessary preliminary to conversion. He also warned against conversions motivated 'by fear and not by love' (we may see here an allusion to the conversions effected by fear during the Bar Kokhba war). After the fall of Beth-Ter the opposite tendency prevailed for a while. It was assumed—and probably rightly—that any Gentile who was ready to join a beaten and persecuted nation was doing so out of full conviction. The Haggadists based themselves on the verse: 'Thou shalt be a father of many nations' (Gen. 17, 4) and argued from it that it was a religious duty to accept converts. They also praised those fathers of Judaism who, as they believed, had made many converts in the past. Rabbi Joshua was even ready to accept a ritual bath as sole condition of conversion, without requiring circumcision. The majority of the scholars was however against this.[151] Rabbi Hiyya, in the fifth and last generation of Tannaim, was the only one who regarded converts as suspect until the twenty-fourth generation.[152] In the next period more and more voices were heard arguing for an intensification of missionary activity. Rabbi Eleazar ben Pedath called the mission to the Gentiles the principal reason for the divine dispensation by which Jews were dispersed into many lands. 'The Holy One exiled Israel among the nations only in order that proselytes might join them.'[153] Rabbis Yohanan and Simeon ben Lakish, the leaders of the second generation of the Amoraim, also insisted on the widening of the boundaries of the Jewish nation. According to the former, Abraham was punished, and his descendants had to undergo their sufferings in Egyptian bondage because 'he prevented people from entering under the wings of the *Shekinah* (Divine Spirit)'.[154] All the prominent pupils of Rabbi Yohanan, Rabbis Abbahu, Judah ben Simeon and Abun, were in favour of missionary activities. In their opinion both the full converts and the 'god-fearing' had their place in Paradise near to the throne of the Almighty.[155]

However, in this generation, the third of the Amoraim, there began the first stirrings of a renewed opposition to converts. Characteristically it could first be observed among their former supporters, the Haggadists and popular preachers. Rabbi Helbo, for instance, said: 'Converts are like scurf unto Israel'.[156] Rabbi Isaac was of the same opinion: 'One evil thing after another may befall those who accept converts (into Judaism)'.[157] The popular attitude was the same. In the Tractate *Gerim* (converts)[158] there are special warnings against those who said to a convert: 'Yesterday you were a servant of idols . . . there is still pork between your teeth'. The rabbis warned against people insulting converts in this way. Such a change of attitude was undoubtedly the result of bad experiences with converts during the period when Christian and Jewish missionaries were competing for proselytes.

The final decision as stated in the Tractate *Gerim* reflects a compromise between the conflicting tendencies. The scholars were especially interested in increasing the number of converts in Palestine proper, where a strengthening of the Jewish community was most urgent. They therefore ruled that converts in Palestine should be accepted at once, without the preliminary hearing of witnesses etc. which was required abroad. A close examination of the candidate was, however, demanded in all cases. The candidates for conversion had to be warned first: 'Why do you wish to become a convert? You see this nation bowed down, despised by all the peoples; blows and suffering are its lot.' Only when the candidate persisted in his intention and was duly received, was he greeted in another fashion: 'Happy art thou in Him who said "Let the world be", because the world has been created for Israel alone and no one is called sons of the Holy One, but Israel, and no one is beloved by the Holy One, but Israel'.[159]

In face of all the prohibitions of the government, the scholars therefore continued their missionary activities, although with many misgivings. Their ambivalent attitude may be summed up in the saying: 'Let your left hand always push (the proselytes) away and your right hand bring them near'.[160]

6. *Conclusion*

The Babylonian Gemara[161] tells an anecdote which aptly illustrates the Roman attitude towards the Jews. An emperor (Hadrian?) once propounded before his counsellors the problem, whether he should not destroy all Jews once and for all. Kitya bar Shalom, a Roman senator and a friend of the Jews (a fictitious person, of course) replied: 'You cannot overcome *all* of them'. This conviction of the Roman government of the indestructibility of the Jewish nation led (after the war of Bar Kokhba and a punitive period) to the restoration of liberty of religion and teaching, of a considerable measure of judicial autonomy, municipal rights and so on. The Jews were allowed practical self-government in all their internal affairs, and were able to set up their own administrative machinery, with the patriarchate as its central pivot. The discriminatory taxes imposed upon them remained in force, as well as the prohibition on entering Jerusalem; but they were eased in practice. The right to make a living and to act freely in internal matters was, however, granted only to the members of the Jewish nation as already constituted—the extension of its numbers by proselytism was forbidden.

The leaders of the Jewish nation accepted the compromise, calmed the people down, prevented further outbursts and permitted a certain degree of adaptation to Graeco-Roman culture. No concession could be made by them in the matter of Jerusalem and the propagation of the Jewish religion amongst the Gentiles.

In principle both sides held to their positions. The Romans continued to govern Palestine, including the Jews living there. The Jews continued to hope for a Messianic deliverance from heaven. Many amongst them also expected to be saved by a more mundane agency, the Parthian army. Yet the common tendency of appeasement led to a *modus vivendi*, which allowed the Jewish remnant to exist in peace in its own land.

This delicate balance between two forces which were unable to compromise on principle, but were willing to collaborate in practice, was put to a rude test in the great crisis which shook the Roman empire in the first half of the third century.

Notes to Chapter III

1. b *Sanhedrin* 13b–14a.
2. For this later type of ordination see below, pp. 60–1.
3. M *Abot* 1, 1.
4. Ezekiel 44, 3; 45, 7; 48, 21, 22.
5. b *Taanit* 29a—correcting the common text to '(Simeon ben) Gamliel'.
6. j *Sanhedrin* 19a–l. 20, bottom.
7. b *Sanhedrin* 11a–11b.
8. b *Horayot* 13b.
9. T *Shabbat* 7(8), 18, p. 119.
10. b *Ketubot* 103b (according to the Munich Ms.).
11. b *Abodah Zarah* 11a.
12. b *Megillah* 11a.
13. T *Sanhedrin* 11, 8.
14. b *Gittin* 59a.
15. b *Sanhedrin* 38a.
16. Theodoretus, *Eranistes seu Polymorphus* Dial. I (*PG* 83, c. 61); cf. A. Büchler, *REJ*, 28 (1894), pp. 64ff.; Y. Levi, ibid., 31 (1895), pp. 202ff.
17. b *Berakot* 43a, end.
18. *Genesis R* 20 (p. 190).
19. j *Abodah Zarah* 2, 10–42a, l. 35.
20. See above, pp. 40–2.
21. See below, p. 120.
22. b *Erubin* 85b–86a.
23. See below, p. 108.
24. See above, p. 40.
25. j *Abodah Zarah* 2, 9–42a, top.
26. b *Ketubot* 103b, end.
27. b *Yebamot* 9a.
28. See above, p. 57.
29. b *Menahot* 104a.
30. See above, p. 49.
31. b *Moed Katan* 17a.
32. j *Bikkurim* 3, 3–65d, l. 65.
33. j *Taanit* 4, 2–68a; *SHA* Alexander Severus, 45, 6.
34. j *Yebamot* 12–13a, l. 12.
35. See below, pp. 99–100.
36. See below, pp. 63–4.
37. T *Niddah* 6, 3, p. 647.
38. See above, p. 16.

39. j *Yebamot* 8, 2–9d end (Krotoshin edition: 'Rhodos' for 'Darom').
40. M *Shebiit* 9, 2.
41. M. Avi-Yonah, *The Holy Land*, Grand Rapids, 1966, pp. 133–5.
42. Epiphanius, *Paenarion* 30, 11, 4 (*GCS* 25, p. 346).
43. b *Sanhedrin* 5a.
44. J. B. Frey, *CIJ*, I, No. 694.
45. See below, p. 166.
46. j *Nedarim* 7, 13–40a; b *Berakhot* 63a.
47. b *Ketubot* 103b.
48. *Leviticus R* 9, 9.
49. A. Büchler, *Der galiläische 'Am ha-'Aretz'*, Wien, 1906.
50. See above, pp. 47–9.
51. b *Pesahim* 49b.
52. See Chapter IV.
53. b *Pesahim*, 49a–b.
54. Ibid., 112a.
55. Ibid., 49b.
56. See above, pp. 57–8.
57. See above, pp. 8–10.
58. b *Shabbat* 33b.
59. *Lamentations R* 1, 13.
60. j *Berakot* 1, 2–3b, l. 17.
61. Sifre *Deuteronomy* 327.
62. j *Abodah Zarah* 3, 1–42c.
63. b *Abodah Zarah* 18a.
64. b *Shabbat* 13b.
65. j *Taanit* 1, 1–64a, l. 9.
66. Ibid., 4, 8–68d, l. 24 bottom.
67. b *Hagigah* 5b.
68. Tanhuma, *Vayesheb* 3, 39a–65a.
69. M *Abot* 2, 3.
70. j *Sanhedrin* 6, 12–23d, end.
71. M *Abot* 4, 15.
72. M *Eduyot* 7, 7.
73. Sifre *Numbers*, IV, 22–a (Friedmann ed.).
74. *Genesis R* 67, 40.
75. M *Uktsim* 3, 12.
76. Mekhilta de Rabbi Ishmael, Pas–ha 8, 45.
77. b *Zebahim* 102a.
78. j *Berakot* 9, 1–13a, l. 31.
79. *Song of Songs R* 32, 7–16c.
80. See below, pp. 127–8.
81. *Genesis R* 9.

82. *Lamentations R* 11, 1.

83. *Derek Erets* 11.

84. T *Abodah Zarah* 1, 19.

85. j *Berakot* 1, 1–2c, l. 26 bottom.

86. *Ecclesiastes R* 11, 5–29b.

87. b *Sanhedrin* 97b.

88. b *Abodah Zarah* 9b.

89. Midrash *Psalms* 36, 6–p. 250 (ed. Buber).

90. b *Yoma* 9b.

91. b *Sanhedrin* 99a.

92. *Genesis R* 2, 3.

93. M *Sotah* 9, 14.

94. j *Taanit* 4, 9–69c, l. 3.

95. b *Pesahim* 112b.

96. j *Yoma* 1, 2–39a, l. 8.

97. b *Baba Metsia* 83b.

98. Ibid., 84a.

99. *Derekh Erets* 'Peace' passim.

100. *Genesis R* 94, 27.

101. j *Terumot* 8, 10–46b.

102. We are told about Elisha ben Abuyah (Aher) that 'the books of the *Minim* (heretics) were gushing out of his mantle' (b *Hagigah* 15b).

103. *Exodus R* 31, 1–64a; ibid., 19, 6–36a.

104. *Mekilta* 5a, ed. Lauterbach, I, p. 35.

105. E. E. Urbach, *IEJ*, 9 (1959), pp. 149ff.

106. M *Abodah Zarah* 3, 4.

107. b *Baba Kamma* 83a.

108. j *Abodah Zarah* 3, 1–42c, l. 8 bottom.

109. b *Baba Kamma* 83a.

110. M *Megillah* 1, 8.

111. b *Baba Kamma* 83a.

112. j *Peah* 1, 1–15c.

113. *Genesis R* 36, 6.

114. j *Peah* 1, 1–15c, l. 7.

115. *Leviticus R* 32, 5.

116. J. B. Frey, *CIJ*, II, s.v.

117. j *Sotah* 7, 1–21b, l. 12 bottom.

118. S. Lieberman, *Greek in Jewish Palestine*, New York, 1942, p. 66.

119. See above, p. 25.

120. Ruth Amiran, *IEJ*, 6 (1956), p. 244; Ruth Hestrin, *Bulletin L. M. Rabinowitz Fund* 3 (1960), p. 66.

121. Amiran, op. cit., p. 241f.

122. H. Kohl—C. Watzinger, *Die antiken Synagogen Galiläas*, Leipzig, 1916.

123. E. R. Goodenough, *Jewish Symbols in the Greco-Roman Period*, III, New York, 1953, Nos. 451–561.

124. Ibid., Nos. 488, 493.

125. M. Avi-Yonah, *Oriental Art in Roman Palestine*, Rome, 1961, pp. 38–40.

126. Goodenough, op. cit., No. 456.

127. Ibid., Nos. 84–5.

128. N. Avigad, *IEJ*, 7 (1957), pp. 77–92, 248; 9 (1959), p. 210.

129. E. E. Urbach, *IEJ*, 9 (1959), pp. 149ff., 229ff.

130. *SHA* Antoninus Pius 5, 4; 'Atque Judaeos rebellantes contudit per praesides et legatos'.

131. See above, p. 130.

132. *Chronicon*, ed. Helm (*GCS* 24, p. 211d).

133. Sulpicius Severus *PL* 95, *c.* 891; Orosius, VII, 17 (ed. Zangemeister, p. 257); Dionysius Telmahrensis 68a (ibid.); Bar Hebraeus, I, p. 55 (ed. Budge).

134. See above, p. 40.

135. E. Renan, *Mission de Phénicie*, Paris, 1864, p. 774.

136. S. Lieberman, *JQR*, 36 (1946), p. 341 has shown that the evidence quoted to the contrary has no relevance here.

137. *Song of Songs R* II, 2, 5.

138. *SHA* Severus 9, 5.

139. See above, p. 71.

140. Dio Cassius—Zonaras 75, 2, 4 (Claudius); Josephus, *BJ* II, 60ff.; *Ant.* XVII, 278 (Athronges); J. Moschus, *PG* 87 (3), *c.* 3032 (Cyriacus).

141. *SHA* Severus, 16, 7.

142. See above, pp. 50–1.

143. b *Baba Kamma* 97b.

144. j *Hagigah* 2, 1–77b, l. 21.

145. b. *Berakot* 14a.

146. *Genesis R* 32, 19, p. 296; 81, 4, p. 974.

147. *Homilia in Jesum*, 17, 1 (*CGS* 30, p. 401f.); b *Berakot* 3a (Yose ben Halafta?); b *Pesahim* 8b (Rabbi Isaac); j *Berakot* 9, 3–13d (Simeon bar Kamtra); j *Maaser sheni* 3, 6–54b (R. Hanina).

148. b *Baba Metsia* 75b, top.

149. S. Safrai in *Scripta Hierosolymitana*, 23 (1973), pp. 62–78 following G. Allon, *Toldot ha-Yehudim bi-tekufat ha-Mishnah veha-Talmud*, II, pp. 116–17 (Hebrew).

150. *Itinerarium burdigalense*, ed. Geyer, p. 21f.

151. j *Bikkurim* 1, 4–64a, l. 15; Levi, *REJ*, 51, pp. 28ff.; *Masseket*

Gerim, 2 (R. Hanina ben Gamliel); b *Yebamot* 46a, 48b end (R. Eleazar ben Hyrcanos); b *Yebamot* 46a (R. Joshua).

152. *Yalkut Ruth* par. 601 (R. Hiyya).
153. *Masseket Gerim*, 4.
154. b *Nedarim* 32a.
155. Ibid.
156. b *Yebamot* 47b.
157. Ibid., 109b.
158. *Masseket Gerim*, 1.
159. b *Yebamot* 47a–b.
160. b *Sanhedrin* 107b.
161. b *Abodah Zarah* 10b.

IV

Palestine Jewry and the Crisis of the Empire in the Third Century

1. *The Crisis and its Causes*

The diagram on p. 20 indicates the gradual shrinking of Palestinian Jewry in the period under discussion. We find in it four critical points. The decline is accelerated in every generation following one of these points. Three of these are connected with well-known historical events: the First War with the Romans, the war of Bar Kokhba and the revolt against Gallus Caesar (351).[1] Between the second and the third there is, however, one more steep decline (especially in Galilee) for which we cannot account by a lost war or suppressed revolt. The time between the annulment of the Hadrianic decrees and the reign of Constantine (*c.* 140–324) was, as we have seen, a period of appeasement and relaxation of political tensions. How is one to explain the evident decline of Palestinian Jewry between these two dates?

The cause is not to be found in anything particular to Palestine, but in the general political and economic crisis of the Roman empire between the death of Commodus and the rise of Diocletian. This crisis was in reality the beginning of the end of the ancient world. At its end the old Roman state did survive in its external aspect, but only in its façade. The changes are visible in all fields of social life, politics, economics and culture. At the beginning of the third century society was still rooted in the Greco-Roman culture; from the fourth century a direct line of development leads to the beginning of the Middle Ages, the Christian-Byzantine period. The Jewish community, as part of the empire, was obliged to face a new situation. It had to revise its tactics and to develop new forms of its age-old struggle for survival in a hostile world.

This is not the place to discuss in detail the causes, beginnings and development of this crisis. Like most great historical upheavals it was the result of a disturbance in the delicate balance required to maintain a stable society. In this particular case the disturbance affected the relation between the centripetal force of the imperial Roman government and the centrifugal developments in the provinces and especially among the provincial armies. From the time of Augustus, the cultural and economic development of the provinces[2] and their assimilation to the Roman way of life kept in step; now one process outran the other, with disastrous results. A succession of dynastic crises so weakened the central government that it temporarily lost control of the provinces. The latter had become largely economically independent through the process of development, carried out or favoured by the imperial government itself. The decline of the old religions dissolved another link which had kept the empire together. The Stoic philosophy which had cemented the Empire disintegrated under the impact of the mystery religions.

The class struggle between the cities and the country added to the general unrest. The Empire had so far rested on the loyalty of the cities, which ruled the countryside. Now the villages began to stir. Their unrest was doubly dangerous, because the Roman army was largely recruited from the peasants. The conflict between city and village soon became one between the civilian and the soldier. The inevitable victory of the armed man was followed by equally inevitable social and cultural decline and the establishment of a totalitarian bureaucracy.

The external symptoms of the crisis were the frequent changes of rulers. Very few of the emperors of these troubled times died in their beds. Some perished by assassins' plots, others were killed by rebel soldiers, some fell in battle, some were executed by order of victorious rivals. Every such change of ruler in an absolutist state shook the whole framework of government. Provincial governors were deposed. Cities and provinces which had chosen the wrong side and fought for the old emperor against the new one were duly punished. The army became the mainstay of each successive government and the prime mover of every revolution. The legions moved away from the frontiers and engaged in civil war for or against the commanders who had revolted. The border provinces were abandoned to their fate. Each one tried to take care of itself as well as it could, with its own emperor and its own army.

The external enemies of Rome naturally profited from the occasion and invaded its frontiers. The chaos spread rapidly. The government ceased to care for the well-being of its subjects, and fought only for bare existence. More and more soldiers were recruited and more and more taxes levied to pay them. The results were confiscations of property, forced labour, a general disorder and lack of security, disruption of trade and communications, economic distress and ruin, famine and epidemics.

2. *Aspects of the Political Crisis in Palestine*

The crisis could not fail to leave its marks in Palestine also. In one hundred and three years the province passed through twenty-five changes of emperors, one every four years on average. If we deduct the three comparatively long reigns of Septimius Severus (20 years), Severus Alexander (13 years), Odenathus and Zenobia (12), who reigned 45 years in all, the other twenty-two emperors ruled for 58 years, and each for little more than two and a half years. Only two of them (Caracalla and Aurelian) ascended the throne peacefully. All the others became emperor after the predecessors had come to a violent end.

The frequent changes of rulers have found their echo even in Talmudic sources, especially in the Haggadah. From the time of Caracalla to that of Diocletian we find many so-called 'Parables of Kings',[3] which reflect in their way the political events of their period.

The first result of the decline of Roman prestige caused by the crisis of the empire was an increase of Jewish self-confidence. In earlier times the rabbis believed the Romans invincible. Now we find Rabbi Isaac saying: 'Rulers come and rulers go, but Israel stands for ever'.[4] The imperial dignity which once evoked respect was now treated with pity or scorn. Rabbi Yohanan said: 'Woe to the dominion which buried those who hold it'.[5] The hint is plain enough. The rabbis had often seen 'a *dux*, whom the legions clothed in purple' (Rabbi Levi).[6] They tell of a 'King' (= emperor) who came into a city and they put up his images and made statues and struck their coins in his likeness; but after some time they destroyed his images, broke his statues, put his coins out of circulation and despised his memory.[7] The emperors of old are described in our sources either as 'just men among the nations' such as the legendary Antoninus,[8] or as monsters such as Titus or Hadrian—'may their bones be ground to dust'. But even such monsters reflected some of the imperial greatness. The ephemeral rulers of the third century evoked nothing but contempt. Their low origins—and this applied especially to the emperors risen from the ranks of the army—and their boorish manners never failed to evoke ironic comments. A simple shepherd could now become governor of a province and even emperor.[9] 'When the Gentiles want to have a king they take him from anywhere and set him over themselves.'[10] 'The Gentile nations are like a ship. In a ship the mast is from one place and the oars from another.'[11] The point is directed against the soldier-emperors such as Maximinus Thrax or any one of the low-born Illyrian emperors. Even the great

Diocletian who was the greatest and most powerful of the Illyrian rulers did not escape mockery. It was generally believed that as a boy he had been a swineherd at Tiberias,[12] perhaps because he became emperor by killing 'the Boar' (Aper), the pretorian prefect.

The mainspring of the revolts was lack of military discipline. From the time of Rabbi Simeon ben Lakish (middle of the third century) to that of Rabbis Levi and Abbahu (in the beginning of the fourth) we find in the sayings of the rabbis numerous and detailed accounts of military revolts. The soldiers in revolt rise up and riot. Some commanders keep faith with the reigning emperor. They try to argue with the mutineers and lose their lives. Others take the *signa* of the legion with the images of the emperor and escape from the camp. Many officers incite their men to revolt. They take the purple and try to rule by the grace of the legions who have proclaimed them. If the revolt fails, the faithful legions are rewarded. The loyal legionaries become *duces* and *eparchoi* (governors). As soon as the emperor hears of the mutiny he assembles his forces and marches against the rebels. As soon as he reaches them, he fights and goes on fighting. If the rebels are defeated and surrender, every mutineer has forfeited his life by law. Sometimes, however, the emperor declares: 'I have no grievance against simple soldiers, but I shall put to death the great ones.' It is obvious from these detailed and concrete descriptions that the authors actually saw these things happen.[13]

As there were hardly any Jews serving in the Roman army[14] they took little active part in mutinies and civil wars. However in these upheavals not only soldiers were involved. Cities and whole provinces sided with one pretender or another. Of course the most violent changes occurred in Rome, the capital, or in military camps located in Germany, Illyria or Syria. In such a case Palestine simply accepted the decisions as they occurred. In a few cases military operations actually extended into the province itself. Palestine was conquered in 194 by Septimius Severus from Pescennius Niger. Quite possibly there was fighting here when Aurelius Uranius revolted in 244 against Philip the Arab, although most of it must have occurred in Syria. In 272, when Aurelian defeated the Palmyrenes, some of the battles may have occurred in Palestine. In any case the Haggadic Midrashim bear ample evidence to the fact that civil war was a common sight in the country. The rabbis describe the rage of the provincial crowd during a revolt. The images of the overthrown emperor are destroyed and his statues stoned. His decrees (προστάγματα) are annulled, torn to pieces and burnt. The hated tax collectors are the first victims of popular fury. When the emperors or their generals (*duces*) set out against a rebellious city, it profits the inhabitants if the *polemarchos* (general) in command is an even-tempered man. Then he is likely to give the rebels a chance to return to their allegiance and escape ruin. Sometimes it was enough to send some 'hard' legion against the city. The provincials were frightened and submitted in haste. But in other cases a regular siege was necessary.[15] In one source we find a detailed description of the siege operations by which a city was reduced: 'At first he (i.e. the emperor) cuts the aqueduct of the city . . . then he attempts a surprise mass attack . . . shoots arrows . . . brings up more legions . . . prepares storming-ladders . . . pours burning petrol (*naptha*) . . . projects stones from *ballistae*. . .'. Thus the property of the citizens is gradually reduced to rubble. If the city is taken by storm, the lives of the rebels are forfeit and depend on the mercy of the ruler. 'A king of flesh and blood against whom a province has revolted, if he is of a cruel disposition he kills everyone; if he is merciful— he kills only half; if he is most merciful—he punishes, but only the great ones' (Rabbi Abbahu).[16] In most cases the emperor 'just lets his legions destroy them (the rebels). Good and bad are treated alike. No one says "this one is a just one, leave him alone". They kill everybody.'[17b] 'He (the emperor) makes a great slaughter (*androlomousia* ἀνδρῶν λοιμός). He kills the good and the bad because he cannot tell the one from the other. (He kills) those who revolted against him and those who did not revolt, those who honoured the king and those who cursed him.'[18]

After the slaughter came the confiscations. 'Two provinces had revolted against the emperor. He then said: this one shall be devastated by fire; and the other shall become the share of the treasury' (*fiscus*).[19]

3. *The Economic Results of the Political Crisis: Conscription, Forced Labour, New Taxes*

Every new ruler who had succeeded in holding the reins of power even for a very short time immediately began to conscript recruits. His opponents at once did the same; for in those stormy times it was the only way to seize power or to hold it. The first act of the '*dux* upon whom the legions had thrown the purple' was therefore 'to recruit legions'.[20] The one sure mark of the 'evil power' (of Rome) was 'that it conscripts recruits from all the nations of the world'.[21] The mass recruitments deprived the economy of much labour. They reduced the number of producers and laid increased burdens on the rest. Jews were as a rule exempt from recruitment, or, if it came to the worst, they could redeem themselves. Rabbi Mana (fourth century) allowed the people of Sepphoris to sell their houses, even if rented by others, to free their sons from the *numerus*.[22] Possibly, however, this was an exceptional emergency in the wake of the failed revolt against Gallus. We find on the whole that in the Talmudic sources the complaints against the other demands of the state, whether in labour or in money, are far more frequent; and this illustrates the degree of their oppressiveness. If they affected the scholarly class who compiled our sources, the complaints are especially violent.

The increase in the size of the armed forces and the military operations within the empire required not only more and more cash to pay the soldiers, but they led to the requisitioning of many other necessities of life: victuals, raw materials of all kinds and means of transportation. The imperial treasury paid the augmented salaries of the soldiers, but it could not afford to pay for all the rest. Paying the soldiers was a vital necessity, because otherwise they would mutiny. The civilian population on the other hand could always be made to supply forced labour or the necessities of war. If they refused, there was the military to 'persuade' them. The increased taxes and the payments in cash burdened mainly the towns. The peasants on the other hand suffered from the deliveries in kind and the burden of forced labour. Most of Palestinian Jews belonged at that time to the peasant class[23] and they had to carry the full weight of those exactions.

Forced labour is called in Talmudic sources *angaria*, a Persian word adopted by the Greeks as ἀγγαρεία. This term denoted at first only the obligation to supply transportation for the postal service of the Roman government, the *cursus publicus*. In course of time the meaning of the term was enlarged to include all other forms of forced labour. In the Mishnah[24] we still find the term used in its old sense. There a decision is recorded about a donkey, 'who was used for *angaria*' that is to say it was taken from its owner to carry travellers or goods for the post. In the following generations the burdens increased as the crisis deepened, and the term *angaria* (also called occasionally *tsumot*) expanded. *Angaria* affected mostly those who were engaged in the victualling or clothing trades (millers, vine-merchants, dealers in cloth etc.). A characteristic story[25] tells of wine merchants who stored their goods in a cemetery, because they heard that *angaria* was being collected in the town itself. Wine was of course very much in demand by the army. In the time of Rabbi Yohanan, the crisis reached its peak. Even members of the municipal councils were liable to forced labour. Even rabbinical students were thus enrolled (e.g. Rabbi Zeira who was 'caught to labour for the King, carrying myrtle wood to the palace' in the time of Diocletian).[26]

Billeting was another trouble which affected most inhabitants. According to Roman law soldiers could be billeted in private houses in the town or village. By law this applied only where there was no inn; however no inn could accommodate the swollen armies of the time. This law was, however, more honoured in the breach than otherwise.[27] As more and more troops marched and counter-marched behind the various emperors and their opponents in the third century, billeting became more and more of a burden. The Talmudic sources discuss whether the soldiers should be distributed by the number of houses ('doors') or by the number of inhabitants,[28] and whether one was allowed to bribe the billeting officers.[29] The burden of billeting was especially heavy in Sabbatical years,[30] and sometimes it caused this religious duty to be suspended temporarily.

Billeting is mentioned as something quite usual. People who had soldiers quartered upon them could at least hope to get rid some day of the unbidden guest. Anyone lodging in an inn could find himself in the street with no hope of other accommodation.[31]

The crisis brought with it also far-reaching changes in the system of taxation.[32] In former times the Romans levied the same taxes in Palestine as were ordinarily collected from tributary provinces. These were (1) the *demosia* or land-tax (*tributum solis*); (2) a *poll-tax* (*tributum capitis*), actually a tax on the value of property; (3) the *anfortah*—according to A. Gulak[33] the payments by lessees of state domains; (4) custom duties.

The *demosia* or land-tax had been fixed once and for all at the time of the Roman conquest. In a time of rapid inflation[34] its value declined as rapidly. Consequently in Talmudic literature we hear of hardly any complaints against this particular tax.

The *anfortah* affected only a limited class of tax-payers, whose complaints (if any) did not easily find an echo in the rabbinical sources. *Custom duties* are mentioned already in the time of Rabban Gamliel II as 'one of the four things by which the government oppresses Israel'.[35] In the following generations complaints against the customs duties as such tend to diminish. There remain the standing objections to the way in which customs were levied. In particular these are directed against the tax farmers who took more than their due; the 'collectors of customs who have no fixed tariff'.[36] The rabbis take special delight in describing the Tantalus-like sufferings of the publicans in the world-to-come. They shall lie on the banks of rivers, their tongues stretched out but unable to reach the water.[37] Our sources describe in detail all kinds of ruses used by smugglers intent on evading the customs. The rabbinical attitude to authority is in this case entirely negative; they discuss the expediency of such illegalities, not their ethical value. In times of prosperity the customs duties were not a heavy burden, for Palestine was largely self-sufficient in the necessities of life.[38] Duties on luxury-goods did not affect the masses. In times of war and anarchy trade between the provinces was much reduced in scope and the crisis led thus to a diminution of the sums levied by the customs.

The *poll-tax* was a much heavier burden. Rabban Gamliel II mentions, in the beginning of the 2nd century, this tax as one of the things 'by which the government oppresses Israel'.[39] In the time of Rabbi Samuel ben Nahman (end of the 3rd century) the poll-tax was still denounced as one of the taxes 'by which the children of Jacob are kept down in this world by the government'.[40] Rabbi Abba maintained in the same generation: 'If you give charity from your property, the Holy One will preserve you from poll-taxes'.[41] The poll-tax was felt as oppressive at all times because it was higher in Palestine than in other provinces.[42] As it was a tax calculated according to the value of property it rose in time of inflation with the rise in the nominal value of the lands taxed.

The saying of Rabban Gamliel II quoted above, mentions for the first time a new tax, which was to become in the future the prime instrument of oppression—the *annona* (*militaris*),[43] which in Talmudic sources has been distorted into the *arnona*. Originally the term *annona* stood for an imperial order to the provinces requiring their inhabitants to deliver supplies to troops on the march. When troop movements became an almost everyday occurrence in the third century, because of the frequency of civil war, the *annona* became a most heavy burden on the civilian population. Its impact was especially great, because it could not be fore-seen, and because its amount was not limited. The *annona* is a subject of execration at all times, from the days of the patriarch Judah I and his son Gamliel III, till the times of Rabbis Samuel ben Nahman and Abba (end of the third century). At this time Diocletian turned the *annona* into a regular tax with a fixed rate.[44]

The *annona* comprised above all the supply of wheat and cattle to the soldiers. In one of the Midrashim[45] we find mention of 'the farmer who was weighing the *annona*' as of an everyday occurrence. A passage in a rabbinical commentary[46] on Deut. 28, 48 ('Therefore shalt thou serve thine enemies . . . in hunger, and in thirst and in nakedness and in want of all things') proves how deeply the oppressiveness of the requisitions was felt. ' "Hunger"—if you hardly have any bread to eat at all, the Gentiles (= Romans) demand white bread and fat meat; "thirst"—if you thirst after a drop of vinegar or beer, and cannot find any, they demand the best wines in the world; "nakedness"—if you search for a cloak or wool or linen, and cannot find it, they ask for silk or fine cloth from goat hair.' In the second half of the third century the *annona* became the financial mainstay of the Roman government. The inflation had by that time caused an almost complete abandonment of a money economy. The state and the individual alike went over to a barter economy. Only towards the end of the century did the emperor Diocletian succeed in stabilizing the economic and political conditions of the empire. He made the *annona* into a regular tax levied on the basis of a property valuation (*census*) which was carried out every fifteen years. From the time of Rabbi Levi (early fourth century) the term *annona* is not mentioned any more. But he could still say: 'The Holy One takes the nations of the world and lowers them into hell saying: "Why did you fine (*konsim* from *census*) my sons (Israel)?" '.[47]

The *annona* weighed most heavily on the peasants. The town dwellers were affected only insofar as they owned land. But they were not spared by new taxes. When Caracalla granted in 212 Roman citizenship to all inhabitants of the empire, his main aim was to levy from them the inheritance tax which had hitherto been paid by Roman citizens only. The tax was levied on all estates exceeding 100,000 sesterces in value; it cannot have affected many Jews, who were mostly too poor to leave so much property. At any rate we read of no complaints against this tax.

Matters stood otherwise with the *crown-tax* (*aurum coronarium, mas ha-kelila*). This tax was originally a voluntary offering in the shape of a gold crown. It was presented by towns or provinces to victorious Roman generals. Later on it was offered to the emperor on his accession or after a great victory. This voluntary gift was, in the usual way of such things, soon turned into an obligatory tax levied every fourth year. In times when rulers changed even more often, indeed on average every two years, this 'crown gold' was a grievous exaction. Every new emperor demanded it as a matter of course; a refusal could be interpreted as treasonable doubt of the legitimacy of his rule. Like the *annona* the crown tax could not be foreseen. This fact increased its destructive effect on economic life. Moreover, the crown tax had to be paid in gold or silver coin, difficult to obtain at a time when such coins had been driven out of circulation by the inflation of a debased currency.

The frequent revolutions had another grievous result. Each new emperor regarded himself as the only legitimate ruler. Not only his active opponents were considered rebels, but all those who had passively refused to admit his authority or to help him against his adversaries. In times of almost permanent civil war the ordinary citizen was in a painful dilemma. He had to guess who would come out on top in the power game. Sometimes this required quite prophetic gifts. If he supported the revolt, and it failed, he was punished by the existing government; but if he remained loyal and the revolt succeeded, he was fined by the new rulers. Thus we can understand why *tsumot* (fines, ζήμια) are mentioned among the evils which Israel suffered from the Roman government in the days of Rabbis Samuel ben Nahman and Abba alike.[48]

The continual changes in fiscal charges can be deduced from the sayings of the pupils of Rabbi Yose (second half of the third century).[49] They mention the following taxes: (a) *pissim*—land-tax (according to G. Allon); (b) *tsumot*—fines (also according to Allon; others think they were additional taxes, which amounts to the same thing, as such extras were collected as fines); (c) *annona*; (d) poll-tax.

Considering the tax burden described above, we need not wonder that very often the tax-payers were unable to meet the demands of the treasury. When the amount due in taxes exceeded the value of their property, their properties were 'sunk' (*shekiin*).[50] The Toseftah and later sources[51] mention that such properties were confiscated. The officials seized the barns of the peasants. In this way many proprietors lost their estates, which became crown property. The lack of security of ownership was another reason why the crisis went from bad to worse. We are told of a very rich man,[52] who refused to be judged before the rabbinical court in a case brought against him by a poor man, for 'all the camels in Arabia would not suffice to carry the leather sacks filled with mortgage deeds which he owned'. Suddenly an order came from the government that he and his properties belonged to the *fiscus*. He implored the rabbis to pray that he might keep at least his personal freedom.

4. *The Collection of the New Taxes and its Abuses*

The new taxation was not only oppressive because of its severity but also because of the abuses in collecting it. In general, complaints against high taxation occur in all periods and in all conditions, and should be treated with caution by the historian: no-one ever pays his taxes cheerfully. However, the outcry against taxes in the third century was so vehement and general that we must assume something out of the ordinary. Clearly there were at this time ample reasons for such complaints. Our sources show that the opposition to the new taxes was not expressed solely in words. People began to hide their property in specially built secret chambers, in tunnels and in caves. Merchants did all they could to conceal their goods from the tax-collectors.[53]

Faced by this 'strike' of the tax-payers, the tax-collectors had recourse to the methods used in the Orient from time immemorial: they employed force. Rabbi Eleazar ben Pedath, who lived in the second half of the third century, said: 'If Israelites give charity—this is for their own good, because if they do not—the Gentiles come and get it by force'.[54] Simeon ben Lakish, his contemporary, likens the collector to a bear who meets a man flying from a lion (Amos 5, 19) and explains the simile as a man 'who entered a city and was set upon by the tax-collector'.[55] Rabbi Levi could tell a story about a legionary soldier who went 'to collect the *demosia* (property-tax) in the province'.[56]

The tax-collectors were especially active during the high holidays. At that time crowds of people, villagers in particular, used to gather in the cities. R. Hanina ben Hama, who lived in the first generation of the Amoraim, attested that 'there is no high holiday but there comes to Tiberias a governor or a centurion or a man with a horse's tail (on his helmet)'.[57] The same fact is handed down in another source as regards Sepphoris: the army comes to the city to collect taxes.

On such occasions no great care was taken to ascertain the true domicile of those caught in the fiscal trap. 'An official was sent to collect taxes from the people of Tiberias and the people of Sepphoris. He saw a man of Sepphoris in Tiberias and caught him. The man said: "But I am from Sepphoris". The collector set him at ease: "No matter, I have written orders for Sepphoris also".'[58] Heavy taxation continued even in quieter times, when Diocletian had restored some kind of order in the empire. In the fifth generation of the Amoraim we are told that in the time of Rabbi Jeremiah a heavy tax was imposed on Tiberias. The rabbi was forced to take the silver candlestick of Rabbi Jacob ben Abin in order to satisfy the tax-collector.[59]

The frequent changes of emperor brought with them equally frequent changes of governors. Many such governors had obtained their posts by bribery in high places. They were naturally anxious to recoup their expenses, and if possible to grow rich at the expense of the provincials. The Midrash tells of an ex-consul (ὑπατικός) who 'if he does not assume his governorship would be unable to collect taxes and if he does not collect taxes will never discharge his debts'.[60] In a time of frequent revolts and lack of strong central government, the ephemeral emperors were unable to control the provincial governors as closely as was usual in earlier times. They were too dependent on the governors' loyalty, and to retain it left them free to exploit their provincial subjects as much as they could.

As is usual in times of crisis, every class affected by it tried to shift the burden on to the shoulders of other people. The rich were supposed to carry the main burden of taxation. However, since under the Roman dispensation they were themselves entrusted with the collection of taxes (and the responsibilities connected with it), they endeavoured to 'pass the buck' as much as possible to the poor. The great land-owners endeavoured to force their tenants and the other small land-holders to undertake forced labour (*angaria*). They exploited their superior status for their private benefit. In the Babylonian Gemara we find an ironical story about how the rich Rabbi Eleazar ben Harsom 'was found by his own slaves (incognito) and forced to do *angaria*'.[61] The story is apocryphal, for this sage lived in the times of the Second Temple, but it is characteristic nevertheless. Doubtless such people treated in the same way many casual passers-by, without their names appearing in our sources.

From all parts of the empire we hear of a strong resistance of the rich to the payment of the new taxes.[62] This is especially evident in Egypt and Asia Minor.[63] The behaviour of the tax-collectors who used force, aroused the ire of the rabbis. Rabbi Samuel ben Nahman said: 'The Holy One decided that the earth should receive its waters only from above, why? Because of the violent ones.'[64] For if he had continued to grant it water from nether springs also (Gen. 1, 7) the 'oppressors' would soon find a way

to get the vital sources into their exclusive power. At the same time delation in the matter of taxes was on the increase. We are told:[65] 'When the
guild of the flax (or linen) merchants had been forced to deliver goods and
had been assembled for the purpose, a certain Bar Hobets was missing.
Those present began to ask each other: "What are we eating to-day?" and
they answered: "*hobtsin*" (cheese). In this way the official in charge
noticed his absence and ordered him to be fetched. Rabbi Yohanan said:
"This is denunciation through a veil".' In a Midrash,[66] the 'Nations of
the World' (the Gentiles) are represented as being interrogated by the
Almighty. He asks them: '"Why did you fine my sons?" And they
reply: "They denounced themselves". And the Holy One takes these
and these (i.e. the Gentiles and the informers) and lowers them into
hell.'

As the time went on and conditions steadily worsened, the Roman
government needed more and more money. Finally it had recourse to a
new way of levying taxes, one aimed at the same time at the rich tax-
evaders and the poor who were unable to pay. From the days of Septimius
Severus onwards the responsibility for the collection of taxes was imposed
collectively on the basic administrative units of the empire, the municipalities. A lump quota was charged to the town. The town council (*boulē*)
had to distribute the tax-burden between its members and the rest of the
inhabitants of the town. The *boulē* was responsible for the collection of the
tax. If one of those bound to pay evaded payment, his share was distributed
among the others. This method became more and more common in the
course of the crisis, till it became standard in the days of Diocletian. This
new way with old taxes partly explains the generosity of the emperors of
the Severan dynasty. They were ready to restore municipal rights to the
Jews and at the same time to make them collectively responsible for the
payment of taxes.

The change in the method of levying taxes explains the change in the
attitude of the rabbis towards tax-collectors in general. 'At first they were
saying: a member (*haber*, i.e. a scholar) who becomes a tax-collector—is
expelled from the *Heber* (because he took on his odious duties voluntarily).
Then it was decided that . . . as soon as he ceased to be tax-collector he
would be re-admitted.' Finally 'an ordinary tax-collector—is allowed' (to
remain in the *Heber*); because at that time the duty to collect taxes might
fall upon anyone.[67]

As usual great property-owners and the very rich still found ways to
evade the taxes. The poor were of course unable to pay. The duty of
supplying the needs of the State thus fell upon the shoulders of the middle
class in the cities. The council and the 'ten good men' (*decemprimi*) were
made responsible for the payment of the crown-tax, the *annona* and the
other taxes. As soon as the full burden of taxation was imposed on this

class, each individual in the group thus 'favoured' tried every possible way to escape from this 'privileged' position. Rabbi Yohanan mentions those 'complaining to the authorities in order to escape service in the *boulē*'.[68] Rabbi Zeira fasted a hundred days in order to prolong the life of Rabbi Ilai and thus to avoid the public duties from falling on his (Zeira's) shoulders.[69] Those elected to the *boulē* often refused to serve and had to be pressed into service. 'Rabbi Yose went to Kafra (a suburb of Tiberias) in order to set up there public officials (*parnasim*) and they refused. He stood up before them and said: Ben Babai was in charge of the wicks (of the seven-branched candlestick) in the Temple; and if he who was in charge of such a small thing is remembered amongst the great men of his age, you who are in charge of human welfare will be the more so.'[70] Rabbi Jeremiah said: 'He who undertakes public duties—is to be compared to one who is busy with the words of the Law'.[71]

As the refusals to serve in the *boulē* became more and more frequent, service was made compulsory. People are mentioned as being seized for the *boulē*. 'The wicked government'—said Rabbi Yohanan—'puts an evil eye on a man's money. It says: this man is a rich man, let us make him an *archōn* (city magistrate); that one is a rich man—let us make him a *bouleutēs* (city councillor).'[72]

Those compelled to serve tried to shift the burden on to their colleagues. On one occasion there were disputes as to the distribution of taxes at Tiberias between the *stratēgoi* (the heads of the council) and the other members. Both parties appealed to the Patriarch Judah I and he decided to divide the charge equally between them.[73]

As the crisis deepened and taxes were piled upon taxes, the task of the city councillor became unbearable. Rabbi Yose ben Hanina (an Amora of the second generation, *c.* 260–290) admitted that 'it is difficult to live in cities'.[74] Many members of the city council were faced with ruin and decided to abandon their property and to run away. This state of affairs had been for a long time so common in Egypt that a special term, *anachōrēsis* (ἀναχώρησις) was coined for it. In the Mishnah the distribution of the tax-burden is discussed in the case of brothers who were business partners, if one of them absented himself to evade tax. When the crown-tax was imposed on Tiberias the inhabitants were much dissatisfied. Half of them fled at once and the other half later.[75] Similar cases are known by inscriptions from other parts of the Empire;[76] but the authorities did not always take them seriously. We are told[77] that once the inhabitants of Paneas threatened the emperor Diocletian with mass flight. A 'sophist' in the imperial suite remarked thereupon: 'They will not go, and even if they do, they will return'. No one would willingly give up his property, unless quite desperate. At the end of the third century Rabbi Yohanan aptly summed up the attitude of his contemporaries in a pithy saying: 'If you are mentioned for the *boulē*—let the Jordan be your neighbour',[78] i.e. run away into the river wilderness.

5. *The Inflation*[79]

During the political crisis the Roman government was forced to take two steps which caused economic distress. One was the increased taxation already discussed; the other was the debasement of coinage, which caused inflation. From the time of Augustus the principal Roman coin was the *denarius*, fixed at the eighty-fourth part of a pound of silver. In the fifty years from Augustus to Nero its silver content remained almost constant. Later on several emperors in time of need chose the easy way out and increased the copper content of the *denarius*, without reducing its nominal value. Thus the percentage of silver sank from 95 per cent to 90 per cent in the time of Nero, to 83 per cent in the time of Trajan, to 75 per cent under Marcus Aurelius, to 70 per cent under Commodus. For several reasons this gradual debasement of the currency did not have its full economic effect. On the one hand the general quantity of coin in circulation in the Roman empire was shrinking at the same time, because of the drain caused by the imbalance of trade with countries abroad. Secondly, no new silver mines of any importance were discovered in that period, while the quantity of silver mined from all existing mines decreased steadily. With the reduction of the amount of silver metal available in the Empire, its price increased. In consequence the smaller quantity of precious metal in the *denarius* was enough to keep its purchasing power stable. In the third century, however, conditions changed. Huge amounts of coined money were needed, especially for the payment of the augmented wages of soldiers. From the days of Caracalla onwards the emperors were forced to reduce fairly rapidly the amount of silver in the *denarius*. As usual in times of inflation this process gathered speed. The resulting fall in the value of money necessarily produced a rise in prices. This caused the state to require greater sums to cover its expenses. No other means being forthcoming, the proportion of silver in the coinage was once more reduced, prices rose again, and so on. In the two centuries between Augustus and Septimius Severus the silver content was reduced, as we have seen, by 50 per cent, i.e. by 5 per cent every twenty years. In the twenty years between the death of Caracalla and that of Maximinus Thrax (217–238) it lost a further 20 per cent. From that time until Gallienus, i.e. in the next twenty years, it fell by an additional 35 per cent, so that in the end the *denarius* contained only 5 per cent of silver. At the end of this period the so-called 'silver' coins were merely pieces of copper thinly coated with silver, by a process of boiling, and this crust soon wore off.

Roman monetary inflation in the third century showed all the well-known symptoms of true inflation. The old, good coins disappeared from circulation; they were hoarded or melted down. Prices, and following them, wages, rose rapidly. Producers and merchants tried to avoid receiving debased coins as far as possible, and turned to barter, exchanging goods for goods. Living costs rose to astronomical figures.

This economic crisis affected Palestine as well as the rest of the empire; the Jewish sector was not immune to this development. One of the effects of inflation was the end of municipal coinage. Another was the adaptation of the law to the changing economic situation.

The beginnings of inflation belong to the days when Rabban Judah I was an old man. (Incidentally, this furnishes further proof that the patriarch was still alive in the days of Caracalla.)[80] 'Rabbi (Judah I) taught his son, Rabbi Simeon, thus: "Gold purchases silver". He replied: "Rabbi, in your youth you taught us: 'Silver purchases gold', and now in your old age you teach us: 'Gold purchases silver?'".' The explanation seems to be that when Rabbi was young, in the time of the Antonine emperors, gold coins were regarded as currency and silver coins as a 'commodity'; according to the law of the Mishnah only the transfer of the 'commodity' and not the payment of the price completed the transaction. In his old age, when Caracalla began to flood the empire with debased *antoniniana* (*c.* 217) the gold coins, which had remained relatively good as regards their metal contents, were driven off the market, in accordance with 'Gresham's law', and became a 'commodity', while the silver coins, however debased, remained the only 'coin' in the market.[81] A Midrash[82] is evidence for the rapidity of inflation. According to it the sons of Jacob on their second departure for Egypt took double the amount they had taken first. For, our source says, 'perhaps in the meantime the prices had risen'. Judah I mentions several cases in which the wages of the workmen had to be doubled. His sayings apparently refer to the days of the Second Temple, but in reality he must have meant his own times.[83]

In the following generations the inflation with all its evil consequences gathered speed. This is shown by the sayings of the Amoraim of the first generation who lived during the time of the sharpest fall in money value (230–260). Rabbi Hanina ben Hama as usual refers to the tribulations of his age when speaking of biblical events. He stated:[84] 'Money mentioned in general in the Pentateuch means a *sela* (4 denarii); in the Prophets—a pound of silver, in the later writings—a *centenarius*' (100,000 sesterces, which at that time equalled in value one *aureus* or gold *denarius*). The Amora felt that in the course of time the value of money had sunk lower and lower, and that this decline should be taken into account in interpreting the Bible in the chronological order of its sections. The rise in prices is for instance expressed in the story (in the Babylonian Gemara) according to which a plain dress cost ten times as much as the gorgeous raiment worn by the High Priests in the Second Temple.[85] However this and other such stories are based on a misreading of the sources.[86]

The end of the inflation came with the monetary reforms of Diocletian and Constantine. From the fourth century onwards the Roman-Byzantine gold coin (the *solidus*) kept its value for hundreds of years. Rabbi Abbahu, who lived at the beginning of the fourth century, praised the new gold coin: 'A man can change it into small change and have enough for many days'.[87]

The monetary inflation greatly increased the severity of the crisis in the economic and hence the political fields. The fall in the value of money affected first of all those whose property consisted of the right to fixed amounts: pensioners, creditors, land-owners who were paid in money etc. The high prices burdened the lives of artisans and labourers living on their daily wages. The funds left to the cities for charity and various public purposes lost value. The patriarch and his house, who had many such funds at their disposal, suffered heavy losses. This explains why the money needs of the patriarchate increased and why money had to be obtained by all possible means. Inflation might thus have been, indirectly, one of the causes for the decline in the status of the patriarchs, which could be observed at that time.

6. *The Social Results of the Economic Crisis*

The greatly increased demands of the state and the consequent reduction of the share of produce left to individuals led in the long run to a diminution of the productive capacity of the economy. This caused a further reduction of the quantity of goods at the disposal of the state and individuals alike. This certainly happened during the economic crisis in the third century, which lasted in all for two generations. Poverty became general, and affected the Jewish community as well. When Rabbi Simlai asked the people of Tiberias to change their dress in honour of the Sabbath, his hearers replied: 'Rabbi, our dress for working days is also our dress for the Sabbath', for they had only one covering.[88] The general distress continued into the next generation. A Midrash complains:[89] 'There is nothing left, no light, no knife, no table'. In the Palestine Gemara we are told, 'Poverty is general'.[90] Rabbi Abbahu[91] tells how the Romans mocked the poverty of the Jews in their theatres. One actor would ask another: 'How many years do you want to live?' And his stooge replied: 'As long as the Sabbath dress of a Jew can last'. Or 'A camel was brought into the theatre in mourning. The clowns asked one another: "Why does the camel mourn?" The reply was: "These Jews now keep the

Sabbatical year and they have no vegetables, so they are eating all the thistles and the camel is mourning".' Or 'Mimus (the clown) enters the theatre with his head shaven. Another actor asks: "Why is your head shaven?" He replies: "These Jews keep the Sabbath, and all they earn on weekdays they eat on the Sabbath; but as they have no wood to cook, they break their beds and cook with them, and so they have to sleep on the ground, and they get dusty and use up the oil (to clean themselves) and so the oil rises in price and the clown has to shave for he cannot afford oil to smooth his hair".'

Under the pressure of economic distress the barrier set up with so much trouble in the preceding generations to keep community life intact gradually began to disintegrate.[92] Scholars started leaving the country. Among them was Rabbi Simeon ben Abba, who was forced to leave for Damascus because he was a 'wretchedly poor man'.[93] Rabbi Hiyya had opposed his departure, saying: 'To-morrow I shall go to (the tombs of) your fathers and they shall say to me: "The One beautiful sapling we had in the Land of Israel, and you allowed it to depart" '.[94] Emigration continued notwithstanding in the time of Rabbi Yohanan. Scholars left the country one after the other: Rabbis Dimmi, Isaac ben Joseph, Abin, Samuel ben Judah, and even Hiyya bar Abba himself.[95] Rabbi Yohanan was forced to allow charity societies to lend money on interest.[96] The number of usurers grew, as always in times of distress. When energetic measures were once proposed to deal with them, they had to be stopped at once, for otherwise 'no great man in Israel would be without blame'.[97]

At that time those forced by need to transgress the Law became more and more numerous. The rules concerning the Sabbatical year became more and more difficult to apply. Rabbi Simeon ben Lakish and his companions once saw a priest ploughing and another trimming his vineyard in a Sabbatical year.[98] The Sabbatical years had already caused hardships in the days of Rabban Judah I. The Palestine Gemara mentions a barber (or scribe—*sofer*) who was suspected of using produce grown in the Sabbatical year. Rabban Judah ordered his release, saying: 'Whatever this poor man has done, he did it for the sake of his life' (i.e. in order to keep alive).[99]

The general distress also affected rabbinical students. Rabbi Simeon ben Lakish was forced for a time to give up his studies and to be engaged as an athlete or a gladiator (*ludarius*).

The distress was endured by all producers, and fell most heavily on the peasants. There was a radical change in the honour in which agriculture was held. Taxes and forced labour used up most of the peasant produce. He began to ask himself for whom he was toiling so hard. The peasants reduced the quantity produced, or abandoned farming. To counteract this tendency, the government was in the end obliged to declare all workmen and labourers (peasant-owners included) members of a hereditary caste. No one was allowed to abandon the profession of his father. The peasants became serfs bound to the soil. In Palestine, however, the rigidity of the system was somewhat modified, a relaxation which remained in force till the year 386.[100]

The evolution of Roman society into a caste society was completed in the time of Diocletian and his heirs.[101] Its beginnings could be already observed in the middle of the third century. Rabbi Eleazar ben Pedath, who was conservative by nature, still used to say: 'A man who has no land is no man'.[102] In the course of time, however, he changed his mind and said: 'There is no trade lower than working the land'.[103] On this point he agreed with the later scholars. Their view has been summed up by Raba in a short saying: 'One hundred *zuz* in land—salt and vegetables only'.[104]

A direct result of reduced agricultural productivity was frequent famine. Such famines were in general much more common in antiquity than in the present day. This was mainly because of the lack of means for transporting wheat in bulk from one place to another. In the Aboth de Rabbi Nathan[105] we find the following lament: 'At first they were saying: "Wheat in Judaea, straw in Galilee and chaff east of the Jordan". Later on they said: "There is no wheat in Judaea but only chaff, and east of the Jordan neither the one, nor the other".' This saying is quoted as a comment on a statement by Rabbi Eleazar ben Shemua, a Tanna of the third generation. It is therefore probably meant as a reference to the period of crisis in the third century. Rabban Judah I, the patriarch, had already been obliged to open his granaries to the people in times of drought.

The crisis in the empire and the famine in Palestine reached their peak in the days of Rabbi Yohanan, who understood well the connection between poverty and famine. He said: 'I remember a time when they were selling 4 *sea*'s (of wheat) for one *sela* (4 *denarii*) but there were many people in Tiberias swollen up with hunger for lack of an *issar* (24th part of a dinar)'.[106] He also said: 'I remember when no workmen could be hired for work in the eastern quarter of the town (in which direction the wind was blowing), for they died from the mere smell of bread'.[107] His contemporary and brother-in-law, Rabbi Simeon ben Lakish, tells us as an everyday occurrence, how 'a man entered his house and found his sons and daughters dead from hunger'.[108] The distress among the Jews continued into the fourth generation of Amoraim. Rabbi Isaac commented on the verse: ' "And thou shalt eat the herb of the field" (Gen. 3, 18)—a man takes the green grass from his field and eats it'.[109] In times when famine was at its worst, in spring, before the harvest, people ate the green wheat in the stalk.

Epidemics, the usual companions of famine, were not slow to make their appearance. Roman historians refer to the severe outbreaks of plague which devastated the empire in times of crisis. One of the worst was in the reign of Gallienus (253–268).[110] This plague is quite possibly referred to in the stories about the 'death at Sepphoris' in the days of Rabbi Hanina ben Hama.[111] A member of the next generation, Rabbi Simlai, mentions the plague in his own time: 'when mortality (*androlomousia* = ἀνδρῶν λοίμος) came upon the world'.[112] Economic distress brought about a crisis in relations between the social classes. Hitherto the two opposed groups were the scholars and the common people (*amme ha-arets*); both groups had some wealthy and many poor members. In consequence of a 'national' crisis social divisions tended to be forgotten. When the economic crisis began, the wealthy classes began to take care for their own interests only. The vertical division of earlier times was replaced by a hardly less dangerous horizontal one. The men of property were now opposed to the poor, and society split into classes. As the crisis deepened the poor hoped for help from the rich. We are told of a 'councillor (*bouleutēs*) who was well-known in his province. The people of the province believed that in times of crop failure he would supply them for ten years running.'[113] They were severely disappointed. The attitude of the wealthy angered the rabbis. They were now saying: 'There are three sins which make the Holy One weep every day'. One of them was 'a *parnas* who lords over the people'.[114] Rabbi Judah (of the fourth generation of Amoraim) said: 'The sin of those robbing the poor is greater than the sin of the generation of the Flood'[115] (which was regarded as particularly corrupt). The rich used the strength of their economic position and oppressed the poor, if necessary by main force. They cared only for the increase of their properties and created the *latifundia* (*patrocinia*) of later centuries. The watchmen (*santerim*— σημάντωρ) chased away the poor going to work on their fields.[116]

Oppression from above was carried out by legal processes and with the assistance of the authorities. The poor reacted in the only way open to them: by transgressing the law, by theft and robbery. The very efforts of the rabbis to stem this evil prove how common it was. Rabbi Yohanan said: 'the generation of the Flood committed all kinds of crimes, but their fate was decided only as soon as they began to rob'.[117] Sometimes the results were grotesque. Rabbi Hanina was once preaching on the same subject at Sepphoris—and that night there were three hundred burglaries at Sepphoris.[118] Rabbis Simeon bar Abba, Judah, Aha, Abba bar Kahana, Levi and other Amoraim of the second or third generation, all spoke against robbery. The greatest of the scholars of the second generation, Rabbi Yohanan, once declared: 'Anyone who robs his fellow-man of anything worth a *pruta* (penny), is to be regarded as if he had taken away his soul'.[119] His pupil Rabbi Ammi said: 'Rains are delayed only because of the frequency of robberies'.[120] Rabbi Simeon ben Lakish, the contemporary and friend of Rabbi Yohanan, said: 'As soon as a man becomes poor here below (on earth), he becomes wicked as regards up there'.[121]

Preaching against the sin of robbery continued till the fourth generation of Amoraim. Rabbi Eleazar said: 'The just ones stick to their properties . . . because they do not put their hands to robbery'.[122]

The Roman officials tried occasionally to exploit the social cleavage for their own purposes. They tried to widen the rift between rich and poor in order to break up the Jewish nation little by little, and thus end the status of Jewry as a 'state within a state'. They tried to pose as friends of the common people—'like the rulers and generals and governors (*hegemōnes*, *duces*, *hipparchoi*) who go about in the provinces to rob and steal. When they return to their seats, they say: "Bring us the poor and we shall feed them".'[123]

7. The Counteraction of the Patriarchate

The national leaders of the Jews understood quite well the dangers of a social cleavage. They made determined efforts to soften the effects of the economic crisis. As usually happens in such circumstances, it was believed at first that charity would allay poverty and hunger. The patriarch Judah I opened his granaries to the poor in the years of crop failure. As the crisis went on everyone soon understood that prosperity would not return soon. The patriarch therefore tried to alleviate the burden of the people by lightening the religious obligations. After the destruction of the Temple various dues had become obsolete (offerings, *shekels* and first fruits).[124] The tithes, however, and the redemption of the first born child, remained in force. After the war of Bar Kokhba the Jewish nation submitted, as we have seen, to rabbinical authority. The bearers of that authority were first and foremost *haberim*, scholars and rabbis. They were very rigorous as regards the strict observance of the Law. The most oppressive of these obligations was the necessity to keep the fields fallow every seventh year. Rabbi Isaac praised in particular those who paid the *annona* and yet kept the Sabbatical year.[125] In ordinary times the supplies stored during the six working years would be enough to feed the people in the seventh. In times of crisis such reserves were used up to feed the soldiers and to supply the other needs of the State. Stores were exhausted long before the Sabbatical year. Those observing the Law were therefore forced to use all kinds of unripe vegetables; we have already referred to the mockery which Jewish misery in a Sabbatical year evoked.[126] As the head of the nation, Rabban Judah I regarded himself under the obligation to help the people; but he had to tread warily in this delicate matter, with an eye to scholarly opposition. He therefore began with small economic concessions: vegetables could be collected at the end of the year, when the hunger was at its worst. In order to help the Jewish farmers living in boundary areas under the rule of gentile cities, he excluded the areas of Caesarea Philippi (Paneas), Eleutheropolis (Beth Gubrin) and Kefar Tsemah, and finally even all Scythopolis (Beth Shean), from the theoretical limits of the Holy Land. Thereby he abolished the obligation of the inhabitants of these areas to keep the Sabbatical year. But even this small step met with opposition. His brothers and his family banded together against him and said: 'The places which your fathers and forefathers declared forbidden, are you allowing them now (i.e. to be worked)?'.[127] It seems that it was his intention to suspend the Sabbatical year entirely. But his first steps already caused 'everybody to speak evil of him'.[128] His more radical proposals met with much determined resistance—especially from the scholars who were close to the Zealots, in particular Rabbi Pinhas ben Yair, the son-in-law of Rabbi Simeon bar Yohai himself. Their suspicions had been aroused by the earlier attempts of Judah I to suspend the fast of the Ninth of Ab,[129] a step dictated by political and not economic reasons.

Rabban Gamliel III, the son and successor of Judah I, and his court continued to follow the same line. They cancelled the prohibition to plough in the season preceding the Sabbatical year; finally, when taxation became especially unbearable, Rabbi Yannai (of the first generation of the Amoraim) allowed ploughing and sowing in a Sabbatical year—as a temporary measure—'because of the *annona*'.[130] Borrowing money at interest, hitherto severely frowned upon, at least in theory, was now allowed in certain cases of urgent need or for charitable purposes.

Judah I also tried to alleviate economic distress in several other ways. He decided on cases involving the distribution of taxes and tried to make the distribution fairer to all parties.[131] He tried to abolish many old prohibitions on export; he allowed the export of fruit from one province to another, and also the export of wine to Syria. His grandson, Rabban Judah II followed the same line, and allowed the use of oil produced by Gentiles. Because of this the common people believed that Judah I had allowed the consumption of bread baked by Gentiles. He once went out into the fields belonging to a non-Jew and remarked: 'How fine is this wheat; why did the scholars forbid it?' He thus hinted that it should be allowed. However, the scholars would not agree with him, and he accepted their decision.[132]

Quite possibly all these measures would have had the desired effect, had the Jews been able to isolate themselves from the rest of the world and conduct their own affairs. They were, however, part of an empire in crisis, and the crisis went from bad to worse. The abolition of a few specially onerous restrictions could not effect a permanent improvement. Even the resources of the patriarchs did not suffice in the end. The patriarch himself was but one of the big land-owners, and hence among the first victims of the inflation and the crushing tax burdens.

Although the measures taken to alleviate the distress of the people did not indeed achieve their principal aim, radically to improve the bad economic situation, indirectly they brought about one important result. The rift between scholars and the *amme ha-arets* gradually diminished. The efforts of Judah I contributed much to that end. At first he opened his store-houses only to the 'students of the Bible, of the Mishnah, of the Gemara, of the Halakah and the Haggadah' and declared 'The *amme ha-arets* should not enter'.[133] Under the influence of Rabbi Jonathan ben Amram the patriarch finally agreed to supply these also. In the following generation the conservative Rabbi Eleazar ben Pedath still declared that 'whosoever gives his bread to one not of the scholars, shall be visited by plagues';[134] but his voice was a solitary one.

From the first generation of the Amoraim the abuse of the *amme ha-arets* disappears from Talmudic literature. The common people began to admit that 'at a time when Israel is in distress its great ones suffer with it'.[135] They noticed that often the outstanding men of their time succumbed to the incessant government demands for money and more money, for material supplies and forced labour. The exemption from taxes accorded to the scholars was at that time abolished, at the insistent demand of the common people. The scholars were very dissatisfied, but it helped to bridge the old cleavage between the various classes of the nation.[136]

Notes to Chapter IV

1. See below, pp. 176–81.
2. See above, pp. 20ff.
3. The 'Royal Parables' have been collected by I. Ziegler, *Die Königsgleichnisse im Midrasch*, Breslau, 1903.
4. *Lam. R* 1, 4–2d.
5. b *Pesahim* 87b.
6. *Exodus R* 15, 13–28a.
7. *Mekilta* 78a (ed. Lauterbach II, p. 262).
8. See above, pp. 40–2.
9. *Mekilta* ed. J. Z. Lauterbach, Philadelphia, 1935, II, p. 237.
10. *Exodus R* 37a, 1.
11. *Genesis R* 83a, 1 (Theodor-Albeck ed. pp. 996–7).
12. Ibid., 63, 8.
13. *Exodus R* 45, 3; *Midrash Proverbs* 6, 32 (ed. Buber, p. 58); *Midrash Zutah*, p. 14; *Numer. R* 20, 19.

14. J. Juster, *Les Juifs dans l'empire romain*, Paris, 1914, II, pp. 269–76; to which add M. Avi-Yonah, *QDAP*, 10 (1944), p. 135, pl. XXVII, 3.

15. *Tanhuma Exod.* (ed. Buber), pp. 40–1; see also *Leviticus R.* 11, 7; *Genesis R* 5, 6 (p. 35); *Mekilta* (ed. Lauterbach) II, p. 262; *Exodus R* 42, 3; *Genesis R* 42, 2 (p. 402).

16. b *Sanhedrin* 39a.

17. *Tanhuma Genesis* (ed. Buber) p. 35.

18. *Tanhuma Numeri* (ed. Buber) p. 91.

19. *Genesis R* 51, 2.

20. *Exodus R* 15, 13.

21. *Genesis R* 42, 4 etc.

22. j *Pesahim* 4, 9–31b.

23. See above, p. 20.

24. M *Baba Metsia* 6, 3. On the subject of the *angaria* see D. Sperber, *L'antiquité classique*, 38 (1969), pp. 164–8.

25. *Leviticus R* 12, 1.

26. j *Berakot* 1, 1–2d, l. 8, bottom.

27. C. F. W. Dittenberger, *Orientis graeci inscriptiones selectae*, Leipzig, 1898–1905, No. 609.

28. b *Baba Metsia* 11b.

29. j *Baba Kamma* 3, 1–3c.

30. j *Demai* 3, 1–23b; for the opposite view see T *Shebiit* 5, 21, p. 69.

31. j *Erubin* 6, 4–23c.

32. L. Goldschmidt, *REJ*, 34 (1897), pp. 192–217.

33. A. Gulak in *Sefer Magnes*, Jerusalem, 1938, pp. 98–100.

34. See below, pp. 102–4.

35. *Abot de Rabbi Nathan* 8, 4.

36. b *Baba Kamma* 113a.

37. j *Hagigah* 2, 2–77d.

38. See above, p. 20.

39. *Abot de Rabbi Nathan*, 8, 4.

40. *Leviticus R* 29, 2.

41. j *Peah* 1, 1–15b.

42. See above, p. 50.

43. Gulak (see n. 33 above), p. 97, n. 2.

44. Judah I—j *Ketubot* 10, 5–34a; Rabbi Samuel ben—Nahman *Lev. R* 29, 2; Rabbi Abba—j *Peah* 1, 1–15b.

45. *Numeri R* 17, 5.

46. *Abot de Rabbi Nathan* 20 (ed. Schechter) 36a.

47. *Genesis R* 20, 1.

48. j *Peah* 1, 1–15b; *Lev. R* 29, 2.

49. j *Shebiit* 5, 9–36a end; cf. j *Peah* 1, 1–15b.

50. Gulak, op. cit. (n. 33 above) pp. 103–4.

51. T *Maaser Sheni* 3, 8, p. 91; *b Sukkah* 29b top.

52. j *Nedarim* 9, 3–41c.

53. *Genesis R* 24, 1, p. 229; *Lev. R* 12, 1; *Esther R* 5, 1.

54. b *Baba Batra* 9a.

55. b *Sanhedrin* 98b.

56. *Leviticus R* 30, 6.

57. b *Shabbat* 145b.

58. *Genesis R* 49, 8.

59. j *Moed Katan* 3, 1–81d, l. 9 bottom.

60. *Midr. Tannaim*, Deut. 32, 40, p. 203.

61. b *Yoma* 35b.

62. H. M. Parker, *History of the Roman World*, London, 1958, pp. 119–21.

63. Diocletian's reform was meant to counter this threat, ibid., pp. 283–5.

64. *Genesis R* 13, 9.

65. j *Peah* 1, 1–16a.

66. *Genesis R* 20, 1.

67. T *Demai* 3, 4; b *Sanhedrin* 25b; cf. D. Sperber, *L'antiquité classique*, 38 (1969), pp. 164–8.

68. j *Sanhedrin* 15, 2–26b.

69. b *Baba Metsia* 85a.

70. j *Shekalim* 5, 2–48d.

71. j *Berakot* 5, 1–8d.

72. *Genesis R* 76, 6.

73. G. Allon, *Tarbiz*, 14 (1942), pp. 145–55.

74. b *Ketubot* 110b.

75. b *Baba Metsia* 8a.

76. C. F. W. Dittenberger, *Sylloge inscriptionum graecorum*, Leipzig, 1915, No. 888, l. 85 (Thrace AD 238).

77. S. Lieberman, *JQR*, 36 (1946), pp. 350ff.

78. j *Sanhedrin* 15, 2–26b.

79. F. Oertel, *CAH*, XII, pp. 262, 266, 724f.; Parker, op. cit. (n. 62 above), pp. 97–8, 278f.; D. Sperber, *Archiv orientální* 34 (1966), pp. 1–25 and his *Cost of Living in Roman Palestine*, Leiden, n.d.

80. See above, p. 41.

81. b *Baba Metsia* 44a–b. On this point see D. Sperber, *Archiv orientální* 38 (1970), pp. 17–22 and his article cited in n. 79 above; also a (hitherto unpublished) article by E. Kleinmann of the Hebrew University of Jerusalem, kindly communicated to me by the author.

82. *Genesis R* 91, 11, p. 1136.

83. b *Yoma* 38a.

84. b *Bekorot* 50a.

85. M *Yoma* 3, 7; b *Yoma* 35b; j *Kilaim* 9, 1–32a. Mr. Y. Klein, Jerusalem, has pointed out to me that according to b *Abodah Zarah* 23b/24a this story refers to the time of a certain Dama ben Nathina, who lived in the times of the Second Temple. However the dating is certainly anachronistic in that setting.

86. j *Maaser Sheni* 1, 2–52d. As D. Sperber has convincingly demonstrated in his *Cost of Living in Roman Palestine* the inflationary prices mentioned in some Talmudic sources refer to nominal amounts in a debased currency, while the actual coins used (gold solidi) each represented millions of denarii.

87. *Genesis R* 16, 2, p. 143.

88. j. *Peah* 8, 8–21b.

89. *Abot de Rabbi Nathan* 9, ed. Schechter 36a.

90. j *Nedarim* 9, 3–41c.

91. *Lamentations R* 17.

92. See above, pp. 25ff.

93. j *Baba Metsia* 2, 3–8c.

94. j *Moed Katan* 3, 1–81c, l. 19 from bottom.

95. b *Abodah Zarah* 73a.

96. j *Sanhedrin* 8, 2–22b.

97. j *Baba Metsia* 5, 1–10a.

98. M *Shebiit* 4, 1; b *Sanhedrin* 26a.

99. j *Taanit* 3, 1–66b.

100. *Corpus juris civilis* XI, 51, 1.

101. E. Stein, *Histoire du Bas Empire* I, Paris, 1959, p. 17.

102. b *Yebamot* 63a.

103. Ibid.

104. Ibid.

105. *Abot de Rabbi Nathan* 27 end.

106. b *Baba Metsia* 91b.

107. Ibid.

108. b *Sanhedrin* 98b.

109. *Genesis R* 20, 9.

110. Parker, op. cit. (n. 62 above) p. 165, n. 5; p. 342.

111. j *Taanit* 3, 4–66c.

112. j *Sotah* 1, 5–17a, l. 9.

113. *Ruth R* 1, 4.

114. b *Hagigah* 5b.

115. *Shoher Tob* 12c.

116. b *Sanhedrin* 98b; A. Marmorstein, *Freimann Festschrift* (*Emet le-Ya'agov*), Berlin, 1936, p. 84f.; A. Büchler, *The Political and Social Leaders of the Jewish Community of Sepphoris in the Second and Third Centuries*, London, 1909, p. 45.

117. b *Sanhedrin* 108a.

118. *Genesis R* 27, 2.

119. b *Baba Kamma* 119a.

120. b *Taanit* 7b.

121. b *Sanhedrin* 103b.

122. b *Sotah* 12a.

123. *Exodus R* 31, 7.

124. M *Shekalim* 8, 8.

125. *Leviticus R* 1, 17.

126. See above, pp. 104–5.

127. b *Hullin* 6b.

128. j *Demai* 2, 1–22c.

129. See above, pp. 70–1.

130. b *Sanhedrin* 26a.

131. See above, p. 101.

132. b *Abodah Zarah* 35b.

133. b *Baba Batra* 8a.

134. b *Sanhedrin* 92a.

135. Rabbi Ahah, *Pesikta R*, ed. Friedmann 50b.

136. A. Marmorstein, *REJ*, 54 (1912), pp. 59–66; *Tarbiz*, 3 (1931), pp. 161–80; *Freimann Festschr.* (see n. 116 above), pp. 81–92.

V

––

The Political Results
of the Crisis

––

1. *Introduction*

Without subscribing blindly to the tenets of historical materialism, one has to admit that there have been periods in history in which economic factors have played a preponderant role. The third century of the Christian era was one of these periods. The origins of the crisis are indeed to be found in the political situation, but its effects were first manifested in the economic field. It was the economic crisis which had a decisive influence on future political developments. The interaction of these two factors moulded the destiny of the Jews in Palestine. The economic crisis has therefore been discussed in detail in the preceding chapter. The political consequences of this crisis were no less important for Palestine Jewry than for the rest of the empire, and deserve an equally detailed discussion.

Not all the results of imperial anarchy were entirely negative from the Jewish point of view. The powerless and ephemeral emperors were obliged to study the wishes of their subjects, to curry their favour and to dispense privileges and concessions. We may define the Roman empire of the third century as an absolutist regime tempered by assassination. In the Midrash we are told how 'a king (= emperor) entered a province and said to them (the inhabitants): "I shall rule over you" and they said: "What did you do for our good that you should rule over us?" What did he do? He repaired their walls, brought them water, fought for them. Then he said: "I shall rule over you". And they said "Yea, yea".'[1] The new rulers owed their power to themselves and not heredity, and in order to keep themselves in the saddle they had to prove their abilities and their capacities to provide material benefits, to win over their new subjects.

Rabbi Levi mentioned 'a *dux* on whose shoulders the legions threw the purple . . . he remits the *loipos* (λοιπός—the 'remainder' of taxes due) and burns the lists of outstanding taxes'.[2]

Whether such concessions remained in effect depended of course on the events. If the rebel *dux* won, his concessions remained valid; if he lost— the victorious government annulled his bounties and fined his adherents.

In this stormy period many of the anti-Jewish decrees of former times were disregarded. The Roman authorities shut their eyes to the revival of Jewish penal jurisdiction.[3] They abandoned for all practical purposes the prohibition to enter Jerusalem. But although Palestinian Jewry profited momentarily from such by-products of the crisis, its general effect was certainly adverse. When so many individuals were ruined, the coherence of the whole community was finally shaken. After all the trouble which had been taken to bolster up the patriarchate after the war of Bar Kokhba, it now lost much of its prestige. The resources of the Jewish community were exhausted to a degree which seriously menaced its political stability.

In this chapter we shall consider the political consequences of the crisis as they affected Palestine Jewry. To do this we shall have to go beyond the third century. By including the fourth and fifth generations of Amoraim we shall have completed the political survey of the age of the Talmud.

2. *The Dissension between the Patriarch and the Scholars*

The general decline of authority in the Roman empire caused a parallel weakness of the patriarchate. The patriarch, who was the visible embodiment of authority among the Jews, as the emperor was amongst the Romans, was another victim of popular discontent.

The general crisis of the third century passed through three stages. The first was political, and affected mainly the imperial government itself. The second was economic, and affected the Jews in Palestine directly. In the third stage the political results of the economic crisis became apparent. As the first factor directly to affect the Jews was economic, the first signs of the internal political crisis likewise appeared in financial affairs. In the days of the patriarch Judah II the exactions of the Roman government increased to such an extent that the patriarch was forced to increase his revenues at any cost. In a Midrash[4] we are told that the patriarch complained to Rabbi Simeon ben Lakish: 'Pray for me, because this government is evil beyond measure'. Rabbi Simeon replied: 'Take nothing from others, and you shall not have to pay anything to the government'. This sage counsel was of no avail to an administration pressed on all sides. The patriarchal revenues were affected by inflation due to the high taxes and the general economic decline. It is not yet clear whether the collection of taxes from the Jews was an obligation of the patriarch. He certainly had to adjust the tax burden between the various classes of the city population,[5] and possibly also between the various towns. In any case he was closely supervised by the Roman government. We are told[6] that once a good woman brought the patriarch a silver plate with a knife upon it. He took the knife and returned the plate. But an agent of the government (*baldar, veredarius*) 'saw it, wanted it and took it' (*vehamitah, vehamdah, venasbah*) a lapidary parody of Caesar's *veni, vidi, vici*).

While there may be doubt whether the patriarch was responsible for the tax payments due from Jewry as a whole, he himself was undoubtedly one of the greatest tax-payers of the empire, considering the extent of his estates and undertakings. He must also have been responsible for much of the forced labour demanded by the authorities, although he was personally exempted from it. The patriarch had to pay the tax due from him out of his revenues, that is from the rents of his farmers and the *apostolē*, collected by his agents in the Diaspora. In times of crisis the income from both these sources declined, just at the moment they were most needed. The *apostolē* diminished, because of the general uncertainty, the civil wars, the disruption of communications, the military campaigns, the thefts and robberies of passing soldiers, the increase in taxes levied on Jews in the Diaspora by the imperial government. All these left smaller amounts free for what was after all a semi-voluntary contribution. In addition came the decline in the value of money, in which the *apostolē* was paid. The patriarchs were therefore forced to look urgently for other sources of income.

The first step in this direction was an attempt to increase the number of tax-payers. Till then the rabbis and their students were in the eyes of the authorities 'priests of a recognized religion'[7] and as such exempt from service in the municipal councils. In this way they escaped personal responsibility for collecting taxes and for the supply of forced labour. This exemption increased the burden which fell upon the rest of the community. In times of crisis, when everybody was suffering from increased taxes, there was naturally much opposition to this exemption. 'When the crown-tax was imposed on Tiberias, the people of the city came before Rabbi (Judah I) and said: "Let the scholars pay as we do". He said: "No". They said to him: "We shall all run away" '[8]—in short, they all threatened *anachōrēsis*.[9] At that time the patriarch refused to impose taxes on the scholarly class. The problem arose again and again in times of distress. At first the tax-exemption of scholars was not attacked directly, but an enquiry was suggested as to who precisely was entitled to such exemption. The discussion centred around the definition of the term 'scholar' (*talmid hakam*). We find a résumé of it in the Babylonian Gemara. Rabbi Yohanan, the foremost scholar of his period, supplied several definitions. Apparently there were many who tried to escape taxation by claiming the status of scholars. Rabbi Yohanan proceeded to define 'scholars' in three ways. According to him, a scholar is one who (a) 'acts as trustee (*parnas*) for the public'. This is in fact the definition of Roman law which exempted the religious functionaries of the Jews from service in a municipality. (b) 'Someone versed in the entire Oral Law'. (c) 'One whom his fellow-citizens have to support because he himself neglects his own affairs and is busy with the affairs of Heaven'—rabbis and students who did not work for gain; thus excluding businessmen who pretended to the status of scholars.[10]

We notice that the head of the scholarly body was himself busy reducing their number. The civil authorities were of course even more interested in reducing the numbers of those exempt from taxation. As one example of the increase of this tendency we may mention the matter of the city wall of Tiberias. In the period of general anarchy and frequent barbarian invasions in the third century, most of the open cities of the empire began to build walls. Even imperial Rome itself was fortified in the days of the emperor Aurelian. Tiberias also was surrounded by a wall and towers in the days of the Severan dynasty, or immediately after.[11] We learn in the Babylonian Gemara[12] that the patriarch Judah II 'levied (the costs of building) the wall from the rabbis'. Possibly he collected other taxes as well which have not been detailed in our sources. The collection of taxes of course aroused strong opposition amongst those affected. Rabbis Simeon ben Lakish and Yohanan, the heads of the scholars, voiced this opposition. In their opinion God protects the sages and they need neither watchmen nor walls.[13] Other scholars joined in the fray. Rabbi Eleazar ben Pedath is reported as saying: 'Our father Abraham and his descendants were punished, went down into bondage in Egypt . . . because they compelled the scholars to do forced labour'.[14] Rabbi Judah ben Levi insisted 'that the tribe of Levi was free from the *leitourgia* (forced labour) in Egypt'.[15] Scholars who were continuing to serve Heaven under similar conditions were hence entitled to a similar privilege. It is even possible that the efforts to make the rabbinate hereditary (similar to the hereditary status then acquired by many other professions) were intended to make them equally responsible for the collection of taxes.

The patriarch Judah II also attempted to increase his revenues by selling the posts of judges. This step evoked strong protests from the rabbis, who till then had manned the Jewish courts almost exclusively. A similar situation had existed once in the days of Rabbis Meir and Yose ben Elisha. They said: 'All the misfortunes which are troubling the world have come upon it because of judges in Israel'.[16] At that time such judges were drawn from among the *amme ha-arets* and the scholars naturally found them wanting. With the establishment of the authority of the patriarchs Simeon II and Judah I, his son, and of the Sanhedrin, only rabbis sat in Jewish tribunals. Now they were faced by a new class of rivals: rich men, who had purchased their appointments from the patriarch. No wonder that the scholars greeted the new judges with derision and contempt. Rabbi Simeon ben Lakish applied to them the verse: 'Your hands are full of blood' (Isaiah 1, 15)—'these are the judges, their scribes and their assistants'.[17] Rabbi Ammi in referring to them quoted the verse: 'Thou shalt not make thyself gods of gold and gods of silver' (Exod. 20, 23). Rabbi Zeira refused to honour them by standing up in their presence.[18] The popular preachers attacked them in still sharper tones. Jacob of Kefar Neburaya quoted once, in the presence of one of the new appointees, who was ignorant of the scriptures, the verse of Habbakuk (2, 19): 'Woe to him that saith to the wood, Awake; to the dumb stone, Arise, it shall teach'.[19]

Our sources are full of complaints against the new judges. They were accused of drinking, of taking bribes, of discriminating between the rich and the poor, of acting in collusion with thieves. The people compared them to coins of the smallest denomination worth three asses or half an ass (*tremissis* and *semissis*).[20]

In the course of time the attack on these appointees passed to the appointing authority, the patriarch himself. Opposition to the patriarchate had already revived in the time of Gamliel III.[21] Rabbi Simeon ben Lakish, the leader of the opposition, said: 'Whoever sets up an unworthy judge sets up an *asherah* (tree worshipped by isolaters) in Israel'.[22]

The first aim of the opposition was to put the patriarch on a level with the rest of the scholars. This egalitarian demand was at first put forward as a matter of theory, but it was finally embodied in a series of legal regulations. The tendency to stress the equality between ruler and ruled is to be found in many of the sayings of Rabbi Simeon ben Lakish and his fellow-rabbis. 'Till now (i.e. up to that time) the herd (Israel) needed a shepherd (the patriarch). What did the "Fathers" look like as they walked before the Lord? Like the patriarch in procession preceded by the scholars, who proclaimed the honour of the patriarch.' This implied that the honour of the patriarch depended on that of the rabbis.[23] 'All ears of wheat are equal one to the other. And thus all Israel are (equal) . . . the elders, the pious, the rabbis and all Israel count equally in a *minyan* (praying group of ten persons or more)'.[24] In contrast to the rule of the emperor, who was above the law, as in contemporary Rome, Rabbi Simeon ben Lakish stressed the responsibility of the rulers before the law courts, even in criminal matters: 'A patriarch who has offended can be condemned to be beaten by a Court of Three' (the lowest of the rabbinical courts).[25] The opinion that all power is based on the consent of the ruled was expressed by Rabbi Azariah in his discussion with a Samaritan. The Jewish sage explained to the Samaritan that the Bible did not say 'I (God) shall set a King over you' but 'You may indeed set a King over you' (Deut. 17, 15)', thereby indicating clearly that power did not come from heaven, but that it derived from the consent of the governed.[26]

In this case too the teachings of the scholars evoked a still stronger response among the popular preachers. One of them, Yose of Beth Maon, preached in the synagogues of his town, which was very near Tiberias, the seat of the patriarch. He dared to attack with great virulence 'those of the House of the Patriarch who appropriate everything'. When he was summoned before the patriarch, he aggravated his offence by saying: 'As the mother, so the daughter, as the generation, so the patriarch'.[27] Rabbi Hanina ben Hama repeated an old argument against the patriarchate which had been already used in the days of Judah I, 'The son of David (the Messiah) will not come till this "kingship" is taken away from Israel';[28] by the 'kingship' he meant undoubtedly the rule of the patriarchs. The coalition between the scholars and the popular preachers is characteristic of this stormy and lawless period. The moderate and enlightened scholars, who in the past were the main support of the moderates and the patriarchal dynasty, suddenly made common cause with the popular agitators, who up to now had always continued the tradition of the zealots. We feel here the influence of that period of anarchy in the outside world.

The opposition to the patriarch was thus revived. An opposition based on similar principles had already existed in the far-off days of the patriarchs Gamliel II and his son, Simeon II. It had been driven underground by the energetic rule of Judah I. Its work was now made easier by the decline in stature of the later patriarchs. As usual in hereditary offices, the sons and grandsons lacked the abilities of their great ancestors. Even the patriarch Judah II, 'who was a great man', met with open resistance; his son Gamliel IV 'who was a small one' was still more dependent on the scholars; 'Rabbi Abbahu intended to "fence him in" '[29] that is to limit his competence and to supervise all his acts.

Of course the patriarch showed some resistance to those who intended to limit his functions. He had at his disposal a force of Gothic slaves, the gift of the emperor; and he apparently did not hesitate to use them. German slaves were still serving the patriarch and his followers in the time of Rabban Judah III (280–320).[30] The most prominent of the opponents of the patriarch, such as Yose of Beth Maon, were occasionally forced to hide from the patriarchal police.[31] Such arrests were legal, for according to our sources the patriarch was entitled to order his men to bring before him by force anyone refusing to obey him, and to have him beaten for contempt of his authority.[32]

The patriarch was also as a rule supported by the Roman authorities against the Jewish opposition. However, the occasional help of the government was but a broken reed against public opinion, which was swayed by the rabbis.

It is probable that the edict of Diocletian, dated 293 and addressed to a certain Judah, bears upon our subject. The edict says: 'The consent of private persons cannot make a man a judge who is not the head of any court, and his decisions have not the force of a judgement'.[33] The intention seems to be to protect the patriarchal courts and to strengthen the hands of the patriarch in the dispute between him and the scholars concerning his appointment of judges. In any case such edicts could not put a stop to historic development, and in the end the patriarch had to compromise with the Sanhedrin.

3. *The Functions of the Patriarchate Limited* de facto *and* de jure

As a result of the conflict between the patriarch and the scholars there was a radical change in the internal constitution of Palestine Jewry. The monarchical rule established in the days of Rabban Simeon ben Gamliel and his son Judah I was replaced by the collective rule of the Sanhedrin leaders. This change found its expression in many fields of public life. In the first place there was the problem which in the past too had served as an indication of constitutional change, the right to make appointments. Part of this right now reverted to the Sanhedrin. In earlier times it was decided that 'a patriarch who has made an appointment against the opinion of the court (sanhedrin), his appointment is valid' and now 'they retracted and decided that the court (sanhedrin) does not appoint but with the consent of the patriarch and that the patriarch does not appoint but with the consent of the court'.[34] The former monarchy was now replaced by a dyarchy, the joint rule of the patriarch and the Sanhedrin. In the following generations a distinction was drawn between the appointment of 'elders' (*zekenim*), the members of the central Sanhedrin, and that of the *parnasim*, the representatives of the central authority in the provincial communities. The 'elders' were nominated by the patriarch himself, of course with the consent of the scholars. Such nominations were usually announced in connection with some festive event in the patriarchal court. Rabbi Pinhas bar Hama said: 'It was the habit of this house (the patriarchal court) to appoint elders in the course of their (wedding) banquets'.[35] On the other hand the appointment of the local *parnasim* was entrusted to single scholars or to commissions of scholars. Rabbi Yose appointed one at Kafra, a suburb of Tiberias; and Rabbi Haggai was setting up *parnasim* in several localities.[36] Rabbi Hiyya was also setting up *archons* (local administrators) either by himself or in conjunction with Rabbis Ammi and Assi.[37] There are even some signs of a return to the state of affairs which existed generations before, when each teacher was ordaining independently. Rabbi Yohanan, who kept up his relations with the patriarchal house, refrained from ordaining on his own; but his contemporary, Rabbi Joshua ben Levi, had no such scruples.[38]

The competence of the patriarch was limited not only *de jure* but also *de facto*. Their privileged positions and their material wealth caused the descendants of Judah I to neglect their studies. The patriarch himself had recognized this state of affairs on his death-bed, when he willed the post of *Ab Bet Din* (president of the rabbinical court) to Rabbi Hanina ben Hama, while his son Simeon remained *Hakam* (president of the Sanhedrin). In the time of his grandson Rabban Judah II the presidency of both court and Sanhedrin was exclusively in the hands of the scholars, in particular of Rabbi Yohanan. Rabban Gamliel IV, the next patriarch, was in all halakic matters entirely dependent upon the decisions of the rabbis. This state of affairs continued into the following generations. Rabban Judah IV was continually consulting Rabbi Pinhas bar Hama.[39] The scholars did not have the slightest hesitation in castigating the shortcomings of the patriarch.

Towards the end of the third century the managing of Jewish relations with the Roman authorities also passed from the patriarch to the rabbis. Rabbi Abbahu, who resided at Caesarea, was the main representative of his nation at the governors' court. The rabbis also took over management of the relations between the Holy Land and the Jewish communities in the Diaspora, a task which had till then been one of the main duties of the patriarch. Rabbi Yose was answering queries which had come from Alexandria. 'He said to Rabbi Mana "Come and sign" but he refused.'[40] A signature of the patriarch is not even mentioned. Rabbi Yose also wrote to Babylonia: 'Even if you are told the order of the feasts, do not change any of the customs of your forefathers who repose in peace'.[41] Many important matters were now decided by single rabbis or by rabbinical commissions. Rabbi Jeremiah went to the Golan where the patriarch had large estates;[42] Rabbis Yohanan and Jonathan 'went and made peace within the cities of the South'.[43]

This loss of face is evident even in matters of representation and protocol. After the death of Judah I the whole nation went into mourning. The priests were encouraged to disregard their ritual purity and to enter the cemetery; 'but when Judah (II) died, Rabbi Hiyya bar Abba had to push Rabbi Zeira into the synagogue of the vineyard in Sepphoris so as to render him ritually impure'[44] against the will of the latter and thus force him into mourning. (Rabbi Zeira who was a priest, was unwilling to take part in the funeral.) Two generations later 'when Nehorai, the sister of Judah IV, died, Rabbi Hanina sent to Rabbi Mana (to persuade him to come to the funeral), but he refused. It was said (to Rabbi Hanina): "If we refuse to defile ourselves for them (the patriarchal house) during their lifetime, this applies *a fortiori* after their death".'[45]

The patriarch nevertheless kept a great deal of his honours and much real power. Officially he was still the head of Jewry in Palestine and the Diaspora. Even scholars had to pay him their grudging respect, for all their efforts to limit his prerogatives. Rabbi Joshua ben Levi stood up before his own son, because the latter was related by marriage with the patriarchal house.[46] Rabbi Abbahu, who was actually in charge of Jewish affairs at Caesarea, the seat of the Roman governor, acknowledged the superior authority of the patriarchal court residing at Tiberias. He regularly consulted the leading rabbis there, Rabbis Ammi and Assi and their colleagues. When judging cases, he and Rabbis Hanina bar Pappa and Isaac Napaha used habitually to decide in favour of the patriarch, till Rabbi Abba was forced to declare: 'You are deciding thus in order to flatter the patriarch and his house'.[47] Rabbi Yose, an Amora of the fifth generation, who was the leader of the scholars together with Rabbi Jonah, admitted: 'The fasts we are proclaiming are not true fasts. Why? Because the patriarch is not with us.'[48] There was always a group of loyal adherents to the patriarchs—the so-called 'men of the house of the patriarch', who were ever ready to mock the rabbis. Thus Rabbi Mana (an Amora of the fifth generation) was 'grieved by the men of the house of the Patriarch'.[49]

4. *The Decline in the Status of Palestinian Jewry*

The political and economic crisis in Palestine not only affected the status of the patriarch, the power relations of the various groups at Tiberias and the constitutional position within the local Jewry; it also affected the position of Palestinian Jewry as a whole *vis-à-vis* the Diaspora. This was especially evident as regards the Jews of Babylonia, who had remained almost unaffected by the crisis, because they lived outside the Roman empire.

The decline in material standards for the Jews in Palestine caused a corresponding decline in the level of their halakic (legal-religious) studies, which had hitherto been the main spiritual activity of the period. Rabbi Isaac explained the position in plain words: 'At first, when money was plentiful, people liked to listen to the Mishnah and the Talmud (the Halakah); now there is no money, and moreover we have to suffer so much from the government, they prefer to listen to the Bible and the Haggadah (legends)'.[50] The latter, which were easier to understand and more popular in form, were more likely to console the people in times of trouble. Rabbi Abba bar Mammal, of the third generation of Amoraim, complained that in this time even rabbinical scholars did not know how to explain the Mishnah. In earlier times people left for Syria in order to make a living;[51] now they went to Babylonia to study. Already in the time of Rabbi Yohanan there were many who emigrated there, especially among the rabbinical students. In the following generations almost all the prominent teachers had stayed in Babylonia for a shorter or longer period: Rabbis Helbo, Jeremiah, Huna, Samuel ben Isaac and others. Finally the old ruling forbidding the emigration of a *haber* had to be rescinded. It was decreed: 'a *haber* who goes abroad does *not* lose his membership thereby'.[52]

Parallel with the decline of learning in Palestine came an increase in self-esteem among the Babylonians; within five generations the relative situation of the two countries had changed places completely. Rabbi Judah bar Ezechiel did not allow his pupil, Rabbi Zeira to go to the Holy Land. 'Anyone leaving Babylonia for the Land of Israel is infringing a positive commandment, for it is written (Jeremiah 27, 22) "They shall be carried to Babylon and remain there".'[53] Although Rabbi Zeira disregarded this order, he prided himself on being a Babylonian. He refused, for instance, to wed the daughter of Rabbi Yohanan, because his descent from Babylonian Jews was purer than that of the Palestinians.[54] A similar story is told of Rabbi Pinhas bar Hama, an Amora of the fifth generation. He said: 'All countries are of mixed descent as regards the Land of Israel, and the Land of Israel is of mixed descent as regards Babylonia. When the descent (of the Palestinian families) was examined, they came to a point of danger and ceased'—apparently it was found that the family of the patriarch (?) was of tainted origin.

Enmity towards the Babylonian 'upstarts' continued to linger among the populace in Palestine, as is witnessed by the incident of Rabbi Zeira and the butcher of Tiberias.[55] Rabbi Kahana, another Babylonian, was so infuriated by the Palestinian 'baiters of strangers' that he forthwith returned home; while Rabbi Yose was bodily assaulted by a 'scoffer' (*letsan*).[56] Yet some of the Babylonians became in the end more Palestinian than the Palestinians themselves. Rabbi Zeira and Rabbi Jeremiah, who both came from Babylonia, called their former compatriots 'fools' (*tipshaya*) because of their eating habits.[57] In spite of the crisis Babylonian scholars continued to come to study in the Holy Land, and to settle there. We know of at least thirty-four such scholars who arrived between 220 and 290, mainly to study under Rabbi Yohanan; only five of them returned home.[58]

The decision of the sages of Palestine in halakic matters began now to be criticized in Babylonia, especially the alleviations proclaimed by the patriarch. In the third generation of the Amoraim (the generation of the pupils of Rabbi Yohanan) the Babylonians begin to rule in the Holy Land itself. The great scholars of that age, Rabbis Ammi, Assi and Zeira, resided at Tiberias but were of Babylonian origin. They paid much respect to the heads of Babylonian Jewry and the scholars living there. 'Even Rabbi

Ammi and Rabbi Assi, important priests in the Land of Israel, submitted to Rabbi Huna (the Exilarch).'[59] Rabbi Ammi used to say: 'Our teachers in Babylonia said, etc.'[60] The only scholar of importance in that generation who had been born in Palestine was Rabbi Abbahu of Caesarea. In halakic matters he followed the opinions of the leading rabbis of Tiberias, who were all Babylonians.

The situation changed only in the fourth and fifth generation of Amoraim. The scholars of these generations were all Palestinians. It seems that at that time the Babylonians were not interested in coming to the Holy Land. Nevertheless the feeling remained that it was superior to other countries. Said Rabbi Nahman on behalf of Rabbi Mana: 'The world cannot exist unless there are at least thirty just men living in it. Sometimes most of them live in Babylonia, and a minority in the Land of Israel, sometimes the majority in the Land of Israel and a minority in Babylonia. All is well with the world if most of them are in the Land of Israel.'[61]

5. *The Relations with the Roman Government in the Times of Crisis. Palmyrene Domination*

While the crisis lasted the civil status of the Jews under Roman rule did not worsen appreciably. The emperors following Severus continued the policy of their predecessors and allowed the Jews their national religious rights as before. Most of the rulers of that troubled period were in any case engaged in a ceaseless war with their internal and external enemies and hardly had the time to deal with questions of internal policy. In the general state of uncertainty they were certainly not interested in adding to the number of their enemies; besides, only a few of them reigned long enough to follow a consistent line of policy. Moreover a new enemy then arose within the empire: Christianity began to make its inroads into the Roman way of life. Whatever energy was left to the rulers after their intensive military duties was directed against the growth of the Church.

The rights of the Jews were observed even in a period of general religious persecution. Diocletian 'ordered all nations to sacrifice (to idols) except the Jews', it is stated in the Palestinian Gemara.[62]

Together with all inhabitants of the empire, the Jews suffered from the military weakness of Rome and the lack of an efficient frontier defence. As we have already seen,[63] the cities within the empire had now to be provided with walls. This included Tiberias, the capital of Galilean Jewry. When the matter was raised in rabbinical circles, some scholars were of the opinion of Rabban Simeon II ben Gamliel, in whose days Rome was still strong. He had said: 'Not all courtyards (cities) need a gate (fortifications) but only those adjoining the street (the frontier)'. But now the rabbis said: 'The sons of the street (the nomad tribes) will press in, enter and come (to rob)'.[64] In this troubled time the razzias of the Arab desert nomads had become more and more frequent.

Some of the Jews agreed with the Roman fear of the German foe. Rabbi Isaac once explained a verse (Psalm 140, 9): 'this refers to the Germania of Edom (Rome)—if they once break out, they would ruin the whole world'.[65] On the whole the Jews kept the peace and followed their moderate leaders, who supported the Romans. When the Persians invaded the empire, the Jews in the Diaspora helped to defend the attacked cities. We are told that when Shapur King of Persia took Mazaca (Caesarea) in Cappadocia, he killed there twelve thousand Jews.[66] The Jews in Palestine seem to have regarded such devotion to the empire as exaggerated. When the refugees from Mazaca arrived at Sepphoris, they were received very coolly. They complained to Rabbi Ammi, 'no pity was shown to us and no one cares for our welfare'.[67] In his 'Annals' Shapur mentions the 'people of Judaea' among the vanquished soldiers of the emperor Valerian—but he meant probably Palestinians, because they are placed together with Phoenicians and Arabians. As the Persian armies did not on this occasion reach Palestine the loyalty of the Jews there was not put to the test.

The loyalty of rabbinical circles towards Rome is also evident in their relations with the Palmyrene dynasty. Odenathus, the ruler of that desert city, saved the eastern half of the Roman empire once the emperor Valerian had fallen into Persian captivity (260). As a reward, Odenathus was put in charge of the Roman Orient, and he ruled it, Palestine included, till 266. In this year he was assassinated. His wife, Queen Zenobia, succeeded, together with her son Vaballathus, in maintaining Palmyrene rule and even in extending it over Asia Minor and Egypt. Only in 273 did the emperor Aurelian take Palmyra and end its domination over Palestine.

It would seem likely that the rule of a Semitic dynasty over their country should have been welcomed by the Jewish leaders. There was a strong Jewish community at Palmyra itself, which had a large stake in the prosperous economy of that city, the control of the desert and of its caravan routes.[68] Palmyrene Jews kept in close touch with Palestine; many of them were buried at Beth Shearim. In Christian sources Zenobia is seen as friendly to the Jews; some of the church fathers call her simply 'the Jewess'.[69] It seems that the struggle between Palmyra and the Persians gave rise to some Messianic hopes among the Jews. Some of them already saw visions of 'the kings of the Orient gathering at Palmyra' and 'Israel going to Palmyra against the kings of the Orient'.[70]

It is quite possible that the common people expected the Palmyrene rulers to restore Jerusalem to the Jews and to allow them to rebuild the Temple. Such expectations, if any, were disappointed very quickly. The

Palmyrenes followed in general the policy of the Roman government. Odenathus took the title of *dux Romanorum*, and Zenobia called herself Augusta. The disappointed Jews began to compare 'Ben Netser' (Odenathus) to the small horn in the vision of Daniel (7, 8).[71] Several rabbis were arrested by order of the Palmyrene government, and remained in prison till the death of Odenathus.[72] Hatred of the new rulers now grew among the scholars; they began to say 'The day on which Palmyra shall fall will be a feast day for Israel';[73] and they lived to see this prophecy come true.

Together with the other citizens of the Roman empire, the Jews looked forward to the re-establishment of stable rule. This hope was expressed by Rabbi Yohanan: 'There should be *one* strong man (lit. "speaker") in each generation, not two'.[74] The strong man who was hoped for did finally appear in the person of the emperor Diocletian (284–305). His personality is reflected in our sources in a peculiar way. He is not represented as an inhuman monster, like the destroyers of Jerusalem and Beth-Ter— Vespasian, Titus and Hadrian. Neither does he appear in the legendary glory of 'Antoninus', the friend of Rabbi. Diocletian appears in the Talmudic sources more or less in accordance with his historic character. His personality seems to have made a strong impression on his Jewish contemporaries. There are many legends concerning his humble origins. According to one of them, 'Diocletianus Caesar was once a swineherd at Tiberias'.[75] His visit to Palestine in 286 and his meeting with the patriarch were described in legendary terms. The emperor is delineated in these stories as a hard ruler; but in the end he changes his mind and shows much favour to the Jewish delegation.[76] He treated with much greater harshness the inhabitants of Paneas, who complained of the taxes.[77] Diocletian is mentioned comparatively often in our sources. His public works are referred to, in particular the building of a dam at Emesa, the establishment of a trade-fair at Tyre, etc.[78] When the emperor visited Tyre, 'Rabbi Hiyya bar Abba was seen stepping over the tombs at Tyre in order to see him', although the rabbi was a priest and as such forbidden to enter cemeteries.[79]

6. *The People Changes its Attitude to Roman Rule.*
The Revival of the Messianic Hopes

As we have mentioned above, the Persian invasion never reached Palestine and the loyalty of the Jews to the Roman government was not tested. Had the event been otherwise, it is very doubtful if Palestinian Jewry would have continued to support Roman rule. In the preceding chapters we have seen how the moderates among the Jewish leaders gained the upper hand after the Bar Kokhba war. They, and the patriarchs who headed them, established a *modus vivendi* with the Roman authorities and thus succeeded in keeping the peace for five generations. This period of peace was based upon Jewish public opinion, as we have described above. In the third century this opinion began to change under the pressure of the worsening economic conditions. The same cause led to a diminution of the hold Jewish authorities had on the masses of the people; it was identified with the oppressive policies of the government. The Jewish attitude to the Romans now underwent a revision. This adjustment occurred in the time of Rabbi Yohanan bar Napaha. The formerly neutral majority now turned against Rome.

For the time being this change of attitude did not have any political results. The moderates, although now a minority, continued in charge of affairs. Nevertheless hatred of the Romans grew among the masses. It was evident that all the troubles which made life difficult resulted from the dependence of the country on the Roman empire. The Romans themselves suffered from the same misfortunes, but this was not understood by the common people. In their antagonism towards the Romans the people put their trust again in the age-old Messianic expectations. The preachers of the Haggadah became more popular, while pure halakic learning was on the decline, as we have already seen. [80] The haggadist preachers were more likely to criticize the 'nations of the world' and the 'evil government'. As the scholars began to leave for Babylonia and the influence of the preachers grew apace, so did opposition to the Roman government.

Rabbi Yohanan was among the first to change his opinion of the Roman rulers; but as a moderate in all things he condemned them but mildly. His pupil and colleague, Rabbi Simeon ben Lakish, who was among the chief opponents of the patriarchate, was also far more extreme in his opposition to the Romans. Rabbi Yohanan said that Edom (= Rome) 'was like the three beasts in the vision of Daniel'—Rabbi Simeon at once added 'much more so'. [81] Rabbi Simeon took over from Rabbi Simeon bar Yohai the Zealot leader the saying: 'A man should never rejoice in this world (because of the enslavement of Israel to its foes) . . . and they say of him (Simeon ben Lakish) that he never even smiled in all his life'. [82] When a high Roman official, a *ducenarius*, presented the patriarch Judah II with a disk full of gold pieces on the occasion of the pagan New Year, and Rabban Judah took one, Rabbi Simeon advised him to throw it straight into the Dead Sea (as a contaminating object). [83]

This (third) generation of Amoraim was the generation of the great Haggadists: Rabbis Levi, Isaac, Hosheyahu, Jeremiah, Simeon bar Pazzi. Most of the Midrashic legends originated with them. There is no limit to the burning hatred for Rome felt by them. Yet, if we compare the expressions used at that time with comparable material from earlier times, when relations with the government were bad (for instance the period of

Hadrian) we note a significant difference. Now there are but few complaints of religious persecution and of the oppression of the just. 'Wicked Edom' is indeed all the time 'writing *diatagmas* (orders) to destroy Israel and to cause them to bow to idols';[84] it 'does not favour the just, but kills them'; 'innumerable oppressive laws and orders are issued daily'.[85] The verse 'the snares of death confronted me' (Psalms 18, 5) was interpreted as referring to the 'Edomite kingdom'.[86] But all such complaints remain general. Among the rabbis of that generation there was not one 'martyr'.

There was apparently more foundation for the complaints about material losses. These are especially numerous among the traditions handed down from Rabbi Yohanan. ' "He robbed" (Ezek. 18, 18)—this refers to Edom'.[87] 'This is the wicked government which casts an evil eye upon the property of a man.'[88] 'All money goes to the government of Edom, and it is never satisfied.'[89] Other expressions of annoyance are directed against Roman officialdom, which never ceased to molest the public with its bureaucratic methods. Rabbi Yohanan said: 'Blame the beast which writes all its doings with a pen';[90] or against recruitment: 'This is the wicked government, which conscripts recruits (*tironia*) from all the nations of the world'.[91]

To such accusations, which were normal in case of foreign domination, were added new ones. As Rome weakened, it used the typical weapons of the feeble, hypocrisy and lies. 'This is the wicked government, which confuses the world and leads it astray with its lies.'[92] 'Like the swine which spreads out its cloven foot (Lev. 11, 3) and says "I am pure" is wicked Esau (= Edom = Rome); he sets up a tribunal and pretends to be a just judge after oppressing, robbing and stealing.'[93]

Hatred of the imperial government finds its expression in a plethora of comparisons with the lowest levels of the animal kingdom. 'The swine— that is Edom.'[94] 'The lizard (*semamit*, Prov. 30, 28)—that is Edom, because there is no creature so hated among the creeping animals as the lizard.'[95] 'Horror—that is Edom.'[96] 'Profligacy—this is the profligacy of the government.'[97] Hatred was also directed against the city of Rome, symbol of the abhorred power. The Haggadists connected its foundation with days of national disaster for Israel: the day on which Solomon married Pharaoh's daughter, or the day on which Jeroboam set up his golden calves, two acts which led to idolatry.[98] Little Rome, that is, Caesarea, the capital of the province, was hated just as deeply. 'Caesarea and Rome—they shall both be destroyed on the Day of Judgement.'[99] 'Ekron shall be uprooted (Zeph. 2, 4) (a pun on the name of Ekron and the root *akor*)—that is Caesarea, the daughter of Edom (Rome), which is seated between the dunes.'[100] Caesarea was regarded as a counterpart of Jerusalem. 'Caesarea and Jerusalem—if someone tells you both are ruined —do not believe him; both are inhabited—do not believe him; Caesarea ruined and Jerusalem inhabited, or Jerusalem inhabited and Caesarea ruined—you may believe him. If this one is full of people, that one is waste; that one is full of people, this one is waste'.[101]

The attitude towards non-Jews in general changed for the worse. Rabbi Eleazar ben Pedath, who was extremist in his views, expressed this feeling in a pointed manner: 'A Jew should never put his finger in the mouth of a Gentile, unless the Gentile puts his finger first into the mouth of a Jew'.[102] The officials and commanders of Rome, who carried out the will of 'Esau', come off badly: ' "Living things both small and great" (Ps. 104, 25)— these are the *duces* and *hyparchoi* and *strategoi*',[103] they and their followers are like ' "the Leviathan which thou didst form to sport in it" (Ps. 104, 26)—they shall be made sport of'.[104]

As in all periods of sharp conflict between the rulers and the ruled, the tools of the government—the secret police, the spies and delators—were singled out for the sharpest scorn.[105] Said Rabbi Abba bar Kahana: 'David's generation was all composed of just men, but because they had delators amongst them, they went out to war and they fell'.[106] Rabbi Samuel bar Nahman compared the delator to a serpent: those 'people of the tongue, speak in Rome and kill here'.[107] Rabbi Simeon bar Pazzi said: 'The rains are not held up, but because of those who denounce others'. Their end will be that 'the Holy One will take them and send them down to hell'.[108]

With the rising hatred against the 'wicked government', the increased influence of the Haggadists and the ever-mounting distress, there arose again the old Messianic hope. At first it was only a vague longing, but soon it changed into a strong desire for immediate redemption. Many Jews now became firmly convinced that salvation must be quite near. The Messianic expectation descended from heaven and became something concrete, a definite hope for freedom from the Roman yoke by means of human factors. In this way the Messianic expectation ceased to be a religious longing and became a matter of politics.

At first this tendency appeared in the form of prayers or wishes. Rabbi Alexander (second generation of the Amoraim) said: 'Lord of the Universe, Thou knowest that it is our will to do Thy will . . . but we are hindered by our enslavement by the government. May it be Thy will that we shall be saved from them and shall come back to follow Thy law with a full heart'.[109] Others said: 'In the dawn of Edom's day, say "May its setting come soon" '.[110]

As the distress grew, the conviction became general that salvation must come soon; for the nation seemed already to have reached the lowest rung of hell, and could not fall any more. Rabbi Yohanan said: 'Tiberias is the lowest of all (cities in which the Sanhedrin resided) . . . and salvation shall come from there'.[111] The verse: ' "Fallen, no more to rise, is the virgin of

Israel" (Amos 5, 2) he interpreted thus: "She is fallen (hence will not fall any more); rise, virgin of Israel" '.[112]

Some members of that stricken generation lost all hope of future redemption. The sages tried to confute them by recalling the past. Rabbi Samuel bar Nahman said: 'Israel would never have been saved from Haman's wickedness, had they despaired of salvation even for one hour'.[113] He also said 'The Holy One, blessed be He, said to him (Jacob): Do not fear, Israel, even if you see him (Esau) sitting beside Me—even from there I shall let him fall'.[114]

Because of the troubled atmosphere of the times, attempts were made to find in the Scriptures texts which could be interpreted in the desired sense. ' "The swine does not chew the cud" (Lev. 11, 7) the swine is Edom who does not drag (a pun on *gerah* "cud" and *gerar* "to drag") after it another kingdom (that is to say, it is the last of them). And why is it called swine (*hazir*)? Because it returns (*mehazereth*) the crown to its (rightful) owner (Israel).'[115] With the fall of Rome will come the end of enslavement and Israel shall have again the crown of freedom.

With the inner certainty, which was based upon such interpretation and similes, that the Messianic period was drawing closer and closer, the Haggadists described the coming reign of the Messiah. The earlier descriptions were generally vague: 'The time of Israel to be saved has come . . . the time has come for the unpruned vine tree (an allusion to the uncircumcized Gentiles) to be pruned'.[116] As the Messianic hope struck roots among the common people, future prospects were related with more and more detail. The preachers speculated upon the direction from which salvation would come—whether from the north or the south; they gave a detailed route of the Messiah: from Tyre to Sidon, to Palmyra and Berea. They described how Israel would assemble in Upper Galilee and how the Temple would be rebuilt in Jerusalem by the Messiah from the House of Joseph.[117] Popular fantasy began to play around such details—a sure sign that its imagination caught fire and that such dreams seemed somehow real.

Hatred of Rome and the Messianic idea combined into one vision of redemption and vengeance. According to Rabbi Levi the Messiah from the House of Joseph will, after rebuilding the Temple, march upon Rome and conquer it as Joshua conquered Jericho; for 'Our father Jacob foresaw that the descendants of Esau shall be delivered into the hands of the descendants of Joseph'.[118] At that moment of salvation the monies paid in taxes shall be returned. Rabbi Levi said: 'All the money in the world is flowing in this world to the kingdom of Edom; from there it shall be dispersed in the days of the Messiah'.[119] Together with the Roman government shall perish its servants: ' "She shall be slaughtered before him . . . and her skin . . . shall be turned" (Numb. 19, 3–5—speaking of the red heifer)—

she (Rome) and her *duces* and *hyparchoi* and *strategoi*'—(the generals, governors and other officers).[120]

In this way the Messianic vision seemed real. Rabbi Yohanan said: 'The Holy One, blessed be he, has said "I shall not come to heavenly Jerusalem till I come to Jerusalem down below" '.[121] The continuation of this development occurred in the fourth generation of the Amoraim, when the rule had already passed to Christian emperors.[122]

7. *Summary of the Effects of the Crisis*

In previous generations, whenever the Messianic vision became over-whelming in the Jewish world, there usually followed some attempt by the nation to give it reality in violent action. The people believed that salvation was near and rose against its oppressors. Some of the most heroic chapters in Jewish history, the Maccabean revolt and the revolts against Rome, were inspired by such expectation. In the third century, however, there was no such immediate result. The reason for this quietism was the difference in the fundamental situation. Formerly the Messianic hope was a result of political or religious oppression. The economic situation was favourable and the nation was possessed of its full strength. This time, however, the root of the evil lay in the economic crisis. There existed no material reserve which could be used for a struggle, unless undertaken in complete despair.

The list of known settlements can give us a picture (with the reservation stated above, p. 19) of the extent of the disaster. The first to suffer were the weak and dispersed Jewish communities which had no strong roots in the land. In the first generation of the crisis (200–230), the number of Jewish villages in the Golan and the Bashan fell below the number of city communities. In the second generation (230–260) the same process appears among the Jewish communities in the coastal plain. It seems that here too the area of settlement shrank and that the surviving communities were henceforth of a markedly urban character, resembling that common in the Diaspora. The Jews of the Jezreel Valley and of western Galilee also suffered severely. The communities in Samaria disappear entirely from our sources. Of all the settlements outside Galilee only those in the Lower Jordan Valley and in the *Darom* stood firm. In Galilee itself a decline can be observed only in the last stages of the crisis (260–290). In the first generations there was no such decline; possibly there was even a rise in the Jewish population. This can be explained on the assumption that in times of crisis the more distant and more isolated communities chose to migrate to Galilee, the stronghold of Palestinian Judaism. Later on Galilee was affected too. The number of known settlements declined visibly. It seems that in Galilee the Jewish population was now only half of the total, and in the other parts of the country only a quarter. The general feeling of decline is also mentioned in Talmudic sources. 'Rabbi Yohanan thought . . . that most of the Land of Israel belonged to Israel' but his pupil Rabbi Eleazar was of a different opinion: 'Most of the Land of Israel is in the hands of the Gentiles'.[123] Of the two branches of Palestinian Jewry, Judaea and Galilee, the one was cut off violently and the other began to wither.

The crisis began in the time of the patriarch Judah I. It worsened after his death in the first quarter of the third century. It was stated in the Tosefta: 'When "Rabbi" died the troubles were multiplied'.[124] It ended with the end of the century, in the time of Rabbi Abbahu, in the third generation of the Amoraim. It reached its peak in the second generation of the Amoraim, in the days of Rabbi Yohanan. In itself this crisis marked a turning-point in world history: the end of antiquity was approaching and the first sign of the coming Middle Ages could be felt. The sense that a 'hinge of fate' was coming was shared by many. When Rabbi Yohanan spoke of Noah, who 'saw a world in its fullness and then in its ruin',[125] he spoke of his own experience. His contemporaries summed up this feeling in a short sentence: 'In the days of Rabbi Yohanan the world was turned upside down'.[126]

Towards the end of the crisis, soon after Diocletian became emperor, Rabbi Ammi, one of the pupils of Rabbi Yohanan, dreamt a strange dream: 'He heard a voice declaring: "Today Magdiel has become king" (referring to the list of the "chiefs of Esau", Gen. 36, 43, in which Magdiel is named before the last one, Iram). And he said: "One more king shall rule in Edom (= Rome)".'[127] His dream did indeed come true. For after Diocletian only one pagan ruled over Palestine; after him came the rule of the Christians. Palestinian Jewry had to face a new situation, which continued until the end of Roman rule.

In order to understand the coming events we shall have to go back and survey the earlier evolution of relations between Judaism and Christianity from their very beginning.

Notes to Chapter V

1. *Mekilta* 40, 73 (ed. Lauterbach, II, p. 229).
2. *Exodus R* 15, 13.
3. See above, pp. 48–9.
4. *Genesis R* 78, 12 (p. 931).
5. See above, p. 100.
6. *Genesis R* 78, 12 (p. 932).

7. A. H. M. Jones, *The Greek City*, Oxford, 1940, p. 228.

8. b *Baba Batra* 8a.

9. See above, p. 101.

10. b *Shabbat* 114a.

11. The remains of this wall were discovered in 1941. Among the stones used in it was the inscribed tombstone of a soldier of the Sixth legion, in which the titles bestowed by Severus on it (*fidelis et constans*) are not included. The wall was therefore built in the time of Septimius Severus or later (M. Avi-Yonah, *QDAP*, 12 (1945), pp. 88–91).

12. b *Baba Batra* 7b.

13. Ibid.

14. b *Nedarim* 32a.

15. Tanhuma *Exodus, Waere* 4 (ed. Buber, p. 20).

16. b *Shabbat* 139a.

17. Ibid.

18. j *Bikkurim* 3, 3–65d.

19. Ibid.

20. b *Ketubot* 17a.

21. j *Shabbat* 6, 1–8a, top.

22. b *Sanhedrin* 7b.

23. Tanhuma *Genesis* (ed. Buber, p. 81).

24. Ibid. *Exodus* (p. 105).

25. j *Sanhedrin* 2, 1–19d.

26. Ibid. 2 end–20d, l. 12.

27. *Genesis R* 80, 1.

28. b *Sanhedrin* 98a.

29. j *Abodah Zarah* 1, 1–39b.

30. j *Shabbat* 6, 10–8c.

31. *Genesis R* 24 (p. 229) and 31 (p. 283).

32. *Ecclesiastes R* 6, 2.

33. B. Dinaburg, *Gulak-Klein Memorial Volume*, Jerusalem, 1943, pp. 76–93. For the text of the edict see *Corpus Juris Civilis*, III, 13, 3.

34. j *Sanhedrin* 1, 3–19a etc.

35. *Ruth R* 7, 8.

36. j *Peah* 8, 7–21a.

37. Ibid. and j *Hagigah* 1, 7–76c.

38. j *Nedarim* 11, 10–42b.

39. *Ruth R* 5, end.

40. j *Kiddushin* 3, 14–64d.

41. j *Erubin* 3, 11–21c.

42. j *Abodah Zarah* 2, 4–41c.

43. j *Berakot* 9, 1–12d.

44. Ibid. 3, 1–6a.

45. Ibid.

46. b *Kiddushin* 33b.

47. b *Ketubot* 84b.

48. j *Taanit* 2, 1–65a.

49. b *Taanit* 23b.

50. Ed. Buber, p. 101b.

51. See above, p. 25.

52. j *Demai* 2, 3–23a.

53. b *Shabbat* 41a.

54. b *Kiddushin* 71b.

55. j *Berakot* 2, 8–5c.

56. Ibid. lines 46–57, 66–75.

57. b *Ketubot* 75a; *Lev. R* 28, 6.

58. For the list see D. Sperber, *Archiv orientální* 38 (1970), pp. 23-4.

59. b *Megillah* 22a.

60. b *Shebuot* 47a.

61. j *Abodah Zarah* 2, 1–40c.

62. Ibid. 5, 4–44d.

63. See above, p. 118.

64. b *Baba Batra* 7b.

65. b *Megillah* 6b.

66. b *Moed Katan* 26a.

67. j *Shebuot* 9, 5–39a.

68. J. Juster, *Les Juifs dans l'empire romain*, Paris, 1914, I, 195, n. 9.

69. Athanasius, *Hist. Arr.* (*PG* XXV, *c.* 777); Orosius VII, 22; Syncellus, *Chronographia* I, p. 716 (ed. Borin); Michael Syrus I, p. 196 (ed. Chabot).

70. *Midrash Zuta* to the Song of Songs, p. 33 (ed. Buber).

71. *Genesis R* 6, p. 903.

72. j *Terumot* 8, 10–46b.

73. b *Yebamot* 17a.

74. b *Sanhedrin* 8a.

75. *Genesis R* 63, 8.

76. j *Terumot* 8, 1–46b/c.

77. See above, p. 101.

78. j *Abodah Zarah* 1, 4–39d; j *Kilaim* 9, 4–32c.

79. j *Berakot* 3, 1–6a.

80. See above, p. 123.

81. *Leviticus R* 13, 5.

82. b *Berakot* 31a.

83. j *Abodah Zarah* 1, 1–39b.

84. *Shohar Tob* 68, 15.

85. Ibid. 104, 21.

86. Ibid. 18, 10.
87. *Genesis R* 44, 15.
88. Ibid. 76, 6.
89. Rabbi Levi in *Ecclesiastes R* 1, 7.
90. b *Pesahim* 118b.
91. *Genesis R* 76, 6.
92. *Song of Songs R* 2, 12.
93. *Leviticus R* 13, 5.
94. Ibid.
95. Midrash *Proverbs* 30, 28.
96. *Genesis R* 44, 17.
97. *Ecclesiastes R* 2, 14.
98. b *Shabbat* 56b (Rabbi Samuel)
99. Midrash *Psalms* 9, 9.
100. b *Megillah* 6a.
101. Ibid.
102. *Genesis R* 80, 7.
103. *Shohar Tob* 105, 21.
104. Ibid.
105. b *Taanit* 7b.
106. j *Peah* 1, 1–16a.
107. *Ecclesiastes R* 10, 11.
108. *Genesis R* 20, 1.
109. b *Berakot* 17a.
110. *Esther R* proem 2.
111. b *Rosh ha-Shanah* 31b.
112. b *Berakot* 4b.
113. *Pesikta de Rab Kahana*, ed. Friedmann, 151b.
114. *Pesikta R* ed. Buber, 151a.
115. *Leviticus R* 13, 5 end.
116. *Song of Songs R* 2, 12.
117. Marmorstein, *Tarbiz*, 3 (1931/2), p. 166.
118. Rabbi Samuel bar Nahman, b *Baba Batra* 123b.
119. *Ecclesiastes R* 1, 7–3d.
120. *Pesikta R* ed. Friedmann, 65b.
121. b *Taanit* 5a.
122. See below, pp. 171–2.
123. j *Demai* 2, 1–22c.
124. T *Sotah* 15, 5.
125. *Tanhuma* 58 (Marmorstein, *Tarbiz*, 3 (1931/2), p. 173).
126. j *Peah* 7, 4–20a.
127. *Genesis R* 83, 4.

VI

Judaism and Christianity to the Accession of the Emperor Constantine

1. *Introduction*

Throughout history the point of interest constantly shifts from one field to another. Sometimes it is politics, sometimes economics and sometimes religion—only to return to politics, and so on. The factors which determine the evolution of human society continue to act from period to period with hardly any change; but those living at each specified period regard one sector as overwhelmingly important, only to dismiss it when the times change. In the history of Palestinian Jewry the centre of gravity passed from politics in the second century to economics in the third. At the beginning of the fourth century the kaleidoscope changed again: religion now came to the foreground.

Such shifts of interest often indicate turning-points in history. The revival of the religious problem in the first quarter of the fourth century marks the beginning of the Middle Ages. The religious attitude now became dominant in the life of society and remained so for several centuries. Simultaneously with this change, and largely as a result, the political and legal position of the Jews in their homeland was also changed completely.

This change did not, of course, occur precisely on the day when the first Christian emperor began to rule over Palestine. History is not created out of nothing. The change only marked the conclusion of a process which had lasted the better part of three hundred years. In this period the Christian faith arose within the Jewish community in Palestine, but was rejected by its majority and forced to seek adherents outside Judaism. The new religion then spread among the Gentiles, till it became the dominant

creed of the Roman empire. This process was already of political importance in the second and third centuries. We have, however, avoided discussing it in the preceding chapters in order not to complicate matters.
Now we must retrace our steps and survey the development of Judaeo-
Christian relations in Palestine and outside it, to the point already reached
in this narrative. In the following chapters we hope to deal with the results
of the situation which developed in this way.

The parting of the ways between Judaism and Christianity goes back
very far—to the moment in which the overwhelming majority of the
Jewish nation refused to admit that Jesus was the Messiah. When the
apostle Paul took Christianity out of the fold of Judaism into the wider
world, he made it into one of the great factors of human history; but at the
same time it ceased to be a matter of importance for the Jews of Palestine.
Preaching to the Gentiles, and the abandonment of the Jewish ritual commandments which it implied, determined the relations between the two
communities both in the Land of Israel and in the Diaspora. Among the
Jews in Palestine there remained only a relatively small Judaeo-Christian
community, a minority among the Jews here and among the Christians
abroad. The Jewish community in Palestine was therefore confronted only
with the stragglers of the great Christian host. In the rest of the Diaspora
the position was reversed. There small and dispersed Jewish communities
were faced with an ever-increasing Christian church which in spite of all
persecutions was steadily growing in numbers and organization. The
attitude of Judaism to Christianity was determined in Palestine as
the relation of a majority to a minority. In the Diaspora the attitude of the
Christian church in relation to Judaism was decided in centuries of bitter
struggle during which Christianity became a historical power of the first
magnitude. Thus the main forces of the two religious groups never really
met face to face.

2. *Palestine Jewry and the Judaeo-Christians. The 'Minim'*

In the Acts of the Apostles the mission to the Jews of Palestine is described
as flourishing; but the communities then established did not continue to
exist for long. In the second century there were—apart from Jerusalem—
Christian communities only at Caesarea (the capital of Christian Palestine), at Ptolemais, which was politically part of Phoenicia, and at Bostra
in Arabia. We know of quite a number of communities in the fourth
century; but even if we assume that all of these already existed in the third
century, Christians lived only in the following places: Diospolis-Lydda,
Jaffa, Azotus, Sebaste, Scythopolis (Beth-Shean), Maximianupolis-Legio,
Gadara, Gedora, Jamnia, Nicopolis-Emmaus, Ascalon, the port of Gaza,

Eleutheropolis and Jericho. All these were urban settlements, and most of them were outside the area of dense Jewish settlement. Eusebius, the bishop of Caesarea in the early fourth century, mentions in his *Onomasticon* only three Christian villages in the whole country: two in the *Darom* and one east of the Jordan. In the Jewish cities, such as Sepphoris or Tiberias, there is no trace of Christians till the time of Constantine.[1]

It follows that the Tannaim and Amoraim of the first generations had to deal only with the few Jews converted to Christianity. The progress of Christianity among the Gentiles did not disturb them. The 'nations of the world' were in their eyes idolaters anyway; if they chose to change their deities, this was no concern of Israel. This point of view is voiced by Rabbi Tarfon: 'The idolaters do not know of God, and deny Him, but those (the Jewish "heretics") do know of Him and yet they deny Him'.[2] And even if the rabbinical leaders could have foreseen the dangers inherent in the spread of the new religion among the Gentiles, the slowness with which it increased in Palestine even among the Gentiles would have reassured them.

There remained the Judaeo-Christians within the fold. These included various groups. One accepted circumcision and the rest of the ritual commandments, and its adherents were thus practically indistinguishable from the rest of the Jewish community. Most of the Jewish contacts with adherents of Christianity were with this group. They alone were sufficiently familiar with the Hebrew original of the Scriptures to dispute with the rabbis on these texts and their interpretation. Among the Christian leaders of the first centuries there was only Origen who took the trouble to learn Hebrew; the others accepted as scriptural the Septuagint version. This text sufficed for their main purpose, which was to preach to the Greek-speaking Gentiles and to the Hellenized Jews of the Diaspora. The Christian leaders of Gentile origin soon gave up the attempt to convert the Jews in Palestine; they recognized that their efforts were in vain.

In the second and third centuries the Judaeo-Christian groups, the so-called *Minim*, were in a state of decline. According to Origen, they numbered in five generations less than 150,000 members, that is about 30,000 in each generation.[3] In the fourth century their numbers dwindled still more. In the days of the apostles Peter and Paul the Judaeo-Christians were still debating the question whether uncircumcised people could become members of the Church.[4] Afterwards, however, the trend changed entirely. Now those Christians who still observed the Jewish usages were suspected of heresy. In the fourth century the Judaeo-Christian groups served only as an object of interest and study for Church historians, as a kind of religious museum piece.[5]

These sects were also divided among themselves. The Ebionites regarded only the text of Matthew in its Hebrew version as a genuine

Gospel. They considered Jesus as the Davidic Messiah, but not as God. The church father, Justin of Neapolis, who lived in the second century, admitted them to his communion, but added that many Christians in his time refused to do so.[6] Another sect, that of 'Judaeo-Christians' proper, themselves observed the Jewish commandments—and in this sense lived separately from Gentile Christians. In their opinion all true Christians were bound to follow Jewish Law. As true Christians they did, however, believe that Jesus was divine. As against this view, the 'Nazarenes' were Judaeo-Christians who regarded only themselves as bound by the Jewish commandments, but not the Gentile converts. They followed indeed the original views of the apostle Paul. The 'Nazarenes' therefore continued to live within the Christian communities, and were gradually absorbed by the Gentile majority. (It should be noted that the terms used above, 'Ebionites' and 'Nazarenes', are used by the Christian authors without much precision). There were, of course, Christians of Jewish origin who had severed entirely all connections with the religion of their forefathers and had been completely assimilated with the Gentiles.

There existed thus a whole gamut of intermediate types between Judaism and Christianity. These could not serve as a bridge between the two religions, because they tried to effect a compromise in matters in which, by their essence, no compromise was possible. The efforts to mediate only led to the complete disintegration of such in-between groups. They remained at the same time isolated both within their people and within their co-religionists, and disappeared without leaving a trace.

Only in Palestine did the Judaeo-Christian groups continue to exist for some time. Here was the origin of historic Christianity, and they were able there to continue the oldest Christian tradition, that of Jesus himself. The Jewish masses among whom they were living, kept the Judaeo-Christians from losing themselves among the mass of other Christians.

Talmudic sources mention the existence of the *Minim* only in four localities: Sepphoris, Kefar Sikhnin (or Kefar Samma), Kefar Neburaya and Capernaum (Kefar Nahum). Christian sources mention Judaeo-Christians living in Cochaba in the Batanaea and several anonymous places in the same vicinity.[7] The Judaeo-Christians were reputed to heal by using the name of Jesus. Two such cases are mentioned in the Talmud: Rabbi Eliezer ben Dama was treated after he was bitten by a snake, and the grandson of Rabbi Joshua ben Levi who swallowed some object. The common people equated such healers with magicians.[8]

The small number of the Judaeo-Christians explains why the rabbis paid so little attention to them, and to Christianity as a whole. After a most diligent perusal of the whole Talmudic literature, which contains certainly no less than 15,000 pages, only 139 passages were found (a total of hardly 36 pages) which deal with the 'Minim' and their opinions; it is not even clear whether this term refers always to Judaeo-Christians, or whether other sects may not be meant.[9]

After the Bar Kokhba war, the relations between Jews and Christians in Palestine had been stabilized. They remained in this stage for the whole period from the fall of Beth-Ter to the ascension of Constantine. Till the time of Bar Kokhba they had passed through three stages within less than a century (*c.* 33–135), which it is necessary to recapitulate in order to understand what follows.

(A) *The First Jewish Revolt.* The siege of Jerusalem marks the first turning point in this story. The Christians who lived in Jewish Jerusalem refused to fight against the Romans with the rest of the people and retired to Pella east of the Jordan. They justified their attitude by recalling how Jesus had foretold the destruction of Jerusalem: 'There will not be left here one stone upon another' (Mark 13, 2 and parallels). They were undoubtedly also influenced by the persecutions they had had to endure from the Jewish authorities in the generation before the revolt. The 'Letter to the Hebrews' which was addressed to them at that time (and which was later attributed to Paul) states, 'now Christ has appeared as high priest . . . through the greater and more perfect tent, not made with hands' (9, 11). Obviously, if the heavenly Temple was coming soon, it was not worth while to fight for the high priest and for the Temple on earth.

The act of leaving Jerusalem did not in itself constitute a break with the Jewish nation. Many of the Jews did not take part in the war. Some, as for instance Rabban Yohanan ben Zakkai and his pupils, had also left Jerusalem during the siege. However, the links binding these early Christians to Judaism were undoubtedly weakened by this act.

The destruction of the Jewish Commonwealth and of the Temple shook the faith of many Jews. The Christians used this traumatic shock for their purposes; they recalled Jesus' prophecy about the coming destruction of the Temple. They profited from the confusion now common among people who used to see in the sacrifices the only way of expiating their sins. Many were asking: 'Who shall cleanse us now?' The Jewish sages replied: 'Prayer is more important than sacrifices'.[10] The Christians had of course another answer: expiation would come through belief in Jesus.

(B) *The 'Blessing Concerning the Minim'.* The leaders of the Jewish nation were in the end obliged to combat the Judaeo-Christian activities. In the first and second generations after the destruction of the Temple disputes with them were fairly common. Their influence was regarded as doubly dangerous because they were still living within the Jewish people, and took part in the synagogue services. With the abolition of Jewish penal jurisdiction there was no way of condemning them for blasphemy, as could have been done before 70.

The 'Blessing concerning the Minim' was therefore composed and included with the 'Eighteen Benedictions' of daily prayer. This text was composed by Rabbi Samuel ha-Katan and approved by Rabban Gamliel II and the Sanhedrin in the last quarter of the first century.[11] It should be noted that the term *Min* was originally not used to describe Judaeo-Christians exclusively. Literally *Min* means in Hebrew 'kind'; anyone of a peculiar 'kind' of thinking could be so defined. Later its meaning was narrowed down to anyone separating himself from the people on religious grounds, a heretic. For instance in the Tosefta[12] various people endangering national unity are listed thus: The *Minim*, the *Meshummadim* (i.e. those leaving Judaism because of the *Shemad*, the religious persecution), the delators and the *Apikorsim* (a word derived from the name Epicurus, but meaning 'heretics' on philosophical and not on religious grounds).

The present form of the 'Blessing concerning the Minim' is in many points different from the original one.[13] It seems that the first version was directed against the *Meshummadim*, the 'evil kingdom', the delators and the *Minim*. An old version, which was found in the Cairo Genizah, contains the version 'the *Minim* and the *Notserim*' (Christians). Some scholars consider this the original version,[14] but there are two reasons against this view. Firstly, as we have seen, the Judaeo-Christians were not, at the time the original text was composed, considered important enemies of Israel; and secondly, all other contemporary sources include them with the *Minim* and there is no reason why they should be mentioned separately. It is true that according to Epiphanius and Jerome (early fifth century) Christians were expressly mentioned in the 'blessing'.[15] It seems therefore that the original text stood as *Minim* and *Moserim* (delators) and that it was changed into *Minim* and *Notserim* during the time of sharp struggle between Judaism and Christianity in the fourth century.

The aim of this 'blessing' was not to exclude the Judaeo-Christians from Israel. This can be proved by considering the first part of the ruling defining those who had 'no share in the world to come':[16] those who doubt resurrection, those who refuse to bow to the Law, and the *Apikorsim*. The *Minim* are not included in the list. The 'blessing' was really aimed at uncovering the *Minim* who pretended to be orthodox Jews and to keep them away from leading the prayers. Already in the Mishnah[17] we find the statement that 'those who say in prayer "We thank you, we thank you" twice (i.e. who admit plurality in godhead) are to be silenced'. Rab said expressly: 'A pre-cantor who erred in all the benedictions is not recalled (from the pulpit) . . . but if he erred in the Blessing concerning the *Minim* he is recalled, for perchance he is one of them'.[18] His contemporary, Rabbi Joshua ben Levi, enlarged this ruling: 'A pre-cantor who made a mistake in two or three benedictions, is not recalled . . . except if he omitted to say: "Who revives the dead" and "who subdues the wicked" (the last words of the "Blessing concerning the *Minim*") and "who builds Jerusalem". For I say: He is a *Min*.'[19] The 'blessing' was intended to test leaders of prayer in the synagogue and to find out their real beliefs.

(C) *The Bar Kokhba War.* From the Jewish point of view this conflict marked the definite parting of the ways between the Christians of Jewish origin and the Jews living in Palestine. Till then these 'heretics' were still regarded as part of Israel. The revolutionary government considered them liable to military service like all other Jews. The Christians refused to serve; this refusal stood out sharply against the general unanimity of national sentiment at a critical time. From their point of view the Christians never could admit the Messianic claims of Bar Kokhba, on which much of his authority was based. They were thereupon regarded as traitors to the national cause and punished by military law.[20]

After the war was lost those of the Judaeo-Christians who were circumcised were expelled from Aelia Capitolina.[21] The new community was composed of Gentiles only; even the bishop was changed. This fact brought out clearly that membership in the church could go hand in hand with a complete estrangement from Judaism, and the separation of the two religions now became complete.

Rabbi Akiba decided, apparently while the war of Bar Kokhba was still going on, that 'whoever is reading in "outside" books (the Babylonian Gemara[22] explains this as meaning "in the books of the *Minim*") and who whispers over a wound (as the Judaeo-Christians were doing while healing by faith) has no share in the world to come'.[23] By this decision the Judaeo-Christians were definitely expelled from the community of Israel.

Once they were outside, the basic elements of the problem were quite changed. From an internal Jewish matter Christianity became an external one. In the generations before the war of Bar Kokhba the contacts between Jews and Judaeo-Christians were still fairly frequent. The Jews did indeed criticize the Christian courts, as we learn of the story of Rabban Gamliel and Imma Shalom, in which a Christian judge is described as corrupt. The 'heretics' of Kefar Nahum (Capernaum) succeeded in causing Rabbi Hanina, the nephew of Rabbi Joshua ben Hanania, to desecrate publicly the Sabbath. As a consequence he had to leave the Holy Land and went to Babylonia. Rabbi Eleazar, the teacher of Rabbi Akiba on the other hand, praised highly the teachings of Jesus, which were transmitted to him by Jacob of Kefar Sikhnin.[24]

After the Bar Kokhba war there came a radical change. The Jewish sages give up all hope of bringing the 'heretics' back to the 'right' path. Their aim is above all to keep whole the faith of their own flock. They took care to 'fence Israel in'. The ruling in the Tosefta[25] lays down cate-

F

gorically: 'Meat which was in the hand of a *Min* is forbidden . . . their slaughtering is idolatrous, their bread is like that of the Cuthaeans, their wine is like wine used for libations, their fruits are impure, their books are works of witchcraft, their sons illegitimate. One may not sell to them, negotiate with them, teach their sons crafts, accept from them any comfort in case of damage to property or to the body.' To make matters doubly sure, it was decided that the 'day of the Nazarenes' (Sunday) was to be regarded as a feast of the idolators. Contact with the Christians was accordingly forbidden three days *before* it (Saturday, Friday and Thursday) and three days *after* it (Monday, Tuesday, Wednesday), in short—always.[26]

The formula with which the discussions with the *Minim* are usually introduced in the Talmudic sources, is characteristic of the attitude of the rabbis. Every such story begins with the words 'A *Min* enquired of Rabbi N. . . .' that is to say the dispute arose because a Judaeo-Christian was interested in beginning it in the missionary spirit of early Christianity. The disputes recorded concern biblical verses which could be construed as admitting a plurality in the godhead, such as 'Let *us* make man' (Gen. 1, 26). Other points concerned the mission of Jesus, the relations of God the Father and God the Son, the Ascension (compared to that of Enoch) and so on. The Judaeo-Christians laid little stress on the doctrine of the Holy Trinity, because the belief in it arose relatively late in Christianity, and was accepted in Judaeo-Christian circles later than elsewhere. It is first mentioned in the fourth generation of Amoraim.[27] The Christians prepared 'Testimonies against the Jews' composed of Biblical passages and commentaries upon them. From these they deduced that Jesus was the Messiah and that the Jews had ceased to be God's chosen. The Jews compiled counter-collections of biblical passages which gave support to their views. Fragments of this compilation have been preserved in various Talmudic books, particularly in the tractate Sanhedrin of the Babylonian Gemara.[28] The disputes became a matter of routine, with set questions and answers. As usual in the discussion of metaphysical matters such disputes were seen to be a waste of time, as one side could never hope to convince the other.

The contacts with the *Minim* appear mainly in the second and third generations of the Tannaim. From the fourth generation (middle of the second century) they cease till the second generation of the Amoraim. This was the generation of Rabbi Yohanan, the time of the great imperial crisis and of the spread of Christianity among the Gentiles. In the second generation of Tannaim Rabbi Eleazar said: 'Be diligent in studying the Torah, so that you may know how to reply to the heretic' (lit. 'Epicurean', the philosophical doubter). Rabbi Yohanan, second generation of the Amoraim, added a caveat: 'This is taught only for the case of a heretic from among the idolators; because a Jewish heretic can only become more stubborn'.[29] Once the rabbis had given up the *Minim*, they put this opinion in the mouth of God. Rabbi Jonathan said:[30] When Moses was writing the Torah . . . when he arrived at the passage . . . 'Let us make man' . . . and he said: 'Lord of the Universe! Why do you leave this opening for the heretics?' And He (God) said: 'Write, whoever wishes to err, let him err'. In general the rabbis were satisfied with a general warning against heresy. Rabbi Eliezer ha-Kappar said:[31] 'Woe to him of the nation which listened to the man who set himself up as God'. He added: 'Do not mix with those saying there is a second God'.

Excommunication, the ban on all contacts, is the typical weapon of a majority which is endangered ideologically by a small minority; we shall see in what follows how a Christian majority used it in the Diaspora against a Jewish minority. Once the *Minim* were expelled, the whole problem lost its importance for a time. The Jews were busy with their own affairs and did not pay much attention to a possible danger from the Christians.

3. *Christianity and its Relation to Judaism till the End of the Second Century*

Let us now take a look at the other side of the problem, the Christians living in the empire and their attitude towards Judaism and the Jews. This matter is much more important than the relation of the Jews with Christianity, because Judaism did not prescribe the way of life of the Christians, whereas the views of the church leaders in the second and third centuries had a decisive influence on the legislation of the fourth and the fifth, and later centuries, and hence also on the lives of the Jews subject to the Roman and Byzantine empires.

The attitude of the Christians towards the Jews is much more difficult to define than the other way round. The Jewish attitude to the Christians was determined within a relatively narrow area, and its sources are to be found within a literature of limited extent. On the other hand, Christian attitude to Jews found its expression all over the empire and in thousands of texts of the church fathers and the martyriologies. In its first centuries Christianity lacked a central institution which could determine its stand on this matter or that. Only towards the end of the period do we find a few canons of church councils which lay down the rulings in the matter of the Jews.

Christian attitudes to Judaism in the first three centuries passed several stages. All of them are determined by one basic fact: the refusal of the majority of the Jewish people to adopt the new religion. This refusal began at a time when the nascent church was weak and persecuted; it remained in force when millions had become Christians, and when the church controlled the machinery of the state.

Jesus and the first apostles were no doubt aiming at the spread of their message among the Jews. Being themselves of Jewish origin and firmly rooted in the Holy Land, their aspirations did not go beyond the boundaries of Judaism.

Even after their first failures in Judaea, the apostles began to preach the Gospel at first in the Jewish Diaspora only. Paul, himself a Jew of Tarsus, was the leader in this respect. The Jews of the Diaspora were more influenced by Greek culture and less zealous than their brethren in Palestine. In the Diaspora there were also many of the 'godfearing' who had almost adopted Judaism, but had not become full proselytes. The Christian apostles could hope to make many converts in these circles.

Paul continued in his efforts with an unusual persistence. He preached in synagogues in Asia Minor, Macedonia and Greece. The Acts of the Apostles ends with the account how he arrived as a prisoner in Rome; immediately upon his arrival he began to preach to the Jews of Rome.[32] His stubbornness in this respect is astonishing. Most of the Jews in every community he visited refused to accept the new teaching; occasionally the apostles were even punished with the full rigour of the Law. As he wrote himself: 'Five times I have received from the hands of the Jews the forty lashes less one' (2 Corinthians 11, 24; cf. Deuter. 25, 3). Paul persisted because, like Jesus, he was essentially a Jew, bound to the Judaism of the Diaspora with a common language and common ways of thinking. To the Gentiles he was obliged to speak as a stranger to strangers; but it is possible that just because of this he succeeded better with them.

Even Paul had to admit early in his apostolate that it was very doubtful that he would convert the Jews. The crisis came at Antioch in Pisidia, when he and Barnabas spoke to the Jews in these terms: 'Since you thrust it (the word of God) from you . . . behold we turn to the Gentiles' (Acts 13, 46). Paul repeated these words in Corinth: 'Your blood be upon your heads! I am innocent. From now on I will go to the Gentiles' (Acts 18, 6). The fact that it was the nation of Jesus which refused to follow him, caused a deep shock to Paul and the other apostles.

In this hour of distress Paul found a marvellous solution of the problem; a solution which influenced the fate of Judaism and Christianity for many centuries. He left the Jewish community, but—in his opinion at least—he took Judaism with him. He denied the Jews their tradition and declared that only the Christians were the real 'Israel', the true Jews envisaged in the Law and the Prophets. In this way the new religion acquired a rich past (a matter of great importance in antiquity, for the ancients believed in the excellence of the forefathers of humanity and in its gradual descent from a Golden Age). Christianity now became equipped with a tradition going back to Creation, with a rich literature, the preachings of the Prophets and the poetry of the Psalms.

Paul still regarded himself bound by the Jewish ritual prescriptions, and agreed that Judaeo-Christians should observe them; but already in his time the Gentile Christians were freed from such restrictions. Paul was opposed to the Judaeo-Christians who tried to force the Gentile converts to obey Jewish Law. He believed that some at least of the Jews would be ultimately saved in the Christian sense—'So too at the present time there is a remnant chosen by grace' (Romans 11, 5) and he expressed the hope that in the end 'All Israel would be saved' (ibid. 26).

When Paul died most of the Christians were probably still of Jewish origin. The period from the time of his death (67 according to the Christian tradition) to the last quarter of the second century is one in which Judaism and Christianity completely parted ways in the Diaspora. This is also the period in which their mutual antagonisms were at their peak.

In the second generation after Paul the number of Christians of Gentile origin went on increasing. The leaders of the church were striving to convince them that they represented the true Israel. Some of these Gentile converts to Christianity may have wanted to get to know what this Israel was. In order to prevent the Gentile converts from being attracted to Judaism by way of Christianity, the leaders of the church did all they could to render Judaism as odious as possible. They related all the blessings in the Bible to themselves, and all the curses to their Jewish competitors. In their opinion God had spurned the Jews and taken away from them their right of seniority. The Christians were Isaac, the Jews Ishmael; the Christians were Jacob, the Jews Esau; Rachel, Jacob's beloved wife, stood for Christianity; the despised Leah for Judaism. Jews were worse than the Gentiles, for they knew the word of God, the Bible, and yet refused to understand it in the 'right' i.e. the Christian way as an allegory.[33]

The so-called 'Letter to Barnabas' is an interesting evidence of this attitude. It was apparently written shortly before the war of Bar Kokhba. It is directed against the Christians who still observed the Jewish practices. The author curses the Jews and calls the synagogues 'the abodes of Satan'.[34] The Judaeo-Christians were by that time almost entirely disregarded by the leaders of the church.

The relations between Judaism and Christianity became worse because both faiths were competing for the same people. Both appealed to the Gentiles who had abandoned the beliefs of their forefathers and who sought new ways because they were 'godfearing' and were looking for a new faith which would grant them eternal salvation. The Christian missionaries dreaded Jewish proselytism, because they knew that proselytes were often the most fanatic of Jews. 'When he becomes a proselyte you (the Pharisees) make him twice as much a child of hell as yourselves' (Matthew 23, 15). The Christian leaders tried to make their flock as zealous, and one way to do so was to stress their antagonism towards the Jews. For this purpose the Christian preachers applied the words of the Prophets against their own people. They called the Jews 'children of the devil' to be avoided by those intending to become Christians. The disputes with the Jews nevertheless continued at the same time, because the Christian leaders had not yet given up the hope of converting them. Such disputes centred on the interpretation of various Biblical passages.

Cyprian, bishop of Carthage, composed a manual for disputes with the Jews, in which he tried to prove the truth of Christianity with seven hundred verses chosen from the Bible. According to the Christian disputants the Jews misunderstood the Biblical text because they interpreted it according to its plain meaning. Only the symbolical-allegorical interpretation of the Christians was the right one. The Christians based themselves of course on the Septuagint, the only Biblical text they could use in the Diaspora. They found in their copies various passages missing in the Hebrew original, and accused their Jewish rivals of forgery and of deliberate omission of verses proving Jesus to have been the Messiah.[35]

In general the Jews who were well versed in the Scriptures, found no difficulty in refuting such arguments. However the Christians possessed one powerful argument: the national disaster which had befallen the Jews. In their view, this was clear evidence that God had spurned Israel. The Jews had been expelled from their country, their Temple was in ruins, their land was given over to strangers, and all this was to remain so to all eternity. Thus the church derived much advantage from the Jewish disaster; and it was clearly interested that this state of affairs should continue *ad infinitum*, that the Jews should never lift themselves from their debasement, and that Israel should not rise again.

The Christian attack on Judaism caused Jewry to react. They had in their hand a very dangerous weapon. According to Roman law,[36] Judaism enjoyed the privileges of a 'lawful religion' (*religio licita*); Jews were absolved from the necessity of taking part in pagan rites, even those enjoined by law. The Christians were not entitled to such rights. Any Judaeo-Christian who was expelled from the Jewish community was by law bound to sacrifice to the emperor and to take his part in idolatrous practices. If he refused, he was punished as an 'atheist'.

Jews in the Diaspora had still other ways of combating Christianity. The Christian fathers complain that the synagogues were centres of anti-Christian propaganda, 'the breeding places of the persecutions'.[37] They accuse individual Jews of taking part in the attacks of the pagan mob on the Christians, and the Jews in general of inciting the Gentile population against the martyrs. It seems obvious that the attempt to spread Christianity among the Jews in the Diaspora caused only Jewish enmity; this reaction of course made Judaism still more odious in Christian eyes.

4. *The Relaxation of Tension and Cessation of the Disputes in the Third Century*

The state of tension between the two communities continued till the last quarter of the second century. At that time it had become quite clear that the future of Christianity lay with the Gentiles. The attempt to spread the new religion among the Jews of the Diaspora had failed just as the earlier one had among the Jews in Palestine. Already in the age of Justin of Neapolis (100–160) the number of Christians of Gentile origin was greater than that of Judaeo-Christians. About 170 a Christian author in Rome calculated that at that time the Christians in the whole world outnumbered the Jews.[38] This might have been an exaggeration at that precise moment, but it is abundantly clear that Christian missionary activity had by and large turned to the Gentiles and away from the Jews. The attitude of Christianity to Judaism had been fixed in principle, and interest in Judaism diminished. Justin's book, *Dialogue with Tryphon the Jew*, which was written in the middle of the second century, already contains most of the arguments which were proffered in the following generations. After Justin literary activity in this field ceased almost completely. From the patristic writings we may conclude that in the Eastern half of the empire disputes with Jews had ceased almost completely after Justin. They were continued only in the West, especially in Africa. There Tertullian wrote his work *Against the Jews* and Cyprian composed his *Testimonies against the Jews*. Both, however, repeated on the whole the arguments already to be found in the epistles of Paul, in the *Letter to Barnabas* and in the *Dialogue with Tryphon*.

In the third century came the great advance of Christianity in the Gentile world. Both Judaism and Christianity benefited from the general feeling that the foundations of the ancient world were tottering. People left in the dark began to grope for individual salvation and bliss in the world to come. There was also a widespread belief that the end of the world was quite near. Many were afraid of what would happen to them in that great hour. Both Judaism and Christianity promised salvation to such perplexed souls.

Judaism had many advantages in its mission to the Gentiles. It was the older religion, and antiquity was always greatly revered in the Greco-Roman world. Its dogmas were simple and corresponded to the natural feeling of what was right. Judaism had no mystic contradictions, no *credo quia incredibile*. Its disadvantage consisted in the heavy yoke of the ritual commandments, which was especially difficult for those not used to them from infancy. Another negative element was the indissoluble bond between Judaism and the Jewish nation. After the great national disasters, and in particular after the war of Bar Kokhba, it was hardly likely that masses of Gentiles would join the cause of a people who had fallen so deep. Proselytism did not indeed cease entirely, but most of those seeking for a new religious way turned to the Christian faith.

Christianity had many advantages in appealing to the Gentiles. It was not encumbered with the ritual practices, it required no circumcision. It was also free from the connection with any particular nation with its historical ups and downs. The new Christians did not lose even the one great advantage of Judaism—its antiquity and its lofty religious Scriptures. The simplicity of the Hebrew texts was of no advantage to the Jews; in a world in which all sorts of mystery religions and sects, such as the Gnostics, were proliferating, it was to their advantage that elements of Greek religious mysticism had from the days of Paul been absorbed into Christian dogma. The fourth Gospel, that of John, was based entirely on Greek philosophical thought. The mystery in Christian belief corresponded to the spirit of the times, and was a great help in spreading the new faith among the Gentiles.

In the third century the Jewish problem had therefore become marginal for the Christians. In many ways the Jews even constituted an advantage for the Christian missions. They served as a living witness to the antiquity and the truth of the Scriptures, the basic text of Christian homiletics, with the addition of the Gospels. The Jews became in this way 'witnesses for the (Christian) truth' (*testes veritatis*). At the same time several Christian writers, in particular Clement of Alexandria and Origen, who were scholars by nature, recognized that the scriptural text used by the church (the Septuagint) was full of mistakes. They did their best to correct it and to follow the Hebrew original as far as possible.

5. *Origen and Eusebius on Judaism and the Jews*

Origen lived for many years in Caesarea. He learned Hebrew there and derived great profit from the teaching of the Jewish sages. Among his teachers was also Hillel (Jullus), the brother of the patriarch Judah II.[39] In his homiletics Origen addressed mainly the Gentiles; he praised Judaism to the skies, but of course only that before the appearance of Jesus. He described the Jews of old as a nation composed of philosophers, full of divine wisdom. It was only their refusal to adhere to Jesus and his teaching that caused their ruin and made them lose their greatness as God's chosen. We must remember of course that Origen's defence of the

Jews was part of his controversy with the Greek philosopher Celsus. Origen's ambivalent attitude is typical of the Christian propagandists. They praised ancient Judaism highly when addressing the Gentiles; but when disputing with their Jewish contemporaries they abused them as much as they could.

Origen had newer things to say on the relations of the church with the Roman state; in this field he is the spiritual father of the Middle Ages. Although in his time the Christians were still being harshly persecuted by the Roman authorities, yet the number of Christians was growing steadily and they could hope for domination in the state in the not too distant future. Origen was the first of the church fathers to foresee the results of such development. He was opposed to the tolerant views prevailing in the ancient world, according to which each nation has the innate right to its own gods. The Roman state which united politically almost the whole *oecumene*, was nevertheless built upon the principle that there was an essential difference between politics and religion. Religious liberty went together with political domination. The Jews profited from this tolerance, at least as long as they remained within their own national sphere and were politically obedient. However Origen pronounced the medieval view, that there was no difference between political and religious matters. He denied the nations the right to their particular gods. There was only one state and it should have only one true religion. That this view of a Christian world state, which dominated the Middle Ages, could not prevail in its entirety was only due to the geographical limitations of the Roman power and the inner divisions between the Christians as to which religious view was the 'right' (orthodox) one.[40]

Eusebius Pamphili, who was bishop of Caesarea from 260 to about 339, is the last Christian historian of the period before the adoption of Christianity by the emperors. He lived to see the triumph of the persecuted religion. In his attitude to the Jews he went one step further than Origen. All members of the new religion agreed that Judaism no longer held the divine truth after the appearance of Jesus. But how was it possible that what was truth at a given moment should afterwards become a tissue of lies? In order to resolve this conundrum, Eusebius constructed a difference between the 'Hebrews' and the Jews, with the former preceding the latter. The 'Hebrews' included the just men that lived before the Patriarchs and the Patriarchs themselves. These were 'Christians' before Christianity. Later Judaism, however, was but a corruption of the earlier 'Hebrew' religion. Moses delivered the Law to the Jews knowing full well that its validity was limited in time. Among the Jewish nation of sinners there appeared from time to time Prophets who were 'Hebrews' and who foresaw the coming of the divine Christian truth. When the appointed time came, Christianity stepped forward and received its 'Hebrew' inheritance. The Jews fulfilled the task of guardians of the divine Law without even knowing what they were doing. With the coming of Jesus they lost their function.[41] Irenaeus, bishop of Lugdunum (Lyons) in Gaul had already written 'if the Jews had known about our future existence, and had they known how we were going to use the evidence of the Scriptures, according to which other nations would be saved, while they, who pride themselves on being the House of Jacob, would lose their inheritance and God's grace—they would not have hesitated to burn their Scriptures with their own hands'.[42] Eusebius adopted this view and went even further. In his opinion God led the Jews astray and deliberately withheld from them the knowledge of their fate. 'The Logos decided to hide from the Jewish nation their end, in order that they should keep the Scriptures without fail for the Gentiles. If they had foreseen clearly their bitter outcome, all the good that the Prophets foretold for the Gentiles . . . in which those circumcised had no share whatsoever . . . they would have destroyed them (the Scriptures).'[43] It is possible that a hint of that Christian view appears also in the Babylonian Gemara.[44] 'Rabbi Ada bar Hanina: If Israel had not sinned—they would have received only the Pentateuch and the Book of Joshua . . . why? because "the more the wisdom the more sorrow" ' (Ecclesiastes 1, 18).

6. *Christian-Jewish Relations on the Eve of the Christian Empire*

Even at a time when the victory of Christianity was approaching, many Christians were still asking themselves: as God has so visibly blessed the Christian mission to the Gentiles, why did He harden to such an extent the hearts of the Jews towards the 'Gospel truth'? In answer it was generally assumed that an event of such importance as the conversion of the Jews was bound to be connected in the providential plan with some great future event. The Day of the Last Judgement was continuously expected in the first centuries of the Christian era: Jesus was going to return to judge the quick and the dead, and on that day the Jews would be converted. This view prevailed already in the days of Justin of Neapolis. It was most useful for the conservation of Judaism under Christian rule. All agreed that God had decided to conserve Judaism till the Last Day. The only difference of opinion was whether all Jews would be converted, or only 'the remainder'—both these views appear in the writings of the apostle Paul.[45] As, however, the Christians could not tell who among the Jews was going to be converted and who not, they had to keep all of them alive for the moment. Moreover, an over-hasty conversion of the Jews might hasten the coming of the Last Judgement. Everyone hopes of course to enter Paradise after death; but no one is in a hurry to die in order to put that hope to the test. The striving after an immediate conversion of the Jews therefore cooled off considerably.[46]

In the last generation before the enthronement of the Christian emperors the leaders of the church adopted more matter-of-fact relations with Judaism. At that time the victory in the competition for the Gentiles was clearly with the church; the number of Christians was far higher than that of the Jews. The church leaders therefore assumed an attitude which on many points resembled that of the Palestinian Jews towards the 'Minim'. They were little interested in spreading their beliefs among the Jews, but tried rather to protect their flock from Jewish influences, as these could shake the faith of the Christians. The Christian missionaries based their preachings to a large extent on the Bible and they made these Scriptures known to the Gentiles. There was always the danger that some of the new Christians would pursue their studies into the Hebrew original, and would then turn their backs on Christianity and adopt Judaism pure and simple. There were also other ways of Judaism influencing Christians, as in the Diaspora the two communities were in close contact in daily life. We therefore find in the decisions of the first councils of the church various canons which did not deal directly with the Jews and Judaism, but were directed only against Christians who came into contact with them.

This tendency continued into the fifth century; to simplify matters we shall deal with all these canons together.[47] The oldest of these canons were adopted at the Council of the Spanish church at Elvira (306); later ones were decided upon at Laodicea (431). The so-called *Apostolic Canons*, which were composed about the same time, also contain provisions concerning the Jews. Hosius, bishop of Cordova, took part in the council of Elvira. He was later an important adviser of the emperor Constantine in religious matters, even if the full measure of his influence only became visible in the days of Constantius II (337–361). The church canons were directed to one thing: to prevent Christians from 'following in the ways of the Jews' (*judaizare*). One way of doing this was to prevent all contacts with the Jews, to isolate them within Christian society. The canons of Elvira forbade Christians to marry a Christian woman to a Jew or a heretic; the punishment was excommunication for five years (Canon 16). It is interesting that there was no parallel punishment in the case of a Christian woman marrying a Gentile, although such marriage was also prohibited. Apparently it was assumed that a Christian wife would draw her husband into the church and not the other way round. Canon 78 forbade extra-marital relations between a Christian and a Jewess. Further canons aiming at the isolation of the Jews were Canon 50, forbidding Christians to eat with Jews, and Canon 49 which forbade Christians to ask Jews to bless their fields.

Such regulations did not indeed counter Jewish aims at that period.

The Jewish sages on their side also forbade mixed marriages, eating with the non-Jewish etc. In the pluralistic society of the fourth century such attempts at isolating one social group from the rest were of no importance. It was only with the creation of a purely Christian society in the Middle Ages that these canons served to lock up the Jews within the ghettoes of Christianity.

The canons of Laodicea were meant to eradicate 'Jewish usages' from among the Christians themselves. Canon 37 forbade Christians to receive from the Jews presents on the occasion of their feast days, and to hold feats jointly with the Jews. Canon 38 forbade the acceptance of unleavened bread from the Jews. Other canons attempt to separate Jews from Christians, by ordering the latter to adopt different dates of holy days. Canon 16 orders the Gospels to be read in churches also on Saturdays (apparently in some communities this was not the usage on a Jewish Sabbath), and Canon 29 requires Christians to work on Saturdays. In the *Canons of the Apostles*, Canon 65 forbids a Christian priest from entering a synagogue and from praying there (there were apparently occurrences of this sort!) and Canons 70 and 71 warn Christians not to fast together with the Jews, not to take oil from the synagogues (for blessing?) and not to light candles on Jewish feasts.

7. *Summary*

By the beginning of the fourth century Judaeo-Christian relations had passed many stages, and a kind of tradition had been established in them. If we try to analyse the state of mind of a church leader in the year 324 for instance, we can observe a mixed attitude to Judaism, composed of layer after layer, and reflecting the long history of three centuries. On top was the practical necessity of separating Christians from Jews in order to protect the members of the community from endangering their faith. Then came the memory of the years in which the two religions competed for the conversion of the Gentiles, and it was vitally necessary to silence the competitor. On the same level there existed the memory of the preaching to the Gentiles and the concomitant necessity of preserving the Jews as 'witnesses for the Christian truth' of the Scriptures, an essential element in the diffusion of the new faith. There also existed a consciousness that it might be ordained for the Jews to stay as such till the Day of Last Judgement, which should not be hastened by any means.

Still deeper went the memories of the great dissensions in the second century and the hatred of the Jews at the time of the separation of the church from the synagogue. This caused a modification in the former attitude: if the Jews had to exist, their existence should be made as miserable as possible. And quite basically there was the conviction, dating from the time of Jesus, that Judaism actually had no right to exist, and that all Jews should adopt the Christian faith. In the following chapters we shall see that as Christianity grew stronger, deeper and deeper layers of this conglomerate were uncovered in the collective psyche of the church leaders; and it was they who guided the civil authorities in this matter.

We have dealt with this matter at length, although most of the events referred to occurred far from Palestine and its Jewry; but they nevertheless had a decisive influence on events and developments in that country, as we shall see in the following chapters.

Notes to Chapter VI

1. For this chapter in general see J. Parkes, *The Conflict of Church and Synagogue*, London, 1934, and M. Simon, *Verus Israel*, Paris, 1948. The Christian communities of the first to third centuries are listed by A. Harnack, *Mission und Ausbreitung des Christentums*, Leipzig, 1902, pp.408–427; cf. also K. Pieper, *Atlas Orbis Christiani antiqui*, Düsseldorf, 1931, p. 24f., map 5 and H. Jedin a.o. *Atlas zur Kirchengeschichte*, Freiburg, 1970, Maps 2, 4 and 5, and pp. 13*f. For the Christian villages see Eusebius, *Onomastikon*, ed. Klostermann (*GCS* 11(1)), pp. 26, 108, 112.

2. T *Shabbat* 13, 5.

3. Origen, *In Joh*. I, 1, 7 (*GCS* 10, p. 4).

4. Acts 15, 1.

5. See Epiphanius, *Panarion* 18, 1, 1 (*CGS*, 25, p. 215); 29, 7, 7; (p. 330f.); 30, 2, 7; 30, 3, 7 (pp. 335, 337–8); 30, 18, 1 (ibid. p. 357). Jerome (*PL* 22, *c*. 924) considers the 'Nazarenes' a Jewish sect.

6. Justin, *Dialogus cum Tryphone* 47 (*PG* 6, *c*. 577).

7. Judaeo-Christians in Sepphoris (T *Hullin* 2, 24); Kefar Sikhnin or Kefar Samma (ibid. 22); Kefar Neburaya (*Ecclesiastes R*, 7, 26); Capernaum (ibid. 1, 8); Cochaba, Batanaea, Golan (Eusebius, *Onomasticon*, *GCS* 11(1), p. 172); ibid. *Historia ecclesiastica* 1, 7, 14 (*GCS* 9, p. 60); cf. Epiphanius quoted above, note 5).

8. T *Hullin* 2, 21; b *Abodah Zarah* 28a; j *Sanhedrin* 14, 19–25d.

9. The Talmudic passages dealing with Christianity are collected in R. Travers Herford, *Christianity in Talmud and Midrash*, London, 1903, and by H. L. Strack, *Jesus, die Häretiker und Christen, nach den ältesten jüdischen Angaben*, Leipzig, 1910. Both works contain evidence which does not seem to be relevant to the subject, and caution is therefore necessary in using them.

10. b *Berakot* 32b.

11. Ibid. 28b.

12. T *Sanhedrin* 13, 5.

13. The present formula is: '. . . may the slanderers have no hope, and may all evil perish at once, and all Thine enemies be destroyed soon, and may the wicked government be uprooted, broken, ruined and subjected . . .'.

14. Strack, op. cit. (note 9), p. 31, par. 21d.

15. Many Christian sources accuse the Jews of cursing Christians in the synagogues (Justin, *Dialogus cum Tryphone* 16 (*PG* 6, *c.* 512); 47 (ibid., *c.* 577); Origen, *Homil. in Jerem.* 19, 12 (*GCS* 6, p. 168); but only Jerome states expressly that the curses were uttered thrice daily and that they referred to the *Notserim* (*In Isai.* 1, 5 18/19 [*PL* 24, *c.* 86]; ibid. 13, 49, 7 [ibid., *c.* 467]; *In Amos* 1, 2, 11 [*PL* 25, *c.* 1001].

16. M *Sanhedrin* 10, 1.

17. M *Megillah* 4, 9.

18. b *Berakot* 29a.

19. j *Berakot* 5, 4–9c.

20. Milik, *RB*, 60 (1953), pp. 276ff.; Justin, *Apol.* 1, 31 (*PG* 6, *c.* 376); Eusebius, *Hist. eccl.* IV, 8, 4 (*GCS* 9, p. 316); cf. Benoit *et al.*, *Les grottes de Murabba'at*, Oxford, 1961, p. 159.

21. Eusebius, *Hist. eccl.* IV, 5, 1–3 (*GCS* 9, p. 304), IV, 6, 3 (p. 306); V, 12 (p. 454).

22. b *Sanhedrin* 100b.

23. M *Sanhedrin* 10, 1.

24. Gamaliel and Imma Shalom—b *Sanhedrin* 116a/b; R. Hanania—*Ecclesiastes R* 1, 8; Rabbi Eleazar—ibid., II, 24.

25. T *Hullin* 2, 20–1.

26. Samuel, according to Rabbi Ishmael ben Yose (?)—b *Abodah Zarah* 6a.

27. *Pesikta R* (ed. Friedmann) 100 b–101a; *Proverbs R* 4, 8.

28. b *Sanhedrin* 38b.

29. Ibid.

30. *Genesis R* 8, 8.

31. Yalkut, *Numbers* 24, 23.

32. Acts 28, 16–19.

33. See in general Justin, *Dialogus cum Tryphone* (*PG* 6, passim); Cyprian, *Testimoniorum adversus Judaeos libri tres* (*PL* 4, *c.* 675–780) and the material collected by Parkes (see above, note 1). For the vehemence of these discussions see J. Juster, *Les Juifs dans l'empire romain*, Paris, 1914, I, pp. 45–8, n. 1.

34. *PG* 2, *c.* 727–782.

35. In the Christian MS. of the Septuagint we find in Psalm 95, 10 after the words: 'Tell it to the Gentiles that the Lord is King' the addition

ΑΠΟ ΞΥΛΟΥ 'from the wood' (cross); the Jews were accused of 'falsifying' this verse.

36. See above, p. 45.

37. Origen, *Homilia in Ps.* 36 (*PG* 12, *c.* 1321); *in Cels.* 6, 27 (*GCS* 3, p. 97); Tertullian, *Ad nationes* 1 (*PL* 1, *c.* 650–1); *Adv. Gnosticos* 10 (*PL* 2, *c.* 143) and the sources quoted in n. 15. See also Seaver, *Persecution of the Jews in the Roman Empire*, Lawrence, 1952.

38. Ps. Clement (Soter) II, Cor. 2 ap. Harnack, *Mission und Ausbreitung* (see note 1 above), pp. 362, 371.

39. Origen, *Sel. in Ps.—Ad. Ps.* 89, 1 (*PG* 12, *c.* 1056); Eusebius, *Historia ecclesiastica* 6, 16, 1–4 (*GCS* 9, pp. 552–3).

40. Origen, *Contra Celsum* 4, 22 (*GCS* 2, p. 292).

41. J. Voigt, *Kaiser Julianus und das Judentum*, Leipzig, 1939, pp. 23–6; Parkes, op. cit. (note 1 above), p. 161f.

42. Irenaeus, *Contra haereses* 3, 21 (*PG* VII, *c.* 946).

43. Eusebius, *Demonstratio evangelica* 7, 1, 83f. (*GCS* 23, p. 313).

44. b *Nedarim* 22b.

45. See above, p. 146.

46. Jerome, *in Jerem.* 4, 18 (*PL* 24, *c.* 829); Parkes, op. cit. (note 1, above), p. 159.

47. K. J. Hefeli, *Histoire des conciles*, tr. Leclerq, Paris, 1907, I, pp. 231 (Elvira 16), 249 (49), 250 (50); p. 1019 (Laodicea 37–38); *Canones Apostolorum*, ed. Frank, Paderborn, 1905, I, Canones 62 (p. 583), 65 (p. 585), 70–71 (ibid.).

VII

The Beginnings of
Christian Rule in Palestine

PART I: THE TIME OF CONSTANTINE I (324–337)

1. *Christian Rule and its Immediate Consequences*

On the 18th September 324 Constantine, then emperor of the West, decisively defeated Licinius, emperor of the East, at Chrysopolis opposite Byzantium. As a result of this battle a Christian became for the first time ruler of the Holy Land.

The possibility that 'the empire shall fall into heresy' (*Minut*)[1] appeared to the authors of the Mishnah as one of the disasters which would announce the coming of the Messiah, but never as something which could really occur at any given moment. Now Rabbi Isaac, of the third generation of Amoraim, repeated this saying with much greater emphasis as something which was actually happening. Till that time Jewry had been engaged on two fronts: on one side Greek paganism in its Roman form (the 'empire') and on the other—the Judaeo-Christian 'heretics' in Palestine. Accordingly the rabbis interpreted the verse in Proverbs 5, 8 as follows: ' "Keep your way far from her" this is heresy: "and do not go near the door of her house"—this is the (Roman) authority'. But the two had become one: ' "Keep your way far from her" that means heresy and authority'.[2]

The change was for the worse. Till that time the Holy Land was the arena of a struggle of a monotheistic-national faith with an international polytheism. Judaism remained in practice (if not in theory) within its national limits, while the pagan religions were by their nature ready to accept the faith of Israel as one more national religion among many. In this way a *modus vivendi* was achieved in practice.[3]

158

Things were different when Judaism and Christianity confronted each other. The new faith took from Judaism one element, monotheism, and another—internationalism—from the pagan world. As a result there arose a new kind of religion, which attempted to dominate all nations because of its universal aspect, and at the same time denied the validity of any other faith, because its God was a 'jealous God' who admitted no other. The Romans had kept their laws within the sphere of political matters; what has been regarded later on as a religious persecution, such as the punishment of Christians who refused to sacrifice for the *tychē* of the emperor, was in their eyes a purely civil affair, a political and not a religious measure. As against this the Christians were convinced that 'the City of God' was infinitely more important than happiness on earth. As eternal happiness was reserved only for Christian believers, it was the duty of the State to save the souls of its citizens whether they wished it or not. The State might use the law, or even physical force, to bring about this happy result. The leaders of the Church were not loth therefore to use the absolute power of the Roman emperor to further their religion.

As we have already seen, the Church leaders had adopted a hostile attitude towards Jews and Judaism, as a result of historical developments dating several centuries back. This found a practical expression in the striving for a separation of the Christians from the Jews in the century preceding Constantine. After his accession, the Church leaders, who were opposed to Judaism as a religion, were joined at the imperial court by the Roman officials who had inherited from earlier times a parallel but secular hatred of Jews and all they stood for. Both groups now joined forces to influence the emperors in the desired direction.

The open hostility now displayed by the Roman authorities limited to a large extent the freedom of manoeuvre of the Jewish leaders. Even the smallest political force can exercise a certain pressure, if it can act freely and choose among the conflicting powers of its time. No political leader or party will increase arbitrarily the number of its enemies. They refrain as a rule from pressing other groups too hard, unless their final aims absolutely require it. In the Orient two powers had faced each other for centuries: pagan Rome and Zarathustrian Persia. As long as the Jews of Palestine were free to choose between the two, they were a free political factor. This choice represented the secret of their political power, even at times when their political strength was on the wane, as happened in the crisis of the third century. The Roman government had compromised with the Jews because of its unwillingness to push them to extremes, and thus force them to pass over to the Persian camp. The Jewish leaders were equally willing to accept the compromise because it ensured the continued existence of the nation in difficult times.

Now the situation had changed entirely. As a result of a combination of religious and political calculations the Roman state took the church as a partner, and abandoned its tolerant attitude towards the Jews; this was part of the price paid by the emperors for the alliance with the ecclesiastical authorities. The Jews now lost the freedom of choice, the basis of their political possibilities. They were forced into a position without issue. They were accounted henceforward natural enemies of the State, as people whom it did not pay to appease and as permanent allies of every enemy of Rome.

In the Holy Land there was an additional factor which complicated matters still further. This was the place where Christianity had originated. In Christian eyes many of its localities (and in particular Jerusalem, Bethlehem and Nazareth) were holy sites. Christian pilgrimages to Palestine had already begun in the third century.[4] With the rise of Christianity not only the situation of the people of Israel changed, but that of the Land of Israel itself. As long as the empire was pagan, Syria Palaestina was one of the least important of the provinces (although a rather unruly one). Even its history was almost unknown to the rulers. There is a characteristic story told by Eusebius in his *Martyrs of Palestine*.[5] Some Christians were brought to be judged at Caesarea before the governor Firmilianus in the beginning of the fourth century. The legate asked them: 'Where are you from?' and they answered: 'We are from Jerusalem' (meaning heavenly Jerusalem, for actually they were Egyptians). The governor of Palestine believed that they referred to some Persian city, the name of which he had never heard, although Aelia Capitolina, formerly Jerusalem, was within his province. Because they were ignorant of its past, there was no reason why the Romans would not be willing some day to restore it to the Jews. In Roman eyes it had no special importance, whether rational or sentimental.

With the rise of Christianity Palestine became the Holy Land of *two* faiths. According to the Christian view, the church represented the true Israel,[6] and all the heritage of the Patriarchs, including the land of Canaan, was rightly theirs. The appearance of this second claimant changed entirely the moral status of the country. It now became an object of controversy between Judaism and Christianity, and remained thus for several centuries. The appearance of the third claimant, Islam, at a later stage, did not change the situation qualitatively but only quantitatively.

This change made the political aim of the Jews, the liberation from foreign yoke, much more difficult to attain by peaceful means; naturally the inclination to achieve it by force became more and more tempting. This tendency grew still stronger when it became obvious that the Christian claim to Palestine was not only a matter of theory. The emperors, the church and the Christian rich took energetic steps to turn it into a Christian country in fact.

The basic conditions for a political crisis in Palestine therefore came into being very soon after the victory of Constantine over his rival. However, these factors did not begin to act immediately. One retarding element was that the Jews of Palestine were still fairly strong and that the new emperor was unwilling to arouse them. Moreover the Christian element in the country was as yet too weak to form a solid base for a consistent anti-Jewish policy.

Another factor which caused delay was the peculiar way in which the original alliance of the empire and church was brought about. This was the result of the political and religious outlook of Constantine himself.

2. *The Character and Policy of Constantine; his Laws concerning the Jews*

Constantine is undoubtedly one of the men who made history. Opinions about him differ to this day. Some think that he was above all a cold-blooded politician, bereft of all religious feeling. He chose Christianity in order to gain the support of the powerful Christian church. This view is based on the rationalism of the 18th and 19th centuries; the historians writing at that time attributed their own views to an emperor living in the fourth century. The truth is, however, quite different.[7] Constantine was a believer, as were all his contemporaries, a few out-of-date sceptics excepted; but he believed in the manner of his own times. He did not put much worth upon the moral or transcendental values of Christianity; but he had a deep trust in the power of the Christian God. This God had made all his enterprises prosper in this world; and He would undoubtedly save him after death. In his private life and his political activities Constantine certainly did little to follow Christian ethics; and he cunningly put off his baptism till the very last moment before his death. In this way he demonstrated the magical foundation of his belief, his trust in symbols and formulas. The sources of his belief were, firstly, the painful death of Galerius, emperor of the East from 305–311 and a zealous persecutor of the Christians; secondly, the vision which appeared to him before the decisive battle with his rival Maxentius at the Milvian bridge before the gates of Rome (313). An angel brought him a standard bearing the Chi-Rho (the monogram of Christ) with the words: *In hoc signo vinces.* Constantine believed, and was victorious. As a young emperor he had worshipped Hercules as the source of his strength, and later the sun-god Helios. Now he had found his true faith, and he was not disappointed. Within eleven years after his victory over Maxentius he became sole ruler of the whole empire; and he continued to rule for many years with great success. As a counter-offering to the Christian god who had saved him, Constantine regarded it as his duty to take care that the church should enjoy internal peace and that its teaching should go out to the heathen. He saw himself as the universal bishop and the apostle of the church to the Gentiles and the Jews alike.

It would be wrong to assume that Constantine regarded politics as his main object and religion only as a means of policy; but it is nevertheless true that his religious aspirations were limited by political necessity. For all the efforts of the Christian missionaries the majority of the inhabitants of the empire still adhered to the old religion. Such 'Hellenes', as they were called, included most of the nobles, of the officials and of the soldiers, and a good portion of the educated classes in general. The religious policy of the first Christian emperor had therefore to be prudent and moderate.

Constantine himself kept the title of *pontifex maximus* and allowed the old sacrifices and auguries to continue. He proclaimed complete religious liberty, and in fact his reign was the only time when no one was molested because of his faith. It formed a kind of era of transition between the times before, when the pagans persecuted the Christians, and the times after, when the reverse was the case.

Constantine was satisfied with proclaiming Christianity a legal faith (*religio licita*), and thus put the church on a level with the Jewish community. The church now was recognized as a public body, it could hold property; the Christians were excused from the pagan sacrifices and their leaders, the bishops, could head courts and judge cases, if the parties were agreeable.

This prudent policy was also followed as regards the Jews. He found this an easy task, because in his time the church leaders demanded no more than the isolation of the Jews from the Christians, as had been set out in the canons of the councils already quoted.

In the time of Constantine the canons were not recognized as legally binding by themselves. In his activities we have to distinguish between the civil legislation, which was formulated according to the Roman tradition, and the administrative actions, or the proclamations of the emperor to the bishops, both of which show already a typically medieval intolerance.

The laws of Constantine concerning the Jews touch upon four subjects only: proselytism, protection of converts to Christianity, the municipal duties of the Jews and pilgrimages to Jerusalem. In all these matters there is almost no difference between his legislation and that of his pagan predecessors. Constantine's religious zeal was moderated by political prudence. In his laws there are only two points in which the legal *status quo* was changed:

(A) As we have already seen, Jewish proselytism was forbidden from the days of Antoninus Pius and Septimius Severus onwards.[8] In 335 Constantine repeated the prohibition; a slave circumcised by a Jewish owner was declared free.[9] Eusebius in his *Life of Constantine*[10] mentions another law according to which Jews were not allowed to hold Christian slaves; but, as no such law appears in the extant codes, Eusebius must have been referring to the edict of 335, mistaking its provisions.

(B) The legal protection granted to Jewish converts to Christianity was a legal innovation. One cannot find it unjust. Two years before his death, in 337, Constantine promulgated a law prohibiting Jews from troubling the converts or causing them any damage; the punishment was graded according to the rank of the offender.

(C) In the matter of the municipal councils (*curiae, boulai*) Constantine made no innovations as far as the Palestinian cities were concerned. In 321,[11] that is three years before he became the ruler over the Orient, Palestine included, he imposed on all Jews (two or three only excepted) the duty of sharing the municipal burden. The few exceptions were meant to serve as a reminder of their former immunity. In fact Constantine only revived an old law of Severus. After the abolition of the pagan worship there was no reason, at least from the point of view of the Roman legislator, to free the Jews from this burden. The privileges of the ministers of religion were preserved in their entirety. As we have seen, Jews were serving on the municipal councils of Palestine a long time before Constantine. In the Diaspora, however, they had been exempted for religious reasons. This exemption was now annulled. After conquering the Orient Constantine decided to proclaim again,[12] and with more emphasis, that those serving in the synagogues, the Jewish patriarchs and the priests, were free from civil and personal obligations. He added that those who had already been made *decuriones* under the earlier law of 321 would be freed from tax collecting and other duties which required them to absent themselves from their normal place of residence. The execution of this law was hampered by local difficulties. The provincial authorities tried to make difficulties for the Jews as far as they could. The governors were of course sensitive to the new anti-Jewish spirit which was now spreading from the imperial court into the provinces. The provision whereby those who had been included in the *curiae* in the years 321–330 were left in the *curiae* made an opening for diverse interpretations, for it made it possible to keep those already drafted subject to their former burdens. Constantine therefore issued in 331 a new law, directed to the 'priests', heads of the synagogues and elders of the synagogues' which freed them and all those employed within a synagogue from all personal burdens (*munus corporale*).[13]

(D) The change which occurred in the matter of the pilgrimages to Jerusalem was not formal but abolished 'illegal' practices hitherto allowed. Eutychius (Ibn Batriq), patriarch of Alexandria in the tenth century, mentions in his history[14] that Constantine prohibited the Jews from living in Jerusalem or passing within it. Obviously this was only a repetition of the old edict of Hadrian, which, as far as we know, had never been formally annulled. It was, however, evaded in practice—at least as far as pilgrimage was concerned—from the third century onwards. We may understand therefore why the edict of Constantine was regarded by Eutychius as a piece of new legislation. In Jewish circles the edict was undoubtedly regarded as a sign of a renewal of the Hadrianic persecution.

The emperor did, however, make two changes in the old edict.

(i) Once a year, on the 9th of Ab, the day of the destruction of the Temple, the Jews were allowed to go up to Jerusalem and mourn on its ruins. This spectacle of Jewish mourning served as a demonstration of the truth of Christianity, as set out by the Fathers of the Church. The Bordeaux Pilgrim, who wrote his account of a pilgrimage to the Holy Land in 333,[15] already mentions this custom. 'Not far from the statue of Hadrian there is a pierced stone; every year the Jewish visit it, anoint it, and mourn loudly, tearing their clothing, after which they go home.' The Jewish sources also contain some hints for this practice in the fourth and fifth generations of the Amoraim. Rabbi Aha stressed the importance of the Wailing Wall: 'The divine Spirit (*Shekinah*) never moves away from the Western Wall'.[16] In another anonymous source,[17] we read: 'The Western Wall of the Temple will never be destroyed'. Rabbi Pinhas bar Hama tells of two brothers, rich people, who lived in Ascalon. They decided to go up to Jerusalem on a certain day. Their wicked neighbours planned to destroy their house on that day; but a miracle occurred and the plotters could not carry out their plan.[18]

(ii) The new prohibition referred only to the city of Jerusalem itself and not to its whole area. Hadrian had prohibited the Jews from entering the whole municipal territory of Aelia.[19] The Christian authors of the second and third centuries state expressly that the Jews were not allowed even to glance at Jerusalem from afar.[20] After Constantine the prohibition seems to have been limited to the city itself. Jerome states that in his time (the beginning of the fifth century) Jews were living in Bethlehem or its vicinity.[21]

It will be seen from the above that in purely legislative matters the edicts of Constantine did not effect a revolutionary change in the status of the Jews.[22] The change for the worse, which undoubtedly did occur at that time, was mainly one of practice. The old laws had been generally forgotten in the anarchical third century. They were now revived, and they seemed new and iniquitous pieces of legislation. Their general tenor was not offensive to the Jews, as was the case with later laws. The old egalitarian spirit of the Roman law was still evident in the laws of Constantine, at least as far as their form is concerned.

Matters look entirely different if we read the other pronunciations of the same emperor. Of course most of the letters and proclamations issued by Constantine were not composed by the emperor himself. They were the work of his ecclesiastical secretariat; but he had undoubtedly read them, and signed them. Constantine's letters to the leaders of the church contain expressions which are particularly offensive to the Jews. In one of these epistles, in which Christians are asked not to keep Easter at the same time at which the Jews keep Passover, the following terms occur: 'The lawless Jews, impure in their crimes' 'Let us not have anything in common with the perjured Jews' 'The impure ones, who were justly stricken with blindness'.[23] Such language seems copied from the sermons against the Jews delivered by Christian zealots.

Constantine's negative attitude to the Jews was expressed not only in words but also in deeds. He and his mother Helena began a series of splendid church buildings in Jerusalem and in Bethlehem. In such a way they placed an additional obstacle in the way of the Jewish longing for a Return to Zion. Possibly this attempt to make Palestine a Christian country is referred to in the words of Rabbi Judah ben Simeon ben Pazzi who said that[24] the cave of Machpelah, the Temple and tomb of Joseph, all of which were purchased and paid for in olden times were the 'three sites which the Gentiles cannot take from Israel by saying: "they were obtained by robbery" '. Constantine also supported the efforts of the convert Count Joseph to spread Christianity among the Jews of Galilee by building churches in the Jewish cities.[25]

Such a change of attitude by the supreme ruler could not but have its effects upon the lower officials. In former times the governors favoured the Jews, because they saw they were in the good graces of the emperors. Now the court had changed its tenor and promptly a series of administrative persecutions started in the provinces. Such acts were illegal, but nevertheless they made life very difficult for the Jews. This campaign of vexations explains the many complaints about oppression at this period. Rabbi Judah ben Simeon ben Pazzi describes Israel as addressing the Creator thus: 'How many persecutions and evil decrees have they made in order to take away Thy kingdom and Thy lordship over us'.[26] The Church canons forbade Christians from sharing in the holidays and the fasts of the Jews and the civil authorities followed suit by forbidding the Jews to keep fasts. We are told in the Babylonian Gemara:[27] 'In the time of Rabbi Zeira a persecution was ordered, and they decreed that there should be no fasts. Rabbi Zeira said: "We shall submit to this order and after the end of the persecution we shall sit and fast".' A similar story is told in another place.[28] Because fasting was forbidden on the Day of Atonement, it was transferred to a Sabbath, so as to avoid the surveillance of the authorities. This event happened in the time of Raba (299–352) that is to say in the times of Constantine.

The close relations between the Jews in Palestine and those in Babylonia did not please the Roman authorities, for both religious and practical reasons. They tried to make such contacts as difficult as possible. The patriarch residing at Tiberias was forbidden to fix beforehand the date of Passover, possibly because there were still Christian sects which obstinately clung to the Jewish date for their Easter feast. If the date of Passover were kept secret, they could not do so.[29] Because of such difficulties with the government, the Sanhedrin at Tiberias was forced to use hints which could be understood in Babylonia.[30] One such letter was composed as follows: 'They tried to set up a governor (an intercalary month) but that Aramean (Roman) did not permit it; so the men of the assemblies (the Sages) met and decided to set up another governor in the month in which died Aaron the Priest (the month of Ab)'. Finally the patriarch Hillel made the rules of the Jewish calendar public (358); but even before that the Babylonians were forced to act independently. Rab Huna bar Abin told Raba that if the month of Tebet (a winter month) arrived when Nisan was due, the year might be intercalated without hesitation.[31]

3. *The Jewish Reaction to Constantine's Policy*

The Jews in Palestine did not react immediately to the change in Roman policy which followed upon the accession of Constantine. This was to a great extent due to the confusion which this unexpected development had caused amongst the Jewish leaders. The division of the Jews into a right wing, a centre and left wing (to use the political terms of our days) was not accidental; it was here based as elsewhere on psychological factors embedded deeply in the nature of man as a 'political animal'. At all periods there are some people who strive to conserve the existing state of things, others who want to change it radically and between them there is the mass of people which is concerned above all to make a living. The period under consideration was no exception, for all its religious veneer.

The rise of an emperor who doubled in the role of a 'heretic' (*Min*) caused the greatest confusion to the leaders of the moderate party, because their programme was based on a close collaboration with the authorities. They now lost all hope for the future. The centre party, which was interested mainly in practical matters, did not despair; they took care to defend energetically the Jewish religion, now under renewed attack from the Christian missionaries. In their eyes this was the most important practical step which could be taken at this difficult time. The extremists renewed their efforts. They began to prepare for a revolt, having revived their Messianic hopes.

The moderate party suffered most from a weakness in its leadership. The patriarchate at this period lost much of its strength, because it was affected by the biological fact of hereditary decline. Some patriarchs inherited their exalted position while still minors. This brought about long periods of guardianship, naturally exercised by the heads of the Sanhedrin. Even those of the later patriarchs who were personally able suffered from their upbringing as descendants of an aristocratic family, delicate in health and weak in character. Such young people, who grew up in wealth and luxury, did not always prove worthy of leadership. The bishop of Caesarea, Eusebius, interpreted in his commentary the verse in Isaiah (3, 4): 'And I will make boys their princes and babes shall rule over them', as a prophetic foresight of the 'Jewish patriarchs, boys or youths young in body but with rotten souls and lacking in good sense'.[32] We need not take the sayings of this enemy of Judaism without the proverbial grain of salt; Eusebius was of course interested in humiliating the Jews and their leaders. For the same reason we may justly doubt the story of the convert Count Joseph about the patriarch Judah IV, whom he represented as surrounded by corrupt companions, and affected by their bad morals.[33] There seems to have been, however, some truth in these allegations, because the Talmudic sources contain at least some hints at the dissatisfaction felt by the rabbis with the patriarchs. 'Rabbi Jeremiah sent a letter to Rabban Judah the patriarch saying: "You should hate those who love you and love those who hate you".'[34] This may well mean that he should turn against his young companions who angered the rabbis, and find himself new friends amongst the sages, even if they were opposed to the patriarchate.

The conversion of the *comes* Joseph is in any case a historical fact, and shows a certain loss of nerve among some at least of the Jewish leaders. The story of this man was as follows.[35] About the middle of the fourth century, in the reign of Constantius II (337–361), a young Christian priest, named Epiphanius, happened to pass Scythopolis (Beth Shean). This Epiphanius was of Jewish origin, and was born at Beth Zadok, in the vicinity at Eleutheropolis (Beth Gubrin). The city of Scythopolis was in these days almost wholly Arian, for this sect was then in favour at the imperial court. Epiphanius, who was himself a pillar of orthodoxy, found refuge in the house of an old man of seventy years or more, who lived isolated in the town because of his orthodox beliefs. In his house there lived also an Italian bishop who had been exiled to Scythopolis by order of the emperor.

The owner of the house was called Joseph. He told Epiphanius the story of his life, mixing, as old people are wont, truth and fantasy. Joseph was originally one of the great men at the court of the patriarch at Tiberias. He acted as counsellor to the patriarch Hillel II and was a guardian of the minor, Judah IV. In Tiberias he read the Christian books kept in the patriarchal archives—undoubtedly because they could serve in disputes with the *Minim*. Later on Joseph learned that the name of Jesus had a magic influence and that it could be used for healing, especially in the cases of sickness of the soul. He thus became a believer in Christ. While on a mission in Cilicia on behalf of the patriarch his conversion became public. He was expelled from the Jewish community and took refuge at the court of the emperor Constantine. There he was honoured with the title of *comes* ('companion of the emperor', Count). With imperial protection he returned to the Jewish cities in Galilee and began to build churches there. In Tiberias he used for this purpose the unfinished Hadrianeum; he built also at Sepphoris, and in the Judaeo-Christian centres Capernaum and Nazareth. His aim was to revive the almost defunct Judaeo-Christian communities in these places. The imperial favour and his official title protected Joseph against the attacks of the Jews, but he could not achieve his principal aim. In the end he left his residence at Tiberias and passed his last days at Scythopolis. There he lived alone, shunned by the local Christians.

As most converts, Joseph wished to justify his change of faith. He therefore told Epiphanius that even the patriarch Hillel had on his death-bed adopted Christianity. According to his story the local bishop had visited him in the disguise of a physician, and baptised him. Now while it is true that Christians in general (and Judaeo-Christians in particular) were popularly supposed to be in possession of mysterious healing powers and magic formulas, it is yet very doubtful if Tiberias had a bishop at all at that time. The first one mentioned in our sources lived in 449. The whole story rests on the evidence of Joseph alone, who is supposed to have 'seen' the happening through a closed door. Some scholars have looked for a confirmation of Joseph's story in the saying of Rabbi Hillel, quoted below. This Hillel was not, however, identical with the patriarch, as he is not given the title of *Rabban* in our sources.

The story of Joseph has yet another significance. On the one hand we note the hostility of the Roman government under Constantine towards Judaism, for all its supposed impartiality. The emperor was apparently most interested in converting the Jews. On the other hand we may note the despair felt by many of the Jewish leaders when they contemplated the victory of Christianity. The change seemed indeed quite miraculous. Within one generation a despised and persecuted sect became the ruling power in a vast empire. The church leaders, such as Eusebius, were deeply impressed by this turn of events. They were filled with enormous self-confidence and dazzled by their success, began to hope for an imminent conversion of the whole of mankind. They could not see the beginnings of the deep rifts which were to come within the church itself, and which were to erode their hopes. They deemed that the second coming of Christ must be at hand, and one of its signs would be Jewish conversion. Conversely, the spirits of the Jews fell. This became evident at the very core of Jewish thought: the Messianic expectation. One—but only one—of the sages, dared to express doubts concerning this hope. A certain Rabbi Hillel is reported as saying: 'Israel has no more a Messiah; for they had devoured him in the time of King Hezekiah'.[36] This *obiter dictum* made the other rabbis furious. One Rabbi Joseph answered Rabbi Hillel, and he began by stating 'May the Holy One, Blessed be He, pardon Rabbi Hillel.'[37] The sages were aware that although Rabbi Hillel's opinion contradicted the Christian argument that the Messiah had come as Jesus, on the other hand it gave up the future Messianic hope altogether. This was in their eyes tantamount to giving up Jewish national existence.

The despair which befell many Jews of this generation found another expression in ever bolder and bolder ways of addressing God. Such sayings might sound strange in the mouths of pious rabbis, and they can only be understood against a background of deep moral distress. Rabbi Berakhiah said for instance: 'So said Israel to the Holy One . . . "For the needy shall not always be forgotten" (Psalms 9, 18)—and Thou art forgetting us!'[38] Rabbi Judah ben Simeon ben Pazzi described Israel as complaining before the Eternal: ' " Shall the throne of iniquity have fellowship with Thee" that Thou art so keen on it (Rome)?'[39]

In the end only a few despaired. Those who followed Count Joseph and became converted to Christianity were still fewer. That they were very few we may even learn from the significant silence of the church fathers. They used to receive every converted Jew with loud shouts of triumph; for every such convert served to confirm the truth of their contention that the church was now the true Israel. Yet they had very little to say about mass conversions in the fourth century.

The accession of a Christian emperor gave a fresh impetus to Christian propaganda among the Jews. As the Judaeo-Christians were by now few in number, this missionary task was undertaken by Gentile Christians. These were especially numerous in the coastal cities, the strongholds of Christianity in Palestine. They did not repeat the attempt of the Count Joseph to spread Christianity in Jewish Galilee, but strove for it in the towns in which the Jews were in a minority. Even there, however, their success was but moderate. After many years of quiet on the missionary front there was a renewal of religious disputes between Christians and Jews. Rabbi Abbahu was the head of the Jewish disputants; he was forced to take up the challenge because he resided at Caesarea, the Christian metropolis of Palestine. Disputing with Christians was now especially difficult, because they were armed with Origen's *Hexapla*, and could refer to the Hebrew original of the Bible. Therefore Rabbi Nahman found it necessary to warn all Jewish disputants:[40] 'He who knows to reply to the *Minim* as well as could Rabbi Iddi, should do so—if not, he should not reply'. The Jewish sages of Palestine who lived in the neighbourhood of Gentiles and who were under Christian rule knew how to deal with the Christian propagandists much better than the Babylonian Jews. Once Rabbi Abbahu had to defend his Babylonian colleague, Rabbi Safra who did not know how to interpret the Bible to the *Minim* as he should. Rabbi Abbahu said: 'We (the Palestinians) are used to them (the *Minim*) and we sacrifice ourselves and study the Torah; they (the Babylonians) do not do so'.[41]

As regards the contents of such disputes very little change is noticeable. The Jewish disputants stressed energetically the Oneness of God, and they denied the relation of Jesus to Him as a 'Son of God'. In this matter there were at that time serious divisions of opinion among the Christians themselves, in particular between the Arians and their opponents. That particular rift ended with the victory of the Orthodox over the Arians. Possibly alluding to it Rabbi Abbahu once said: 'For example—a king of flesh and blood, he rules and has a father or a brother or a son. The Holy One said: I am not thus. "I am the first" (Isaiah 44, 6)—I have no father; "I am the last"—I have no brother; "and beside me there is no God"—I have no son.'[42]

The Christians compared the ascension of Jesus to heaven with that of Enoch. The rabbis replied by diminishing the stature of Enoch himself. Rabbi Abbahu said: 'Enoch was a hypocrite, sometimes just, sometimes wicked. God said: "Let us take him away while he is still just" '. The verse in Proverbs 24, 21: 'And meddle not with them that are given to change (*Shonim*)' was interpreted 'Do not meddle with those who declare that there is a second (*sheni*) god'. Rabbi Aha said: 'God was angry with Solomon when he uttered the above verse . . . thereupon Solomon expressed it more clearly: "There is One . . . he has neither son nor brother" ' (Eccl. 4, 8).[43] The dogma of the Holy Trinity[44] aroused still sharper opposition.

The Christian claim that only they represented the true Israel was treated by the rabbis with scorn. As against the written law (the Bible), on which their adversaries based their claims, the Jewish sages pointed to the Oral Law, which was theirs only. Thus said Rabbi Judah ben Shalom: 'Moses asked for the Mishnah to be also written down, but the Holy One, blessed be He, foresaw that the nations of the world would translate the Torah and read it in Greek, and that they would say "We also are Israel". So the Holy One said to him: "I shall write for you most of my Law . . . but the Mishnah is the Holy One's mystery, and He does not disclose His mystery but to the just.'[45]

At the same time the rabbis hinted at the divisions of opinion among the various Christian sects, as contrasted with the unity of Judaism. Rabbi Berakhiah said: 'The nations of the world are thus—these say "We are Israel, the world has been created for us" and those say: "We are Israel" etc'.[46]

In the disputes with the Christians we may well marvel at the boldness with which the Jews refuted the arguments of their adversaries. In the Middle Ages the position of the Jewish disputants in such cases was a most difficult one. They had to be very careful what they said, lest they should be accused of insulting the established Christian state religion. The situation was quite different in the fourth century. Although the victory of the church was already in the offing, its opponents still had complete freedom of speech, and they made good use of it. When a Christian emperor proposed to Rabbi Tanhuma bar Abba: 'Let us all be one people' the rabbi replied: 'We who follow the Covenant of Abraham cannot be like you; you should join the Covenant (be circumcised) like us'.[47] Even at the end of the century, when John Chrysostom asked the Jews: 'Why did you crucify Jesus?' they replied: 'Because he led the people astray and was a magician'.[48]

The same energy was also displayed in face of the Roman authorities. In spite of all prohibitions, proselytism continued. As against Rabbi Helbo, who had argued: 'All the proselytes are as a scab to Israel',[49] Rabbi Berakhiah said: 'The proselytes shall be like priests who serve in the Temple'.[50] In the second century the 'wicked' government terrorised the Jews by its cruelty and its energy. In the third they could scorn its weakness and its divisions. In the fourth, Rome, now having turned Christian, was despised as using not only force, but also the weapons of the weak: hypocrisy, false piety and lies. 'This is the wicked government which incites all the peoples and leads them astray with its lies.'[51] Rabbi Berakhiah derided the 'princes of Edom who would like to "set their nest among the stars" (Obadiah 4) . . . but who tear the flesh of Israel with pincers and steal its money'.[52]

Hate of the Roman 'Esau' fed in the second century on political subjection, and in the third on the economic distress. Now the economic position had improved, but the future of Israel in its native country appeared more and more doubtful. At the same time there grew the hope that salvation could come after the fall of the 'wicked government'. This view, which in earlier times had been held only by a few fanatical zealots, became widespread among the sages. Already in the fourth generation of the Amoraim Rabbi Aha had said: 'When Esau comes, hell comes with him'.[53] His contemporary Rabbi Abin said: 'As the rose withers when there is a burning heat, but blossoms forth when the dew comes, so it is with Israel. As long as the shadow of Esau falls on them, they fade away in this world, but once the shadow passes, they become well again'.[54] Rabbi

Judah ben Simeon ben Pazzi added: ' "And God called the light day"—this is Jacob; "and the darkness night"—this is Esau. "And there was evening"—, this is Esau, "and there was morning"—that is Jacob'.[55] In such a reckoning the rule of Jacob comes after that of Esau. Rabbi Nahman repeated the same saying in a slightly different form: 'As long as the light of Esau shines, the light of Jacob cannot be seen; once the light of Esau is dimmed, that of Jacob shines forth'.[56]

The tension led to the belief that salvation was near and that it would come through the ruin of Rome, the last of the 'four kingdoms'. Rabbi Pinhas ben Hama said: 'As the world began with the four kingdoms . . . it shall end with the four kingdoms . . . Babel, Media, Greece and Edom (Rome)'.[57] People also began to calculate the advent of the Messiah, an arithmetic exercise which has always been typical of periods of excitement. Sayings began to circulate which stressed the nearness of the salvation and of an ingathering of the Exiles. We find in one passage this saying: 'Thus said the Holy One: "Do not be dismayed, Israel, for I will save you from afar, and your offspring from the land of their captivity" (Jeremiah 30, 10)—from Gaul and Hispania and its provinces "Jacob shall return" from Babylonia, "and have quiet"—from Media, "and ease"—from Greece, "and none shall make him afraid"—from Edom (Rome)'.[58]

In the eyes of that generation the Messianic victory was gradually assuming the aspect of a 'Blitzkrieg', a sudden and violent upheaval. Rabbi Berakhiah said: The Holy One shall punish Esau the wicked in three hours and tame him'.[59] Many were expecting the arrival of the Messiah, from hour to hour and from moment to moment. Rabbi Jeremiah ordered that he should be buried dressed in white, with sandals on his feet and his staff in his hand; placed on his back, he would be ready to rise at once to welcome the Messiah.[60]

In the end the Messianic hope descended from the realm of fantasy into the calculation of political realities. Instead of hoping for miracles from heaven, people began to long for a victory of Rome's enemies on earth. Rabbi Eleazar bar Abbina said: 'If you see the kingdoms quarreling with each other, expect to hear the steps of King Messiah'.[61] As soon as the Messianic hope had become concrete in this way, the ground was prepared for self-help by force and for an armed encounter with the Romans. The decline in the prestige of the moderate patriarchate also helped to speed the conflict.

Other voices were not however lacking. Many of the leaders of the nation wished to continue with the old waiting policy. They warned all the time against a hasty confidence in 'calculating the (Messianic) end'. Rabbi Zeira said: 'Three things come unexpectedly: the arrival of the Messiah, the finding of an object and a scorpion's bite'.[62] Rabbi Huna said: 'Four oaths were sworn against four generations who tried to hasten the end and failed. These were: in the days of Amram (Korah), in the days of Dinay (the Zealots), in the days of Bar Kozziba (Bar Kokhba) and in the days of Shuthelah ben Ephraim.'[63]

Mention of Shuthelah (1 Chron. 7, 20) refers on the face of it to the days of Joshua, but the chronological order of the other references indicates that this pseudonym covers some event which occurred after the revolt of Bar Kokhba. Was there in the days of Rabbi Huna some revolt which had failed? There are two possibilities in this respect: we may interpret this saying as referring to the revolt against Gallus Caesar in 351;[64] or to a revolt in the days of Constantine.

There is only one source for such an event. In his sixth oration *Against the Jews*, delivered in 387, John Chrysostom, who lived then at Antioch, before becoming the patriarch of Constantinople, enumerated the various attempts of the Jews to re-build the Temple. After mentioning the defeat of Bar Kokhba he continues: 'And again in the days of Constantine they tried . . . and the emperor seeing this attempt cut off their ears . . . and had them led thus around from place to place . . . But these are matters of old. Now I shall speak of a subject which is known to all of you who are of a certain age' . . . and then he passed on to the events in the reign of Julian.[65] Apart from Chrysostomus this Jewish revolt against Constantine is mentioned in the Syriac Chronicle of 846, and in the history of George Cedrenus, a Greek historian of the eleventh and twelfth century; both obviously copying Chrysostomus; Cedrenus mentions him as the source.[66] The Syriac historian Bar-Haebreus (Abu-l-Faraj) mentions the business of the cut-off ears in connection with the revolt of Bar Kokhba.[67]

Some historians doubt the existence of this revolt; they appeal to the silence of Eusebius and other writers of the Constantinian era. They also point out that Chrysostomus omitted to mention the revolt against Gallus, which is referred to by all other sources, and goes on straight to the events under Julian after speaking of Constantine. They propose therefore to correct the revolt 'against Constantine' to 'against Constantius'. There are however several arguments against this theory. Chrysostomus spoke in 387 of this revolt as of an old and forgotten affair, but of the events under Julian, that is to say in 363, as something known to the aged among his hearers. It is not reasonable to assume that he regarded an event of 351 as old and forgotten, and one of 363 as fairly recent.

We might attempt to solve this problem by returning to the text before us. From what Chrysostomus tells us of the punishment inflicted, the cutting off of ears, the revolt seems to have been neither widespread nor dangerous. It is most unlikely that thousands of rebels were mutilated and paraded thus through the cities of the empire. What was meant was probably the act of a small group. Chrysostomus in his oration spoke only of the attempts to restore the Temple, and hence passed over in silence the revolt against Gallus, which spread in Galilee and coastal Judaea. Probably some zealot group attempted a coup-de-main in Jerusalem in order to keep Jerusalem from becoming a Christian city; their failure was immediate. Most of the people and its leaders did not believe in the permanence of the Christian victory, and continued the policy of waiting and of passive resistance. In the meantime matters grew steadily worse.

PART II: THE REIGN OF CONSTANTIUS II (337–361)

Constantine died on the 22nd May 337. His three sons divided the empire between them. Palestine with the whole Orient fell to the eldest, Constantius II. After a period of wars between the brothers and several revolts, Constantius became in 350 ruler of the whole empire. As he was childless, and as he was interested in easing for himself the burden of government, he appointed on 15th of March 351 his nephew Gallus to the rank of vice-emperor or Caesar, and let him rule the East.

The fate of biological decline, which had afflicted the Hillelite dynasty, did not stop before the imperial house. As compared with his father Constantine, Constantius was a little man, even if he was superior to his brothers. He was also luckier and kept his head and his empire; but in matters of state and religion his views were of the narrowest. He was dependent on his advisers among the officials and the clergy to a degree unheard of under Constantine. Moreover as the second in the succession of Christian emperors, he felt much more secure in religious matters, and was accordingly much more severe in his dealings with non-Christians.

4. *New Anti-Jewish Legislation*

Constantine was personally an enemy of the Jews, but in his laws he did not pass beyond what was normal in the ancient Roman legislation. He only made the laws more severe and insisted on their being followed to the letter. Constantius II acted otherwise. On the 13th August 339 he and his brothers published a law, which was the first step towards carrying out the full programme sketched out in the Canons of Elvira.[68] The main aim of these canons was to separate the Jews from the Christians and to keep Judaism confined within its existing boundaries. Three of the laws of 339 have been preserved in the Theodosian code:[69] (a) intermarriage between Jews and Christians was forbidden; (b) additional protection was decreed for converts (c) Jews were forbidden to hold Christian and Gentile slaves.

One paragraph forbade Jews under pain of death to marry and to convert Christian women. From the point of view of the Roman law-giver this was but the closing of a loophole in the laws against proselytism. So far only circumcision was prohibited in Roman law; now the law was extended to the conversion of females. In fact this provision was intended to limit the freedom of action of the individual Jew. It did not, however, evoke much protest, for in the matter of mixed marriages the rabbis and the church leaders were of one mind.

Another paragraph of the same law is more interesting. It annuls the mixed marriages of women who had once formed part of the imperial *gynecaeum*; such women were ordered to return at once to their former place. It seems that cases of this kind, which could not have been very numerous, were the real motive behind the provision against mixed marriages. We notice the economic motivation of this law. The imperial *gynecaeum* was a spinning and weaving factory. Women who left it to marry Jews enabled the latter to compete with the imperial manufactures, and thus aroused the wrath of the Treasury.

Another section of the law is addressed in general to 'the Jews, their elders and patriarchs'. It menaces with death by burning anyone who would dare to attack converts by throwing stones or in any other way. Non-Jews who joined in the act would be punished in the same manner.

The third section, that dealing with the conversion of slaves, had *prima facie* a purely religious motivation. The emperor extended the prohibition on holding Christian slaves to slaves of all religions and of all nations except Jews. According to Jewish Law, a Hebrew slave did not retain this status for long; he had to be set free within seven years at the utmost. The provision that Jews could not hold Gentile slaves was a direct blow aimed at Jewish slave-holders in general. According to the new law only the Christian slaves owned by a Jew were set free entirely; the others were confiscated for the benefit of the Treasury. A Jew found holding a Christian had all his property confiscated; if he circumcised a slave, whether Christian or pagan, he was punished with death.

This law concerning slaves, ostensibly meant to protect their religious beliefs, had a far-reaching economic significance. At that time the Jewish artisans and manufacturers were as dependent on slave labour as were their Gentile competitors. The difficulties caused by the new law to Jewish industries were undoubtedly one of the causes—and possibly even the principal cause—for the revolt against Gallus Caesar, which broke out a few years after its promulgation.

Another law of Constantius II, published in 353,[70] prohibited the conversion of Christians to Judaism; the proselyte lost all his property. This law was slightly less harsh than the former one as far as Jews were concerned; a pagan proselyte was not punished at all, whereas the earlier edict punished Christians and pagan proselytes alike.

G

The laws of Constantius II were offensive not only by their contents but also in their wording. The edicts of his father Constantine were formulated in a careful and apparently impartial manner. It was only in his letters to the church leaders that the emperor allowed free rein to his feelings. In the laws of Constantius II, however, the anti-Jewish sentiments were to be found in the very wording of the text. The Jews are a 'savage' (*feralis*) or an 'abominable' (*nefaria*) sect. Judaism is a 'disgrace and an infamy' (*flagitium, turpitudo*). The Jewish assemblies are 'meetings of blasphemers' (*sacrilegi coetus*). Such language from a legislator was enough to arouse the gravest doubts as to his impartiality amongst those subject to him. [71]

5. *The Revolt against Gallus Caesar*

The situation which preceded the outbreak of this revolt was in many ways similar to that existing in 66 before the First Revolt against Rome. There were three factors which seemed to favour the insurgents: a revolt in the West, which kept Constantius busy, the weakness and corruption of Gallus, and hope of a Persian intervention.

On 18th January 350 the general Magnentius revolted at Augustodunum in Gaul against Constans, Constantius' brother and co-regent. On the 1st of March of the same year the general Vetranio followed suit at Mursa in Illyricum. Constans perished soon afterwards. A prolonged period of negotiations followed, and then Constantius in June 351 started a campaign against Magnentius. At its beginning he suffered a reverse at Atrans. This fact seems to have become public in the Orient early in the autumn of 351.

Gallus had in the meantime absolutely failed as a ruler. Within a short time he succeeded in arousing the enmity of the officials both in Syria and at the imperial court. A capable general, Ursicinus, was sent to take charge of the army of the Orient. Gallus kept only the command of his personal guard, and this was clearly the first step towards his removal from all his offices. [72]

In 336 Shapur II, king of Persia, had started to wage war against the Romans. His first aim was to reconquer northern Mesopotamia, which Galerius had taken from the Persians in 297. In 350 Shapur besieged Nisibis for the third time, after two earlier failures, in 337 and 346. This time he almost succeeded. It was quite clear in 351 that Persian attacks would continue for some time.

The combination of these three factors seemed to have encouraged the Jewish rising against Gallus. The Jewish rebels were headed by a leader known to us only by his Roman name Patricius. The name was not unusual among the Jews in the fourth century, [73] although it must have

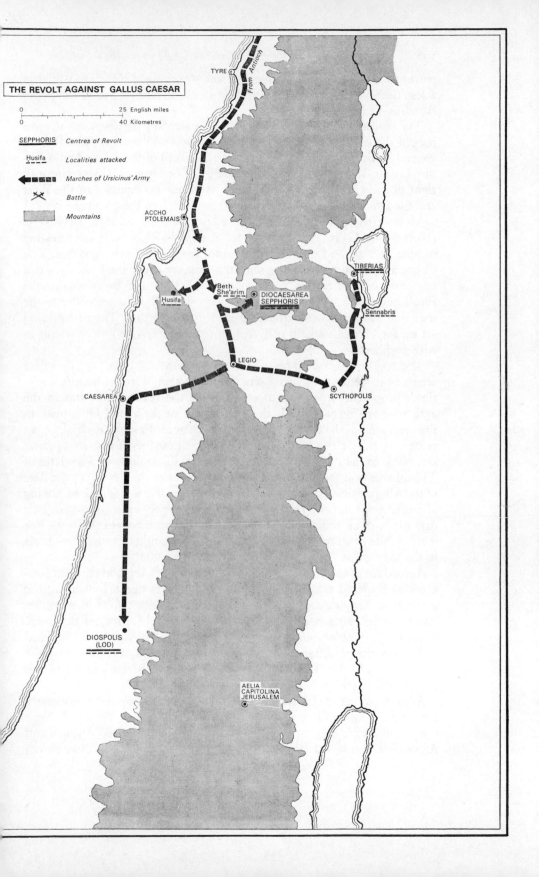

THE REVOLT AGAINST GALLUS CAESAR

0 — 25 English miles	
0 — 40 Kilometres	

SEPPHORIS — Centres of Revolt

Husifa — Localities attacked

◄▄▄▄▄ — Marches of Ursicinus' Army

✕ — Battle

▓ — Mountains

TYRE

From Antioch

ACCHO
PTOLEMAIS

TIBERIAS

Husifa

Beth
She'arim

DIOCAESAREA
SEPPHORIS

Sennabris

LEGIO

CAESAREA

SCYTHOPOLIS

DIOSPOLIS
(LOD)

AELIA
CAPITOLINA
JERUSALEM

corresponded to a Hebrew name. We know nothing of this commander in a lost cause save his name; it survives in the history of the Latin writer Aurelius Victor.[74]

The official leaders of the Jewish community in Palestine seem to have judged the situation with much more coolness and caution. The Roman general Ursicinus, who was in command instead of the debauched weakling Gallus, showed quickness and energy. The sages of Tiberias proved right in their judgement. Constantius overcame his enemies in the West and the Persians were unable to penetrate deep into the empire.

Most of the people followed the advice of the moderate party. The revolt against Gallus remained the act of a band of zealots. It is interesting to note that all we know about it comes from non-Jewish sources. The Talmudic literature mentions only the military occupation which was a consequence of its failure. Some scholars[75] have argued therefore that the revolt never took place, and that Patricius was a Roman pretender to the imperial crown. However the text of Aurelius Victor: 'They (the Jews) set up for Patricius a kind of kingdom (*sub regni speciem*)' does not fit in with such a view.

The revolt broke out at Sepphoris in the month of June 351. This date seems to fit better the general situation than that of 352, which is sometimes proposed. According to our sources the revolt broke out in the 15th year of Constantius II, the fourth year of the 282nd Olympiad, in the year 2368 of the era of Abraham (which according to Eusebius began in 2016/5 BC) or the year 5843 of the Creation (beginning in 5492 BC according to the Alexandrian chroniclers and Theophanes). The dates of Theophanes and the Olympiad reckoning point to the year 351; the date of the Abrahamic era allows a dating to this year, and so does the reckoning of regnal years, for the 15th year of Constantius began in June 351. This date fits best, as we have seen, the general circumstances of the time. For it seems likely that the news of the defeat of Constantius reached Sepphoris in the autumn of 351.[76]

According to our sources the revolt did not last long, even if its suppression required some hard fighting. The rebels began by seizing the armoury at Sepphoris (Diocaesarea), probably in the course of a sudden attack on the garrison which camped in the citadel (*castra*) of the town. Armed with these weapons they spread all over Galilee which was denuded of Roman troops. After its initial success, the revolt was joined by the inhabitants of other Jewish cities, in particular Tiberias and Lydda; it also spread in the coastal plain southwards to Lydda.[77]

After these successes the rebels seem to have set up a revolutionary authority, a 'kind of kingdom' in the words of Aurelius Victor. By their capture of Lydda they cut the coastal road which connected Antioch and Alexandria, the two centres of Roman power in the Orient. Our sources mention no attempt to take Jerusalem. As we have already seen, the revolt against Gallus is passed over in silence by Chrysostom, just because it involved no effort to restore the Temple.[78] The rebels seem to have thought it necessary to await their encounter with the Roman troops approaching them from the direction of Antioch, before attempting the attack on Jerusalem, which was defended by a troop of Moorish cavalry.[79] It seemed unwise to disperse their forces; after repelling the main forces of the enemy they could always go back and complete their task of freeing the Holy City.

It seems that the rebels did not attack the Christians, perhaps in order to avoid raising the ire of the emperor. They seem, however, to have injured many 'Hellenes' (pagans) and Samaritans. The Christian historians, who note carefully every injury done by the 'impious Jews' to the members of their community, do not mention such doings, and their silence is eloquent.

The foci of the revolt, Tiberias, Sepphoris and Lydda, were also the centres of Jewish industry, in particular that of spinning and weaving textiles. This seems to support the view that the principal motive of the revolt was an economic one, the result of the damage done to the Jewish textile manufactures by the decrees of Constantius concerning slavery.

The news of the revolt moved Gallus (or, more likely, Ursicinus) to action. All available troops were sent forward to suppress the rising. Since the days of Diocletianus each of the emperors had at his disposal a field army, which served as a mobile reserve to the border forces (*limitanei*) settled along the frontiers. Part of this field force must now have been ordered from Antioch southwards. On its way to Galilee, the centre of the revolt, it entered the region of Ptolemais-Acre. An old lamentation has been preserved,[80] which is based on the biblical text of Zephaniah 1, 10. It seems to refer to the revolt against Gallus: ' "A cry will be heard from the fish gate"—this is Acco . . . "a wail from the Second Quarter"—this is Lydda . . . "a loud crash from the hills"—this is Sepphoris . . . "a wail of inhabitants of the Mortar"—this is Tiberias'. The text mentions three out of the four cities which are listed by Jerome as having taken part in the revolt. One may well ask why Acre is also mentioned. Sepphoris, Tiberias and Lydda were well-known Jewish towns, but it seems hardly likely that the rebels would have succeeded in taking an important harbour city such as Ptolemais-Acre, which was inhabited mostly by Gentiles. It seems most likely that this passage refers to the destruction resulting from the fighting in the vicinity of the city. It seems likely that the rebels had massed their forces to stop the advance of the Roman troops in the hill passages on the road between Acre and Sepphoris, and that the Romans used Ptolemais as their base. The same had been done by Vespasian in his campaign against Galilee in 67 (see map, p. 177).

No siege is mentioned in connection with this revolt. It seems therefore that its fate was decided by a battle in the Acre plain. The fighting continued from Acre south-eastwards towards Jewish Galilee, for the approach to Sepphoris is easier from that direction than by the direct Acre-Sepphoris road. Several Jewish townlets in the vicinity of Sepphoris suffered in the fighting and some were destroyed. The excavations at Beth Shearim have shown that the city was completely destroyed at that time, with bodies left in its streets. The burials in its necropolis ceased about the same time. When the Romans took Sepphoris, they sacked and burnt the city—there too traces of burning were found in the excavations. All non-Jewish sources mention that Sepphoris was destroyed as a result of the rising. Jerome adds Tiberias and Lydda for good measure. It appears however that the open country suffered much more than the cities. The operations continued along the coastal road; but even Jerome has to admit that the losses in life were not very great—at least as compared to the terrible slaughter in the two revolts against Rome. He mentions several thousand dead, including women and children. After the revolt of Gallus no more Jews are mentioned in three cities and fifteen villages, most of them in Galilee or the Western part of the Jezreel Valley, the rest in the coastal plain. But the main cities, which Jerome mentions as destroyed, did somehow survive. In the time of Valens, late in the fourth century, Sepphoris was not only settled, but a purely Jewish city.[81] Tiberias continued its former role as the capital of Jewish Galilee. Only Lydda seems to have suffered more, but even there a Jewish community survived.

After the military operations came the occupation. Ursicinus the *magister militum* (general-in-chief) of the Orient, gave his name to this period in the Talmudic sources. The occupying forces seem to have in the beginning acted with great severity. Many of the people of Sepphoris who were involved in the revolt, had to flee in disguise. Rabbi Hiyya bar Abba said: 'In the time of Ursicinus "the king" the people of Sepphoris were put on trial, they placed masks on their noses and were not recognized; but after that they were denounced and all caught'.[82] The persecutions and searches were also carried out in other localities. Rabbi Huna tells that in Tiberias 'We had fled before the "Goths" and hid in a certain cave at Tiberias, and we had lamps in our hands, if they burned low we understood it was day, and when they burned brightly it was night'.[83] The 'Goths' mentioned in this text might be barbarians serving in the Roman army, or the police of the patriarchs, or Roman police (*agentes in rebus*). Possibly the flight of Rabbi Yudan, one of the chiefs of the Sanhedrin at Tiberias, was also connected with this occupation.[84]

In the long run, however, neither the revolt nor its suppression affected the position of Palestine Jewry. There was indeed loss in lives and property. The worst we know of Ursicinus' soldiers was the burning of a

Torah scroll in the Galilean village of Sennabris south of Tiberias.[85] The official leaders of the nation, the patriarchs and the rabbis did not take part in the revolt and were not punished. The few of them who were mixed up in the rising went into hiding; the others continued their avocations peacefully. Rabbi Yose, the colleague of Rabbi Yudan, remained at Tiberias and continued to teach. There is no mention of any executions or martyrdoms among the rabbis at that period.

The matter which most agitated the rabbis in the areas occupied by the Romans was that of supplying the troops with warm food on the Sabbath. On the whole they took up a permissive attitude. Rabbi Mana allowed the bakers to work on the Sabbath when Tiberias was occupied by the regiment of one Proclus, a commander under Ursicinus.[86] The same occurred at Sepphoris; at Naveh bread was allowed to be baked at Pesah, although the command to avoid all unleavened food was much more severe. As the occupation continued into the spring of 352 this transgression was justified in two ways. Firstly the matter did not involve a danger to faith: 'Ursicinus did not intend to persecute religion but only to make sure that the troops should have warm food'.[87] Secondly, the matter was for the public good 'possibly many shall still need him (Ursicinus)'.[88]

One of the results of this attitude of compromise was that the Jewish national authority was not affected and that no special laws were passed against the Jews.

When a rabbinical delegation (with Rabbi Jonah and Rabbi Yose at its head) visited Ursicinus at Antioch (probably in the winter of 351–2) in order to obtain some mitigation of the occupation regime, he stood up before them. His companions were astounded and asked him: 'Why are you rising before these Jews?' and he replied: 'I have seen their faces as victors in the war'.[89] Clearly this reply is apocryphal and based on the no less legendary encounter between Alexander the Great and the high priest,[90] and the vision of Constantine before the battle at the Milvian bridge.[91] However, the mere fact that such a story should be attributed to Ursicinus shows that he was regarded as a humane and just ruler.

The Jews continued to live for ten more years under the rule of Constantius. Gallus was indeed deposed and executed in 354, but the anti-Jewish legislation remained in force and was acted upon. Only after ten years did hope revive; paradoxically so, because Julian, the last of the Hellenes, mounted the imperial throne. The Jews then applied to themselves the verse from Daniel (11, 34): 'When they fall they shall receive a little help'.

Notes to Chapter VII

1. M *Sotah* 9, 15.

2. b *Abodah Zarah* 17a.

3. See above, p. 45.

4. See the pilgrimages listed in T. Tobler, A. Molinier, *Itinera hierosolymitana et descriptiones Terrae Sanctae bellis sacris anteriora*, Paris, 1877–80 (Société de l'Orient latin); some of the references to the first and second century are doubtful, cf. D. H. Windisch, *ZDPV*, 1925, pp. 145–58.

5. *De martyr. Palaestinae* 11, 9–10 (*GCS* 9, pp. 937–8); Syriac text ed. Cureton, London, 1861, pp. 40–1.

6. See above, p. 148.

7. For the old view see Gibbon, and J. Burckhardt, *The Age of Constantine the Great* (tr. M. Hadas), London, 1949; the new one is based on the researches of N. H. Baynes, *Constantine the Great and the Christian Church* (*Proceedings of the British Academy*, XV, 1929); ibid., *CAH*, XII, pp. 678ff.

8. See above, p. 45.

9. *Codex Theodosianus* XVI, 9, 1 (21 October 335), cf. O. Seeck, *Regesten der Kaiser u. Päpste*, Stuttgart, 1918/19.

10. *Vita Constantini* IV, 27, 1 (*GCS* 7, p. 127).

11. *C Th* XVI, 8, 3 (11 December 321).

12. Ibid. XVI, 8, 2 (29 November 330).

13. Ibid. XVI, 8, 4 (1 December 331).

14. Eutychius, *Annales* I, 446 (*PG* 3, *c.* 1012).

15. *Itinerarium burdigalense*, ed. P. Geyer in *Itinera hierosolymitana saeculi IIII–VIII*, Wien, 1898, p. 22.

16. *Exodus R* 2, 2.

17. *Pesikta de Rab Kahana* (ed. Buber) 49b.

18. *Song of Songs R* 7, 2.

19. See above, pp. 50–1.

20. See above, p. 51.

21. Jerome, *Epistola* 84 (*PL* 22, *c.* 745).

22. *C Th* XVI, 8, 1; XVI, 8, 6; XVI, 9, 2. O. Seeck has proved that the laws quoted, which were ascribed partly to Constantine and partly to Constantius II, are all part of the same law of 13 July 339.

23. *Vita Const.* III, 18 (*GCS* 7, p. 85).

24. *Genesis R* 79, 7.

25. See below, p. 168.

26. *Shoher Tob* 5, 6.

27. b *Taanit* 8b.

28. b *Hullin* 101b.

29. S. Lieberman, *JQR*, 36 (1946), p. 333f.

30. b *Sanhedrin* 12a.

31. b *Rosh ha-Shanah* 21a.

32. *In Isaiam* III, 3–4 (*PG* 24, *c.* 109); Jerome ad loc. (*PL* 24, *c.* 64).

33. Epiphanius, *Panarion* 30, 7, 3 (*GCS* 25, p. 342).

34. j *Megillah* 3, 2–74a.

35. Epiphanius, *Panarion* 30, 4–12 (*GCS* 25, pp. 338–48).

36. b *Sanhedrin* 99a.

37. Ibid.

38. *Yelammdenu*, ed. A. G. Wertheimer, *Batey Midrash* I, p. 42.

39. *Shoher Tob* 13a.

40. b *Sanhedrin* 38b.

41. b *Abodah Zarah* 4a.

42. *Exodus R* 29, 5.

43. *Deuteronomy R* 2, 33.

44. *Genesis R* 25, 1.

45. *Tanhuma* Genesis, ed. Buber, p. 88.

46. *Song of Songs R* 7, 3.

47. b *Sanhedrin* 39a.

48. *In Ps.* 8, 3 (*PG* 55, *c.* 110).

49. See above, p. 82.

50. *Exodus R* 19, 4.

51. *Song of Songs R* 2, 11.

52. Haggadah *Genesis* 56.

53. *Genesis R* 16, 2.

54. *Song of Songs R* 2, 2.

55. *Genesis R* 2, 3.

56. *Genesis R* 6, 3.

57. *Ecclesiastes R* 5, 15.

58. *Leviticus R* 29, 2.

59. *Song of Songs R* 4, 8.

60. j *Kelaim* 9, 6–32b.

61. *Genesis R* 42, 4.

62. b *Sanhedrin* 97a.

63. *Song of Songs R* 2, 7.

64. See below, pp. 176ff.

65. *Adv. Iudaeos* V, 11 (*PG* 48, *c.* 900).

66. Cedrenus, ed. Bonn, I, p. 499; *CSCO* (*SS*) III, 4 Chron. A. D. 846, p. 148f.

67. Bar Hebraeus (ed. Budge), I, p. 53.

68. See above, p. 153.

69. *C Th.* XVI, 8, 1; 8, 6; 9, 2; Sozomen, *Historia Ecclesiastica* III, 17 (*PG* 67, *c.* 1093).

70. *C Th.* XVI 8, 7 (8 July 353).

71. E.g. *C. Th.* XVI, 8, 1; 8, 7; cf. J. Juster, *Les Juifs dans l'empire romain*, I, p. 253.

72. See above, p. 174.

73. J. B. Frey, *CIJ*, I, index.

74. Sex. Aurelius Victor, *Liber de Caesaribus*, 42, 9–12 (ed. Pichlmayer, p. 128).

75. S. Lieberman, *JQR*, 36 (1946), pp. 340–1.

76. Sex. Aurelius Victor (see note 74 above); Jerome *Chronicon* (*GCS* 24, p. 238); *Historia miscell.* XI (*PG* 95, *c.* 915); Cedrenus (ed. Bonn I, p. 524); Sozomen, *Historia ecclesiastica* IV, 7 (*PG* 67, *c.* 1124); Socrates, *Historia ecclesiastica* II, 33 (ed. Bright, Oxford, 1893) p. 106; Theophanes, *Chronographia*, a.m. 5834 (ed. de Boor), p. 40, 20); Michael Syrus (ed. Chabot, I), p. 268; Agapius of Membidj (*PO* 7, p. 571f.).

77. Aureli usVictor, loc. cit.

78. See above, p. 174.

79. *Notitia dignitatum*, ed. Seeck, Berlin, 1876, p. 73.

80. *Pesikta R* ed. Friedmann, 8, 29.

81. Theodoretus, *Historia ecclesiastica* IV, 22 (*GCS* 19, p. 259f.).

82. j *Yebamot* 15, 1–15c.

83. *Genesis R* 31, 11.

84. j *Ketubot* 11, 1–34b.

85. j *Megillah* 3, 1–74d.

86. j *Sanhedrin* 3, 6–21b.

87. j *Shebiit* 4, 2–35a.

88. j *Betsah* 1, 6–60c.

89. j *Berakot* 5, 1–9a.

90. Josephus, *Ant.* XI, 331–335.

91. See above, p. 161.

VIII

The Emperor Julian
and the Jews

1. *The Rise of Julian and his Political Principles*[1]

A year after the execution of Gallus Caesar, the emperor Constantius again felt the need for someone to help him to carry the burden of power. By now his only surviving relative was Julian, Gallus' younger brother. In 355 the youth of twenty-three was recalled from his studies at Athens and invested with the rank of Caesar. He was at once sent to Gaul, to contend with revolt within and German invasions from without. Julian had been brought up in the study of philosophy and literature. Once in Gaul he revealed himself, however, as a born statesman and general. He succeeded in defeating his foes in the field; he even outwitted his no less dangerous enemies in the councils of Constantius and the imperial emissaries who came to control him. In 360 an enthusiastic army proclaimed Julian Augustus, thus ranking him with the elder emperor. Constantius refused to acknowledge Julian as his equal. Both sides were preparing for war, when the issue was suddenly decided by the unexpected demise of Constantius in the little village of Mopsucrene near Tarsus (November 361). Julian remained the undisputed master of the whole empire.

The new emperor believed that the alliance of church and empire brought about by Constantine was fatal for the Roman state. He therefore set about to undo the work of his two Christian predecessors. His policy was the reflection of his firm belief in the old Hellenic religion, in its neo-Platonic formulation—the latter being itself strongly influenced by the Gnosis, and Jewish and Christian mysticism. Julian's religious attitude was attuned to the mood of his age; for the fourth century was entirely pervaded by a sense of the metaphysical, not to say mystical.

185

The short reign of Julian (November 361–June 363) was marked by three main lines of policy: the reform of the state, the war with Persia and the struggle with the church. His attitude to Judaism and the Jews was conditioned by the two latter factors, and especially by the last. From the beginning of his reign Julian strove to give the Hellenic religion a new lease of life by the reopening of the temples, the restoration of the cults of the old gods and the establishment of a pagan priesthood of a high moral quality. He refused, indeed, to persecute his enemies. The past persecution of Christians had taught him that such acts of repression could only affect weaklings. Each religion worthy of its name has a kernel of firm believers who are ready to keep faith with it up to, and including, martyrdom. A new persecution would only strengthen the church. A small minority could perhaps be wiped out in this way, but not a body of believers who already numbered thirty to forty per cent of the population.

Julian's plan for attacking the church was much more subtle. At his accession he proclaimed full religious liberty and kept his promise to the letter. This did not hinder him from trying to convince the citizens of the empire that the old faith was both better and stronger than the new one, and that one could put one's trust in the old gods. Julian hoped that a victorious campaign against the Persians would amply demonstrate the power of the Olympians.

His provisional plan of action shows that he had learned much from the methods of his ecclesiastical opponents. The leaders of the church knew how to take over the 'good' parts of Judaism and to reject the 'bad'. In the same way Julian tried to revive the old religion by using the Christian model. Thus he attempted to create a firm institutional infrastructure for the pagan world, which would serve it as the church organization served Christianity. He himself stood at the head of this anti-church as the high pontiff; the old republican title of *pontifex maximus*—which had been kept by the emperors as a matter of form was no empty title in the eyes of Julian. It implied an active involvement in the matters of the pagan 'church' on the model of Constantine. Julian appointed chief priests for all provinces, the opposite numbers of the metropolitan archbishops. The new 'church' was meant to aid the poor and the sick, and to provide charity where necessary. Julian abolished too the special privileges of the Christian clergy which were granted by Constantine and Constantius II.

The second point of Julian's programme was to replace the Christian rite with a pagan counterpart, including absolution for sins. Julian did not order the closing of any church built by Christians, but he insisted on the restoration of the old rites in the temples, which had been rededicated as churches. He took care that the temples abandoned in the past should be reopened and the feasts and prayers renewed therein. Sacrifices were especially important in his eyes. Julian believed in the doctrine of his teacher Iamblichus, the head of the neo-Platonic school, according to which no prayer would be complete without sacrifice, because 'the life of the victim carries the prayer on high'.[2]

Propaganda was the third point of Julian's programme. He tried to encourage everywhere the adherents of the old religion, granting special privileges to cities which had remained faithful to it and refusing such favours to those who had adopted Christianity. He wrote in this sense to the main cities of his empire, to Alexandria, Athens etc.[3] In these manifestos he endeavoured to persuade the inhabitants and the magistrates of these cities to return to the beliefs of their fathers. One of these letters was addressed to the people of Tiberias;[4] unfortunately only the superscription of this message has been preserved.[5]

Julian was also out to sow dissension in the enemy camp. As a born strategist he understood the importance of dividing his enemies and keeping his own forces together. With this aim in view he annulled the penalties decreed by his predecessors against bishops who had strayed from orthodoxy. He allowed all of them to go home, hoping that the Christian sects would resume their old quarrels, thus paralysing the church establishment.

The fifth point was the gradual removal of Christians from public life. Their number had grown, especially in the army, and the emperor was obliged to leave them in their posts. He tried, however, to cut off their replacements by prohibiting Christians from teaching or learning Greek literature. He stressed with supreme irony that only those believing in Homer's gods could understand his poems and could convey their meaning to others. As in this period literary productivity was at a very low ebb and all education and culture were based on the Greek literature and learning of the past, Christian authors too had to study and imitate pagan literature. They even made desperate efforts to interpret it in a Christian sense. If Julian's order had been carried out systematically, there would be within one generation no Christian who could be counted among the educated, within the meaning given to the term at that time. They could neither have taken part in social life nor filled any public office.

This order was intended to cut off the Greek root of Christianity; but the other root, the Jewish one, likewise did not escape Julian's attentions.

2. Julian's Relation to Judaism in Theory and Practice

In describing Julian's attitude to Judaism we have to distinguish between the philosophical propagandist and the emperor. His theoretical writings betray the fact that up to his accession he had no contact with the Jews, either as a body or as individuals. In his youth he had affected to follow

Christianity, although even then he was already suspected of paganism; any approach to the Jews would only have confirmed the suspicions of the clergymen who watched his every step. His knowledge of Judaism up to 361 was based on a thorough study of the Septuagint version of the Bible. The familiarity of the emperor with his Jewish subjects and their problems could only have resulted from his brief stay in the East in 362–363.

As in most other matters Julian's attitude to Judaism was a reverse image of that adopted by the Christian church.[6] Its 'fathers' idealized the Hebrew past in theory. They could hardly do otherwise; for the church had acquired from it, together with the text of the Bible, its whole historical background, which was of much use in its missionary activity. In practice, however, the leaders of this same church were engaged in a bitter day-to-day struggle with the descendants of the same patriarchs and prophets they were honouring as the forerunners of Jesus. Julian condemned the Jewish past unreservedly when he wrote as an anti-Christian propagandist. He disputed Jewish pretensions to be God's 'chosen people' and derided the past exploits of a nation which was subject to foreign rule throughout almost the whole of its history.

On the other hand Julian the emperor favoured the Jewry of his time, the enemies of his enemies, and he endeavoured to bring them over to his side. In his positive approach to contemporary Judaism Julian followed the footsteps of his neo-Platonic masters. Like them he praised the attachment of the Jews to the religion of their forefathers. He contrasted it with the Gentile convert's desertion of *his* ancestral beliefs in favour of Christianity. Julian also extolled Jewish tolerance of other religions; although, as we have seen, this tolerance sprang from necessity rather than from conviction. In the fourth century at any rate Jewish tolerance contrasted in Hellenic eyes favourably with the intolerant zeal of the Christians. Because of his neo-Platonic leanings Julian attached special value to the sacrifices prescribed in Jewish ritual.

Julian, as other Hellenic statesmen and writers, held that the Jews were entitled as a nation to an 'ethnic' god of their own. Him they should serve and worship just as all other nations should serve and worship their national gods. The neo-Platonists tactfully ignored the universal claims of the Jewish god. It is interesting to note that a faint echo of this pagan attitude may be heard even in the Palestinian Gemara. Rabbi Abba bar Zamina tells the story of a Jew who was employed by a Roman tailor.[7] Once the master invited the workman to share his meal. The Jew declined of course the ritually impure viands. Thereupon his Roman master praised him saying: 'Indeed you may know that if you had eaten, I would have killed you. Let a Jew stay a Jew and a Roman a Roman.'

Beside such reasons as were derived from his philosophical and religious convictions, Julian had two practical grounds for favouring the Jews, and in particular those of Palestine. One reason, applying to the Jews in general, was connected with his plans for a war against Persia.

Julian planned his campaign carefully. He trusted his ability as commander in the field, which he had proved by his victory over the Germans at Strassburg. His administration was strong and well directed. He took good care of his finances and had made short shrift of the wasteful court of Constantius, dismissing wholesale its multitude of barbers and cooks. Everything was ready therefore; a victory in the East would make his rule secure and revive the trust in the Hellenic gods. His projected line of advance would carry him through parts of Mesopotamia densely settled with Jews. If he could gain their sympathy (or at least ensure their neutrality) his advance would be made much easier. Nor was he quite mistaken in this assumption. The Jews of the Persian borderlands had indeed been brought up in enmity to everything Roman since the days of Trajan. When the empire turned Christian, this hostility could have hardly diminished. No one could expect therefore that they would welcome a Roman emperor appearing at the head of a Roman army. Nevertheless their resistance to Julian was by no means as desperate as their fight against Trajan. The fortress of Piri-Shapur, an important Jewish centre, surrendered after only two days. The Jews of Birtha abandoned their city on the approach of the Roman army. Thus far Julian's letters and proclamations seem to have at least tempered somewhat the deep-seated hostility of the Mesopotamian Jews to everything Roman.

In Palestine itself peculiar local conditions gave the Jews the status of a balancing force. Their adherence to one of the opposed camps would turn it into a majority of the population. As has been shown above,[8] Christianity advanced but slowly in Palestine in its first three hundred years. Even in the fourth century its progress was by no means rapid. By Julian's time even the strong support given by Constantine and Constantius II to the Christian communities of the Holy Land had not been enough to turn them into a majority. The case of Bostra, the capital of the province of Arabia, may serve to illustrate the point. There a Christian community had existed since at least the middle of the third century.[9] Indeed Bostra was one of the local centres of Christianity. Nevertheless we learn from a letter of Julian to the people of Bostra[10] that in his time the Christians formed barely one half of the local population. If such was the position in one of the oldest Christian centres, it is obvious that the new religion had made still less headway in the old centres of paganism. The great cities of the Philistine coast were still very strongly attached to their old gods. Gaza and Ascalon in particular remained for centuries strongholds of Hellenism. A celebrated school of rhetoric and neo-Platonic philosophy flourished at Gaza from the third to the fifth century. The common people of the two cities remained fanatically attached to their gods, Marnas and Atargatis. This pagan zeal (which burned as fiercely in the inland cities of Caesarea Philippi (Paneas) and Sebaste) burst out into riots upon the accession of Julian as soon as it was noticed that the imperial favour was withdrawn from the Christians. The town mobs attacked individual Christians and burned down the local churches.[11] Quite apart from the excesses of the city mob, always ready to burn and to loot, the attitude of these cities under the Christian emperors showed how strongly they were attached to the old faith. Constantine had to accord the port of Gaza (Maiumas) a separate city status, in order to create at least one Christian municipality in this area.[12] Jerusalem seems by what appeared in Jewish eyes as an irony of fate to have been the only city in Palestine in which there was a Christian majority. For the Jews were still forbidden the city, while many Christians had settled there since Constantine and his mother Helena inaugurated an era of lavish church building and charitable works of all kinds. Imperial liberality encouraged also many pilgrims to settle permanently as monks or nuns in the Holy City.

The Jews in Palestine had indeed lost much of their power and numbers by the middle of the fourth century. Nevertheless they remained the balancing group between Christians and pagans. Julian's aim of a compact anti-Christian majority could be achieved by their adherence to his cause, especially if the Christian community could at the same time be weakened by the withdrawal of official aid.

Yet even if we discount all reasons of religious belief or political strategy, there remains in Julian's attitude to the Jews a substratum which defies analysis. His letters undoubtedly convey an undertone of personal sympathy with the Jews of his time. Anti-Semitism appears in the fourth century in its new, medieval, version, quite different in form or tone from the older anti-Semitism of the pagan writers. With Julian there appears at the same time the first of the philo-Semites in the modern sense of the word. Julian was by nature a man of warm humanity. He was always ready to share the sorrows of the oppressed and he tried honestly to alleviate their sufferings. Even the cold and official language of his edicts (and still more so the personal letters) show an unusual degree of sympathy with the 'underdog'. Poor taxpayers crushed by the exactions of the Treasury, or the Jews vexed by the officials of Constantius could be sure of his good will—Julian even regretted the heavy burdens imposed on the Jews by their own patriarchs. His strong sense of justice forced him to take the side of the weaker party. In his eyes the Jewish masses were being unjustly persecuted and he wished in all sincerity to help them, even against their own authorities. In any case he annulled the anti-Jewish decrees of Constantius. As a statesman Julian was used to decide quickly, and to execute his decisions at once. This was also the case in the matter of the Jews.

3. *Julian's Meeting with a Jewish Deputation at Antioch.*
His Decision to Return Jerusalem to the Jews

In May 362 Julian left Constantinople; after a slow but busy progress across Asia Minor he arrived at Antioch on the 19th July. Here he occupied himself with affairs of state and the preparations for the Persian war. Nevertheless he found time to receive a deputation of the Jews. He invited to this audience the 'chiefs of the Jewish community'. We cannot tell from this wording of our sources whether this refers only to the heads of the community of Antioch, or whether it was meant to include the presidents of the provincial synods of Syria and the adjacent provinces, the 'little patriarchs' of Syria, Cilicia and Pamphylia. The composition of the Jewish delegation becomes, however, considerably clearer, if we compare the various accounts of this historic audience, as recorded by the Christian writers and historians. John Chrysostom, addressing the Jews of Antioch in 387 states that Julian was speaking to 'some Jews' ('Ιουδαίων τινάς); he then adds: '*you all* (i.e. the Jews of Antioch whom he was haranguing) did thus and thus'.[13] Rufinus[14] is another almost contemporary witness, as he wrote at the beginning of the fifth century. Moreover, he had access to official sources, as we shall see.[15] He speaks of 'all the Jews called in to the emperor' (*omnium convocatos ad se*). Rufinus seems to imply thereby that the audience was held at the emperor's request; as will appear subsequently, this is a fact of some importance. Sozomenus[16] wrote in the later half of the fifth century; but as he was a native of Palestine, he was at least aware of the local traditions. He is our only source to define the delegation as the 'chiefs of the Jews'. That he is referring to the 'little patriarchs', the heads of the Jewish synods in the provinces, may be inferred from his subsequent story of a proclamation addressed by Julian to 'the patriarchs and chiefs' (πατριάρχαις in the plural) and 'heads of the communities' (ἀρχηγοῖς). We may conclude from the silence of all these sources that *the* patriarch of the Jews, i.e. the one residing at Tiberias, did not appear among the delegates at Antioch either in person or by representative.[17]

The details of the meeting have come down to us in the form of a dialogue between the emperor and the Jews. Julian is reported to have asked the Jews: 'Why do you not sacrifice to God, as required by the Law of Moses?' The Jews replied: 'We are not allowed by our Law to sacrifice outside the Holy City. How can we do it now? Restore to us the City, rebuild the Temple and the Altar, and we shall offer sacrifices as in the days of old'. Julian: 'I shall endeavour with the utmost zeal to set up the Temple of the Most High God'.

Even after the lapse of sixteen centuries it is obvious that there was more behind this scene than what was said in public. Julian, who knew the

Scriptures by heart must have been well aware that the Jews were not allowed to sacrifice anywhere else but in the Temple of Jerusalem. We can only assume that he needed a solemn supplication on the part of the Jews in order to declare publicly a policy upon which he had already decided in private. He was thus able to proclaim his decision in the most public manner in the presence of the assembled court and officials. The statement of Rufinus that the Jews were convoked by the emperor, adds strength to this assumption. Such an understanding of the value of publicity for propaganda purposes is by no means an isolated phenomenon in Julian's career.

It seems therefore most probable that Julian had considered his Jewish policy on the way to Antioch and that he arrived there with his mind already made up. His decision appears very unexpected—especially if we remember that it originated with a Roman emperor, and one traditionally-minded at that. It must have been a personal policy, and not due to the advice or the influence of any official. Julian was anyhow rarely influenced by his official advisers. The opinion of his Neo-Platonic philosophers, to whom he listened occasionally, would hardly be in favour of such a decision. For it implied much more than the mere re-erection of a ruined edifice. It seems to have involved the return of Jerusalem and its territory to the Jews and the consequent re-erection in Palestine of an autonomous Jewish entity.

By realizing the age-old Jewish aspirations Julian could hope to attain several ends. He could gain Jewish adhesion to the league of peoples and religions which he was busily mobilizing against the church. The renewal of sacrifices in one more temple, and in particular the resumption of sacrifices in Jerusalem (which would assure him the favour of the God of the Jews) would, in his eyes, constitute an additional guarantee for victory in the Persian war, and for the success of his policy in general.[18] Julian's passion for erecting sumptuous buildings, which were meant to commemorate his reign, was noted by the historian Ammianus and must also be taken into account in explaining his policy in Jerusalem.[19]

There was also a special reason for the rebuilding of the Temple at Jerusalem. The destruction of the city and its sanctuary had been used for three centuries as an unanswerable argument for the truth of the Christian message. The Christian apologists advanced this fact in proof of three of their favourite topics. Firstly, they argued it proved that the Jews had lost their status as the Chosen People; obviously God favoured them no longer, since He allowed His temple to be destroyed in their midst. Secondly, the Jews in asking for the condemnation of Jesus had been really guilty of deicide; for although God had restored them to Zion after the First (Babylonian) Exile, this, their Second Exile, had already outlasted the other by 230 years and would last for ever. Thirdly, it showed that Jesus was a true prophet; he had predicted that not one stone of the Temple would be left upon another,[20] and this prophecy had come true for all to see. By restoring Jerusalem to the Jews and by rebuilding the Temple Julian undoubtedly intended to strike a crushing blow at this line of argument. It would invalidate at the same time the claim of the church to the status of the 'true Israel', its assumption of Jewish guilt and the veracity of Jesus as a prophet.

The interest of historians in later ages was focused almost exclusively on 'Julian's attempt to rebuild the Temple'. The church historians of the fifth and sixth centuries wrote long descriptions of the miracles which had prevented the execution of the 'wicked design'. Quite naturally they were mainly interested in the propaganda value of the failure of this attempt. Modern historians, on the other hand, have been mainly interested in the romantic aspect of the matter. A re-examination of the sources shows that Julian's act of state had a double significance, religious and political.

The political aspect is already well in evidence in the very first steps which followed the solemn proclamation of policy at the audience in Antioch. After it Julian addressed at least four letters to the Jews. Two of these have been lost, but their existence is certain, for Julian mentions them in his third epistle. The contents of these two can be reconstructed in outline.

Obviously the proclamation of the emperor's decision at Antioch required the promulgation of one edict addressed to the Jews of the empire to acquaint them with his intention. Another letter was sent to the patriarch and the authorities in Palestine and concerned the execution of the project. These were modelled on the epistles of Constantine, of which more below.[21]

A summary of what one may call Julian's first proclamation, the one presumably addressed to the Jews of the whole empire, we can find in the fifth diatribe 'Against Julian' by Gregory of Nazianzus.[22] Gregory was a fellow-student of Julian at Athens and knew his style very well; as a zealous Christian he was a strong opponent of the emperor and his policies. According to this contemporary source, Julian adjured the Jews and 'proved' to them from the Scriptures that the time had come for them 'to return to their native land, to rebuild the Temple and to set up the rule of their ancestral ways (τῶν πατρίων τὸ κράτος).[23]

4. *Jewish Reactions to Julian's Proclamation*

According to all contemporary sources this declaration of Julian evoked a wave of wild enthusiasm throughout the whole Diaspora. This is attested by eye-witnesses dispersed through many lands. Ephraim the Syrian wrote at Nisibis: 'The Jews were seized by a frenzied enthusiasm, they blew the *shofar* (ram's horn) and rejoiced'.[24] Gregory of Nazianzus wrote in Asia Minor that the Jews stood ready to depart with the greatest alacrity.[25] Rufinus wrote in Italy that the Jews felt as if the Messiah had come. 'They (the Jews) arrived at such a degree of impudence, that it seemed to some of them that the days of the prophets had returned. They began to abuse our people (i.e. the Christians) as if the days of *their kingdom* had already arrived (*reparatis sibi regni temporibus*).[26] The last words are an additional proof that Julian's proclamation contained something beyond the mere permission to restore the Temple, and that it had an added political significance. Rufinus mentions also the beginning of the ingathering of the dispersed Jews in Jerusalem. Other authors recall the collection of great sums in money and jewellery, the gifts of Jewish matrons from all parts of the world.[27]

The second letter of Julian was addressed in particular to the patriarch Hillel II, the head of the Palestinian Jewry. Its existence is vouched for by the mention Julian makes of it in his third epistle, of which more below. We may reconstruct the contents of this message from the two letters sent by Constantine in similar circumstances, though to a different address. One was to Macarius, the bishop of Aelia Capitolina, in which Constantine ordered the construction of the Church of the Anastasis. The other letter was sent by Constantine to Eusebius, the archbishop of Caesarea, and concerned the erection of a Christian sanctuary near the presumed site of the Oaks of Mamre.[28] In both epistles we find a set formula for the co-operation between the secular and the spiritual authorities in the erection of a place of worship. The emperor appoints a delegate-general to supervise the work. This was either the governor of the province concerned or a special commissioner. In the latter case the governor was requested to furnish the delegate all the assistance in his power. The construction itself was entrusted to the ecclesiastical authority. This was a mere matter of convenience as regards the Christian churches; but it was an absolute necessity in the planned re-erection of the Temple. Without the actual participation of Jewish priests no building could be erected fit for lawful sacrifice. This had been already seen by Herod in his reconstruction of the Temple, as we know from Josephus. The emperor requested the religious authority to submit an estimate of the expenses and of the materials required (in particular as regards the more costly materials, such as marble, rare timbers etc.), and the number of expert workmen necessary. Although the whole work was done by imperial order and with imperial assistance, the members of the community concerned were allowed, nay invited, to contribute to its embellishment each according to his means.[29]

Julian's message concerning the re-erection of the Temple contained probably also his order restoring to the Jews Jerusalem and the area surrounding it. There they were to live according to the customs of their forefathers. He probably also ordered the Christians to restore the properties they possessed in Jerusalem—illegally in his opinion.[30]

One consequence of this act was the creation of a Jewish authority entitled to levy taxes. In consequence of this the emperor requested the patriarch to give up the *apostole*, the levy collected by his emissaries from the Jews of the Diaspora, and which weighed heavily upon them. This levy now appeared superfluous, for the local government of Jerusalem would have its own revenues. This detail also goes to show that Julian's undertaking was inspired by the Jews of the Diaspora. It was they who suffered most from the patriarchal levies. The emperor complied probably the more readily with their request, as it fell into line with his general policy. Throughout his reign Julian was trying to lighten the burden on the tax-payer (thus, for instance, he abolished the *aurum coronarium*). His aim was to save the resources of the state for its future tasks, in particular for the expedition against Persia.[31]

In the conclusion of his letter Julian must have granted the patriarch the honorary status of a *praefectus praetorio* (one of the four ministers, each administering a quarter of the empire). We can deduce this from the fact that later on the patriarch Gamliel VI was deprived of this dignity under Theodosius II. As it seems most unlikely that a patriarch should have been invested with such high rank by any one of the Christian emperors who succeeded Julian, it must have happened in his reign.[32]

We may also assume that parallel orders were issued simultaneously to the governor of Palestine, informing him of the imperial decision. Another part of this edict must have revoked the decrees of Hadrian forbidding the Jews to enter Jerusalem. As we have seen Hadrian's decree had gradually fallen into desuetude in the third century. It had never been formally annulled, and had been put in force again in the days of Constantine. The Jews in consequence established a provisional synagogue in one of the ruined porticoes surrounding the Temple Mount.[33]

The special commissioner charged with the execution of the imperial edict was also appointed at the same time. Julian's choice fell on Alypius, a native of Antioch, and a close friend of the emperor. Julian wrote to him as 'my brother', according to the usage of the Hellenistic courts (the patriarch Hillel was accorded the same honour). While Julian was administering Gaul, Alypius was his representative in Britain. He remained loyal to Julian during the war with Constantius. Alypius was a man of scholarly interest; Julian mentions in one of his letters a map of Britain which Alypius had sent to him.[34] The delegate-general was a pagan, but not a fanatical one; after Julian's death he had no scruples in accepting high offices under the Christian emperor Valens.[35] His moderation in religious matters influenced the course of events considerably, as we shall see.

The patriarch and the Sanhedrin must have regarded the imperial letters and proclamations as the harbingers of an impending revolution. The restoration of Jerusalem and its territory to Jewish rule, together with the re-erection of the Temple, would radically change the whole structure of Jewish public life. It would most likely bring about a restoration of the ancient form of government, headed by a high priest in a restored Temple. It was by no means clear how all this would affect the destiny of the nation. The existing authority of the patriarch and Sanhedrin had been created with enormous exertion after a great national disaster. For several centuries it had succeeded in overcoming external and internal difficulties. It had kept together the remnants of the nation on its old soil, and kept it from destruction and hunger. Now there was to be a complete change. The old and tried authority was to be superseded by a new and untried one; for the House of Hillel was not of priestly descent. The patriarch could not hope to take up the function of the high priest in the new theocracy about to be established.

A state of parallel authorities, of high priest and secular *nasi* (Prince or Ethnarch) had, indeed, existed already in the days of Bar Kokhba. But this happened in the middle of a war. The actual power was then naturally concentrated in the hands of the secular commander-in-chief. Now the ruins of Jerusalem were to be restored by the Roman emperor himself. The new Jewish authority would therefore be constitutionally a creation of the Roman state and hence would be pacific by its very nature. The patriarch and the leaders of the Sanhedrin could not have failed to remember the days of Hillel the Old (the ancestor of the patriarchal line). This Hillel was head of the Pharisees, themselves the spiritual ancestors of the present Sanhedrin. He and his fellow-Pharisees waged a strife with the Sadducee high priest and his adherents. There was no certainty that a similar quarrel would not arise now. The hardly-won national unity would then be in danger again. The very first demand of a friendly emperor, the abolition of the *apostolē*, was in itself a clear indication of the difficulties to come. It would deprive the patriarchal court of its means of support and influence in the Diaspora. The taxes levied in substitute and the revived Temple due of half a shekel would be at the disposal of the new high priestly authority, in which the patriarch could, at best, play but a minor part.

The patriarch and the Sanhedrin were of course loyal Jews, faithful to their religion and to their nation. They could hardly oppose for selfish reasons the realization of a hope for which the whole nation had been praying for nearly three centuries. However, there were also weighty reasons of public interest, which must have caused them to hesitate before embracing the new policy with any show of enthusiasm. Ultimately, the whole undertaking depended on one individual life. Athanasius, the metropolitan of Alexandria and a great leader of the church, had already asserted that Julian and his works were but 'a small autumn cloud, soon to pass away'.[36] In spite of all the efforts of Julian, the Christians were still a very large and a very strong body, certainly the strongest of all the institutions in the empire after the imperial government itself. Julian was a childless widower, and they might be waiting confidently for the end of his reign. Moreover, Julian was about to expose himself to the imminent risks of a campaign in Persia; the leaders at Tiberias felt the need for caution. Being responsible for the welfare of a whole nation, they must have felt many misgivings as to whether they should entrust the fate of Judaism to a single mortal.

Side by side with doubts arising from the political situation there were others of a religious nature which influenced the attitude of the rabbis. For many generations the Jews had firmly believed that the rebuilding of Jerusalem and the restoration of the Temple would happen when the Messiah arrived. A scion of the House of David would come and restore the rightful dynasty. The restoration of the Temple would not and could not therefore be undertaken by a Gentile ruler and moreover one addicted to idolatry. The adherents of the new policy replied that King Cyrus of Persia had also been the ruler of a Gentile nation, and that God had nevertheless stirred up his spirit to restore the Temple.

For the time being, there could be no open resistance to the imperial order. The Jewish leaders in Palestine had to submit in silence. This attitude explains the curious fact that there is an almost complete silence in both Talmuds concerning Julian and his plan. Some scholars have tried to explain this silence as a sign of confusion after the failure of the scheme.[37] Such an opinion cannot be maintained for several reasons. Firstly, the Jewish leaders had no reason to be ashamed for their part in this affair; it was the result of an imperial decision which they did not solicit. Secondly, Talmudic sources were not in the habit of glossing over national misfortunes. Disasters can be always explained on the Biblical model, as the punishment for the sins of an unworthy generation. The downfall of Bar Kokhba was a much greater catastrophe than that which occurred under Julian; and yet there is a whole crop of stories and legends connected with the siege and ruin of Beth-Ter. The silence of the Jewish sources is therefore rather the result of the neutral attitude observed by the majority of the Jewish leaders in Palestine as regards the whole of Julian's project.

A minority of rabbis, however, supported Julian's plan wholeheartedly. Rabbi Aha said for instance: 'The Temple shall be built *before* the coming of the Kingdom of David'.[38] He also laid stress on the fact that many of the most sacred objects of the First Temple were missing from the Second, and yet it was a valid sanctuary. In consequence the erection of a Third Temple under the same conditions could be regarded as lawful.[39] An indication of a Messianic ground-swell in the time of Julian may be also found in another saying of the same sage: 'Why did the Saviour of Israel (God) make the Sabbatical year a blessed one? To show that Israel shall be saved in a sabbatical year'.[40] The year 362/3, in which Julian attempted to restore the Temple, corresponds to a sabbatical year (4122 of the Jewish era).

Rabbi Yudan was apparently also numbered amongst the supporters of the undertaking. We have already noted that this rabbi inclined to the views of the zealots. According to him 'the salvation of Israel will come step by step . . . now they are in great distress and if salvation were to come at once, they could not stand such great relief'.[41] The gradualness of Israel's redemption would naturally allow for the rebuilding of the Temple; that would mark only the dawn of the Messianic era.

Some of the zealots were ready to consent to the new policy and to accept the help offered by their old foe, the now repentant 'Esau'. The easily inflammable masses were overwhelmed with wild enthusiasm. The Jewish mobs in Gaza and Ascalon[42] took a joyful part in the persecution of the Christians and the burning of their churches.[43] Had they been permitted to do so, they would probably with equal alacrity have joined the Christian mobs attacking the Hellenic temples.

The Jewish priests, of course, must have heard the news with much satisfaction. Undoubtedly part of the workmen engaged in the project came from their ranks, in accordance with the precedent set in the time of King Herod.

The Christian reaction was equally clear and unmistakable. The whole affair was the work of Satan, intent on afflicting God's church. What especially roused their anger was the spectacle of the monotheistic Jews accepting the favours of a pagan emperor. The Hellenic pagans received the news on the whole favourably. Although they had suffered at the hands of the Jewish zealots in the days of the revolt against Gallus, the Hellenes did not now refuse their assistance to the Jews. We may perhaps date from this time the friendly relations between Jews and pagans, which continued after Julian's death. They are vividly reflected in the letters of Libanius, one of Julian's closest friends.[44]

5. *The Beginnings of the Restoration of the Temple.* *The Work Interrupted. Julian's End*

The preparations for a building enterprise of such size must obviously have taken much time. Even if the declaration of Julian was made in the early days of his stay at Antioch (and there is no reason to assume this, for he had many other matters to attend to) it could hardly have occurred earlier than in the autumn of 362. The actual building operations could not have started before the spring of 363, considering the climate and the means of transport in antiquity. Considerable time must be allowed for the gathering of the Jewish multitudes from the Diaspora (there were hardly any winter sailings at that time) and for the collection and transport of the building materials and other necessities. According to the ecclesiastical historians everything was ready on the spot when the workmen began to uncover and to remove the ruined foundations on the site.[45] We are told that special silver tools had to be prepared. This was not so much the sign of lavish generosity or wastefulness on the part of the Jews but a legal necessity. Such tools had to be used because the Scriptures expressly forbade the use of iron in the construction of the altar (Deut. 27, 5; I Kings 6, 7).[46]

Julian must naturally have been somewhat disappointed by the cool reception of his proclamation by the patriarch and the Sanhedrin. As was his habit he thereupon appealed to the Jewish masses against their official heads. This was Julian's way in his struggle against Constantius. A similar appeal seems to have been the reason for his famous letter, addressed 'To the Community of the Jews' in general.[47] The full text of this letter has been preserved, but its authenticity has been contested. In any case it did already exist in the fifth century, for part of its wording is quoted by Sozomenus.[48] The researches of Heck and H. Levy[49] seem to have proved beyond doubt that the letter is genuine, both as regards style and contents. In this letter the emperor proclaims the annulment of the taxes which the evil counsellors of Constantius had schemed to impose on the Jews. Julian declares that he had ordered the lists of tax-payers found in the imperial chancery to be burnt. He recalls his request to the patriarch to abolish the *apostolē*. This was an appeal to the Jews of the Diaspora and an attempt to counteract a possible obstruction coming from Tiberias. Before setting out on the Persian campaign Julian repeats solemnly his promise to rebuild the Holy City. He concludes with the expression of the hope that he will be able to offer after his victory sacrifice to the Most High God in the newly built Temple together with the Community of the Jews.

As Julian left for Persia on the 5th March 363,[50] it is clear that as far as he knew the rebuilding of the Temple had by then hardly started. One single sentence has remained from another letter written by the emperor in the course of his campaign.[51] This was apparently part of a proclamation addressed to the Jews of Mesopotamia and Babylonia. The one sentence reads: 'I am building with all zeal the new Temple of the Most High God'. Clearly at the time the letter was written the work had already begun, and Julian was not aware of any interruption.[52] The building itself started under most auspicious conditions. The imperial treasury supplied considerable sums of money. Skilled craftsmen and masons were brought to Jerusalem from all sides. Timber, stones, lime and other building materials were held in readiness. A multitude of Jews gathered in Jerusalem to assist the workmen.

The first step was of course the removal of the existing foundations. The Church historians describe this part of the work as involving the destruction of the remnants of the Second Temple.[53] They of course derive particular satisfaction from the thought that the Jews themselves were busily uprooting their own ruins, at the same time completing the work of Titus and fulfilling to the last the prophecy of Jesus. The existence of ruined edifices on the Temple Mount was of course exploited long before that time by ignorant guides, who demonstrated by them to the pilgrims how the prophecy had been fulfilled to the letter. It seems, however, much more likely that the foundations now removed belonged to the temple of Jupiter built by Hadrian in the Quadra, the former Temple esplanade of Aelia Capitolina. This pagan sanctuary was certainly abandoned from the time of Constantine onwards. We may reasonably assume that its ruins were still visible. It seems hardly likely that the Jews would begin the work of erecting the Third Temple by removing the ruins of the Second. Such remnants would have been invaluable as evidence of the exact position of the former edifice, and in particular of the Holy of Holies.

The work must have gone on through April and May. On the 27th of May (according to the Abyssinian menology, i.e. in the month of 'Iyar' according to the Syriac chronicle of 724)[54] there occurred the event which led finally to the abandoning of the whole enterprise.

This event has been the subject of innumerable descriptions from the pens of the ecclesiastical historians. In their eyes it was a miracle; and as usual with the stories of miracles, this story too was embellished throughout the ages. It acquired subsidiary miracles and branched out into more and more marvellous details. We are told that fire came down from heaven and devoured the workmen. Earthquakes happened again and again. Everything built during the day fell to pieces by night. A mysterious cave was discovered by the workmen in the foundations of the Temple; in this cave they found a pillar, and on the pillar was open a book, the Gospels of St. John, which had lain hidden under the foundations of the Temple since Creation. A great cross was seen in heaven, stretching from the Mount of Olives to the Anastasis. Crosses appeared on the garments of the inhabitants of Jerusalem, Christians, pagans and Jews. Other crosses appeared on their utensils, their books and their houses. Crosses were seen in the other cities of the Orient. One author adds the interesting detail that the crosses on the vestments of the unbelieving Jews and pagans were black, those on the dress of the Christians white, and so on.[55]

In fact there is only one reliable and impartial source, the history of Ammianus Marcellinus.[56] Ammianus was a native of Antioch, a Hellene free from religious bias. He was not however an eye witness of the events themselves. He served as an officer of the Roman army, and accompanied Julian throughout the Persian campaign. The history was written by Ammianus in 379, when he lived at Rome in his old age. Obviously he had to rely for the account of events in Palestine in 363 on some written source, most likely an official report. Alypius, the commissioner responsible for the project, must have submitted such a written account to Julian's successor, justifying his decision to stop the work. Ammianus probably follows this state paper when ascribing the cessation of the building to 'balls of fire' (*globi flammarum*), which had suddenly issued from the foundations of the building and had burnt several workmen. He then adds laconically 'and the undertaking stopped' (*cessavit inceptum*) without specifying who gave the order to cease.

Because of the scale of his history Ammianus gave only a short summary of the official report; he could hardly give more room to such a minor matter. He stressed only the 'wonders of nature' which he found mentioned in his source. This agreed with the bent of his mind towards the miraculous, of which there is plenty of evidence in the other parts of his book. When speaking of the incidental 'balls of fire' he forgets to mention the earthquake which was the principal cause of the trouble.

Here the gap is filled by Rufinus, who also wrote in Italy, a generation later.[57] He too seems to have used the same official report, for the 'balls of fire' turn up again in his history, mixed up with a plethora of miracles. Rufinus has, however, copied from the original report two items of essential importance, which Ammianus had omitted as either too commonplace or too trifling. Firstly, the outbreak of the fire was preceded by an earthquake the previous night. Secondly, the fire broke out in a subterranean building between the two porticoes (*aedes . . . aditum inter duas porticus*). This description gives us a clue as to the locality; for in the whole Temple Mount there is only one spot which fits this description. These are the subterranean vaults now called 'Solomon's Stables', situated in the south-eastern corner of the Temple esplanade in the angle between the eastern and the southern porticoes (see diagram overleaf). The earthquake might have caused an explosion of gases accumulated in the closed underground room. More likely still, it might have been followed by an outbreak of fire amongst the building materials, especially wood, stored there, as indeed implied by Rufinus himself.

Of the other contemporary authors, the one, Ephraim the Syrian, gives only a general poetic description of a storm, earthquakes and fire; the other, Gregory of Nazianzus[58]—who was followed by John Chrysostom in the next generation—describes only the fire from heaven, which came

down to devour the Jewish unbelievers. Chrysostom was so much pleased
by this miracle that he repeated the story three times in three different
sermons.[59]

If we were to believe Rufinus and the other Christian sources, we would
have to assume that this was a case of arson. According to these authors,

Diagram of the Temple Mount in the Time of Julian

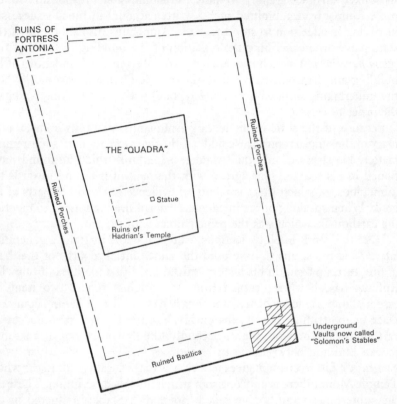

Cyril, the bishop of Jerusalem, foretold several days in advance that the
building would not be completed. To support this view he quoted Daniel
and the Gospel of Mark. Fires did at that time serve well the propaganda
of the church: when Julian ordered the re-opening of the Temple of
Apollo at Daphne near Antioch, the building was burnt down. The
emperor was convinced that this was the result of a crime; the Christians
of course regarded the fire as sent from heaven.

It is, however, hardly necessary to assume the work of a pious fire-bug;
the annals of the period are full of earthquakes in the Orient in general,
and in Palestine in particular. We can hardly believe, however, that the

destruction of some building materials and the deaths of a few workmen or spectators would by themselves lead to the stoppage of the whole undertaking. We must therefore look elsewhere for the real cause.

Who was responsible for the order to cease work? Some writers have attributed the suspension of all activity to the Jews, who are supposed to have been frightened by the 'miracles', others to the Jews and pagans jointly. In any case, it is almost impossible to assume that the order to cease work could have been given by Julian. The eyewitnesses to the event may have been deeply impressed; but their emotions could hardly have been shared by a pagan philosopher several hundred miles away. The stories told by Chrysostom[60] and others concerning Julian's alleged repentance (obviously modelled on the deathbed repentance of Antiochus Epiphanes in the Second Book of the Maccabees, chapter 9) are also in conflict with chronology. From Julian's letter, of which only one sentence has been preserved, we note that while he was already engaged in warfare he wrote of the construction of the Temple as a thing of the present.[61] Obviously he never heard of the stoppage at the time of writing. Julian crossed the Tigris at the end of May or the beginning of June 363, and he advanced into the heart of the Persian empire. By his orders the bridge of boats over the Tigris was burnt and communication between the empire and the army ceased for the time being. After the 20th of April 363 the records of the empire contain no decree signed by Julian.[62] The news of his death on June 16th reached Alexandria and probably also Palestine only in August.[63] The news of events in Jerusalem from the end of May cannot therefore have arrived in camp while Julian was still alive.

With all communications cut with the imperial camp, the fate of the Hellenic revival and of the restoration of the Temple were both left in suspense. For the officials in charge of the work, with Alypius at their head, the earthquake must have come at a very opportune moment. They could now with good reason adopt a policy of 'wait and see'. Should Julian return victorious from Persia, or at least return alive, they had a valid excuse in the occurrence of a natural event of which they could always give an exaggerated account in their reports. If he perished, there would be a new emperor, who would decide what should be done. They were not mistaken in their calculations. Early in August the news reached Palestine that Julian had been mortally wounded in battle on June 16th, 363. The new emperor was Jovian, a Christian. With the death of the last Hellenic emperor the attempt to restore the Temple fell in abeyance.

Historians are as a rule very sceptical about the chances of Julian's success. They judge by results; the attempt to restore the old religion appears hopeless in their eyes because it failed. In fact, however, Julian was by no means 'a romantic on the throne of the Caesars' and nothing else. In his time the old religion was still a potent force. It remained as such for at least one or even two generations after Julian's death. The first Christian emperors following Julian were very circumspect in their policy towards the pagans. Moreover, Julian reigned in all only eighteen months; what would have happened had he remained on the throne, like Constantine, for thirty-one years? The final judgement how near Julian came to success, is given by his opponents, the leaders of the church. They pursued the dead emperor with unparalleled vehemence of abuse and venomous hatred beyond the grave. This in itself is the sufficient measure of their fears while he was alive. In the words of Seeck 'every live donkey kicked the dead lion'. Obviously they were the better judges of what was possible and what not than historians living in the nineteenth century.

The Jewish historian has to approach Julian's activity from another angle. Undoubtedly Julian could have turned Jerusalem into a Jewish city and could have had the Temple rebuilt as the symbol of its freedom. But can we assume without hesitation that the emancipated nation would accept the Roman overlordship willingly and gratefully? For Julian remained, after all, a Roman emperor, and he neither could nor would give up his sovereign rights. Would the conflict between Rome and Israel be resolved peacefully in the fourth century, as it was not in the first? How would the future relations develop between the Jewish religion and Hellenic paganism, once their common enemy had been overcome? Would there be a revival of the Jewish aspirations to complete political independence? Would there be a repetition of the tragedy of the year 70 and a third destruction?

The spear of the Christian Arab which put an end to Julian's life deflected the course of history and these questions must remain unanswered.

Notes to Chapter VIII

1. In general see: P. Allard, *Julien l'Apostat*, Paris, 1910, especially pp. 130–48; J. Bidez, *La vie de l'empereur Julien*, Paris, 1930; Ricciotti, *Giuliano l'Apostata*, Roma, 1956, pp. 280–4.

2. Iamblichus, *De mysteriis*, 5 ed. Parthey, pp. 199ff.

3. *Juliani epistulae et leges*, ed. Bidez et F. Cumont, Paris, 1924, Nos. 54, 59–60, 73, 110–11, 114–15.

4. Ibid., Nos. 154, 209.

5. See below, p. 193.

6. J. Voigt, 'Kaiser Julian und das Judentum', *Morgenland*, Heft 30, Leipzig, 1939; H. Levi, *Zion*, 6, pp. 1–32.

7. j *Shebiit* 4, 2–35a, b.

8. See above, pp. 138–9.

9. Eusebius, *Historia ecclesiastica* VI, 20, 2 (*GCS* 9, p. 566).

10. Ep. 114, ed. Bidez, p. 196.

11. Gregor. Nazianz. *Oratio* IV *contra Julianum*, 87 (*PG* 35, *c*. 616); ibid. IV, 93 (*c*. 626); ibid. V, 29 (*c*. 701f.); Rufinus, *Historia ecclesiastica* XI, 28 (*GCS* 9, p. 1033f.); Sozomen, *Historia ecclesiastica* V, 9, 1 (*PG* 67, *c*. 1237); Theodoret, *Historia ecclesiastica* III, 7 (*GCS* 19, p. 182); *Chronicon paschale* I, ed. Bonn, p. 546f.; Cedrenus, ed. Bonn, I, p. 533f.; Michael le Syrien, ed. Chabot, I, pp. 283, 288, cf. also the inscription: 'God is One. Victory to Julianus' of 362/3 (467 of Ascalon), M. Avi-Yonah *QDAP*, 10 (1944), p. 160f., and the Ma'ayan Baruch inscription (from Caesarea Philippi) praising Julian as the 'templorum restaurator' (A. Negev, *IEJ*, 19 [1969], pp. 170–137.

12. Eusebius, *Vita Constantini* IV, 38 (*GCS* 7, p. 132).

13. *Adversus Judaeos* V, 11 (*PG* 48, *c*. 900); *de S. Babyla* 22 (*PG* 50, *c*. 568).

14. Rufinus, *Historia ecclesiastica* X, 38 (*GCS* 9, p. 997).

15. See below, p. 201.

16. Sozomen, *Historia ecclesiastica* V, 22 (*PG* 67, *c*. 1284).

17. Socrates, *Historia ecclesiastica* III, 20 (ed. Bright, pp. 160–2); Theodoret, *Historia ecclesiastica* III, 20 (*GCS* 19, p. 198); *CSCO(SS)* III, iv, Chron. ad a. 846, ed. Chabot, p. 153.

18. H. Levi, *Zion*, 6, pp. 15ff.

19. Ammianus Marcellinus 23, 1 (ed. Eyssenhardt, Berlin, 1871).

20. Mark 13, 2.

21. *Vita Constantini* III, 30–2, 52–3 (*GCS* 7, pp. 91–3, 99–101).

22. *Oratio* V *contra Julianum* 4 (*GCS* 35, *c*. 668); cf. J. Bidez, *Oeuvres de l'empereur Julien; lettres*, Paris, 1922, p. 129.

23. G. Allon has tried to interpret this text thus: 'to restore the usages of the fathers'; however, as the Jews of Palestine—and indeed of the whole empire—enjoyed at that time full religious liberty, this would amount to a 'restoration' of something they already possessed.

24. Ephraem (trsl. A. Rücker, *Bibliothek der Kirchenväter*, 20, 1919, I, p. 218).

25. Cf. n. 22.

26. Cf. n. 14.

27. Chrysostom, *Adversus Judaeos* V, 11 (*PG* 48, *c*. 901); Gregor. Nazianz. *Oratio* V, 4 (*PG* 35, *c*. 668); Philostorgius VII, 9 (*GCS* 21, p. 95f.); Sozomen V, 22 (*PG* 67, *c*. 1284).

28. See note 21.

29. For Mamre see Eusebius, *Vita Constantini* 52–3 (*GCS* 7, pp. 91–3, 99–101).

30. Philostorgius VII, 9 (*GCS* 21, p. 95).

31. W. Ensslin, *Klio*, 18 (1923), pp. 104–9.

32. E. Jerg (*Vir Venerabilis*, Wien, 1970, pp. 130–8) has recently discussed this problem. His conclusion is opposed to a grant of the rank of *praefectus praetorio* to the patriarch by Julian, because (a) ecclesiastical dignitaries were not thus honoured, (b) the task was not hereditary, (c) the titles 'illustris' and 'spectabilis' mentioned in this connection in *CTh* XVI, 8, 22 were not used in the time of Julian. The author suggests that the rank of 'illustris' etc. was granted *ad personam* to the patriarchs Judah IV by Theodosius I, and to Gamliel VI by Theodosius II, who later on deprived him of it. In this connection we may point out (a) the patriarch was honoured as a national, not a religious leader (so also Jerg p. 132); (b) the appointment might well be *ad personam* for every patriarch from Hillel II onwards; (c) the titles were attached to the grant when the civil *praefecti praetorio* were thus honoured. If the patriarchs were individually honoured by Theodosius I and II, the custom must have gone back before the time of the two Theodosii. It is true that both tried to protect the patriarch as part of the social establishment of their time, but to assume that they would take the initiative in according him a signal honour is to fly in the face of all we know of these emperors and their basic anti-Judaism. We maintain therefore that the grant—under whatever title—was first made by Julian and was repeated by later emperors as a routine matter till Theodosius II put an end to this usage.

33. Philostorgius VII, 9a (*GCS* 21, pp. 95–6).

34. *Ep.* 10 (Bidez, p. 12f.).

35. Ammianus Marcellinus XXII, 1, 2.

36. Socrates III, 14 (p. 154).

37. Voigt (op. cit., note 6 above) p. 60.

38. j *Maaser Sheni* 5, 2–56a.

39. j *Taanit* 2, 1–65a.

40. j *Berakot* 2, 3–4d.

41. *Shoher Tob* 18, 36.

42. See above, p. 190.

43. Ambrose, *Epistola* XL, 15 (*PL*, 16, *c.* 1154).

44. Sozomen V, 22 (*PG* 67, *c.* 1284); see also below, p. 225.

45. Socrates III, 20 (p. 161); Sozomen V, 22 (*PG* 67, *c.* 1284); Theodoret III, 20 (*GCS* 19, p. 199).

46. Artemii Passio (Philostorgius VII, 9a *GCS* 21, p. 96); Theodoret III, 20 (*GCS* 19, p. 199).

47. *Ep.* 204 (Bidez-Cumont) op. cit., note 3 above.

48. Sozomen V, 22 (*PG* 67, *c.* 1285).

49. *Ep.* 25; cf. M. Heck, *Yabneh*, 2, 118–39; H. Levi, *Zion* 6, pp. 2ff.; esp. 27–9; Ensslin, *Klio*, 18, pp. 119, 189f.

50. Socrates III, 20 ed. Bright p. 161 notes that immediately after ordering the restoration of the Temple Julian left for the Persian war

(καὶ αὐτὸς ἐπὶ Πέρσας ἤλαυνε); only then he resumes the story of the building activities. See also Seeck, *Regesten*, p. 212.

51. Joh. Lydus, *De Mensibus* IV, 53 (ed. Wünsch, p. 110); Ep. 134, p. 197 (Bidez).

52. The apparent contradiction with Ep. 89 (Bidez, p. 163) addressed to Theodorus (cf. Ricciotti, p. 284) has been explained by Levi, op. cit.

53. Sozomen V, 22 (*PG* 67, *c.* 1285); Theodoret III, 20 (*GCS* 19, p. 199).

54. *Synaxaire ethiopien* (*PO*, I, p. 533). *CSCO(SS)*, III, iv, Chron. ad. a. 724 (ed. Brooks), p. 104. The event is connected with the discovery of the relics of John the Baptist at Sebaste and their translation to Egypt.

55. Ambrose, *Epistola* XL, 12 (*PL* 16, *c.* 1152–3); Philostorgius VII, 9a (*GCS* 21, p. 96); VII, 14 (ibid., pp. 99–100); Theodoret III, 20 (*GCS* 19, pp. 199–200); Socrates III, 20 (ed. Bright, p. 161); Sozomen V, 22 (*PG* 67, *c.* 1285); Zonaras XIII, 12 (ed. Dindorf III, p. 211); Glycas, *Annales* IV (Bonn), p. 470; Theophanes s.a. 5855 (de Boor, p. 52, 10); Michel le Syrien (ed. Chabot), I, pp. 283, 288–9; Agapius de Membidj (*PO* I, p. 418f.).

56. Ammianus Marcellinus XXIII, 1, 2.

57. Rufinus X, 39–40 (*GCS*, 9, p. 997f.).

58. *Oratio* V, 4 (*PG* 35, *c.* 669).

59. *Adversus Judaeos* V, 11 (*PG* 48 *c.* 901); *in Ps. CX*, 5 (*PG* 55, *c.* 285); *de S. Babyla* 22 (*PG* 50, *c.* 568).

60. *Adversus Judaeos* V, 11 (*PG* 48, *c.* 901).

61. See also note 52.

62. Seeck, *Regesten der Kaiser und Päpste*, Stuttgart, 1918/9, p. 212.

63. The news arrived in Alexandria on August 19th, 363 (ibid., p. 213).

H

IX

The Great Assault
on the Jews and Judaism,
363-439

1. *The Division of the Period*

After the death of Julian a Christian general, Jovian, was proclaimed emperor. After him all the emperors belonged to the dominant religion. The Hellenes made one or two attempts to enthrone a pagan emperor, but all these efforts miscarried.

The period to be dealt with in this chapter embraces the years from the death of Julian to the split in Eastern Christendom following the Council of Chalcedon (451). This period can be subdivided into three parts: the first lasted till the accession of Theodosius I (363–383). This was a period of a truce between the hostile religions. The popular response to Julian's paganism was still remembered by the rulers. In consequence the Christian emperors followed a policy of prudence as regards non-Christians. In this period, therefore, the situation of the Jews did not change for the worse. The second sub-period includes the time from the accession of Theodosius I to the death of his son Arcadius (383–408). This is a period of an energetic attack on Judaism by the leaders of the church, mainly through pressure on the imperial government. The government ceded here and there, but did not cause serious injury to the Jewish community as a whole or to Jews as individuals. The third sub-period lasted from the accession of Theodosius II till the publication of his third Novella (408–438). During this time the power of the church overcame the scruples of the government, and both turned against the Jews. Their rights, whether as communities or as individuals were seriously curtailed, and the patriarchate was abolished.

2. *The Period of Transition*

The news of the death of Julian provoked in southern Palestine a Christian reaction, which led to the destruction of most of the Jewish communities in the *Darom*.[1] They had already suffered much damage in the earthquake of May (Iyar) 363—the same one which had caused the stoppage of the rebuilding of the Temple of Jerusalem. In the Syriac chronicle of 724 we read:[2] 'In these days the Lord was angry with the cities . . . of the Jews in the South (*Darom*). And the Lord's anger came forth and began to destroy these cities . . . and their inhabitants . . . in the month of Iyar in the year 674' (Seleucid era = 363). It is clear from this account that the destruction did indeed begin with the earthquake, but did not stop with it; an earthquake does not normally put an end to a settlement. The Jewish villages in the *Darom* had succeeded in escaping the ruin of Judaea which followed the Bar Kokhba war. They continued to exist till the fourth century; but now most of them disappear from history. We may assume that they were affected not only by natural events, but were also attacked by their hostile neighbours, who prevented reconstruction after the earthquake. Rabbi Pinhas ben Hama tells the story of 'an old student, who studied the lore of intercalation for three years and half with his rabbi. He then went and intercalated in Galilee, but he did not have time to do the same in the South, because the times were troubled.'[3] Rabbi Hiyya Rabba explained the verse: 'lest he (Esau) come and slay us all (Gen. 32, 11)—this refers to our brothers in the *Darom*'.[4] Some places such as Engedi, Eshtemoa and Susiya survived, however: witness the recent finds of synagogue remains there, continuing into the Arab period.

But Christian vengeance did not go any further. Jovian died very soon, on the 17th February 364. He was replaced by Valentinian, who made his brother Valens co-ruler and appointed him emperor of the East. Valens was an Arian, a sect once favoured by Constantius II. However since the times of that emperor the situation had changed radically. In the time of Constantius the Arians could hope to become dominant; accordingly they took towards the Jews the attitude of a church triumphant. In the days of Valens it had become clear that the Arians were a minority and destined to remain such; they felt themselves accordingly isolated. The emperor was struggling hard with an orthodox majority, which did not hesitate to call the Arians 'Jews'.[5] He was forced to send several bishops into exile; among them were Egyptians who to their disgust found themselves in Sepphoris, a purely Jewish city. Valens was not interested, therefore, in adding to the number of his enemies, and hence treated the Jews and pagans with relative tolerance. The only law touching Jewish affairs which was promulgated during his reign forbade the billeting of soldiers in syna-gogues.[6] From Syriac sources[7] we learn that in 378 the emperor gave the Hellenes and the Jews in Antioch permission to continue their worship without interference. In a law of 397[8] we find a reference to an earlier law of Valens by which Jewish religious functionaries were freed from the obligation to serve in the *curiae*, confirming an earlier edict of Constantine of 321. On the other hand, the special laws of Julian favouring the Jews were abolished after his death.

3. *The Rise of Theodosius I, the Orthodox Emperor*

After Valens had lost the battle and his life at Adrianople, fighting the Goths (379), the Spaniard Theodosius I became emperor. He was a zealous Christian and firm in his orthodox beliefs. He was influenced much more than his predecessors by the leaders of the church, although even he sometimes showed some reluctance to fulfil all their wishes. In his time, and that of his sons Honorius, emperor of the West (395–423) and Arcadius, emperor of the East (395–408), the forces which in the end led to the abolition of the civil rights of the Jews gained the upper hand.

This movement began within the church. Till the fourth century the ecclesiastical organization as a whole was based on the bishops and the priests who were in charge of the cities and villages. This organization was mainly intended to protect the Christian communities from the pressure of hostile pagan governments. The bishops, priests and their assistants were only a small organizational nucleus within the mass of believers. Now a new force was added to the church, composed of people who devoted all their energy to the furtherance of its aims—the monks.

Already at the end of the third century many zealous Christians had left the cities and went to live as hermits in the desert. Monasticism began in Egypt and spread from there to the other countries of the East. By their isolation and their asceticism the early monks aroused the admiration of the other Christians. At that time the forces of rationalism were on the decline, and those of emotion, in particular religious emotion, were in the ascendant. Religion was based on mysticism and visions; asceticism and bodily suffering became one of the main keys to heaven. The lives of the first *anachoretai* were in agreement with the spirit of the times. They were honoured by the masses and the rulers alike.

In the fourth century there occurred a radical change in the character of the Christian monasticism. The earliest monks lived isolated in the desert far from the abodes of men. Now their pupils formed large groups, which developed into the earliest monastic orders. Their numbers grew apace. Joining the monastic organization carried with it freedom from civic duties, from taxes and from military service. The monks now returned to the cities and became a great and active force, always at the beck and call of the leaders of the church.

The church acquired in the monks an excellent instrument of warfare against both Hellenism and Judaism; for they had no other occupation besides their religious activities.

The first aim of the monks was the conversion of non-Christians. The pagan reaction in the days of Julian had shown that there were still big reserves of power among the believers in the old gods. The foremost duty of the militants of the church was hence to prevent a repetition of the relapse into paganism. In this they were completely successful. From the fifth century onwards Hellenism disappears as a historical factor of importance. Only a few communities (and the Jews as the foremost of these) were still outside the Christian world and remained deaf to its message. The original plan of action of the church authorities (as explained in chapter VI above) was now put into action against them. They were firstly to be isolated within the Christian society, then humiliated, and, if possible, finally eliminated entirely.

At the same time there was a period of peace within the church. After the accession of Theodosius I Arianism began to decline rapidly. For the time being no other dogmatic differences disturbed the ecclesiastical peace. The bishops and the monks did not therefore turn their energy to disputes within the Christian fold, but could use it against those outside the church.

Their main lever of action, used both by the ordinary clergy and the monastic orders, was a constant pressure on the imperial authorities. The great church leaders, who lived at the imperial court and who met the emperors frequently, tried to influence them by preaching and indoctrination, to awaken their 'Christian conscience'. The minor bishops acted on the provincial administrators; and the monks, as well as some of the bishops, tried to rouse the rabble against individuals or institutions which they regarded as hostile to the 'true religion'.

The division of the empire into an Eastern and Western part became permanent after 395.[9] This division was in general to the advantage of the church. If the government in the East proved obdurate to its demands, it could apply to that of the West, and vice versa. Between the two, there was always one which was the weaker, and therefore readier to compromise. If one of the two tried to carry out some decision in favour of the Jews, the other could be appealed to. With bitter irony Rabbi Judah the son of Rabbi Simeon remarked:[10] 'Lord of the Universe, when you decided to condemn the world, you delivered it to two rulers, Romus and Romillus (the rulers of the East and West, the names remind us of Romulus and Remus)—if one of them intended to do something, the other one prevented him'. A law passed by one of the two was binding in the other half of the empire, if not annulled explicitly by the second authority. As the Western empire contained smaller Jewish communities, we see that most of the anti-Jewish legislation was first passed in the West, and only later on applied in the East in general, and in Palestine in particular.

The disasters which befell the empire from the beginning of the fifth century onwards, only served to strengthen the hands of the church. These were the invasions of the Germans and the Huns, and the epidemics, disasters which in the end caused the downfall of the Western empire. The Christian preachers explained them as signs of the wrath of God, directed against the authorities who still favoured the unbelievers. With the decline in the status of the rulers and the rise of the authority of the church, this pressure increased steadily. The forces which acted at that time against the Jews were of a permanent nature, and were growing in strength all the time; whereas those which favoured them were only intermittent, and grew weaker all the time. It was clear, therefore, what the final outcome would be.

The emperors intended on the whole to keep public order and to prevent injustice, to defend those who were injured and to punish the disturbers of the public peace. The equitable justice of the early Roman law was as yet not quite forgotten. However the actions of the authorities against the pressures of the church were limited in scope and temporary in nature. Repeated orders on paper proved powerless against the force of the mob. Moreover, such orders were limited to a particular case and a particular place. Even if effective on one occasion, they could not prevent a renewal of disorders after a short interval in another form and another locality. The imperial edicts had therefore only a very limited effect.

A typical case occurred in 388.[11] The bishop of Callinicum on the Euphrates instigated the local mob to burn down a synagogue. The governor of the province did not dare to punish the guilty, but appealed to the emperor Theodosius. The emperor censured the governor and ordered the bishop to set up a new synagogue. But Ambrose, the bishop of Milan and one of the great leaders of the church in his generation, intervened. By menacing the emperor with the fires of hell and by using the full force of his spiritual authority—to the point of refusing him entry into his cathedral—Ambrose forced Theodosius to annul his orders. This happened to Theodosius I, who was one of the strongest emperors of the Late Empire. In the time of his son Arcadius, some of the court officials were inclined to Hellenism, and the emperor himself hesitated whether to prosecute good tax-payers who happened not to be Christians.[12] His son, Theodosius II, was completely dominated by his elder sister Pulcheria, a bigoted church-woman. In the reign of this emperor most of the anti-Jewish legislation was promulgated.

The only people who were interested in exercising counter-pressure were the Jews. Their power was, however, very limited when compared to the enormous resources and the power of their opponents. They were therefore trying as far as possible to gain time, to obtain anew confirmation of old privileges, to protect the main point and to give way on minor ones. They were handicapped not only by their isolation within the empire, but by unfavourable external circumstances. The relations between the Roman emperors and the kings of Persia were unusually peaceful in the first half of the fifth century. The Persian ruler Yezdegerd even agreed to serve as guardian of the emperor Theodosius II while he was a minor, and in fact refrained from anything which might injure his ward. The Jews had therefore no hope of any succour from beyond the Euphrates. The factors which in former times had motivated the emperors to agree to a compromise, and to let the Jews live their own life, lost their validity one after the other.[13] The spirit of the times, the sympathy of the rulers, the support of the 'god-fearing', the number of the Jews, their wealth, their relations with the outside—all these were now ineffective or non-existent. Nothing remained to the Jews but their own strength. The pressure exercised on them was indeed tremendous; but even the greatest and most powerful state cannot entirely subdue the will of a determined nation, short of physical extermination. For all its weaknesses, fifth-century Jewry still represented a real power. On this point it differed from the dying paganism. Owing to this hidden strength the Jews succeeded in fending off the forces which now mounted one attack after another on them.

4. *The New Legislation concerning the Jews*

The play of the forces and the counter-forces described above caused the legislators of that period to waver continuously. In the decade 383–392 only laws limiting Jewish rights were passed. This was the result of the accession of the orthodox emperor Theodosius I. Theodosius was nevertheless strong enough to resist the more extreme demands of the church. From 392 to 395 he issued several laws protecting the Jews. After his death the same line was followed for two years (till 397). Then began a fresh struggle. From 398 to 404 contradictory laws were promulgated, but in 404 the anti-Jewish policy was victorious. Except for four laws (of the years 412, 420 and 423) all the legislation of these years (17 laws in all) was intended to limit Jewish rights. But if we look at the legislation of these years as a whole, we shall note a common general line despite all the oscillations. This line followed the policy proclaimed by the ecclesiastical authorities: the Jews were to be isolated, their growth was to be stunted, their status lowered, and they should be pulverized by the suppression first of their central and then their local authorities.

The Jews did not resist all the stages of this legislation with equal force. Their isolation within a Christian society was favoured by their own leaders. For a long time these had tried to keep their flock from contact with external influences. After the destruction of its state, Judaism had secluded itself within the ancient world, even before it was cut off by the Christian authorities. Hence the Jews accepted without a murmur the law forbidding mixed marriages, which repeated in more general terms that of 339.[14] From 388 onwards the emperors did not have to promulgate another edict on this matter. Another law, of 393, forbade polygamy among the Jews.[15] This was indeed an innovation and an interference in their internal matters. The law in itself only confirmed a situation already existing within the community and was therefore not challenged.

The second aim of the church leadership was to reduce as far as possible the number of Jews, and to prevent the spreading of the Jewish faith. For this purpose they proposed laws which protected converts from Judaism to Christianity and bestowed special privileges on them. Other laws renewed the prohibition of proselytism, the holding of Christian slaves by Jews and the purchase of non-Jewish slaves in general. From the Jewish point of view the laws protecting the converts were of no particular importance. The Jewish leaders certainly did not approve mob attacks on the persons of the converts or on their property. In any case the number of such cases was probably not very large. The Jews as a whole held fast to their religion, despite all pressures and temptations whether by the church or the government. The attacks on converts seem to have ceased at that time, because the laws protecting them were not re-enacted, as was normally the case of legislation which was often infringed. In the end the Christian emperors themselves had to deprive the converts of the right to seek asylum in churches. Too many of them seem to have been touched with grace only in order to escape the attention of the fiscal officials or their private creditors.[16] In 429 a law was promulgated in which all restrictions on the right to inherit, contained in the testaments of Jewish parents against converted children were declared null and void. The converts were entitled to inherit with the other children against the express will of the testator. Their rights were protected even if they had committed an offence against the parents; they inherited nevertheless the part allotted to them according to Roman law, any legal disinheritance being set aside.[17]

We have already seen[18] that at the time when a *modus vivendi* was established between the Roman government and the Jews, the Jewish leaders refused in practice to accept one of the points of the compromise, that concerning the prohibition of proselytism; although a concession on this point could be counterbalanced by many important advantages in other matters. All the more so, the Jews could now refuse with good conscience to obey the orders of a hostile government on this point, which was vital to them. Proselytism was continued as long as there were Gentiles ready to embrace the religion of Israel. In the period we are discussing certain Christian circles were still inclined towards Judaism. For this we have the evidence of John Chrysostom from fourth-century Antioch. In the first quarter of the fifth century Jerome still speaks of Palestinian Christians who were 'inclined to Judaism' (*judaizantes*).[19]

While the Christian legislator was attempting to punish the converter of proselytes, he also diminished the civil rights of the proselyte. In 383 their right to leave a testament or to inherit was abolished; in 391 they were forbidden to appear before the courts.[20] The laws against proselytism were severe enough already under pagan emperors. The new edicts only repeated the ancient ones; it is certain of course that they were now applied with much more energy. In 423 the mere circumcision of a Christian was punished by confiscation of property and perpetual exile, exactly as in the days of Severus.[21]

The *Novella* of 31st January 438 published in the name of Theodosius II, sums up the whole of the legislation against proselytism. It forbids any act of proselytism under pain of death, the prohibition applying to males and females in equal degree (till then only the proselytising of men was punishable, and that of women only by way of marriage, as stated in a law of Constantius II). This law, however, only applied to the conversion of Christians to Judaism.[22]

The danger of proselytism was the greatest in the case of slaves who belonged to Jews. In this matter the Jews consistently refused to accept the imperial edicts, for the prohibition to hold slaves endangered their economic position. This law was therefore frequently infringed and was accordingly re-enacted in 384 (when the purchase and conversion of Christian slaves by Jews were forbidden). In 417 the acquisition of slaves was again prohibited, but the Jews were now allowed to acquire and to hold slaves in other ways than by purchase (for example by testament or gift), on condition that they did not try to change their religious beliefs.[23] The purchase and holding of non-Christian and *a fortiori* of Jewish slaves was allowed. In this point the edict of Constantius II which had been annulled by Julian, was not re-enacted. In 423 this law was again promulgated without any change.[24] The energetic opposition of the Jews to any limitation of their right to hold Gentile slaves apparently produced some effect. The many legislative acts in this matter, and their different rulings prove by themselves that they met with much resistance.

The next chapter in the anti-Jewish legislation concerned the diminution of their civil rights. Even should they succeed to multiply or to keep their number intact, it was intended that they should live in a state of perpetual abasement, as citizens of the second class. Their right to hold public (state) offices was affected, as well as the right (or rather the duty) to sit on city councils *curiae* (*boulai*). The first was a genuine privilege, even if there were probably few Jews serving in the army or in the civil establishment. On the other hand the imperial treasury was very much interested in having the Jews sit on the city councils. In this way they became responsible for the payment of taxes together with the Gentiles. As long as reasons of state were predominant, the Jews were kept in the *boulai*. Later on, with the increase in power of the ecclesiastical elements, a series of laws was promulgated with the aim of removing them from this public service together with others.

At first matters on this point took a twisting course. In 383, a short time after the fall of Valens, Theodosius annulled the law freeing 'Jewish men of religion' (i.e. the rabbis) from the obligatory participation in the *curiae*.[25] However in 397 the emperor again freed the '*archisynagogoi*, the patriarchs (provincial), the elders and all those taking part in religious services and who are subject to the illustrious patriarchs'. This law was issued on the 1st July 397; but already on the 30th September 398 it was annulled as regards the Western empire.[26] Between 398 and 438 the legal situation did not change. In the general anti-Jewish law of Theodosius II all privileges of non-Christians were abolished summarily.[27]

While the 'rights' of the Jews to share the burdens of the *curia* was disputed between the ecclesiastical and the fiscal authorities, both were agreed that non-Christians should be evicted from all public offices. Between 404 and 438 the Jews were gradually forbidden to hold the offices of the *agentes in rebus* (a kind of secret service), to act as representatives of the cities (*defensores civitatis*), to serve in the army and the bar; finally they were evicted from every public office which they were not expressly allowed to hold.[28]

As far as the Jews were concerned, these laws were of symbolical rather than practical importance. They resulted from the vision of churchmen of a purely 'Christian state'. Basically this idea was not different from that held by the Jewish leaders in the time of Ezra and Nehemiah. In the liberal period of the Roman empire Jewry separated itself of its own will from the rest. At that time the military camps and the state and municipal offices were open to the Jews. The right not to serve in the army was then regarded by them as a valuable privilege. Hence they accepted without protest the new laws, which undermined their civil status as it is understood today. There was no need to re-enact them for a long time. In any case not many Jews served in the military or civil offices under the Theodosian dynasty. The few who tried to enter the imperial service were not regarded favourably by the Jewish leaders.

When the first anti-Jewish laws were passed in the time of Constantine, all Jewry was seized with trepidation. Many began to despair; some were ready to abandon Judaism, while others decided on armed resistance. Now a much cooler view was taken. The Christian state did but little to endanger the material existence of the Jews. The original laws concerning the holding of non-Jewish slaves, and their subsequent mitigation, show that when an economically vital matter was concerned Jewish opposition to persecuting decrees could still count on a measure of success. The state did not interfere in any other economic matter. The freedom to trade was not infringed, and most economic life went on as before. Jews could still own land and work it. Even within the framework of the new laws the ordinary Jew could still hope to earn a living. However the ecclesiastical leaders, who had instigated the anti-Jewish legislation, were of course not satisfied with this state of affairs. In accordance with their basic policy they took the next step, and attacked Judaism as such.

The assault on Judaism, to be distinguished from that on individual Jews, developed in two directions. This was in conformity with the two forms in which the life of the nation expressed itself. One was an attack on the local Jewish communities, which were concentrated around their synagogues. The other was directed against the patriarchate as the central institution of Judaism. The aim of the double assault was therefore to limit, or if possible, to abolish the autonomy of the Jewish communities, their jurisdiction and their religious worship, and to abolish the patriarchate, the keystone of the national organization, representing national unity after the destruction of the Jewish state.

The legal change as regards the communal autonomy occurred in 415. Till then the Roman government followed the traditional line of supporting the Jewish self-governing communities. In 392, while promulgating laws against the Jews in the matters of mixed marriages and proselytism, the emperors were still defending the Jewish courts instituted by the patriarch. They discouraged for instance appeals to the civic courts against excommunications pronounced by these courts. In 396 all intervention by strangers in Jewish markets which aimed at interference with the free movement of prices was forbidden.[29] In 397 the community officials, who were under the authority of the patriarch, were freed from the *curiae*. If the patriarch dismissed them, they would lose the privilege; in this way the power and authority of the patriarch were much enhanced by the Roman government.[30] In 398 a law was made which seemed *prima facie* to subject the Jews to the authority of the Roman courts and their laws. In fact it left a loophole, in that it authorized the Jews to have recourse to courts of arbitration in civil matters. The rabbinical courts continued to act in the guise of arbitrators and the civil courts were instructed to carry out their decisions.[31] In 412 the right of Jews not to appear before the civil courts on Sabbaths and Jewish holidays was confirmed.[32] It seems that many Christians had great confidence in the uprightness of the rabbinical courts. They asked such courts to judge their cases, especially if the defendant was a Jew. In 415 this practice was forbidden. All cases between Christians and Jews were henceforward to be tried by the ordinary civil courts.[33] This was the first real infringement of Jewish judicial autonomy.

The synagogues were the main field of dispute between the church and the Jews. From 388 there begins a period of concentrated mob attacks on Jewish places of worship, usually instigated by zealous Christian preachers. At first the government reacted with vigour. The Christian leaders were ordered to restore the buildings at their own expense. The attacks did not however cease. Ten separate edicts had to be published in the years 393–426 which were intended to protect the synagogues and the right of the Jews to pray in them. The unceasing efforts of the ecclesiastical leaders, however, in the end wore down government resistance.

On the 29th September 393 a most energetic order was published by the emperors,[34] directed against all those who would destroy or damage a synagogue under the pretence of furthering Christian faith. The government reaffirmed its position that 'it was well known that the Jewish sect is not forbidden by law'. Within four years another order had to be reissued, directed to the provincial governors (17th June 397). They were ordered to take care that synagogues should not be molested.[35]

After the death of Arcadius the spirit of this legislation changed. The first law passed by Theodosius II on this subject (29th May 408) was directed against the Purim festivities, which were alleged to include matters offensive to Christianity.[36] Save for such insults to the dominant faith, the Jews were, however, allowed to continue with their ritual as before. In the same year (24th November 408) the government of the Western empire published a law protecting the African church from offences committed by the Donatist sectarians and Jews.[37]

In the meantime the destruction of synagogues continued. In 414 the famous and splendid synagogue of Alexandria was destroyed, in 419 that of Magina. On the 6th August 420 a new edict was issued,[38] announcing that no innocent Jew was to be molested, and that their synagogues and (private) houses were to be safe from fire and other groundless damage. Even if a Jew was found committing an offence, he should be handed over to the public authorities, and no one should be allowed to lynch him. At the same time the legislation also warned the Jews to refrain from insolence and from insults to the Christian faith, and to trust that the law would protect them. In practice, therefore, this law marks a serious change for the worse in the status of the Jews. We learn from it that Jews were being attacked, and that not only their synagogues but also their private houses were no longer safe. The instigators of these acts used the pretext that the

Jews were offending the Christian faith. The legislation pretended to blame the excesses of the mob, but actually he gave them licence to carry on, while pretending to be impartial.

Three more years passed, and the situation did not improve. In 423 no less than three laws were passed on this subject.[39] It seems that the Christians now used a simple and effective expedient to prevent the rebuilding of a ruined synagogue. They dedicated it on the spot as a church. The Christian legislators were now in a quandary. The act was clearly illegal, but its result was the creation of a consecrated building, an act which could not be undone under ecclesiastical law. A compromise solution was found in the end: the general prohibition on depriving the Jews of their places of worship was repeated, and no one was to be allowed to burn them. However, if they had been already consecrated as churches, the Jews were to receive another piece of ground of the same size or value as their original property. At the same time the emperor forbade the construction of new synagogues, and ordered that no changes should be made in those already existing. In fact this law gave the mobs both legal justification and what amounted to a reward for their illegal acts. When the Jews asked for this evil law to be repealed, the emperor replied on the 9th April 423, reaffirming it and adding insult to injury. 'It is our duty' so we read in his reply 'to diminish the power and the impudence of the abominable Hellenes, Jews and heretics. Therefore we inform the Jews, that we do not agree to fulfil their offensive requests, but order only . . that in future they should not be persecuted and that their synagogues shall not be seized and burnt.' The prohibition of building new synagogues was maintained. Everything already taken from the Jews was lost for ever.

This invitation to fresh persecutions fell on fertile ground. Two months later the government had to publish a new edict forbidding 'real Christians and those calling themselves thus' from doing violence to Jews and Hellenes who were living peaceably. This time the law was provided with a sanction: the stolen property had to be returned threefold or fourfold. As some governors allowed the mob to do its will, the law menaced them also with the same punishment. In matters of substance, however, the existing laws were maintained: no new synagogues were to be built and the old ones could not be enlarged.

The third *Novella* of Theodosius II (438) summed up all the previous legislation. It laid down definitely that new synagogues were not to be built, and that old ones could be repaired only if they were likely to fall down. Every newly built synagogue was to be turned into a church. Whoever decorated a synagogue which needed no repair was liable to a fine of fifty pounds in gold.[40] The archaeological evidence, however, proves conclusively, that all these prohibitions remained on paper only.

The attack on the patriarchate began about the same time (415) as the attack on the synagogues. As it was connected directly with the history of the Jews in Palestine, we shall deal with it in that context.

5. *The Christians Become the Majority in Palestine*

An important change occurred in Palestine in the period between the death of Julian and the Council of Chalcedon. The majority of the population now became Christian. We have already seen that at the time of the accession of Constantine the adherents of the new religion were still relatively few.[41] The efforts of the first two Christian emperors to change this situation remained largely without effect. This is shown, *inter alia*, by the behaviour of the city masses during the short reign of Julian. The number of Christian communities in Palestine (even if we disregard the question whether they were numerous or not) can be divided chronologically as follows: 9 were founded in the time of the apostles; only one additional community in the second century, 8 in the third century, and even in the fourth century only 18. In the fifth century, however, there was a rapid increase: 58 new communities are now mentioned.[42] A comparison of the list of Christian localities given by Eusebius in his *Onomasticon* with the Latin edition of the same work made by Jerome leads to the same result. Eusebius wrote at the beginning of the fourth century, Jerome at the beginning of the fifth. The former mentions only three Christian villages; but the latter adds to his descriptions of the various biblical localities a long list of churches built in them. It is clear that in the meantime a determined effort had been made to give the Holy Land a Christian character. The fanatic monk Bar-Sauma states that even at the time of his arrival in Palestine (in the middle of the fifth century), the number of Christians there and in Phoenicia was small, while that of Jews and Samaritans was very considerable.[43]

The anti-Christian outbreaks in the time of Julian had proved to the leaders of the church that this situation needed to be changed urgently. The monks were called upon to carry out the missionary task. The Christian propaganda started from two centres, both outside Palestine. Monks from Egypt influenced the south-western part of Palestine. Hilarion, a pupil of Antony, the father of the Egyptian monasticism, settled in the vicinity of Gaza. He and his disciples were active in Gaza itself, in Ascalon, Eleutheropolis and the cities of the southern wilderness.[44] Parallel activities went on in the northern and eastern parts of Palestine, starting from Syria. In the time of Theodosius I, John Chrysostom dispatched monks from Antioch to take care that the imperial order closing the pagan temples was duly executed; they could also act as Christian missionaries.[45] In 428 the monk Euthymius founded the first monastery in the Judaean desert, and monasticism became endemic in the country.

Christianity in Palestine derived strength also from another source. Disasters had befallen the western half of the empire in the beginning of the fifth century, such as the German and the Hun invasions. In particular the capture and sack of Rome by Alaric the Goth in 410 caused refugees from Italy and other countries of the West to flee to the Holy Land. Many of these were rich and noble Roman ladies. Under the influence of Jerome they settled in Jerusalem or Bethlehem. The refugees strengthened the Christian element in Palestine with their numbers, their wealth and their social position, all of which influenced the local officials.

While a Christian majority was thus being created in Palestine for the first time in its history, its importance grew in Christian eyes for another reason. It became in fact one of the main suppliers of relics of saints. Already in the time of Julian the alleged remains of John the Baptist and of the prophet Elisha were smuggled out to Egypt. In the fifth century the discovery of such relics and their veneration grew apace. Among such relics were not only those of Christian saints but also of heroes of the Old Testament. Naturally the former Land of Israel enjoyed an almost complete monopoly in this respect. In 395 the bones of Joseph were transferred from Shechem to Constantinople and in 406 those of the prophet Samuel. In 412 the body of the prophet Zechariah was found; this time the relics remained in Palestine and a church was built over the tomb. The same procedure was followed with the prophet Habakkuk. In 415 the relics of the proto-martyr, the deacon Stephen, were found at Kefar Gamala, together, as was confidently believed, with those of Rabban Gamliel, the teacher of Paul, and of his sons. This discovery was made in a most mysterious manner, involving dreams and nighly visions; the news was spread far and wide and made a profound impression on the whole Christian world. When the empress Eudocia returned from her first visit to Jerusalem, she took with her part of the relics of Stephen. Later on she built a splendid church outside the north gate of Jerusalem over the rest. As late as the time of the emperor Leo (457-474), the garments of the Virgin Mary were found in the possession of a Jewish woman at Jerusalem; these too were transported with great pomp to Constantinople.[46] From the material point of view, this growth of interest in such finds profited the country; taxes were reduced and many pilgrims came to visit the holy sites, spending money on their way.

6. *The Jewish Share in the Material Prosperity of the Byzantine Period*

The Jews also profited from the general prosperity. They were, after all, the exclusive holders of traditions regarding the people and localities of the Old Testament. The biblical stories had by then become the common property of the Christian masses, side by side with the Gospels. Christian interest in the identification of the 'holy sites' of the Old Testament was not less than in those of the New. There was, however, a difference. The places mentioned in the Gospels do not number much more than a score; those of the Old Testament are over six hundred. The Jewish guides found therefore plenty of work in taking round parties of Christian pilgrims. Jerome mentions expressly that it was a Jewish guide who showed him the birthplace of Nahum the Elkoshite. The Samaritans too guided the pilgrims in their itineraries.[47]

In the period between the completion of the Palestinian Talmud and the earliest 'Salvation Midrashim' our first-hand information concerning the state of Palestinian Jewry and its spiritual life is much reduced in quantity. We are perforce obliged to use the evidence of patristic literature, fundamentally hostile to Judaism. While using such sources we must of course take into account this general tendency, as well as the ignorance of their authors in Jewish matters. This ignorance was due partly to the general difficulty in understanding an alien religion, and partly to the fact that the Jewish leaders were not interested in disclosing their real aims to strangers. Nevertheless from the Christian writers we may obtain a fairly clear picture of what went on among the Jews of Palestine. The works of Jerome are of prime importance on this point, because he lived in Palestine from 385 to 420, studied Hebrew and commentaries on the Bible with Jewish teachers, and became well acquainted with them, as far as this was possible for a Christian priest who hated everything Jewish.

Jerome states with emphasis that 'the Jews had no right to serve in the army and to carry arms' and that 'they have no judges of their own'.[48] The first part of this statement is true, even if it represented a state of affairs which had continued from the pre-Christian centuries. However, the second part of Jerome's statement did not correspond to reality: Roman law, as we have seen, prohibited Jewish jurisdiction inasmuch as the ordinary courts were concerned, but allowed its existence as courts of arbitration. As such they were recognized by the authorities. There can be no doubt that the Jews continued to take their suits to their own courts, as before.

The number of Jews in Palestine was throughout this time on the decline, but the rate of this decline was apparently not determined by the anti-Jewish legislation. Jerome admits that the Jews were bringing up many children and grand-children 'just like worms'.[49] Chrysostom also observed that the Jews were very numerous in 'Palestine, Phoenicia and every other place'.[50]

The new laws slowed down Jewish activity in trade and agriculture, but they kept up these activities even so. Their wealth and property provoked the greed of the Christian mobs; the laws prove that in most cases the destruction of a synagogue was accompanied by widespread looting. The tendency evident among the Jews to amass wealth was understandable and even vital; for parting with some of their wealth was the only way to gain sympathy from Roman officials. It also made it possible for them to escape when necessary, and to hope for better times. We therefore note at this time the beginning of a social tendency which has continued to our own days in the Diaspora. Against this background we can understand the complaints of Jerome and other writers about the 'materialism' of the Jews and their cupidity.[51] It is of course quite possible that in these difficult times many Jews found some consolation in material pleasures.

7. *The Spiritual Situation of Palestinian Jewry.* *The Messianic Hopes*

In Jerusalem the situation remained unchanged. One of the successors of Julian, perhaps even Jovian, re-enacted the edicts of Constantine concerning the Holy City. As before the Jews were allowed to visit it only on one day in the year, the Ninth of Ab, in order to mourn the destruction of the Temple. Jerome has left a moving account of this procession, in his commentary on Zephaniah 1, 15.[52] With evident relish he describes how the Jews bribed the Roman soldiers to grant them the right to lament, how a whole people came mourning, women feeble with age, old men burdened with many years and so on. The Jews came pale and weeping, their hair disordered and their garments torn and worn out. While they were wailing over the ruins of the Temple and blowing the *shofar*, the Roman soldiers came and demanded more money to allow them to go on mourning. All this went on while golden crosses rose triumphantly above the city from the Anastasis and the Mount of Olives.

We may contrast with this story, which rejoices at distress of others, the pathetic account given by Rabbi Berakhiah.[53] He compared the mournful pilgrimages of his own time with the joyful going-up to Jerusalem on the three festivals of pilgrimage while the Temple was still standing. 'They come silently and they go silently, they come weeping and they go weeping, they come in the darkness of the night and they depart in darkness.'

But even if the Jews were for the time being deprived of their rights in earthly Jerusalem, they did not lose their assurance in a heavenly Jerusalem and a future return to Zion. All our sources are unanimous in stating that the Jewish spirit remained unbroken, in spite of all the troubles which befell them. Chrysostom states that 'that people (the Jews) are strong in their spirit, impudent, warlike, daring and ready for an affray'.[54] The disappointment which they had suffered in the time of Julian, did not end their Messianic hopes. They still believed that there would be a Jewish future, that in the day of the Messiah they would rule other peoples and would return to Jerusalem. Voices were still heard among the Jews: declaring that 'a ruler would arise from the House of Jacob and destroy utterly Constantinople the guilty city and he will besiege and ruin the rebellious metropolis of Caesarea'.[55] This assurance impressed even many Gentiles. Jerome derides 'our Jews and semi-Jews, who are all looking forward to a Jerusalem of gold and precious stones, which shall descend for them from heaven'.[56]

Many writers attest the strength of the Jewish spirit for all the injuries and insults which they had to suffer. Jerome himself confirms that lately the situation of the Christian religion had become parlous in the vicinity of Tiberias, and that many Jews 'persisted in their errors'.[57] Even the Jewish names of that time indicate a spiritual return of the people to their origins. The Greek names disappear in the fifth and sixth centuries and are replaced by Hebrew, mostly biblical, names.[58] Jerome also mentions the fact that many Jewish scholars of great learning were still residing in Palestine,[59] even if the activity of the rabbinical schools had become much reduced after the completion of the Palestinian Talmud.

The hopes of seeing Jerusalem rebuilt with the consent of the Roman authorities did not cease entirely, for all the failure of Julian. In 443 the empress Eudocia came to Jerusalem for the second time, this time for good. With her coming Jewish hopes rose again. Eudocia had once been called Athenais, and grew up as a Hellene in the house of her father, a teacher of Greek at the University of Athens. Only when the emperor Theodosius II chose her to be his empress in 421, did Athenais change her name and become a Christian. She kept, however, her inclination towards Greek culture, wrote poems and composed set pieces in the spirit of Greek rhetoric. In 439 she visited Jerusalem for the first time. In 443 relations between her and her husband had become tense, and she chose to retire and to leave the imperial court for a semi-exile in Jerusalem. It is not quite clear, why the Jews had such high hopes of her. A text of a letter has been preserved, sent purportedly from the 'Priests and heads of Galilee' to the Jewish nation, in which they are told 'the time of our exile has passed, the day has come for the ingathering of our tribes, because the kings of the Romans have decided to give us back Jerusalem. Hurry to go up to Jerusalem for the feast of the Tabernacles, because our kingdom shall rise in Jerusalem again.' This letter is undoubtedly spurious, but it reflects the Jewish feelings at that time. The only practical result of such hopes was that Jews were now allowed to visit Jerusalem (perhaps even to settle there). This permission remained in force even after the anti-Jewish excesses instigated by the monk Bar-Sauma.[60] In 419/22 this monk succeeded in having several synagogues destroyed—in particular a very splendid building at Rabbath-Moab.[61] The riots at Jerusalem so to speak crowned his activities.

8. *The End of the Patriarchate*

For the leaders of the church who intended to humble the Jews, the patriarchate was like 'pricks in their sides and thorns in their eyes' (Numb. 33, 35). They saw in it the institution which served as a link between the Jewish communities dispersed throughout the empire. It was the corner stone of Judaism and so long as it lasted, the latter would only be half destroyed. Once the patriarchate was abolished, the whole of Judaism would fall, for the isolated communities, so they hoped, would be unable to stand up to a united church.

This policy was dictated by religious motives only, without taking any other factor into account. It is characteristic of the spirit of the times that the leaders of the church succeeded in imposing their policy on the civil government, and caused the abolition of the patriarchate. For almost three centuries this institution had served to restrain the Jewish zealots. By following a cautious and prudent policy the patriarchs had succeeded in keeping the Jewish community in Palestine in being, preserving the peace of the country and maintaining more or less normal relations with the Roman government. The great economic crisis of the third century, the revolt against Gallus, and even the exciting times of Julian, did not undermine their position. Now the Roman government itself gave up the political advantage of having an institutionally moderate leadership in order to obtain a doubtful religious advantage.

The prudent policy of the patriarchate in the time of Julian caused its position and influence to emerge unscathed from the failure of his policy, and to remain intact in the period of the 'religious armistice' after his death. From the letters of the pagan rhetor and writer, Libanius of Antioch we learn a good deal about the high honours of the patriarch and his friendly relations with the official world, and the Hellenes in general.[62] These letters were written in the years 388–393 and we may conclude from them that there was a good deal of correspondence between the patriarch and the leaders of the Hellenes. Each party recommended its friends and asked for the good offices of the other. The patriarch was able to communicate with the Greek rhetors as an equal, because he had been educated in the Hellenic culture of his time. His sons were studying at Berytus under a pupil of Libanius, and after that continued their studies under the master himself. The Greek writer, who wrote a most artificial and elaborate prose following the complicated rules of Greek epistolography, addresses the patriarch in this style, apparently because he was sure that his correspondent would understand the most delicate hints. From these letters we may learn about the status of the patriarch as the leader of the Jews of the whole empire. The Jewish communities of Syria appealed to him when in distress, and he intervened on their behalf with the high officials of that province, including Libanius himself. The patriarch appointed each year in consultation with the Sanhedrin, the archons (rulers) of the Jewish communities (probably what is meant by that were the 'little patriarchs', the heads of the Jews in each province). If the Jewish communities did not like the appointees, they addressed themselves to prominent Gentiles of their provinces and asked them to intervene with the patriarch. It was most important to ensure that the patriarch should recognize the officials of the communities, because, as we have seen, by the law of 397 only those who were recognized as 'under the jurisdiction of the patriarch' were free from service in the *curiae*. Moreover, the judgments of the Jewish tribunals (including excommunications) were acted upon by the authorities (according to the law of 392) only if the patriarch recognized such courts as valid.[63]

The goodwill of the patriarch was moreover most valuable for the officials governing Palestine. He could smooth their path, because he was at the head of a considerable part of the population, a part which was always inclined to unrest. The patriarch could also ease the way of young teachers and advocates who tried to make a career in Palestine. Every injury to his status and every insult to his honour was punished heavily by the government. Only he could forgive the offender and obtain a pardon.

Because of a certain delicacy implied in his spiritual attitude, Libanius does not mention another cause for the influence of the patriarch—his wealth. With the re-establishment of political and economic order under Diocletian and the dynasty of Constantine, the material position of the patriarchate was greatly improved. His messengers again went out to the communities of the Diaspora—they are mentioned in the story told by the *comes* Joseph to Epiphanius. Jerome, who wrote almost 80 years later, also states that 'the emissaries (of the patriarch) are being sent to this day to the provinces'.[64] After Theodosius I the western half of the empire did indeed suffer much from the German invasion; but the eastern half was relatively quiet and prosperous. As it happened, most of the Jewish communities of the empire were in the Orient. In Egypt and in the other oriental provinces economic conditions improved definitely in the fourth century. The Jews must have also profited from this new wave of prosperity, and part of their wealth was certainly contributed to the patriarch through his emissaries. The Jewish leaders were naturally interested in amassing reserves with which to counter possible attacks on their people and on their own authority.

The funds which were flowing from all parts of the Diaspora to Palestine caused a rift between the governments of the eastern and western halves of the Roman empire. In 399 Stilicho, who ruled the West in the name of the emperor Honorius, quarrelled with Eutropius, who ruled the East, this time in the name of Arcadius. Among other acts, intended to needle their eastern colleagues, the western rulers forbade the collection and transmission of money destined for the patriarch, who resided in the East. When the two governments had made up their disputes, the prohibition was repealed in 404.[65] The whole matter was superficially unimportant, but it was a signal for the coming intervention of the government in the inner affairs of the patriarchate.

The church leaders did not neglect any opportunity to remind the emperors of the 'treasures' of the patriarch and to appeal to their greed. John Chrysostom calls the patriarchs 'merchants' and 'traders'; Jerome also refers to their wealth.[66] At first the authorities defended the honour of the patriarchs from such attacks from outside, just as they protected it from attacks by dissatisfied Jews. In 396 an edict was published threatening 'all those who dared to insult in public the illustrious patriarchs'.[67] In 404 the privileges of the patriarchs were confirmed again, for the last time.[68] The emperors were in fact at that time still protecting the patriarchs against official intrigues. When a serious quarrel arose between the governor of Palestine, Hesychius, and the partriarch Gamliel VI, the governor tried to implicate his opponent in a trial involving real or imaginary conspirators against Theodosius I. He bribed the secretary of the patriarch to hand over to him the correspondence of Gamliel. The intrigue failed; when the patriarch complained directly to the emperor, Hesychius was condemned and executed.[69]

In the end, however, the influence of the enemies of the patriarch proved too strong. The patriarch was accused, as we learn already from Chrysostom, of infringing the anti-Jewish laws. In 415 Theodosius published a severe reprimand,[70] in which the patriarch was accused of building new synagogues, causing Christian slaves to be circumcised and judging in cases between Christians. The patriarch is represented as an official with certain legal powers, who had overstepped the bounds of his lawful authority. It should be noted that most of the laws which the patriarch was supposed to have infringed were part of the most recent anti-Jewish legislation. These laws were in direct conflict with the aspirations of the patriarch as head of the Jewish community. No compromise, however subtle, could bridge over such basic conflicts. The patriarch was accused of transgressing that part of the new laws which was totally unacceptable to the Jews: the prohibition of proselytism, of the building of new synagogues and of their autonomous jurisdiction. Matters between the patriarch and the government now came into the open.

As the patriarch was still relatively powerful, the formulas used in the reprimand indicate a reluctance of the government to push matters to extremes. The emperor deprived Gamliel of his honours as *praefectus praetorio* and degraded him from the rank of *illustris* to the next one, *spectabilis*.[71] He moreover ordered all Christian slaves to be freed, as prescribed by the law of Constantine; and all new synagogues to be destroyed, but only in deserted localities, and on condition that this could be done without tumult. In the end Theodosius warns the patriarch that he will be punished with the full force of the law, should he dare to circumcise a non-Jew. Punishment for acts in the past is not mentioned in the decree.

In any case the patriarchate of the House of Hillel came to an end before many years had passed. In a law of 429 mention is made of the 'end of the patriarchs' (*excessus patriarcharum*).[72] The emperor seems simply to have refused to approve a successor after the death of Gamliel VI. Obviously there must have been descendants of the Hillelite dynasty still living and available at that time, even if Gamliel VI lacked sons. The Hillelite dynasty, which had lasted for five centuries, came to an end in the direct line, and with it the patriarchate itself.

The Roman authorities used this occasion to split the Jewish authority in Palestine. In the law referred to, dated 429, mention is made of 'the heads of the Jews who are appointed by the *synedria* (in the plural!) of the two Palestines, or who function in the other provinces'. In Palestine the right to appoint the community officials passed to the two *synedria*, each functioning in its own province. Palestine was in 429 divided into three provinces: *Palaestina prima*, which included Judaea and Samaria, the coastal plain and the Peraea east of the Jordan; *Palaestina secunda*, which included Galilee and the former Decapolis; and *Palaestina salutaris*, or *tertia*, which included the Negev and southern Trans-Jordan. As there were hardly any Jews living in the third province, reference is made to the *synedria* of only two.

The intention is obvious, to split up the Jewish community by dividing its authorities. In this way the traditional differences between Caesarea (in *Palaestina prima*) and Tiberias (in the *secunda*) could be exploited for the benefit of the Roman government. The plan miscarried, for Tiberias remained the centre recognized by Jews in the whole of Palestine. In the Diaspora the disappearance of the central authority had more effect. The Jewish communities became isolated, for the provincial general authorities (the 'little patriarchs') who had depended on the 'great patriarch' at Tiberias, did not have enough authority; they too disappeared. The emperors ordered that the taxes formerly levied for the patriarch should now be diverted to the imperial treasury. This was an additional benefit which they derived from the dissolution of the patriarchate. The *fiscus* profited from this new disaster, as it had profited from the destruction of the Temple.

The religious advantage hoped for by the ecclesiastical leaders after the destruction of the patriarchate did not however materialize. The Jews remained loyal to their religion not less than before, or even more so. The political results were, however, far-reaching. For the time being the Jews of Palestine remained depressed and isolated in their trouble. As soon as there arrived an occasion to act against the Roman government, the authorities felt the absence of the only institution which had been able to restrain the Jewish masses.

Notes to Chapter IX

1. See above, p. 16.
2. Philostorgius, *Suppl.* VII, 38a (*GCS* 21, p. 237); *CSCO(SS)* III, IV, Chron. ad a. 724 (ed. Brooks), p. 104.
3. j *Erubin* 5, 1–22c.
4. *Genesis R* 76, 3.
5. Theodoret, IV, 22, 35 (*GCS* 19, p. 260).
6. *CTh* VII, 8, 2 (6 May 368 or 370 or 373?).
7. Ibid. IV, 24, 2 (*GCS* 19, p. 262); Jacob of Edessa *CSCO(SS)* III, IV, p. 224; *Historia miscellanea* XII (*PL* 95, *c.* 928); Michel le Syrien (ed. Chabot), I, p. 294, VII, 7.
8. *CTh* XVI, 8, 13 (1 July 397).
9. See above, p. 210.
10. *Genesis R* 49, 9.
11. Ambrose, *Epistola* XL (*PL* 16, *c.* 1101ff.).
12. Marcus Diaconus, *Vita Porphyrii*, 41 (ed. H. Gregoire and M. A. Kugener, Paris, 1930, p. 35).
13. See above, pp. 35–9.
14. *CTh* III, 7, 2.
15. *CJC* I, 9, 7 (30 December 393); the law has not been included in the Codex Theodosianus.
16. *CTh* IX, 45, 2 (17 June 397).
17. Ibid. XVI, 8, 28.
18. See above, pp. 81–3.
19. Chrysostom, *Adversus Judaeos* I, 3 (*PG* 48, *c.* 847); Jerome, *In Zachariam* III, xiv, 9 (*PL* 25, *c.* 1529); *In Malachiam* IV, 5–6 (ibid., *c.* 1578); *In Joel* III, 7–8 (ibid. *c.* 982).
20. *CTh* XVI, 7, 3 (21 May 383); XVI, 7, 4 (9 June 391).
21. Ibid. XVI, 8, 26 (9 April 423).
22. *Nov. Theodos.* 3 (31 January 438).
23. *CTh* XVI, 9, 4 (10 April 417).
24. *CTh* XVI, 9, 5 (9 April 423).

25. Ibid. XII, 1, 99 (18 April 383).

26. Ibid. XVI, 8, 13 (1 July 397); XII, 1, 158 (13 September 398).

27. See note 21 above.

28. *CTh* XVI, 8, 16 (22 April 401); XVI, 8, 24 (10 March 418); *Nov. Theod.* 3 (438).

29. *CTh* XVI, 8, 8 (17 April 392); XVI, 8, 10 (28 February 396).

30. Ibid. XVI, 8, 13 (1 July 397).

31. *CTh* II, 1, 10 (3 February 398).

32. Ibid. II, 8, 26 (26 July 412).

33. Ibid. XVI, 8, 22 (20 October 415).

34. Ibid. XVI, 8, 9 (29 September 393).

35. Ibid. XVI, 8, 12 (17 June 397).

36. Ibid. XVI, 8, 18 (29 May 408).

37. Ibid. XVI, 5, 44 (24 November 408).

38. Ibid. XVI, 8, 21 (6 August 420).

39. Ibid. XVI, 8, 25 (15 February 423); XVI, 8, 26 (9 April 423); XVI, 8, 27 (8 June 423).

40. *CJC* I, 9, 18; *Nov. Theodos.* 3 (31 January 438).

41. See above, pp. 138–9.

42. Pieper, *Atlas orbis christiani*, Map 5, p. 24f.

43. Nau, *ROC*, 1913, p. 274.

44. Jerome, *Vita Hilarionis* (*PL* 23, *c.* 29ff.).

45. *CSCO(SS)* III, IV, Jacob of Edessa (ed. Brooks), p. 227.

46. The relics of Joseph: *CSCO(SS)* III, iv, *Chronic.* ad a. 846, p. 159; Samuel—Leo Grammaticus (ed. Bonn), p. 105; Zacharias—*CSCO(SS)* III, iv, *Chron. minor.* p. 160 and the Madaba Map, M. Avi-Yonah, *The Madaba Mosaic Map*, Jerusalem, 1954, p. 68; Stephen, Gamliel etc.— *PL* 41, cols. 807–18; Sacchetti, *Studi Stefaniani*, Beitgemal 1934; *Chron. minor. Syr.* p. 158; Eudocia—*Bullet. corresp. héllenique*, XIII (1889), p. 294f.; Maria's robe—Leo Grammaticus p. 114; Georg. Cedrenus (ed. Bonn) I, p. 614; Elisha—Leo Grammaticus, p. 115.

47. Jerome, *Prologus in Naum* (*PL* 25, *c.* 1232); *Synaxaire arabe-jacobite*, ed. Basset (*PO* I, p. 276).

48. *In Isaiam* III, 2 (*PL* 24, col. 59).

49. Ibid. XLVIII, 17 (*PL* 24, *c.* 462).

50. Chrysostom, *Contra Judaeos et Gent.* XVI (*PG* 48, *c.* 835).

51. For example: Jerome, *Prologus in Osee* (*PL* 25, *c.* 820); *In Ezechielem* IV, 13 (ibid., *c.* 49f.).

52. *In Sophoniam* I, 15 (ibid., *c.* 1354).

53. *Lamentations R* 1, 17–19a.

54. See note 50 above.

55. *Targum Jonathan*, Numbers 24, 19.

56. *In Isaiam* XVII (LX, 1 seq.) (*PL* 24, *c.* 587).

57. Ibid. III (*c.* 124).

58. For instance the son of a man called Olympius is named Theodorus (Mattanyah) in a synagogue inscription found at Caesarea: M. Avi-Yonah, *Bulletin Rabinowitz Fund*, 3 (1960), p. 44.

59. The source of this statement is Origen, *Homilia in Jerem.* X (*CSG* 6, p. 74f.); Jerome (VIII, *PL* 25, *c.* 645) translated the text while adding to it and fitting it to the conditions of his time.

60. Nau, *ROC*, 1914, pp. 119–23.

61. Ibid. 1913, p. 383f.

62. M. Schwabe, *Tarbiz*, 1(2), (1929/30), pp. 85–107.

63. *CTh* XVI, 8, 8 (17 April 392).

64 *Commentarium in Epist. ad Galatus* I, 1 (*PL* 26, *c.* 311).

65. *CTh* XVI, 8, 14 (11 April 399); ibid., 8, 17 (25 July 404).

66. Chrysostom, *contra Judaeos et Gent.* XVI (*PG* 48, *c.* 835); *adversus Judaeos* VI (ibid., *c.* 911).

67. *CTh* XVI, 8, 11 (24 April 396).

68. Ibid., XVI, 8, 15 (3 February 404).

69. Jerome, *Epistola* LVII, 3 (*PL* 22, *c.* 570).

70. *CTh* XVI, 8, 22 (20 October 415); see also above pp. 219–20.

71. Ibid.

72. Ibid., XVI, 8, 29 (30 May 429).

X

Division in the Christian Camp:
Two Generations of Peace
and Strengthening for the Jews

The time between the promulgation of the third *Novella* of Theodosius II and the accession of his successor Marcianus (439–451) was a period of deep distress for the Jewry of Palestine. It was a time of pressure from the outside and loss of hope within the community. However with the schism in the church which followed the Council of Chalcedon in 451, matters improved somewhat.

1. *The Division in the Christian Camp*[1]

Centrifugal tendencies are always present in any public body of considerable size; they are still more in evidence in great empires, comprising a multitude of peoples and countries, each of which has interests of its own. These often conflict with each other. In the third century such conflicts weakened the Roman empire with almost fatal effect. They did not cease in the following centuries, even after the emperors had tried to strengthen the empire by a union of Church and State.

In the period under discussion in this chapter the divisive forces appeared in different guise in the West and the East of the Roman world. In the West political power passed to the Germanic tribes—the Goths, Franks, Vandals and so on. These nations conquered the various provinces of the empire, and set up kingdoms of their own. Their inevitable disputes were carried out in the open, by wars of sovereign states. Religious life in the West, however, remained uniform in character. After the fall of the Western empire the church remained the one unifying factor in society; it served as protector of all centripetal forces. Gaul, Spain, Italy and Africa, each of which had a political authority of its own, all submitted to the spiritual authority of the bishop of Rome, the real inheritor of imperial greatness.

In the East the situation was exactly the reverse. The emperors residing at Constantinople succeeded in preserving the unity of the state. They repulsed all attempts of the German barbarian to seize parts of the empire. They also defended the empire successfully in the North against the Slavs and in the East against the Persians. Political unity was thus preserved in the East, but the divisive forces found a free field in the religious sphere.

This religious sectarianism was made possible by the special structure of the Christian faith, composed of many elements of conflicting nature. In the course of its phenomenal rise this disparity benefited the expansion of the church. Every Gentile could find in it something to suit his own views. One of the original elements of this conglomerate was the old oriental belief in a god who takes human shape and comes down to earth to save suffering humanity. Another was the Gnostic belief in the vital importance of magic formulae. Only he who uses the right spell or holds the right belief can hope for salvation. The formula served as a key to heaven, because it was supposed to force the supranatural agencies to obey the human will. The great task was to find the right key or creed. Early Christianity had inherited from Greek philosophy a tendency to refined definitions, not to say hair-splitting. One result of this philosophical heritage were a great many formulae and creeds, which showed only very slight differences in their wording. But it was just these minute changes which assumed immense importance in the eyes of the believers. They were sincerely convinced that these small divergences—often no more than a *iota*—made all the difference between heaven and hell. The precise formulation of creeds was refined still further by the fact that many of the bishops and their advisers had passed through the Roman law-schools, and had learnt to regard an exact formulation of legal material as sacrosanct.

The many differences which arose regarding dogma would, however, have had no political significance, were it not for the terrestrial forces which stood behind them. One of these divisive forces was the sharp competition between the three main patriarchal sees in the East: Constantinople, Antioch and Alexandria; the claims of Rome augmented the conflict. Each of the holders of these great sees tried to enhance its importance, quite apart from personal antagonisms which often existed between the bishops. The pope at Rome relied on his undisputed sway in the West, and on the tradition which made the apostolic leaders of the early church, Peter and Paul, the first heads of the Roman church. He could also appeal to the century-old sentiment in favour of the former imperial capital, which still gave its name to the whole empire. As against these claims the patriarchs of Constantinople demanded the rule of the Eastern church, as befitted the ecclesiastical leaders of the new capital of the empire, a real capital and not a fictive one. Many of the bishops of Alexandria were most forceful personalities, such as Athanasius and Cyril. They were backed by the Egyptian nation which abhorred Byzantine rule. The Egyptian church became soon the exponent of Egyptian nationalism, which expanded also to Syria. Antioch, the capital of the whole diocese of the Orient (which also included Egypt), had its own claims, of course.

When Dioscurus, the bishop of Alexandria and Eutyches, a priest of Constantinople, proclaimed in 449 the complete unity of the two natures of Christ (in Greek *mone physis*, 'one nature'), this attempt to impose the opinions of Alexandria on the Christian world failed. The bishops of Rome and Constantinople allied against Dioscurus. They were supported by the emperor Marcian; at the Council of Chalcedon in 451 a compromise formula was adopted, which proclaimed the unity of Christ 'in two natures'. The Monophysites (those in favour of 'one nature') opposed vigorously the decision taken at Chalcedon, and they found much support in Egypt and Syria.

Juvenal, then bishop of Jerusalem, had at first supported the Monophysites. At Chalcedon he changed his opinion and joined the majority. In recognition of his timely change his see was elevated to the rank of a patriarchate and given primacy among the churches of Palestine and Arabia. The former authority of the see of Antioch over Palestine was abolished. When the new patriarch returned to Jerusalem, he was met by a revolt of the monks and the masses of the people, who had remained faithful to the Monophysite creed. Another priest was enthroned as bishop in Jerusalem. It took Juvenal twenty months (and the intervention of the imperial army, with much bloodshed) to regain his see.

2. The Influence of the Ecclesiastical Divisions on Byzantine Policy

From 451 onwards the division between the 'Orthodox' and the 'Monophysites' becomes a determining factor in the internal politics of the Byzantine empire. Its influence is felt even in foreign policy. Religious policy changed from emperor to emperor. Marcian and Leo (451–474) supported the Chalcedonian decrees. Zeno and Anastasius (474–518) tried to appease the Monophysites. Justin I and Justinian (518–565) veered again in the Orthodox direction.

These variations were to a large extent determined by the general policy of each emperor. There appeared a certain alternation in Byzantine history. In the fifth–sixth centuries, prudent emperors replaced adventurous ones and vice versa. The former tried above all to preserve the *status quo* and to strengthen the inner structure of the state, politically and economically. They followed a cautious policy and amassed great reserves of gold. Their enterprising successors endeavoured to restore the past glories of the Roman empire. They made plans to restore Roman rule in the West. For this purpose they used up the treasures collected by their predecessors and endangered the economic structure of the empire by wars of conquest.

A restoration of the Roman empire in the West obviously required the winning of the goodwill of its population. The peoples of Italy, Gaul, Spain and Africa were under the spiritual leadership of the Roman pope. They therefore supported the decrees of Chalcedon. Moreover a policy of conquest required political calm at Constantinople itself. The people of the capital (and of Asia Minor in general) were also mostly supporters of the orthodox creed of Chalcedon. The energetic emperors therefore supported the decision of the Council of 451, and risked the wrath of the majority of the orientals, who were inclined to the Monophysites. On the other hand the prudent emperors tended to look to the oriental provinces, especially Syria and Egypt, as these were the most prosperous regions of the empire. They hoped by appeasement and by timely concessions to keep the empire intact and to avoid uneconomic disruptions. The revenues of these rich provinces were indeed badly needed to fill their treasuries.

Among the emperors who ruled in this period Leo belonged to the adventurous kind. He attempted to re-take Africa (in 468). The invasions cost enormous sums and led to no results. For thirty years after, the imperial finances were still suffering from that ill-conceived expedition. To fill the treasury again a very cautious policy was needed; this was the line taken by Leo's successor, Zeno the Isaurian. He succeeded in 488 in turning the German tribes westwards from the Balkans. The danger of a German invasion of the Eastern empire which had menaced Constantinople since 379 was thereby banished for ever. Zeno was indifferent to the fate of Italy. The treasury deficit and the frequent revolts in the empire obliged him to take first and foremost care of internal matters. He tried to calm the Monophysites, and advocated a religious compromise in his *Henoticon* (482). The moderate party among the Monophysites accepted the compromise and made its peace with the government. Only a small minority continued to object. The West refused to accept the *Henoticon*, but Zeno did not care for the West.

Anastasius, who succeeded Zeno, followed the same cautious policy. He worked hard to improve the economic position of the empire, and died leaving a treasury surplus of 320,000 pounds of gold.

After Anastasius Justin I mounted the throne (518). His accession marks another change in imperial policy in the direction of 'Orthodoxy' and aggressiveness.

3. *The Influence of the Byzantine Divisions on Palestine Jewry*

The political situation within Palestine was changed entirely by the politico-religious divisions within the Christian camp. The disputes between the Monophysites and their opponents split the Christian majority, which had come into existence in the fifth century. The moderate emperors strove for domestic peace and did not intend to create more difficulties for themselves by a policy of religious persecution. The ecclesiastical leaders were busy with their internal disputes and had no energy left for dealing with the Jews. The monks, who had been the leaders of the attacks upon the synagogues, were restrained by one of the decisions at Chalcedon. According to it they were placed under the strict control of the bishops. Besides they too turned their energy to fighting with their Christian opponents and to resisting the imperial government. As a result of this peculiar constellation the Jews enjoyed one last period of peace before the end of Byzantine rule over Palestine. This relative quiet lasted for 76 years, from the council of Chalcedon to the accession of Justinian (451–527).

It is interesting to compare this period of relative peace with that which prevailed in the second century. As formerly, this time too there was a kind of unwritten compromise between the Jews and the government. Both sides made concessions *de facto*, if not *de jure*. In the second century, however, the policy of appeasement had positive aspects; this time both parties were only refraining from open hostilities. The Byzantine government chose to leave the Jews in peace so as to ensure quiet. The Jews, on the other hand, were quite bewildered; for just at that time their brethren in Babylonia were being persecuted cruelly by Kavad I the king of Persia (488–531). They could not hope to find support in the East against the Byzantines. The compromise was not therefore the result of a change in the spirit of the times; it merely arose out of political calculations. In any case it was short-lived.

From the Byzantine side the striving after peace was expressed mainly in the cessation of new legislation. The existing laws were not repealed, but from the promulgation of the Third *Novella* of Theodosius II in 438 till the resumption of anti-Jewish legislation under Justin and Justinian in 527, no new laws were made on this subject. As before, the government refrained from interfering with Jewish economic activities, and allowed the Jews to make a living as they could. Attacks on synagogues did not cease entirely, but became much rarer; no new edicts were necessary to restrain them.

As an example of this policy of appeasement we may study the attitude of the emperor Anastasius towards the Jews of Jotaba. In the time of Leo, a Persian, named Amorcessus, occupied that island, which dominated the Gulf of Elath (Akaba). He expelled the Byzantine customs-men and began to levy tolls from the ships passing along the gulf. It seems that a community of Jewish merchants was settled there; they also held Makna on the eastern shore of the gulf. The rule of Amorcessus was recognized by the emperor Leo in 474. In 498 Anastasius ordered an assault on the island and occupied it. The Jews residing there were left unmolested, apparently for financial reasons. The autonomous community of Jotaba continued to exist till the time of Justinian (about 535).[2]

4. *The Situation of the Jews in Palestine towards the End of Byzantine Rule*

The Jews had to accept the abolition of the patriarchate, but as they could not exist as a community without a central institution, within a short time they created a substitute. The attempts of the government to separate the communities of Palaestina prima from those of Palaestina secunda by setting up two Sanhedrins failed miserably. The rabbis residing at Tiberias were still regarded as the heads of the whole nation. The people continued to honour the memory of the patriarchs for centuries after the abolition of that institution.[3] As we have already seen, the actual direction of affairs had passed out of the hands of the patriarchs into those of the sages many generations before the patriarchate was formally abolished, and hence it caused less difficulty than the Byzantines expected. For about a century the school at Tiberias was headed by a rabbi called *archipherecytes* (a Greek form of the Hebrew title *rosh ha-perek* 'head of the school', or literally 'head of the chapter'). About 520 there arrived in Palestine Mar Zutra, the son of the Babylonian exilarch. The rabbis of Tiberias received him with great honour and 'introduced him among the heads of the chapter'. Shortly afterwards Mar Zutra became the head of the Sanhedrin. He was succeeded by his son, grandson and other descendants for seven generations, till the transfer of the whole school from Tiberias to Jerusalem after the Arab conquest.[4]

The history of the period proves clearly that the Jews in Palestine continued to act as one body. Their new authority followed the same line as the old one—it was both realistic and prudent.

The local Jewish authorities acted within the framework of the national organization. They were less important in Byzantine eyes, and hence subject to less external pressure. After the completion of the Palestine Gemara we have little information about the inner life of the communities. By comparing the Talmudic data with those from the time of the Gaonate, we can observe that the local communities continued to act much as before. With the relative decline of the great schools of learning the authority of the rabbis declined also. The influence of laymen, the formerly despised 'people of the land' (*am ha-arets*) began to rise. The rich among them now became leaders in their communities as the 'good men of the town', jointly with the local rabbis and judges.

The economic condition of the Jews did not worsen at that time; it may even have improved somewhat. The Byzantine period was on the whole a period of material prosperity for Palestine.[5] The huge investments which the Christian emperors made in the 'Holy Land', by building churches and monasteries and encouraging pilgrimages, had their repercussions in all spheres of economic life. The archaeological surveys in Palestine have shown that at this time the area of cultivation was increased to an extent not reached till our own times, especially in the Negev. The Jews too seem to have profited to some extent from the general prosperity. This can be proved from the remains of synagogues which were then constructed or repaired. One of them, that of Beth Alfa, is dated by an inscription to the reign of 'King Justinus', probably Justin I (518–527).[6] Many synagogues can be assigned to this period on stylistic grounds. We find them at Hammath Gader, Hammath Tiberias, Husifa (Isfiya), Jericho, Naaran, Maon, Gerasa, Ascalon, Gaza, Azotus etc.[7] It is true that the ornamentation of existing synagogues, and still more so the building of new ones, was against the law,[8] but this was apparently often ignored In the style of the contemporary synagogues we may notice a certain resemblance to contemporary churches; the symbolic values of the Jewish religion were, however, observed.[9]

The characteristics of this later type of Palestinian synagogue are a basilical plan and a mosaic pavement with figurative representations of men and beasts. The basilicas are divided almost without exception by two rows of columns into a nave and two aisles. The nave was higher than the aisles, leaving space for a gallery over the latter and for clerestory lighting. The galleries were probably used by the women attending the synagogue. The entrance to the building was through three doors placed on the side opposite the apse. The apse itself pointed to Jerusalem and was a semi-circular niche; a square apse occurs at Gerasa (middle fifth century). The floor of the apse and of the small podium in front of it was slightly elevated above the floor of the nave. This kind of tribune was usually separated from the main room by a chancel screen. It was used for the precentor and the Torah reader. The Ark of the Law was placed in the apse itself and was apparently hidden behind a veil. Two seven-branched candlesticks stood on both sides of the apse. Below the apse was a hollow space which was used either for keeping the community chest or for a depository of damaged Torah scrolls or other sacred texts.

The ornaments of the later synagogues were much more modest than those of the earlier type, at least on the exterior. Reliefs were used almost exclusively for capitals or chancel screens. The dominant motif is the seven-branched candlestick (*menorah*) together with the vine-scroll rising from an amphora, pomegranates and rosettes. In the first half of the fourth century the rabbis began to allow the use of figurative imagery in the mosaic floors of the synagogues. The great series of mosaic pavements found in the synagogues dates from the fourth to the eighth century. The main elements of such pavement decoration were three: the Ark of the Law flanked by candlesticks and lions; the Zodiac signs in circle segments, with the Sun (Helios) in his chariot in the centre, and personifications of the Seasons in the corners; thirdly, scenes from the Scriptures, in which miraculous salvation occurred: Noah's Ark (Gerasa), the Offering of Isaac (Beth Alfa), Daniel in the Lion's Den (Naaran). Symbols of Paradise (peacocks, vine scrolls, animals living in peace with each other) occur on some pavements. The artistic value of these mosaics varied; in all of them the design is lively, sometimes bordering on the naive. Many of the motifs used occur also on church pavements of the same period. We may draw the conclusion that the mosaic artists worked indifferently for both Jewish and Christian holy places. On the whole more figurative images were used in synagogues than in churches, because the edict of 427, which forbade the use of religious symbols or (by implication) of biblical scenes in pavements was not operative in the synagogues. Thus at Beth Alfa anyone could walk over the images of Abraham, Isaac and even the symbolic 'hand of God' depicted on the floor.

As pressure on the Jews in Byzantine times continued and even grew stronger and stronger, there was an evident retreat from the liberal interpretation of the Second Commandment, and a movement in the direction of greater rigour. The representations of human beings and animals were removed from the synagogue pavements. Later pavements show no human figures, and later still no beasts; in the end only symbols are left, together with floral and geometric ornament. It should be noted that while the images were removed, the inscriptions beside them were left untouched (as at Naaran); the letters were more sacred than the images.

The synagogue inscriptions throw much light on the economic situation of the Jews. In comparison with the inscriptions of the earlier type of synagogues (those of the second or third century), a certain decline in the amounts donated can be noted. In earlier times individual donors gave whole stoas, staircases, columns; now a whole community had to combine

I

to complete the mosaic pavement of the synagogue. This happened at Beth Alfa and Jericho.[10] Private donors were now able to give only parts of pavements, as we note at Naaran, Hammath-Gader, Caesarea etc. The most detailed information concerning donors is to be found in the pavements of Hammath-Gader and Maon.[11] At Hammath there were many visitors from outside the town, who came to bathe at the famous hot springs. Many of them contributed to the synagogue pavement. Their contributions were on the whole modest enough. The largest one was five gold pieces, which were given by a whole family, including one *comes*. A woman gave one gold piece, a couple half a gold piece. Most donors gave one third of a gold piece, some even less. Others donated textiles instead of money. At Maon a gift of two gold pieces was solemnly commemorated in a special mosaic inscription. Only in Gaza could one individual afford to give a whole column, and a couple of wood merchants the pavement of an aisle. It should be noted that it was apparently not easy to collect the donations. Indeed, at Husifah the inscriptions contain a special blessing upon those who 'donated and brought their donation'.[12] It seems that the dominant class among the Palestinian Jews were small proprietors or merchants, who could afford to give, but not overmuch.

In spite of all the ordinances to the contrary there were still Jews who served as civil servants and as local officials. Among the donors at Hammath-Gader there appears a *comes* Pheroras, one of a large Jewish family. It is true that at the time of this inscription (fifth or sixth century) the title of *comes* had become much depreciated; but even then it denoted officials or civilians of some standing. It was bestowed on heads of town councils or even of village councils; it seems most likely that Pheroras was only one of these 'honorary *comites*'. The renewed ban by Justinian in 527 against Jews holding government offices was apparently published just because in the period of 'armistice' which preceded this emperor there were many such cases, upon which the authorities turned a blind eye until prodded into action by the emperor.

We know of 43 settlements in Palestine inhabited by Jews at this time, 31 of them villages and 12 towns. In the coastal plain and east of the Jordan Jews lived in towns only; most of the Jewish villages were concentrated in Galilee. A few villages remained in the Jordan Valley, and in the *Darom* (Esthemoa, Susiya). In the Negev there were hardly any Jews left.

It should be noted that at this time, as in the previous period of appeasement in the second and third centuries, Jews succeeded in infiltrating also into Jerusalem. This was probably connected with the residence there of Eudocia. In the *Life of Sabas* (439–531)[13] we are told of Jews walking in the streets of Jerusalem, and becoming important tax-payers there. We are also told that in the time of Phocas Jews in Jerusalem were baptized forcibly.[14] Christian authors accuse the Jews of delivering Jerusalem to the Persians, which they could hardly have done unless they were residents of the city.[15] It seems that some Jews settled in the Holy City and that the local authorities preferred not to notice that their presence was illegal. We know also that at this period Jews visited Hebron, and prayed at the Machpelah cave and at the Oaks of Mamre.[16]

The number of Jews still left in the country can be estimated from Eutychius' story of the armed Jewish warriors who helped the Persians during their invasion in 614. He estimates their number at 20,000, which would correspond to a total population of 150–200,000. We may arrive at the same conclusion by counting the number of Jewish settlements at different periods. After the war of Bar Kokhba there existed about 200 such places, while the total number of the Jewish population was 750–800,000.[17] Now there remained but a quarter of the settlements, which would correspond to about 150,000–200,000 souls. According to this estimate the Jews constituted 10–15 per cent of the total population. Such estimates are not, of course, exact; but it is clear that a sharp decline had occurred in the number of the Jews in Palestine, both absolutely and in proportion to the rest of the inhabitants. This fact was to have important political consequences.

5. *The Jews and the Samaritan Revolts*

The Jews found it easier to observe calm during the period of the 'armistice' we have just described, when they contemplated the sad fate of the Samaritans. Ever since the days of the Return to Zion in the Persian period, the Samaritans had taken up an ambivalent position; they were believers in the God of Israel, and non-Jews at the same time. This ambivalence proved fatal in the end. It was possible that they had once hoped to profit at the same time from the advantages of being Jews and from those enjoyed by the Gentiles. In fact they suffered from the disadvantages of both estates. The Jews regarded them as outside the pale and the Roman authorities refused to accord to them the privileges they had granted the Jews. Already in the third century the Samaritans were forbidden to circumcise their children, because as non-Jews they were regarded as subject to the general penal law, and were not granted the indulgence given to the Jews.[18] In the time of Diocletian the Samaritans were obliged to sacrifice to the pagan gods, together with all other nations (always excepting the Jews). After this the Jewish rabbis regarded them with contempt as so many idolaters.[19] In the time of the revolt against Gallus relations between the two nations were still bad. The mutual hatred ebbed only when both began to suffer from the hostile policy of the

Christian emperors. They did not, however, reach the point of joining forces.

The ill-luck of the Samaritans was due to their bad timing. They did not sense rightly the moments for action and for lying low. The Jewish revolts occurred at a time when the Roman emperors were still convinced of the value of tolerance, and followed the Virgilian *parcere subjectis et debellare superbos*. The Jewish revolts were suppressed with a heavy hand, but the defeated were spared. Besides, Judaism had spread by that time beyond the boundaries of the empire, and because of that it had assured to itself a certain amount of independence. At that time most of the Samaritans refused to take action. Now, when times had changed they revolted against emperors, who were only too ready to destroy them utterly. The Samaritan policy was on the whole the result of ill-advised despair. They had become suddenly aware of the fact that because of the spread of Christianity in Palestine they had no future within the country; and yet they lacked an outside base, such as was provided by the Jewish Diaspora.

The Samaritans, who had been pliant and submissive to the tolerant Rome of paganism, now became rebellious when confronted with Byzantine Rome, merciless when facing unbelievers. In the fifth and sixth centuries it was they who formed the centres of rebellion in Palestine. The Jews generally kept away from such desperate moves. Only towards the end of the Byzantine period did some Jewish zealots join the rebels.

The Samaritan revolts were hopeless undertakings from the start; they were left in the lurch by the Persians. The first unrest broke out in the time of Marcian, shortly before the Council of Chalcedon (451). In a Monophysite revolt Samaritan soldiers in Roman pay were active in fighting the sectarians.[20] But in the next generation, in 484, they revolted against the emperor Zeno. This revolt broke out after the emperor had succeeded in overcoming his rival Illus, who ruled at Antioch. Zeno suppressed the Samaritan revolt with great cruelty and built a Christian church (the remains of which are still visible) over the Samaritan place of sacrifice. After that the Samaritans kept the peace for some time. Another attempt to raise Neapolis against the emperor Anastasius failed. Most of the inhabitants refused to join the few zealots who had occupied the church on Mount Garizim and had raised there the standard of revolt. In the second year of Justinian (529) a great Samaritan revolt broke out. The revolt was connected with the invasion of Syria by the Arab prince al-Mundhir, the ruler of Hira who was supported by Persia. He even reached the walls of Antioch.[21]

The revolt of 529 is of special interest for us, because late sources claim that the Jews joined the rebels. This mistaken opinion is based on a passage in the *Chronicle* of Malalas,[22] who wrote: 'The Samaritans clashed with the Christians and the Jews'. Later Byzantine authors who used this source (for instance Theophanes, Cedrenus and the Latin epitomator of Theophanes)[23] read: 'Clash of Samaritans and Jews with the Christians', and wrote accordingly in their books. The authors who lived at the time of the revolt or shortly after (Procopius of Caesarea, Zacharias the Rhetor, the *Chronicon paschale* and others)[24] refer only to a Samaritan revolt. The evidence of Procopius is most important, for he was born in the country and his estates had suffered greatly during the revolt and the repression which followed it. It seems probable that in the beginning of Justinian's reign, before the anti-Jewish intentions of the emperor had become evident, the Palestinian Jews did not wish to be involved in the Samaritan revolt. They seem to have judged the situation with more coolness than the Samaritans, who acted out of despair. As a result the latter were crushed and could not rise, when the proper moment arrived at the time of the Persian invasion.

Both Samaritan revolts, that of 484 and that of 529, took a parallel course. The rising started at Neapolis (now Nablus) the Samaritan capital, which was situated in the heart of Mount Ephraim. The rebels broke out into the coastal plain and the Valley of Jezreel through the mountain passes. Sometimes they even menaced Jerusalem. On their way they burnt churches and monasteries, and killed bishops and clerics. In 484 they occupied Caesarea, the seat of the Byzantine governor. In 529 they seized Scythopolis, the residence of the governor of Palaestina secunda. Their first successes were due to the strict separation of civil and military power in the Byzantine empire. There were no troops at the disposal of the governor, for the army, commanded by a *dux*, was disposed along the frontier. After their first easy successes the Samaritans set up in both revolts a kind of government and crowned a 'king' (in 484 it was one Justus, in 529 one Julianus). They collected taxes, and arranged even for feasts with horse-races etc. The civil governors of Palestine were unable to stop them. In the meantime, however, the *dux* collected his forces on the Arabian border and mobilized his Arab allies. His seasoned troops had no great difficulty in defeating the raw rebel forces. Many Samaritans perished and their 'king' and other prominent leaders were executed. After that there came a series of punitive measures, fines, religious persecutions and forced baptism. In the revolt in the time of Zeno ten thousand Samaritans perished. In the time of Justinian the number of victims was doubled, and twenty thousand youths of both sexes were sold by the Arabs in the Persian and Indian slave markets. In the end the position of the Samaritans was much worse than in the beginning, and worse even than that of the Jews.

Notes to Chapter X

1. J. B. Bury, *History of the Late Roman Empire* I–II, London, 1923.
2. See below, p. 253 and Choricius, *Ad Aratum* (Teubner ed.), pp. 65–8; Abel, *RB*, 1938, 529–32. The identification of Jotaba with Tiran fits the data of Procopius (*De bello Persico* I, 19, ed. Haury, p. 100f.) but a careful archaeological survey of the island in 1956 did not find any Byzantine remains there. It seems that we must give up the distance of 1,000 stadia given by Procopius and opt for an identification of Jotaba with the Jeziret el-Far'un (Crusader Isle de Graye) where excavations on land and under water have produced many Byzantine remains.
3. J. Mann, *The Jews in Egypt and Palestine*, London, 1920, I, pp. 172–174; II, pp. 205ff.
4. *Sefer ha-Yishub*, II, ed. S. Assaf and L. A. Mayer, Jerusalem, 1944, p. 89.
5. M. Avi-Yonah, *IEJ*, 8 (1958), pp. 39–51.
6. *Sefer ha-Yishub*, I, Jerusalem, 1939, ed. S. Klein, p. 12.
7. Ibid., pp. 45–7, 109, 113, 114; cf. M. Avi-Yonah, *QDAP*, 3 (1934), pp. 118–31.
8. The Synagogue inscription at Nabratein, dated to 565, commemorates the renewal of the synagogue; it was cut into a lintel of the third century. (N. Avigad, *Rabinowitz Fund Bulletin*, 3 (1960), pp. 49–59.)
9. Avi-Yonah, *Bull. Jewish Palestine Exploration Society*, 1 (2) (1933), pp. 9–15; *Rabinowitz Fund Bulletin*, 3 (1960), pp. 31–5.
10. See note 6 above and Avi-Yonah, *QDAP*, 6 (1938), pp. 73–7.
11. E. R. Goodenough, *Jewish Symbols of the Greco-Roman Period*, I, New York, 1953, pp. 239–41; S. Yeivin, *Rabinowitz Fund Bulletin*, 3 (1960), pp. 36–40.
12. M. Avi-Yonah, *QDAP*, 3 (1934), pp. 129–30.
13. Cyrillus Scythopolitanus, *Vita Sabae* 57 (ed. Schwartz, p. 154).
14. See below, p. 254.
15. Eutychius, *Annales* (*PG* 111, c. 1089) mentions Jewish villages in the vicinity of Jerusalem.
16. Antoninus Placentinus, *Itinera*, ed. P. Geyer (see above, p. 182, note 15), p. 179 (AD 570).
17. See above, p. 19.
18. Origen, *Contra Celsum* II, 13 (*GCS* 2, p. 142).
19. j *Abodah Zarah* 5, 4–44d.
20. Zacharias Rhetor, *Church History* I, 5 (ed. K. Ahrens-G. Krüger, p. 14).
21. Revolt against Marcianus—Mansi, *Collectio conciliorum* VII, p. 512;

Zeno—*Chronicon paschale* (Bonn, ed.), pp. 603–4; Malalas, XV (ed. Bonn, p. 382f.); Procopius, *De aedificiis* V, 7 (ed. Haury, pp. 165–6); Anastasius—Procopius, ibid.

22. Malalas XVIII (Bonn ed., pp. 445–6).

23. Theophanes, a.m. 6021 (ed. de Boor, p. 178, 23); Cedrenus (ed. Bonn, I, pp. 646–7); *Historia miscell.* XVI (*PL* 95, *c.* 981); Agapius de Membidj (*PO* VIII, p. 427) mentions only a revolt of the Jews.

24. Procopius, *Historia arcana* 11, 24–30 (ed. Haury, pp. 74–5); Zacharias Rhetor, IX, 8 (ed. Ahrens-Krüger, pp. 176–7); *Chronicon paschale* (ed. Bonn, I, pp. 619–20); Bar-Hebraeus (ed. Budge, I, p. 74).

XI

The Emperor Justinian
and the Jews

---

1. *Renewal of the Anti-Jewish Legislation*

As we have seen, the Jews had refrained from taking part in the Samaritan risings, but not out of any love for the Byzantine government. In fact even the moderate emperors, those who tried to make a compromise with the Monophysites, were full of deadly hatred for the Jews. We are told that when the emperor Zeno was informed that the bodies of some Jews had been burnt in the course of a riot at Antioch, he replied: 'What a pity that the living were not burnt also'.[1] Anastasius and his Monophysite friends used the term 'Jews' to abuse their enemies, the supporters of the Chalcedonian orthodoxy.[2] In general the Monophysites accused their archenemies, the Nestorians, of holding Jewish views on Jesus. The Council of Ephesus, where the Monophysites predominated, wrote to Nestorius in the following terms: 'The holy assembly to Nestorius, the new Jew'.[3] In the time of the emperor Marcianus the Monophysites distributed a letter allegedly written by the Jews to the emperor, saying: 'To the merciful emperor Marcianus from the nation of the Jews. For a long time people have been of the opinion that our fathers had crucified a god, and not a man. But now the Council has assembled at Chalcedon and has decided that they had crucified a man and not a god, we supplicate you that we should be forgiven this mistake and that our synagogues be returned to us.'[4] In the book of 'Jacob the Convert' whom we shall meet again, we are told that while the hero of the story was still a Jew, he attacked Orthodox Christians together with the Monophysite mob, calling them 'Nestorians and Jews'.[5]

With the accession of Justinian to the imperial throne (527) there was a radical change in Byzantine policy. The new emperor planned a re-conquest of the West. He dispatched his generals with large armies first to Africa (533–535) and then to Italy (535–554). As he was interested in gaining the support of the Westerns who obeyed the Roman pope, he annulled the compromise of Zeno (the *Henoticon*) and returned to Chalce-donian orthodoxy. The Monophysites again became opposed to the government. In the first half of Justinian's reign this rift was not felt as yet, because his energetic empress Theodora was a secret supporter of Monophysitism. After her death (548) opposition to the government grew apace in the Eastern provinces; it endangered the whole structure of Byzantine power in the East.[6]

The policy of repression, which was adopted by Justinian, was felt by the Jews as well as by the other religious minorities. There began a new period of hectic legislation. In the circumstances then prevailing this could only mean more laws against the Jews.

After a pause of 89 years a new law regulating Jewish affairs was promulgated.[7] This edict was published while Justin I was still nominal emperor; but as Justinian, although only heir-presumptive, was in fact already the ruler, we can attribute this piece of legislation to his initiative. In any case it conforms with his later edicts. According to its preamble this law was made because there were so many 'heretics' (that is: non-orthodox) who had infiltrated the army and the civil service. The main innovation of this law was the definition of the term 'heretic'. Till then its legal meaning was 'a Christian whose opinions differed from those of the established church'. Now, however, this definition was enlarged to mean 'anyone who is not orthodox'; therefore it now included also the Jews.

In itself the new law did not contain much that was new. The emperor again prohibited the appointment of Jews to civil and military charges. He excluded them from the teaching profession (meaning of course teaching in public universities, in which the professors were regarded as civil servants). Such prohibitions did not amount to much as far as the Jews were concerned. They were in any case separated from the cultural world surrounding them, and avoided as far as possible all contacts with the 'evil government'. Their expulsion from all city offices was a more serious matter; it included the prohibition to serve as city advocate (*defensores civitatis*) and as members of the city council (*curia*). The emperor allowed the Jews only the right to serve as lower-grade officials (*cohortalini*), because this involved more trouble than honour. As Justinian later on declared expressly (in his *Novella* 45 of the year 537)[8] his aim was to make the Jews bear all the burdens connected with municipal charges, without allowing them to enjoy any of the benefits. It seems astonishing that the emperor now gave up the right to force Jews to serve in the *curiae*. In past centuries the emperors had been interested to keep them there, because in this way they became co-responsible for the collection of taxes and had to make good any tax deficits from their own pockets.[9] The reason for this sudden change is not far to seek. Among the other fiscal reforms of Anastasius there was one which involved the abolition of the tax-collecting duties of the municipal councils; these were now taken over by officers of the treasury appointed for this purpose. After that there was of course no further need to keep the Jews in the *curiae*. This law had especially grievous consequences in the two Jewish cities in Galilee, Tiberias and Sepphoris. There municipal rule passed again into the hands of strangers, as it had in the darkest days of the Hadrianic persecution. Still worse was what happened during the revision of the laws which were taken over from the Code of Theodosius into that of Justinian. The exemption of Jewish religious personnel from the municipal burdens was conveniently forgotten on that occasion. The anti-Jewish tendency of the Justinianic legislation is evident in other laws. An old law of 421 promised the Jews triple or quadruple compensation for property of which they were unjustly deprived. In the Code of Justinian this law was kept on the statute book, but the compensation was reduced to double the damage only.[10]

The emperor did not refrain from meddling in the old matter of the Christian slaves held by the Jews.[11] Because of its economic importance this matter had been already, as we have seen, the subject of a violent conflict between the government and the Jews. Justinian did not interfere with the substance of the law. He did, however, increase the penalties for a Jew holding a Christian slave to fifty pounds of gold. He also obliged Jewish slave-holders not only to release all their Christian slaves, but also every slave wishing to accept baptism. If the slave was baptized first, and then freed, and his former owner became baptized later on, the slave was not to be returned to his former status. As in the case of his predecessors, Justinian met with much resistance when trying to enforce this law. He had to repeal its provisions in 533.

Other laws regulated the status of the Jews in the imperial courts. They were declared unfit to give evidence against Christians (of course only those of the orthodox variety). Later on this law was amended; the testimony of a Jew was declared irrelevant only if it was hostile to a Christian. If it happened to be in his favour, it was declared acceptable in evidence. The emperor added that the testimony of a Jew would be also accepted in the case of a member of the municipal council who was evading his tax duty. In such cases the interests of the *fiscus* outweighed the orthodoxy of the defendant.[12]

Justinian also made regulations concerning the case of a Jewish family, part of which only had adopted Christianity. He confirmed the old regulations protecting the inheritance of a convert son. He added that in case one of the parents wished to baptize an infant and the other opposed it, the will of the former should prevail. It was immaterial whether it was the father or the mother who favoured Christianity. In general, of course, the will of the male parent prevailed in Roman law.[13]

In his *Novella* 131 of 545 the emperor forbade the Jews to acquire, or receive in mortgage or in any other way landed property on which a church had been erected. The church was to receive the estate of anyone who had transgressed this prohibition.[14]

All these laws formed a series of pin-pricks against the Jews, but there was nothing revolutionary in them. Even after their promulgation the Jews could continue to exist, and to make their living. Matters were different as regards other legal changes, which affected either the general status of the Jews or the execution of the laws. Moreover, Justinian arrived at last at the point of direct intervention in the internal affairs of the community.

The groundwork for such action was laid carefully. While the law officers of Justinian were going over the Theodosian Code in order to ascertain which laws should be taken over into the new Code of Justinian, they resolved to omit the old law by which Judaism was declared a *religio licita*. In this way the whole legal basis of Byzantine Jewry was taken from under its feet, and the path was left open for legal attacks on the Jews and a persecution of their religion. At the same time it was declared (*Novella* 131, and *Codex* I, 3, 44) that the canons of the church should henceforth have the force of a law.[15] In this way the civil government finally capitulated before the church—but only in Jewish affairs. The church in general did not derive much benefit from this decision. Under Justinian's Caesaropapism the ecclesiastical establishment was but part of the machinery of imperial government.

The manner of executing this decision added insult to injury. The Jews were handed over to their old enemies, the leaders of the church. The execution of the laws against them (and against the other religious minorities) was entrusted jointly to the bishops and the provincial governors. The law enjoined the bishops to appeal directly to the emperor, should they notice that the civil authorities were lax and delayed the execution of the law.

The authorities began now to interfere in the internal affairs of the Jewish community. The emperor, for instance, forbade the Jews to keep the Passover holiday at its proper date, if it fell before the Christian Easter. Even Procopius had to admit that in this way Justinian forced the Jews 'to neglect the divine service and to transgress their laws'.[16]

The urge to meddle in all the affairs of his subjects, which was characteristic of the whole reign of Justinian, is demonstrated in his *Novella* 146 of 553. The emperor used an internal dispute in the synagogue of Constantinople in order to further his divisive aims. The dispute occurred between those worshippers who wished to have the Bible read only in the original Hebrew, and those who wanted it read also in a Greek translation. The emperor at once issued a general law addressed to all synagogues and not only to those directly concerned. His law shows that his aim was to bring the Jews nearer to Christianity. The belief of the Jews in the plain sense of the Scriptures is rejected by him in favour of the allegoric-symbolic interpretation, by which the church fathers found the coming of Jesus foretold in the Bible. In order to close the gap between the Jewish and Christian texts of the Scriptures, the emperor ordered that the Greek version of the Scriptures be allowed in the synagogues. He recommended the Septuagint version, the one used in the Christian churches, but he allowed the use of other texts, including even that of Agilas (Aquila), probably in ignorance of the fact that this translation was prepared under the guidance of Rabbi Akiba and followed literally the Hebrew original. At the same time he forbade the heads of the synagogues to excommunicate anyone advocating the proposed liturgical change. On the other hand he demanded that the ban be applied against those doubting the Resurrection of the Dead, the Last Judgment, and the existence of angels. These provisions seem to have been directed against the Samaritans and those Jews who shared their views.[17] At the conclusion of his law Justinian forbids the use of the 'Second Law' (*deuterosis*), possibly meaning the haggadic commentaries in the Midrashim, used in synagogue services.

The carrying out of this law was enjoined upon the 'archipherecytes, elders etc.'. The mention of the former shows clearly that the law was intended to be applied in Palestine also. There can be no doubt, however, that it remained on paper as regards most of the Jewish communities, and certainly those of the Holy Land.

Another subject, which was usually dealt with at length in former laws, does not appear in Justinian's laws at all. There is no mention whatsoever of attacks on synagogues. This omission is not accidental. By the time of Justinian both the bishops and the monks were entirely submissive to the government. Moreover, there was now no need to incite the mob to interfere with Jewish places of worship, for the emperor took charge of this task himself. In *Novella* 131 (545) he only repeats the old prohibition to build new synagogues. On this point the Jews were certainly in a better position than the Samaritans, who were not allowed to have synagogues at all. In Africa, which had been reconquered under Justinian, a special law (*Novella* 37 of 535) which regulated the religious affairs of the province in general, forbade the establishment of synagogues.

In the eyes of the Jews the acts of the emperor must have loomed larger than his laws. In the time of Justinian there occurred also the first case of forced baptism in the Byzantine empire. In the Cyrenean town of Borion there stood a magnificent synagogue, which local legend attributed to king

Solomon. Justinian turned it into a church 'and forced all the Jews to relinquish the religion of their forefathers and to become Christians'.[18] This was not an isolated case. In the liturgical poems of the great Byzantine poet Romanus (who was himself of Jewish origin) we find a mention of the fact that many Jews had been baptized 'for fear of the existing laws'.[19]

There is much archaeological evidence that in these times one synagogue was destroyed after another. In Gerasa a church was built already in 450 over the ruins of a synagogue. In Caesarea, Husifah on Mount Carmel and Engedi traces of fire were discovered on the mosaic floors of synagogues; in Caesarea the evidence even included particles of sulphur.[20]

Under such circumstances we may well understand why many Jews took part in the riots which started at Caesarea in 556. A mob, composed mostly of Samaritans, but with not a few Jews among it, profited from the usual disputes of the two established Byzantine factions, the 'Blues' and the 'Greens', and attacked the Christians of the city.[21] Many were killed, and several churches were plundered and burnt down. Stephanus, the civil governor of the province, tried to protect the endangered Christians. Thereupon the rioters attacked his palace. He himself perished and his property was looted. The prefect of the Orient, Amantius, intervened in person. He came to Caesarea, arrested some of the rioters, executed a few, maimed others, and confiscated the property of many. Thereupon 'a great fear fell upon Caesarea and all the countries of the East'.[22]

This event was of no great importance in itself. The place of the outbreak and its course prove that it was but a local riot. Nevertheless it demonstrated the weakness of a regime, which was unable to keep order even in the capital of a province. It was also significant that after several centuries the zealotic spirit arose again amongst the Jews. They felt oppressed to such a degree, that they forgot to weigh coolly the chances of a rising. It was also important that common trouble made Jews and Samaritans forget the hatred which had divided them for so many generations.

2. *The Conflict between Byzantines and Jews in the Red Sea*

The Byzantine authorities came into conflict with the Jews not only in religious matters, but also in the field of foreign trade. From times immemorial Byzantine commerce moved in two directions. The trade in raw materials with the peoples of the north went by way of the Black Sea; the trade in Eastern products, especially of those from China and India, crossed Persia. When the empire was at war with Persia—a state of affairs which occurred with distressing regularity—this Eastern route was of course closed. The Persians dominated all the land roads leading eastwards, with the exception of the northernmost one which passed the lands of the Huns and Mongols and was very unsafe. The Persians controlled as well the sea-routes through the Persian Gulf. There was only one way by which the Byzantines could turn the sea-blockade of the Persians, the sea-route along the Red Sea. From that sea Byzantine ships could reach India and Ceylon through the Straits of Aden. Energetic emperors made therefore great efforts to pierce a sea-route for their trade to India through the Red Sea. They had at their disposal two harbours, one in Palestine (Aila, now Elath) and one in Egypt (Clysma, now Suez). The Byzantines were greatly assisted by the fact that the western shore of the Straits of Aden (Bab el-Mandeb) was in the hands of their Christian allies, the kings of Ethiopia. The common religion made the Ethiopians the natural allies of the Byzantines. For at that time religion mingled with all aspects of life, including foreign commerce.

In order to make their control of the Straits of Aden doubly secure, the Byzantines needed also its eastern coast. This area was in the sixth century inhabited by the Himyarites, a South Arabian nation. The Ethiopians did from time to time gain a foothold in their country. Himyar had, however, also a strong Jewish community. The leaders of the national party, who were opposed to Ethiopian domination, had adopted Judaism. Himyar thus became an area of conflict between Byzantine and Jewish interests. This confrontation soon assumed the aspects of an overt political struggle.

The kings of Himyar and the Jewish leaders who resided at Tiberias were in constant communication. In the 'Book of Himyar'[23] the anonymous Syro-Christian author describes the persecutions of Christians by the Jewish kings of Himyar. He tells that 'Jewish priests' from Tiberias accompanied the king on his travels. They also served as his messengers to the rebellious Christian cities of his realm. According to Simeon of Beth Arsham, another contemporary Christian author, the 'Jews in Tiberias sent every year priests (rabbis?) and instigated disputes with Christians'.[24]

The Himyarites succeeded under the leadership of their Jewish kings in shaking off twice the hated Ethiopian yoke. The great Byzantine empire thus found itself in direct confrontation with a small Jewish kingdom. However, this little nation occupied an important strategic position, which the empire needed in order to realize its commercial ambitions. Each of the two parties to this conflict attempted to exercise pressure in favour of its co-religionists who lived under the domination of the other. According to our sources the king of Himyar arrested Byzantine traders on their way to India, and executed them, because 'in Roman lands the Christians were oppressing the Jews'.[25] The information about the situation of the Jews under Byzantine rule was most probably derived from the rabbis who were dispatched annually from Tiberias to Himyar. The Jewish leaders in Palestine hoped apparently for an easing of Byzantine pressure, using the geographical position of Himyar and Jewish preponderance there as a lever. The Christians tried to use counter-measures. Simeon of Beth Arsham writes in his account as follows: 'Let them (the rabbis of Tiberias) be told that if they do not cease (to send rabbis and books to Himyar) their synagogues will be burnt and they themselves will be molested in all places where the Crucified one is reigning'.[26]

The attempt of the Jewish leaders to make use of the independent Jewish state of Himyar to ease their situation under Byzantine rule shows that they supported Byzantine rule only under duress. The strength of their position in this conflict depended of course on that of the kings of Himyar. Had the position of the Jewish kings there been absolutely secure, the plan might have succeeded. However, the Byzantines were able to use the Ethiopians in order to checkmate the Himyarites. In this way they could free their trading routes, without having to make any concession to the Jews living within the empire. Because of the Ethiopian danger Dhu-Nawas, the Jewish king of Himyar, asked for Persian help. He sent messengers to al-Mundhir, the Arab ruler of Hira under Persian suzerainty. Al-Mundhir was in charge of the western border of the Persian kingdom and was well acquainted with the problems of Southern Arabia. However, Dhu-Nawas was unlucky in his timing. At this very moment (the beginning of the twenties of the sixth century) there was a short lull in the wars between Persians and Byzantines. The Persians did not come to the assistance of Himyar and the Ethiopian invasion was successful. Dhu-Nawas fell in battle in 525. A Christian Ethiopian viceroy reigned again in Himyar. Only later on did the Persians understand that the rule of allies of Byzantium over Himyar was to their disadvantage. They thereupon helped Saif ibn Dhu-Yazan (a scion of one of the chief helpers of Dhu-Nawas) to organize a revolt against the Ethiopians. In 575 the Persians became the dominant power in Himyar, and the Ethiopians were expelled from the country. But by then the whole matter had ceased to have any influence on developments in Palestine.[27]

A change for the worse occurred in this connection also at Jotaba. As we have seen above,[28] the island had come under Byzantine domination in the time of Anastasius, who did not, however, molest the autonomous community of Jewish merchants living there. This community survived until the age of Justinian. He put an end to their independence and subjected them to Byzantine law. This was probably another step in his aggressive policy in the Red Sea.[29]

3. *The Successors of Justinian*

The continuing oppression of Palestine Jewry revived in the end its militant spirit. Justinian's successor, Justin II, had to suppress a Judaeo-Samaritan revolt in 578; his general Theophilus did it with the cruelty common at that time.[30] Some leaders of the revolt joined a band of robbers assembled by one Cyriacus in the vicinity of Emmaus. In the Jordan Valley conflicts between Jews and the Christian settlers became also more and more frequent. Jewish fanatics (such as the Jacob who was later converted) took an active part in the disputes between the various Christian sects. In order to do them injury freely, they adopted the slogans now of one party, now of another. This Jacob had no special preference; if the 'Greens' were the stronger party, he persecuted the 'Blues' calling them 'Jews and bastards' (*mamzirous*, a Greek form of the Hebrew word *mamzer*). If the 'Blues' became powerful, he molested the 'Greens', calling them 'Manichaeans'. When the 'Greens' murdered the governor Bonosus, he assisted in this deed; he also incited the dock workers of Rhodes against the 'Blues'.[31]

In the time of the emperor Mauricius (582–602) there were again cases of forced baptism. Domitianus, a brother of the emperor, who was bishop of Melitene, forced the Jews in his diocese to adopt Christianity, 'but' adds a Christian chronographer 'they became only Christian hypocrites.'[32]

Such and similar events explain why the Jews of Sycaminum rejoiced when they learnt of the death of Mauricius, who was assassinated by Phocas. However, one of the 'priests' (sages) who had witnessed their joy, warned them that the new ruler would still bring greater troubles upon them.[33] He was soon proved right. In the time of Phocas the cases of forced baptism were no longer isolated events; a concerted attempt was now made to force the Jews of the whole empire, Palestine included, to adopt Christianity. The story of the imperial order is handed down in a similar form by two sources. One of these, dating to 650, is the *Didascalia of Jacob now baptized*;[34] the second is the history of Dionysius of Tell-Mahre, an Egyptian historian who wrote about 775.[35] Both state that 'the emperor Phocas (variant: Heraclius) ordered all Jews within his dominions to be baptized'. The continuation of the story differs in the two sources. In the 'Didascalia' the story is told of Sergius governor of Africa and Carthage is given as its locality. Dionysius refers it to one Georgius, a governor of Palestine and locates it at Jerusalem.[36] We cannot now decide which version is the better one, although the former seems more reliable.

This is the story as told by the *Didascalia of Jacob*: 'The governor ordered the Jews to appear before him and asked us: "Are you slaves of the emperor?" And we answered and said: "Yes, lord, we are the emperor's slaves." He said: "The Gracious One (meaning the emperor) orders you to be baptized." When we heard this we were very much afraid and no one dared to answer. He said "Why do you not answer?" and one of us, Nonus said: "We shall not do it, because the time for holy baptism has not yet come." Then the governor stood up in a rage and slapped Nonus' face with both hands, saying "If you are slaves, why do you not do as your lord wills?" and we were all as if turned to stone from fear. The governor ordered us to be baptized. They did this to us whether we willed it or not. We were now in great doubt and mourning.'

'Jacob' describes himself as a merchant, and pretended to be a Christian. Once, however, when he had an accident, he cried out '*Adonai!*' ('Lord' in Hebrew). He was arrested at once. When it was found that he was circumcised, he was put in a dungeon. There he stayed for a hundred days; then he was forced by threats of fire and tortures to accept baptism.

Baptism had thus become a matter of politics, a sign of fidelity to the emperor. The Jews could not object to it, unless they wished to appear as traitors to the state.

The linking of religion and state created a situation not dissimilar to that which existed in imperial Rome, with the only difference that what was once a sacrifice to the emperor's genius now became baptism.

On the whole Jews regarded the new persecution as one more of the signs announcing the coming of the Messiah. The Jews in Palestine in particular were sure that their salvation was coming nearer every day. They saw the Persian armies spreading over the Byzantine empire, and they began to hope that they would soon reach the borders of the Holy Land.

Notes to Chapter XI

1. Jean d'Asie (ed. Nau, *ROC* 1897, p. 462); Malalas XV (ed. Bonn, p. 389f.).

2. Zacharias Rhetor VII, 8, p. 123.

3. *CSCO(SS)* III, IV, Chron. minor. p. 161.

4. Michel le Syrien, ed. Chabot, II, p. 91; VIII, 12.

5. Nau, *Didascalie de Jacob* 53 (*PO* 8, p. 776f.); 'Sargis d'Aberga' (*PO* 3, p. 637). The Greek text has been published by Bonwetsch, *Göttinger Abhandlungen* 1910, NF, XII, No. 3.

6. E. Stein, *Histoire du Bas Empire*, II, Bruxelles, 1949, pp. 623–5; G. Ostrogorsky, *History of the Byzantine State*, Oxford, 1968, p. 78.

7. *CJC* I, 5, 12 par. 2.

8. Ibid., III, *Novella* XLV, proem. p. 278.

9. See above, p. 216 and *CTh* XVI, 8, 8; 8, 9; 8, 13; II, 1, 10.

10. *CJC* I, 11, 6; cf. *CTh* XVI, 10, 24.

11. *CJC* I, 10, 2 (527); I, 3, 4 (56) par. 8 (533).

12. *Nov.* XLV, 1, p. 278f. (537); *CJC* I, 5, 21 (531).

K

13. *CJC* I, 5, 13.

14. *Nov.* CXXXI, c. 14, par. 1 (545); ibid., p. 662f.

15. Ibid. c. 1, p. 655.

16. Procopius, *Historia arcana* 28, 16–18; ed. Haury, p. 174.

17. Origen, *in Matthiam* 22, 23–33 (*PG* 13, c. 1561–1564); Epiphanius, *Panarion* 9, 2, 3 (*GCS* 25, pp. 198–9); M. Gaster, *The Samaritans*, London, 1925, pp. 78, 88; C. H. Thomson, *The Samaritans*, London, 1919, pp. 187, 197.

18. Procopius, *De aedificiis* VI, 2 (ed. Haury, p. 175).

19. A. Maas, *Byzantinische Zeitschrift* 15 (1906), p. 30f.

20. Avi-Yonah, *IEJ*, 6 (1956), p. 261.

21. See also below, p. 254.

22. Malalas XVIII (Bonn ed., p. 487); Theophanes a.m. 6048 (ed. Boor, p. 230, 5–15); *Hist. miscell.* XVI (*PL* 95, c. 991); Cedrenus (ed. Bonn, p. 675).

23. A. Moberg, *The Book of the Himyarites*, Lund 1924, p. 7a, CV.

24. J. Guidi, *Atti della R. Accademia dei Lincei*, 3, VII, 1881, pp. 501–15; Moberg, op. cit., p. XXV, note 2.

25. Michel le Syrien, ed. Chabot, II, p. 183.

26. See note 24.

27. H. Z. Hirshberg, *Israel be-'Arav*, Jerusalem, 1945, Chaps. IV–VI, pp. 50–111 (Hebrew).

28. See above, p. 237.

29. Procopius, *de bello Persico* I, 19 (ed. Haury, p. 100f.).

30. John of Ephesus, *The Third Part of the Ecclesiastical History*, trsl. R. P. Smith, Oxford, 1860, p. 209.

31. 'Sargis d'Aberga' (*PO* 8, 1912, ed. Nau, p. 776f.; Joh. Moschus, *Pratum spirituale*, 163 (*PG* 87, c. 3032); Palladius, *Historia lausiaca*. 110 (*PG* 34, c. 1212); Moschus ibid. 12 (c. 2861).

32. J. Nikiou ed. Zotenberg, 1883, p. 535 (ap. Nau, *PO* VIII, p. 733, note 2).

33. 'Sargis d'Aberga' 82 (*PO* 13, p. 51).

34. See note 5 above.

35. Ap. Nau, *PO*, 8, p. 720; Chabot, *REJ*, 28 (1894), p. 291f.

36. Bonwetsch (op. cit., note 5 above), pp. 1–2.

XII

The Persian Invasion
and the
End of Byzantine Rule

1. *The Last War between Persia and Rome*

The first half of the seventh century was a decisive period in the history of Palestine. It saw the end of Christian rule which had lasted since 324; the end of Roman domination which had begun in 63 BC, and even the beginning of the end of the Greek cultural domination, which reached back to the time of Alexander the Great (or even earlier) over at least a millennium. The importance of this historical turn can be measured by the fact that Islam, which then flooded the whole Orient, is still the ruling religion in much of its area thirteen hundred years later.

This historical change was felt also by contemporaries. Among the Christians, prophecies multiplied about the approaching Day of the Last Judgment. A new tempo can be noticed in that generation, much quicker than before. It seems as if everyone was feeling that the time left for action was getting less and less. The new tempo affected also warfare. Persia and Rome had by then been fighting for four hundred years across the Euphrates border. In all that time the Persian army had reached Antioch four times, and the Romans had arrived at Ctesiphon thrice. In the beginning of the seventh century however, war between the two powers became total in character. Accordingly each put forward all its strength. Astounding victories and terrible defeats followed each other almost without pause. Within a few years the Persian army had conquered Syria, Palestine and Egypt, and had reached the gates of Constantinople. Of all the splendid empire of Justinian the capital alone remained unconquered. Then matters changed as suddenly. A Roman emperor attacked Persia

257

through the Armenian mountains and advanced into the heart of the enemy kingdom. The victors of yesterday became the vanquished, and had now to beg for peace. In the end the frontier between Rome and Persia remained unchanged. All the tremendous efforts of both sides had remained without any result. The only real consequence of the great war was the complete exhaustion of both rivals. This prepared the way for the easy conquests of a third party. The Moslem Arabs, and they only, profited from the war between Rome and Persia. It seems almost as if the two old empires had conspired together to commit a joint suicide.

The last war between Rome and Persia began in 603, in the third year of the emperor Phocas. Within two years the Persians had conquered the Roman fortresses beyond the Euphrates. In 606 they invaded Syria, and raided Phoenicia and Palestine. In 609 the main Persian army crossed the Euphrates and advanced upon Antioch.

In the meantime a revolt had broken out in Constantinople against Phocas. He was deposed and executed on the 5th October 610. His place was taken by Heraclius, the son of the governor of Africa.

The new emperor was at once forced to fight desperately against enemies on every side. The Avars and the Slavs invaded the Balkan peninsula and menaced the capital from the north, while the Persians advanced from the east. Heraclius made indeed an effort to stop the Persian progress. He fought them at the gates of Antioch but suffered a defeat, and was forced to evacuate Syria. After this lost battle Antioch capitulated, in 611. The land route between Palestine and Constantinople was now cut, and the Byzantine army was left with the sea route only. In 612 the Persians invaded Asia Minor and took Caesarea in Cappadocia. Then they turned again southwards. In 613, the fourth year of Heraclius, the Persian general Khoream Rhumizan, also called Shahr-baraz ('the wild boar') took the city of Damascus. The Persian army had now arrived at the gates of Palestine.

The reason for Persian successes was not so much their own strength, as the weakness of their opponents. The Persian army, which now advanced almost unopposed, had been beaten a few years ago by the same Roman troops, and even by Arab tribesmen. However the Roman army was deeply divided at the time of the Persian invasion. Phocas had become emperor by the murder of his predecessor Mauricius. The rule of Phocas was regarded as that of a usurper. There were many conspiracies against him; they were suppressed with much cruelty. This again increased the gap between the ruler and the leaders of the army and civil service, the dominant establishment at Constantinople. At the very beginning of the Persian invasion the commander of Urfa-Edessa, a most important border fortress, refused to obey the emperor. In the seventh year of the war the governors of Cyrene and Africa revolted, and this time with success. It now became clear that Phocas could not trust any of his commanders or governors. Under such conditions he could hardly hope to make headway against his external foes.

It may happen under such desperate circumstances that the people itself will rise to repel an invader. There was but little hope of such a rising in favour of Phocas. He had continued the policy of Justin and Justinian and had supported the Chalcedonic decrees. He had thus forfeited the loyalty of the many Monophysites living in the Eastern provinces of the empire. They, taken together with the other non-orthodox, formed undoubtedly the majority of the population in Syria and Egypt. In Palestine the situation was indeed somewhat different. In this country the orthodox were in a majority, because of the special conditions prevailing in the Holy Land. However, in Palestine there were two more elements who were bitterly opposed to the official establishment: the Jews and the Samaritans. Hence here too there was no popular resistance to the invaders. The lack of support for the Byzantine rule was tragically revealed at the time of the Persian invasion. One city after another capitulated, almost without resistance. The inhabitants preferred Persian rule, of which they knew nothing as yet, to the domination of the orthodox emperors, who shared their faith but whose heavy hand they had felt for the last century and a half.

2. The Persian Invasion and the Jews

The Christian population thus remained passive, but the Jews had every reason for becoming active. They had only waited for the approach of the Persian armies in order to revolt. Their hatred of the Byzantines had already caused much trouble to the generals of the eastern march of the empire; for the Jews lived within the fortresses and could hasten their fall. Already during the wars of Anastasius and Justinian with the Persians there had been cases of Jewish attempts to deliver the besieged cities to the Persians. In 503 the Jews of Constantia conspired to hand over their town to the enemy.[1] In the time of Justin a Samaritan delegation visited the Persian king, Chosroes I, immediately after the great Samaritan revolt of 529 (this was the grandfather of Chosroes II, the conqueror of Jerusalem). The delegates tried to influence the Persian king not to make peace with the Byzantines. They promised him their support and that of the Jews.[2] Many other cases of this kind are mentioned in our sources. The relations between the Jews living under Roman rule and the Persian government were made easier by the fact that many Jews served in the Persian army. We are told that before one of the battles between Byzantines and Persians in the days of Justinian, the Persian commander requested an armistice for one day, because of a feast of the Christians and of Jewish soldiers in his army.[3] In the time of the great invasion, the Persians were assisted by Jews also outside Palestine. When the army of Chosroes II approached Antioch in September 610, the Jews in the city revolted. The commander of the garrison, Bonosus, suppressed the revolt and punished them heavily.[4] The Jews of Caesarea in Cappadocia were luckier; the local Christians fled the city and the Jews opened its gates to the Persians (612).[5] We may well compare their attitude with that of their forefathers in the third century. Then the Jews of Caesarea resisted king Shapur of Persia to the utmost. 12,000 of them were killed at the time.[6] Now the Jews received the Persians with open arms. This change in behaviour illustrates the difference in their attitude to the Byzantine rule. The policy of Justinian and his successors had deepened the rift between the Jews and Byzantines. No forced baptism could turn the Jews into loyal supporters of the empire. The Jews were forced to bear the persecution, and hope for better times. When Benjamin of Tiberias, a Jewish notable, who had been active against the Byzantines, was asked by the emperor Heraclius in the hour of Byzantine victory: 'Why did you do evil to the Christians?', he replied simply: 'Because they are enemies of my religion!'[7]

The moment the Persian armies arrived on the borders of Palestine, the Jewish leaders were faced with a special problem. In all other conquered provinces the Jews were only interested in living in peace under a government which would respect their civil rights and allow them freedom of worship. In Palestine the situation was different; here the Jews had political demands of a far reaching nature. It seems that at this time there were no differences of opinion among the Jews: all were agreed that the decisive moment had arrived to attain the freedom from foreign rule. All parties were ready to revolt. The zealots because they had always been ready to do so. The majority of the people, who had stood aside from the desperate undertakings of the zealots was now ready to act, because it was quite clear to them that no Jew could hope to live unmolested under Byzantine domination. Even the leaders of Tiberias, who had hitherto followed a moderate policy, were forced to admit that if they did not act now, a second opportunity was not likely to recur. It is possible that they had changed their attitude at the moment the Byzantine government broke the 'armistice', which had lasted from Zeno to Justinian. The problem was therefore not whether to revolt, but when. The only possible answer was: at once.

The excitement, which arose among the Jews at the approach of the Persian army, is evidenced by the revival of Messianic hopes which had always accompanied periods of spiritual ferment. 'Jacob the Convert' states that while he was at Tiberias as a young man, a 'priest' prophesied that within eight years a Messianic king would come and restore the glory of Israel.[8]

This time the Messianic hopes were given a literary form. We are confronted now for the first time with the so-called 'Salvation Midrashim' as historical sources. This seems therefore the place to evaluate their value as evidence. Every work of this kind, from the book of Daniel onwards, is composed of two parts. In the first the author describes the troubles of his own times; for without such catalogue of disasters no proper coming of the Messiah could be expected. This part of the book can be therefore used as a historical source, but of course with due caution. The fantasy of the writer may colour his account of the events. At a certain point, the writer leaves reality behind, and launches his imagination on pure fantasy. He then begins to describe things to come and not things which have been. This point, at which the author leaves reality behind, is the focal point of the whole work, because it gives us the date of the composition. Up to this point he might have been describing past events in the guise of prophecy— as a *vaticinium ex eventu*—but from now onwards he is on his own. This point can usually be established by some such phrase as 'then came the Messiah etc.'. The book then ceases to serve as an account of historical events and can only be used as evidence for the temper of the age.

The first of these Midrashim which we can use here is called *The Midrash of Elijah*.[9] It contains but little material before the 'point of Messianism'. The author refers to three years of Persian invasion— apparently the book was composed about 607. We learn from it that the roads to Constantinople were already cut. The Byzantine army is described as using the sea route. The time was one of troubles for the Jews. There was a 'king . . . the lowest of kings, the son of a serving maid. He began to lift his hand against the people of the Lord.' This description suits Phocas best. This Midrash was therefore composed before the accession of Heraclius in October 610. 'A king comes against the holy mountain and burns it . . . a cursed among women gave him birth!—and on that day there is sorrow and war against Israel.' The author seems here to allude to Phocas' orders for forced baptism—the equivalent of the burning of the Temple. The book is evidence of the spiritual ferment in Judaism; this is more important for us than what is actually written in it.

3. *The Persians Conquer Palestine with Jewish Aid*

The Persian invasion of Palestine, the capture of Jerusalem and the captivity of the 'True Cross' made a tremendous impression upon the whole Christian world. The events have been mentioned by a great many historians. Most of them restrict themselves to the story of the taking of the Holy City by the Persians, of the doings of the Jews during the conquest and the ensuing ruin of the churches. The only connected account of the events has been left by the Armenian historian Sebaeus.[10] The account by the monk Strategius of Saint Sabas,[11] who was an eyewitness to the destruction of the city, contains some important details. The two poems composed by the patriarch Sophronius, add to the picture.[12] Many other sources supply details of the dates of the various events, or of the route taken by the Persian armies.[13]

Sebaeus supplies us with the most important facts for the history of the invasion up to the attack on Jerusalem. 'When the Persians approached the Holy Land' he writes 'the remains of the Hebrew nation rose against the Christians. They committed great crimes out of national zeal and did many wrongs to the Christian community. They went and joined the Persians and made common cause with them.' From this we can learn that the Jewish revolt broke out before the Persian army arrived in Palestine, and that at the moment of their approach the revolt had come out into the open. The motive for the revolt was 'national enthusiasm', that is to say a definitely political reason. When the Persians arrived, the two parties came together and made an alliance. The Jewish forces remained a separate unit even after the juncture. Sophronius too tells how the enemy arrived before the gates of Jerusalem: 'The Parthian came accompanied by the Hebrew, his friend'.

An alliance between the Persians and the Jews was at that time profitable for both. The Jews must have demanded the restoration of their rule in the Land of Israel and in particular the return to them of Jerusalem. The new Jewish authority would of course be under Persian suzerainty. The Persian kingdom was—unlike its Byzantine rivals—not based on religion. The Persians kept in general the principles of tolerance which had guided the Achaemenids. The Babylonian Jews, who had lived for centuries under Persian rule, enjoyed, in normal times at least, an uncommon degree of autonomy. The Jews of Palestine, who formed a compact group living in its old homeland, could hope for a similar, or even greater, degree of independence. They may well have remembered the times of the First Return to Zion. Then too the Jews lived under their own laws under the rule of the first kings of Persia, Cyrus and Darius I. There were occasional waves of religious persecution in Persia also; yet these were but passing episodes, not to be compared with the constant and relentless grind of the Byzantine imperial machine. Even a semi-autonomous Christian state could exist in Persian Armenia under Persian rule. The Jewish leaders might well have hoped to enjoy a similar status under the Persians and to see the basic hopes of Jewry—hopes held since the destruction of the Temple—realized in their time. The Persians too were interested in an alliance. Their reasons were not political and long term, but military, and short term. The Persian army advanced upon Palestine from the direction of Damascus. Its first aim was Caesarea, the capital of the province. The shortest and easiest road in that direction crossed the Jordan at the Bridge of the Daughters of Jacob, and continued by way of Tiberias, Sepphoris, Legio (Megiddo) and the Megiddo pass into the coastal plain, and so on to Caesarea. This road cut across the main areas settled by Jews. The attitude of the Jews of Tiberias, the mountains of Galilee and Nazareth, could make possible an easy and quick advance of the invaders (see map, p. 264).

The details of the agreement between the Persians and the Jewish leaders have not been preserved. It seems clear, however, that there was such a pact. The Jews of Tiberias, the Galilean mountains and the vicinity of Nazareth now joined the Persian army which arrived at Caesarea in record time. In the eyes of the Persians this campaign was aimed at the conquest and annexation of the occupied regions, and not as a quick plundering raid. The invaders were therefore interested in gaining the goodwill of the inhabitants. The Persians promised the people of Palestine that they would not injure them, and they seem to have kept their promise. From Caesarea the army advanced along the coastal road to Apollonia (Arsuf, Rishpon) and then turned inland. They passed Lydda-Diospolis and began the ascent in the direction of Jerusalem.[14]

For what happened afterwards we have two accounts. One is that of Sebaeus, who tells in detail about the surrender of Jerusalem, followed by a Christian revolt, and a renewed assault by the invaders. The second story can be found in the account of the monk Strategius. It is repeated in a poem of the patriarch Sophronius. According to these sources the city refused to submit and was besieged and stormed.

Those who favour the second version stress that fact that Strategius was an eye-witness to the events, which Sebaeus was not.[15] It seems, however, that the two accounts do not contradict each other. Strategius was not an eye-witness of the events *before* the siege; for he arrived at Jerusalem together with the other monks of Mar Saba who were flying before the Persian invaders. Moreover, the story of Sebaeus justifies to a certain extent the behaviour of the Persians towards the Christians. Such an admission from a Christian writer seems to us to add credence to his story.

According to Sebaeus' version, Jerusalem did indeed surrender at first, as did the other cities of the empire which had been attacked by the Persians. The conquerors appointed commissioners to watch over the inhabitants, at the request of the latter. After several months (probably at the beginning of the spring of 614) the hot-heads among the Christian youth of the city revolted. The reasons for this revolt are passed over in silence by Sebaeus. Possibly there were Jews among the Persian officials and soldiers garrisoning in Jerusalem; this fact may have given rise to grave suspicion in the Christian community regarding the fate of the Holy City. They may well have suspected that according to the pact between the Persians and the Jews it would be delivered to the latter. Possibly they

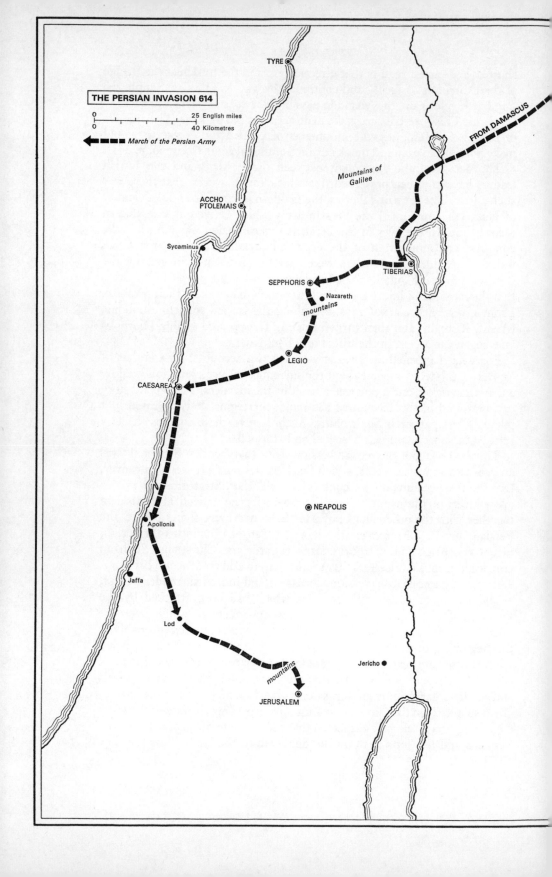

THE PERSIAN INVASION 614

0   25 English miles
0   40 Kilometres

◀▬ ▬ ▬ March of the Persian Army

TYRE

FROM DAMASCUS

Mountains of
Galilee

ACCHO
PTOLEMAIS

Sycaminus

SEPPHORIS   TIBERIAS

Nazareth

mountains

LEGIO

CAESAREA

NEAPOLIS

Apollonia

Jaffa

Lod

mountains   Jericho

JERUSALEM

even obtained exact information on that point. In the ensuing fight between the Jews and the Christian youths the latter were victorious. The Christians killed or wounded many Jews, and the survivors escaped to the Persians stationed in Caesarea.

On hearing of this breach of the capitulation agreement, Shahr-baraz collected his troops, including his Jewish allies. In Jerusalem there existed a peace party, headed by the patriarch Zecharias. However the mass of the people and the monks were intent on fighting under any conditions. It seems that they hoped for a miracle, and their opinion prevailed in the end. Although they had no regular forces, the Christians of Jerusalem made all the preparations necessary for a siege. It lasted twenty days. The Persians destroyed first all the churches outside the walls of the city, including the Eleona on the Mount of Olives and the Gethsemane church in the Kidron valley. Then they commenced their attack on the city proper. The besieged threw stones, shot arrows, and chased the besiegers away from the vicinity of the walls. They defended themselves bravely. The Persians brought battering rams to bear upon the walls, and bombarded it with *ballistae*, but without effect. Finally they dug a tunnel under the wall on its north-eastern side near the present Herod's Gate.[16] The roof of the tunnel was supported by wooden posts. When the tunnel was completed the posts were set on fire, the roof collapsed and brought down part of the wall over it.[17] A breach was thus made in the city wall and at the end of May 614[18] the city fell to the Persians. For three days there was much killing, plunder and destruction.

Having done their work, and set fire to many of the main churches of the city, including that of the Holy Sepulchre, the Persian army withdrew, leaving the Jews in possession.

4. *Jewish Rule in Jerusalem*

The Jews were thus again the rulers of Jerusalem. The form and acts of their government are shrouded in obscurity, apart from information supplied by its enemies. Clearly in Jewish eyes the new authority was legitimate and was invested with the full powers of government. Its first task must have been to restore order to the city. There was at that time complete anarchy in Palestine. Groups of Arabs and Jews were wandering all over the country, seeking for monks, an object of hatred to all non-Christians.

Christian writers, including modern ones, have much to tell about the cruelty with which the Christians in Jerusalem were treated by the Jews. Such complaints have one basic source: the opinion that Jews have *eo ipso* less rights than Christians, and that the latter are allowed to do what is forbidden to the former. Persecution is a one-way street on this view. If we study the behaviour of the Jews after the conquest of Jerusalem objectively, we note at once that their intention was to set up their rule in the same way and by the same methods as did the Byzantines. Modern historians, who quite rightly condemn such cruelties, ignore the prevailing spirit of the seventh century. No man or nation should be condemned because they were unable to rise above the common morality of their times.

The enthusiasm which reigned at that time among the Jews is evidenced by one more 'Salvation Midrash', the one called *The Book of Zerubbabel*. This work was in fact composed after the disillusionment which the Jews had experienced later on about the Persians; but in any case it tells us what had happened before that. The Jews in Jerusalem had at their head a leader, who is mentioned only by his symbolic name Nehemiah the son of Hushiel the son of Ephraim the son of Joseph. His real name is unknown. He ruled in Jerusalem and 'made sacrifices'.[19] Apparently Temple services were resumed for the third time after the destruction of the Temple, following previous efforts under Bar Kokhba and Julian.

After the renewal of the Temple services an effort was made to remove the alien places of worship, including the churches which were still standing after the Persians had left the city. This action, which can be compared to the systematic destruction of Greek temples and of synagogues by the victorious Christians was part and parcel of the seventh century religious atmosphere.

The problem of what to do with the surviving Christian inhabitants had also to be solved one way or another. After the killing which followed the capture of the city, the Persians announced a general amnesty. They ordered the survivors to leave their hiding places and promised them their lives. The Christians were collected in one place and each one was asked what was his profession. The Persian official in charge then selected those likely to be useful, and sent them into exile to Persia. At their head went the patriarch Zecharias, together with a chest containing the fragments of the 'life-giving cross'. The number of those exiled was 37,000. The rest, 4,500 approximately,[20] were placed in the (presumably empty) Mamillah pool outside the city. They were ransomed from the Persians and asked to change their religion—if not, they would be killed. It was a case of forced baptism in reverse. According to the accounts of the Christian sources—the only ones we have—all the captives decided to die for their faith. This event—if it is a fact—only shows to what an extent the religious oppression by the Byzantine rulers had aroused a parallel fanaticism on the part of their victims. It was one of those atrocities lamentably common in revolutionary times.

The apparent successes of Judaism caused at that time many conversions. Anastasius, a monk of Mount Sinai, tells of a fellow-monk from his monastery, who saw a vision in his dreams, and as a result abandoned Christianity, was converted to Judaism and lived as a proselyte among the Jews of Naaran and Livias in the Jordan Valley.[21] 'Jacob the Convert' tells of a priest from Acre called Leontius, who adopted Judaism under duress after the capture of the city.[22] These were certainly not the only cases of this kind.

After the occupation of Palestine, the Persians began to plan an invasion of Egypt in one direction and an attack on Constantinople in the other. Palestine was a useful base for an attack on Egypt, but the way of the invader was beset by many difficulties. Another Persian army invaded Asia Minor at that time and reached Chalcedon (Kadiköy) on the coast opposite Constantinople. In view of the huge distances between their northern and southern armies, the Persians were most sensitive to any threat from the sea. This was a real danger, as the Byzantine fleet still ruled the Mediterranean, in spite of all the defeats of the land forces. The Persians were good riders but bad seamen. The Jews were therefore given the task of seizing the harbours of the Phoenician coast. The first place to be attacked was Ptolemais—Acre; the assault was successful with the help of the Jews living in the city.[23]

After the fall of Acre the Jewish forces turned upon Tyre. According to the historian Eutychius the whole of their army was engaged in this attack, including, besides the units from nearby Galilee, contingents from Jerusalem and Damascus. The whole force numbered 20,000. The attack failed. The Jews in the city, who numbered 4,000, were unable to help because they had been jailed by a cautious commander. After a prolonged siege, the Jews suffered a defeat by a flanking sortie of the troops from Tyre.[24]

The siege of Tyre is important not only because it marked a military turning point in the history of the Jewish community, but also because it enables us to ascertain the length of Jewish rule in Jerusalem under Persian suzerainty. This rule began with the recapture of the Holy City in 614. After some time the Persians changed their policy, went back on their undertakings and betrayed their allies. They expelled the Jews from Jerusalem and returned the city to the Christians.

The Christian authors mention this reversal in the same breath as the story of the fall of Christian Jerusalem and its destruction. They are naturally enough interested in combining the 'crime' and its 'punishment' in one story. It is however clear that at the time of the assaults on Acre and Tyre this change in Persian policy still lay in the future. The Jews would hardly have fought for the Persians after the latter had betrayed them. Therefore the fixing of the date of the siege of Tyre is of great importance. Eutychius, who is the main source for this matter, does not

mention any date.[25] However the Arab historian Ibn Khaldun, who repeats the story of Eutychius,[26] states that the siege of Tyre was contemporary with the Persian siege of Constantinople. He states 'the king
of Persia retired disappointed from before Constantinople, then the Jews
gave up the siege of Tyre and fled away'. As the Persians camped before
Constantinople for a whole decade, and as it is most unlikely that the Jews
held Jerusalem for such a length of time, it seems that Ibn Khaldun
referred to the siege of Chalcedon, the eastern suburb of Constantinople.
This would fix the date of the siege of Tyre to the summer of 617, at which
time the Persian army retreated from the vicinity of Constantinople, after
taking Chalcedon itself. It seems that the siege of Tyre lasted from the
winter of 616/7 to the summer of 617. The renewed Jewish rule in
Jerusalem continued therefore for less than three years.

The *Book of Zerubbabel* states that the 'King of Persia went up against
Jerusalem in the fifth year'. This discrepancy in dating is more apparent
than real. We must remember that Jewish rule in Jerusalem began in the
spring of 614, in the Jewish year 4474. If the Persian 'king' came to
Jerusalem after the Jewish New Year of 617, he would arrive in 4478, in
the fifth year after the former date.

5. *The Change of Persian Policy. Expulsion of the Jews from Jerusalem*

The story of the change in Persian policy in Palestine is told by many
Christian authors. Amongst them are the Armenian Sebaeus, the author
of a Syrian *Chronicle*, Abu-l-Faraj (Bar Hebraeus) and Michael the
Syrian.[27] They all agree that the Persian king decided to rebuild Jerusalem
as a Christian city, to restore the churches and to expel the Jews. They
only differ in their account of the causes of this reversal. Most of them
attribute it simply to divine providence. The author of the Syrian *Chronicle*
tells us that the Jews promised the Persian commander the treasures which
were—so they said—buried under the Church of the Holy Sepulchre. As
they could not keep their promise, the Persians decided to break with
them. Others relate the change to the influence of a Christian queen of
Persia, or a Christian court physician.

It is of course possible that some court influences may have been
brought to bear upon the aging king Chosroes. There could have been
unsatisfied greed, the wiles of courtiers or of Christian members of his
harem etc. Basically however there can be only one real reason for this
sudden change in Persian policy. The Jews now suffered the common fate
of revolutionaries after a successful revolution. While the fight was still
going on, the Persians accepted Jewish aid because they were interested in
upsetting the existing state of things. They tried to unite all the opponents

of Byzantine rule. After the conquest they were as naturally interested in ruling the country in peace. For this they needed the acquiescence of all peaceful and law-abiding elements in it. Such submission they could hardly expect from the Jews, who had opposed the established rulers for several centuries, and for whom opposition to the government had almost become second nature. The Persians might possibly have accepted this, had the Jews been able by their number to rule the country effectively. It seems, however, that the Persians quickly noticed that they were relying on only 10–15 per cent of the population, too weak a base for a permanent domination. As they got to know the situation on the spot, it became clearer every day that they would have to come to an agreement with the Christian majority. The Christians were worth persuading, for they were able to choose their side. They could support either Byzantium or Persia. It was worthwhile, therefore, to buy their support. The Jews were in a different situation. A return of Byzantine rule would in any case bring disaster upon them. There was then no need to appease them and no danger in oppressing them. The military failure before Tyre undoubtedly influenced the Persian commanders, and weakened the Jewish position.

There seems to have been some Jewish resistance nevertheless. They tried first of all to regain the favour of the Persian commanders. Modestus, who was in charge of the affairs of the Jerusalem patriarchate after the exile of Zecharias, wrote in a letter to an Armenian bishop:[28] 'They (the Jews) were full of envy and rage, and they asked on several occasions to be allowed to return to the Holy City, and gave many gifts, but they were not deemed worthy of it.' Those who saw in 'Nehemiah son of Hushiel' a Messiah, 'the son of Joseph', tried to resist by force. 'Jacob the Convert' tells how the Jews who did not wish to follow Jesus were led astray. They were confused and confounded because they followed 'the evil dragon' who was 'impure and led to sin'—whose name (again symbolical), was Armillius.[29] Quite possibly he meant by these mystical terms the Messianic movement which had then spread in Jerusalem. In the *Book of Zerubbabel* we are told that 'Shiroy (the son) of the King of Persia went up against Nehemiah and all Israel . . . and he pierced Nehemiah through and they exiled Israel into the desert . . . and there was woe in Israel such as there had never been the like'. The Jews were expelled from Jerusalem after energetic resistance. To overcome it Persian troops under ten 'kings' had to be called up to the city. The new exiles left by the eastern gate of the Temple Mount like their Christian predecessors, and set their steps towards Jericho and the desert. 'Nehemiah' himself was apparently executed at Emmaus.[30]

This change in Persian policy was an event of very great importance in Jewish history. By betraying their Jewish allies the Persians put an end to the national hopes of the Jews for many centuries. The Persian power was the only one of those existing at the time which was not based on a narrow religious dogma. It was therefore the only one from which the Jews could hope for an autonomous existence in the land of their fathers. The two other great powers, Byzantium and Islam, were both inspired by a religious vision, in which a pluralistic society had no place. The deception, which the Jews suffered in their alliance with the Persians, marks therefore the real end of the political history of Judaism in Palestine. Having to give up their hope of liberty and independence, they ceased to be a political power. All that remained to them was a noble vision without substance. The Jews in Palestine lost their political aim. They became thus adapted in their profile to the Judaism of the Diaspora. This was one of the most tragic moments in the history of our nation.

6. *The Restoration of Byzantine Rule in Palestine.* *The Revenge of Heraclius*

In the meantime the fortunes of war began again to favour the Byzantine cause.[31] After several years of preparation the emperor Heraclius left Constantinople in the spring of 622 and attacked in his turn. His plan was bold and original. He refused to counter-attack the enemy in the usual field of battle between Persians and Byzantines—south-eastern Asia Minor and Syria—where the Persians were ready to encounter him. Instead he decided to outflank them by invading the mountains of Armenia and taking up a fortified position there. He crossed the Black Sea, entered Armenia and was helped by the local Christian population. From Armenia he conducted a lightning campaign into the very heartland of the Persian empire. The whole plan of campaign was carried out in six years. While the Persian army was still in occupation of many Byzantine provinces, and Persian governors ruled in Alexandria, Jerusalem, Damascus and Antioch, Heraclius arrived at the borders of Persia proper. In the autumn of 627 and the spring of 628 he stood before the walls of Ctesiphon, the capital of Persia. There he learned that his adversary Chosroes had been deposed. The various pretenders to the Persian throne began to fight each other. All of them were interested in making peace with the Byzantines as soon as possible, for only thus could they hope to overcome their internal enemies. Heraclius obtained without the slightest difficulty the evacuation of the Byzantine provinces occupied by the Persians, the release of the captives and the return of the relics of the Holy Cross. In the spring of 629 he arrived on the borders of Palestine on his way to Jerusalem.

The leaders of the Jews were in a desperate situation. Nevertheless they made a last effort to come to terms with the victorious emperor. They tried to have the past forgiven and forgotten. Heraclius was by his nature neither vindictive nor an enemy of the Jews. In the previous summer he had pardoned the Jews of Edessa, who had continued to defend their city after the departure of the Persians. Heraclius' general, his brother Theodosius, wanted to put them to the sword; but the emperor spared them.[32] Heraclius was also interested in preserving the peace of his realm after the long and devastating wars, which by 629 had continued for twenty-five years. He agreed therefore to receive at Tiberias the leaders of the Jews from the city and from the mountains of Galilee and Nazareth. After receiving their presents, he gave them letters of grace, in which he promised pardon for past offences. He confirmed his declaration with an imperial oath.[33]

At Tiberias the emperor was staying at the house of one Benjamin, a very rich Jew, who entertained the emperor and the army at his expense. The attitude of this Benjamin is typical of the confusion which now reigned among the Jewish leaders. Having been betrayed by the Persians they lost hope in the future of their nation. Benjamin accompanied the emperor on his way to Jerusalem. On the way he was persuaded to adopt Christianity. He was baptized at Neapolis, in the house of Eustathius, a prominent Christian. The disappearance from Jewry of this strong personality seems to have had considerable influence on his contemporaries.[34]

Heraclius arrived at Jerusalem in March 629. On the 21st of March he entered the city at the head of a splendid procession. He went on his way to the Church of the Holy Sepulchre, where he put back in their place the relics of the Cross he had received from the Persians. This was the greatest moment in the life of Heraclius, and the last great hour of Byzantine Jerusalem.

In Jerusalem the emperor soon noticed that, if he wished to keep the sympathy of the Christian population, he would have to sacrifice his new protégés, the Jews. He found some of the churches of the town half built, others still in ruins. The leaders of the Christian community, priests and monks alike, were passionate in their demands for revenge. They argued that in the time of the Persian invasion the Jews had caused more Christian deaths than had the Persians. Heraclius was by nature a conscientious man and one who tried hard to keep his promises. We know that on his death-bed he asked his son Constantine to allow a certain Armenian to return from exile, 'because I have promised it to him on oath and my oath is not in vain'.[35] In Jerusalem he argued that he was bound by his oath and that no person would in the future trust his word, if he were now to break it. However the priests knew how to lull his conscience. They took the sin of a broken oath upon themselves and as an atonement decreed a special fast. For centuries the Copts in Egypt continued to keep the 'Fast of Heraclius'.[36]

The emperor was the readier to accept the arguments of the clergy, because he became convinced that the Jews in Palestine were too weak to resist. After the incident of Benjamin of Tiberias he thought that it would not be difficult to convert most of the Jews, if not all of them. He promulgated an edict in Jerusalem, ordering all Jews to leave the city to within a radius of three miles. There began also a series of trials of Jews accused of killing Christians and destroying churches in Jerusalem and in Galilee. Many were executed, others went into hiding or fled to the desert. Some went as far as Edessa, but they were not left there in peace, and had to continue their way into Persia. Others hid in the mountains or went to Egypt.[37] Those who remained suffered various tribulations: 'The blessed Mar Yehudai said that the people of the Land of Israel were prohibited from saying the *Shema* or from praying. They were only allowed to assemble on Sabbath mornings to sing hymns.' They did assemble and say the prayers surreptitiously, disguising them as *piyyutim* (liturgical poetry).[38] It is from that time that Jewish liturgic poetry began to flourish.

7. *The Arab Conquest*

Five years had not passed after Heraclius' triumphant entry into Jerusalem, before a new enemy arose against him. Within a few years the Moslem Arabs took away from him Syria, Palestine and Egypt. Their quick conquests resulted not only from the weakening of the empire and its army by the tremendous efforts of the Persian wars, but also because the emperor did not know how to make good use of his opportunity after his military victories. Obviously he could expect no loyalty from his Jewish subjects after breaking his oath to them; but he failed even to unite the Christians. He made indeed several efforts to effect a compromise between the orthodox and the Monophysites. For this purpose he created a new dogma of 'Monothelism', according to which Jesus had two natures (as was held by the orthodox) with one will (this was a concession to the Monophysites who considered the human and divine nature of Jesus to be one). However as often happens, both sides refused to compromise. The matter was complicated by problems of ecclesiastical jurisdiction. During the Persian invasion the orthodox bishops had been ejected from their seats to the general joy of the Monophysites; now they returned in the wake of the Byzantine army. Their adversaries were in consequence ready to join the growing mass of those dissatisfied with Byzantine rule.

The Moslem invasion began in 634.[39] In February of this year the Arab armies reached the outskirts of Gaza. There they defeated the governor Sergius and his army. The battle occurred near Thadun (Anthedon). In July of the same year the Arabs gained another victory at Ajnadeyn near Beth Gubrin. Other armies invaded the Golan and besieged Damascus.

In 635 Bostra, the first Byzantine city to do so, submitted to the invaders. In the beginning of 636 the Arabs occupied Galilee and Tiberias. They retreated to the Yarmuk River on the approach of large Byzantine forces. There the decisive battle occurred on the 20th August 636. The Byzantine army was defeated and evacuated Palestine and Syria. The Arabs continued their slow and steady progress. They began the siege of Jerusalem in July 637; the city surrendered to the Caliph Omar in March–April 638. In 640 Caesarea, the last Byzantine stronghold, was captured after a siege of seven months. This was the end of Byzantine Palestine.

The Jews remained largely passive during this change of rulers. There can however be no doubt which side they were on. According to 'Jacob the Convert' they rejoiced greatly when the news was received at Caesarea that Sergius the governor had been defeated and killed.[40]

We have already noticed that in hours of danger the Byzantine emperors were wont to take measures against internal opposition, first and foremost against the Jews, in order to make sure of the solidity of the 'interior front'. This was also the case at the beginning of the Persian invasion in 609. It happened again after the first Arab attacks. In 634 Heraclius ordered a general forced baptism of all Jews in the empire. He even tried to give this policy a larger scope, and sent messages to Dagobert king of the Franks and to Sigibert king of the Visigoths in Spain, asking them to force the Jews in their realms in the same way. According to a legend Heraclius had been warned that 'a circumcised nation will fall upon you and will take away from you the Holy Land'. Heraclius assumed that this prophecy referred to the Jews, the only circumcised nation he knew of; as usual in such Pythian sayings another circumcised people, the Arabs, was meant.[41] In any case he must have known at the time he gave his order (634) from which directions the Byzantine empire was threatened. The real reason for his policy was, as in the time of Phocas, the desire to eliminate hostile elements within his realm. The order remained merely on paper; for a few years after it was given the Byzantine emperor had no power over the Jews of his former provinces.

There can be no doubt that the Jews hoped that the Ishmaelite rule would save them from the evil government (of Byzantium).[42] There is, however, no information in our sources of any real collaboration with the invaders. Sebaeus the Armenian does indeed state that, after the order of Heraclius, Jews of 'all the twelve tribes' assembled at Edessa, and from there went to all the Arab tribes, one thousand to each tribe. These Jews later on served the Arabs as guides in their invasion into Palestine.[43] This romantic story is of course pure invention. In the time of Sebaeus the Jews were no longer organized in tribes. The Jews of Edessa, and of Syria in general, must have been largely ignorant of the roads to and in Palestine. The Arab historians would not have passed over in silence a stream of thousands of Byzantine Jews into Arabia. The most important detail of this story, the reference to guidance in the roads of the Holy Land, does indeed occur also in another source, but in a quite different context. We are told that Heraclius refused to continue to pay the usual subsidies to the Arab tribes allied with Byzantium, in return for which they guarded the borders of the empire. The disappointed tribes joined the Moslems and led the invaders, by the routes known only to themselves, to their objectives.[44] This story bears the stamp of historic truth. Sebaeus must have combined two separate facts: that the Moslems had expert guides and that the Jews were hostile to the Byzantines; from these facts he concocted his story. There is another story, according to which during the siege of Caesarea a Jew showed the Arabs the way to enter the city by its sewers.[45] This account agrees with what we know of the attitude of the Jews in sieges of Byzantine towns, and also with the archaeological discovery of underground sewers in Caesarea, of a man's height or more.

In fact the Jews had no special reason to sacrifice themselves for the new invaders. They could hardly expect anything good from them in the positive sense. The only thing they could hope for would be some relief from oppression. The Arabs appeared, like the Byzantines (but unlike the Persians) as bearers of a specific religious message. Islam could not by its very nature agree to give the Jews satisfaction in their national hope. It is true that it was on the whole more tolerant as regards non-Moslems (at least in theory). Both religions refused, however, to submit the 'true believers' to the rule of 'unbelievers'.

This attitude to the Jews became evident from the first acts of the invaders. In their first attacks, which were aimed at destruction and not at conquest (as in their attack on Gaza in 634), they did not exempt Jews from the general destruction. In the battle of Tadun (February 634) and its follow-up scores of villagers, Jews, Samaritans and Christians, were killed or injured indiscriminately.[46] Even later on, when they did not raid but tried to conquer and hold, the Arabs made no distinction between Christians and Jews. Both groups were in the eyes of Islam 'people of the Book'. According to the Prophet's revelation, they were entitled to live in peace under the protection of the Moslems, provided they paid the prescribed poll-tax or ransom. Of course, this equation between themselves and the Jews was a deep debasement for the Christians, compared to their status (or rather to that of the orthodox among them) under Byzantine rule. The Jews on the other hand enjoyed their freedom from the oppression of the 'evil government' and from the constant fear of forced baptism. We read in the source quoted above: 'Now that the Holy One, blessed be He, has put an end to the rule of Edom (Byzantium as heir to Rome) and has abolished its oppressive decrees'.[47] This result came about however without any special intention on the part of the Arabs to favour the Jews. In case of need they did not hesitate to sacrifice Jewish interest to an accommodation with the Christians. When Jerusalem surrendered, the Caliph Omar promised the patriarch Sophronius not to allow any Jews to settle in Jerusalem. The few families who moved in soon afterwards did so with the consent of the patriarch. However, this condition was very soon set aside; and the possibility of settling freely in Jerusalem was perhaps the greatest boon derived by the Jews from the Arab conquest. On the other hand they had lost for centuries the hope of living in a Jerusalem of their own.

8. *Conclusion*

We have surveyed in this book five hundred years of Jewish history in Palestine, from the fall of Beth-Ter to the Arab conquest. Even in the long history of Israel this is no small stretch of time. We have seen how the survivors of the great catastrophe closed their ranks, how they set up a new national authority, how the political and economic position of the Jews in the country was strengthened and how they achieved a compromise settlement with the Roman government.

This new national-religious structure had to undergo heavy trials in the time of the imperial crisis in the third century; it lost much of its strength in that cruel test. As soon as that crisis was over, there began a long drawn out struggle with the Christian state. When the Jews could at last hope for a renewal of their power in Palestine, they suffered a crushing blow in the betrayal of the Persians.

The story of the political decline of Palestinian Jewry does not of course give a complete account of Jewish history. Side by side with the external struggle, a tremendous amount of work was done within. The leaders of the nation used the occasion to create the protective armour of the normative law, which served to preserve Judaism for forty-three generations.

In these centuries the fate of the Jewish nation resembled that of the wanderer in the fable, for whose cloak the sun and wind contended. All through the Middle Ages, which from the Jewish point of view lasted till the eighteenth century, they continued to suffer under the consequences of the Byzantine legislation and the diminution of their civil rights formulated therein. This was true even for the Islamic countries, the enemies of Byzantium, and all its successors. Nevertheless the Jewish nation kept its character throughout all persecutions. The 'stiff-necked' people lived stubbornly on; even if its political will was broken, there were always from time to time great popular movements, such as the Messianic commotion in the seventeenth century.

The Jewish emancipation, which started in the end of the 18th century and continued into the 19th, enabled the Jewish individual to become politically active; but only on condition he left his nation, which was now in serious danger of melting away in the new and more friendly environment. The emancipation did however achieve a thorough modernization of Jewish economic and social structures, and as such made further political activity effective. When under the influence of the romantic movement one nation after another began to recall its national past and to strive for national unity, and when Italians, Germans and Poles achieved their national freedom, political consciousness awakened also among the Jews. It took the shape of a striving after the seemingly almost impossible revival of a Jewish state in the old country, which had been abandoned for centuries. With the revival of their national will, Jews awoke to their historical past. The history of the Second Jewish Commonwealth is only perfunctorily mentioned in the Talmud; now the Books of the Maccabees and the history of Josephus were reintegrated into Jewish historical consciousness. The first centuries of the post-biblical period acquired at last a clearly defined profile. However, the period after the destruction of the Jewish state remained as the so-called 'period of the Mishnah and the Talmud', the preserve of specialized historians who regarded it as a 'history of suffering and scholarship' and nothing more. This book has been written in order to restore it to its proper place in the political history of the Jewish nation as a whole.

Notes to Chapter XII

1. *The Chronicle of Joshua the Stylite*, ed. Wright, London, 1882, pp. 47–8.
2. Malalas (ed. Bonn, p. 455f.); Theophanes, a.m. 6021 (ed. de Boor, p. 179, 1ff.).
3. Michel le Syrien, ed. Chabot, II, p. 191.
4. Agapius of Membidj (*PO* 8, p. 449).
5. Sebaeus, *Histoire d'Heraclius*, trans. F. Macler, p. 63.
6. See above, p. 126.
7. Theophanes, a.m. 6120 (ed. de Boor, p. 328, 19–20); abbreviated in *Historia miscell.* (*PG* 95, *c.* 1041).
8. 'Sargis d'Aberga' 101 (*PO* 13, p. 76).
9. J. Eben-Schmuel (J. Kaufmann), *Midrashey Geula* ('Book of Elijah' pp. 29–48; Perek Eliyahu 49–54) (Hebrew).
10. Sebaeus (op. cit., n. 5 above), Cap. XXIV, p. 68f.
11. A. Couret, *La prise de Jérusalem par les Perses*, Orléans, 1876, p. 29f.

12. Sophronius, *PG* 87, *c.* 3809f.

13. *CSCO(SS)* III, IV, *Chron. syr.* ed. Guidi, p. 22f.; Eutychius, *Annales* (ed. Cheikho, p. 216); Vita Georgii Chozebitae, cap. 34 (*Analecta Bollandiana* VII, p. 133); *Chronicon paschale* (ed. Bonn, p. 704); Georgius Pisides (ed. Bonn, pp. 17–18); Zonaras XIV, 15 (ed. Dindorf III, p. 307); Theophanes, a.m. 6106 (ed. de Boor, pp. 300, 30–301, 5); *Historia miscellanea*, XVIII (*PL* 95, *c.* 1025); Cedrenus (ed. Bonn, I, p. 715); Leo Grammaticus (ed. Bonn, p. 148); Ephraemus (ed. Bonn, p. 64); Barhebraeus (ed. Budge, I, p. 87); *History of the Patriarchs* (*PO* 1, p. 484).

14. Couret, *La prise* (see above, n. 11); *Analecta Bollandiana* VII, p. 133.

15. Hillkowitz, *Zion*, 4, pp. 307–18 (Hebrew).

16. Avi-Yonah, *Jerusalem*, 2 (1949), pp. 228–30 (Hebrew).

17. Cf. the siege works which led to the fall of Dura Europus, *Excavations at Dura Europus, Provisional Report* VI, 1936, pp. 188–206.

18. For the date see Vailhé, *ROC* 7 (1901), p. 647 (614); Butler, *The Arab Conquest of Egypt*, Oxford, 1902, p. 61, n. 4 (615).

19. *Midrashey Geula* (see n. 9 above), pp. 55–88.

20. The list of those killed at the taking of Jerusalem is quoted differently in the various sources. The list has been found in Arabic (A. Couret: *La prise* etc. (see above, n. 11); Peeters, *Mél. de la faculté orientale de l'Université St. Joseph*, Beirut, 9, pp. 1–42; cf. J. T. Milik, ibid., 37 (1960/1), pp. 128, 182–3.; in Georgian (Cleophas Koikylides, *RB*, 1903, p. 492; Peeters, *Analecta Bollandiana*, 31, 1912, pp. 301–8. The Arabic source gives the number as 24518; one Georgian source lists 4618, the other 4518.

21. Anastasius Sinaita, *Homilia* 84 (*PG* 89 *c.* 1692).

22. 'Sargis d'Aberga' 90 (*PO* 13, p. 62).

23. Ibid., 90 (p. 62); 109 (p. 84).

24. Eutychius, *Annales* (*PG* 111, *c.* 1084–5).

25. See below, note 27.

26. *Sefer ha-Yishub* (ed. L. A. Mayer–S. Assaf), II, p. 68, No. 5 (Hebrew).

27. Sebaeus, cap. XXIV, p. 68f.; cap. XXV, p. 71f.; *CSCO(SS)* III, iv, *Chron. syr.* ed. Guidi, p. 23; Bar-Hebraeus, ed. Budge, I, p. 87; Michel le Syrien, ed. Chabot, II, p. 400—XI, 1.

28. Sebaeus, cap. XXV, p. 71f.

29. 'Sargis d'Aberga', cap. 94 (*PO* 13, p. 70).

30. *Sefer Zerubbabel*, 99–101 (*Midrashey Geula*, note 9 above), p. 80; Marmorstein, *REJ*, 3 (1906), p. 183, 'The ninth sign'.

31. For a chronology of the campaigns of Heraclius see Gerland, *Byzantinische Zeitschrift*, 3 (1894), pp. 330ff.

32. Agapius de Membidj (*PO* 8, p. 466).

33. Eutychius, *Annales* (*PG* 111, *c.* 1089–90).

34. Theophanes, a.m. 6120 (ed. de Boor, p. 328, 15–23); *Hist. miscell.* XVIII (*PL* 95, *c.* 1041).

35. Sebaeus, cap. XXX, pp. 99–100.

36. Eutychius (*PG* 111, *c.* 1090).

37. Cedrenus (ed. Bonn, I, p. 735); *Hist. miscell.* XVIII (*PL* 95, *c.* 1041); F. Dölger, *Regesten der Kaiserurkunden des oströmischen Reiches*, I, München–Berlin, 1924, No. 197.

38. Edelmann, *Oriens christianus*, 3rd series, 7, p. 19f.

39. For the chronology of the Arab conquest of Palestine see de Goeje, *Mémoire sur la conquète de la Syrie*, Leiden, 1900 (s.A.H. 13); Caetani, *Annali del Islam*, III, Milano, 1910, p. 16f.

40. 'Sargis d'Aberga', cap. 117.

41. Dölger, *Regesten der Kaiserurkunden des oströmischen Reiches*, I, p. 24, Nos. 206–7, s.a. 634; Michel le Syrien, ed. Chabot, II, p. 414; *Synaxaire arabe-jacobite*, ed. Basset (*PO* 11, p. 562); Ibn Khaldun ap. *Sefer ha-Yishub*, II, p. 68, No. 5 (Hebrew).

42. *Sefer ha-Yishub*, II, pp. 69–70 (Hebrew).

43. Sebaeus, cap. XXX, pp. 94–7.

44. Theophanes a.m. 6123 (ed. de Boor, pp. 335, 233–6); *Hist. miscell.* (*PL* 95, *c.* 1044).

45. Caetani, *Annali del Islam*, IV, pp. 158–9.

46. *CSCO(SS)* III, iv, *Chronica minora*, p. 114.

47. Edelmann (op. cit., note 38 above).

Index

(b.: *ben* or *bar*, 'son of'; R.: Rabbi)

Ab Beth Din 57, 60, 122
Ab, ninth 164, 223
R. Abba 95, 96, 123
R. Abba b. Kahane 69, 107, 130
R. Abba b. Mammal 123
R. Abba b. Zaminan 188
R. Abbahu 44, 47, 48, 67, 82, 92, 93, 104, 120, 122, 123, 125, 133, 165
R. Abin (Abun) 82, 105, 171
Abraham 82, 118, 239
Acra 3, 4
Acre (Ptolemais) 22, 26, 72, 138, 179–80, 267
Adiabene 79
Aelia Capitolina *see* Jerusalem
Africa 250
agentes in rebus 216
Agilas (Aquila) 250
agriculture 20–2, 105–6, 217, 222
Agrippa I 9
R. Aha 21, 107, 164, 170, 171, 197
Aher *see* Elisha b. Abuyah
Aila (Elath, Akaba) 237, 252
Ajnadeyn 272
R. Akiba 12, 55, 64, 65, 66, 143
Akraba 16
Alarich 221
Alcimus *see* Eliakim
R. Alexander 130
Alexander the Great 2, 7, 181
Alexander Jannaeus 5, 6
Alexander Severus 42, 91
Alexandria 38, 122, 218, 234
al-Mundhir 242, 253
Alypius 195, 201, 203
am ha-arets 63, 107, 110, 238
Amantius 251
Amazons 76

Ambrose 212
R. Ammi 48, 107, 119, 121, 123, 124, 126, 133
Ammianus Marcellinus 201
Amorcessus 237
anachōresis 101, 117
Anastasius, emperor 235, 236, 237, 246
Anastasius of Sinai 267
androlomousia 93, 107
anfortah 95
angaria (*tsumot*) 94, 97, 99
annona (*militaris*) 96–7, 100, 108, 109
Antioch 68, 178, 179, 181, 191, 210, 258, 260
Antioch in Pisidia 146
Antiochus III 3, 6
Antiochus IV 3–4, 6
'Antoninus' 39–42, 58, 91; *see also* Caracalla
Antoninus Pius 13, 15, 37, 39, 40, 45, 77
Aper 92
Aphrodite 72
Apikorsim 142
Apollonia 263
Apollonius of Tyana 36
'apostle' 61
apostolē 61, 117, 195, 199
Apostolic Canons 153
Appian 36
Arabah 19
Arabs 16, 242, 272–5
Aramaic 73
Arbel 22
arbitrators 48, 217
Arcadius, emperor 212
arche 47
archipherecytes 237, 250
archisynagogus 38
archon 101, 121, 226

Arians, Arianism 167, 170, 209–11
Aristobulus 6
Ark of the Law 238, 239
arms industry 24
arnona see *annona*
Artabanus 68
Ascalon 138, 164, 189, 198, 220
R. Assi 48, 121, 123, 124, 125
assimilation 72
Astreia (Esther) 73
Atargatis 190
Athanasius 197, 234
Atrans 176
Attilianus, P. Calpurnius 43
Augustus 90, 102
Aurelian 91, 92, 126
aureus 103
aurum coronarium see crown-tax
R. Azariah 119
Azotus 16, 138

baale batim 21
Babylonia, Babylonian 8, 9, 26, 36, 38, 60, 74, 124–5, 166, 172, 199
balls of fire 201
balsam 16, 59
R. Bannah 48
baptism *see* forced baptism
Bar Hobets 100
Bar Kokhba 12–13, 16–19, 23, 28, 36, 50, 54, 56, 65, 66, 67, 143, 147, 173
Bar Kozziba *see* Bar Kokhba
Barnabas 146
'Barnabas, Letter to' 147
Bar-Sauma 224
basilicas 238
Benjamin of Tiberias 260, 271
'Ben Netser' 127
R. Berakhiah 169, 171, 223
Berea 131
Berytus 68
Beth Alpha 239, 240
Beth Guvrin *see* Eleutheropolis
Beth-Horon 27
Bethlehem 51, 160, 164, 221
Beth Maon 120
Beth Mehoza 22
Beth-Shean 22, 109, 138, 167, 168, 243
Beth Shearim 19, 23, 25, 27, 38, 74, 76, 126, 180
Beth-Ther 67
billeting 94–5, 210
Boethus, Flavius 43
Bonosus 254, 260
Bordeaux, Pilgrim 164
Borion 250
Bostra 138, 189, 273
boulē, bouleutēs (curiae) 47, 101, 107, 163, 210, 216–17, 226, 247–8
Byzantine policy 234–6, 251–3

Caesar, Julius 7
Caesarea 22, 36, 47, 67, 123, 129–30, 138, 150–1, 169, 224, 228, 243, 251, 263, 265, 273, 274
Caesarea in Cappadocia *see* Mazaca
Caesarea Philippi *see* Paneas
calendar 62, 166
Caligula 10
Callinicum 212
candlestick 40, 41, 59, 75, 99, 101, 239
Capernaum (Kefar Nahum) 140, 168
Capitolias 22
Cappadocia 38, 126, 260
Caracalla ('Antoninus') 39–42, 45–7, 77–9, 91, 97, 102, 103
Castra 78
census 96
Centaur 76
centenarius 103
centurion 98
Chalcedon, council of 234, 246
chōra 9
Chorazin 76
Chosroes I 259
Chosroes II 268, 270
Christians, Christianity 11, 137–55, 158–81, 185–90, 232–4
Christians, = 'true Israel' 146, 147, 170, 193
church and state 159, 185–7
circumcision 42, 45, 46, 143, 228
cities *see* towns
civil status 46
Clarus, Gaius Erucius 43
Claudius (the robber) 78
Clement of Alexandria 150
Clysma 252
Cochaba 140
cohortalini 247
collaboration with Rome 71; *see also* denunciation
colony, Roman 12, 40
comes 168, 240
Commodus 39, 40, 102
Community of the Covenant *see* Dead Sea Sect
compromise with Rome 79–83; with Byzantium 236–7
Constantia 259
Constantine the Great 104, 158–66
Constantinople 221, 235, 249, 258, 267, 268
Constantius II 174–85
consuls 37, 42–3, 66, 99
converts 163, 168, 169, 174–5, 214, 248
Corinth 146
Councils 153, 234, 246
crafts, craftsmen 22–3, 76
cross, appearance of 200
cross, relic of 261, 266, 270
crown-tax (*aurum coronarium, mas ha-kelila*) 97, 100, 101, 117, 195
curiae see *boulē*
cursus publicus 94
custom duties 71, 95
Cyprian of Carthage 148
Cyriacus 'the wolf' 79, 254
Cyril of Alexandria 37, 234

Cyril of Jerusalem 202

Dabberat 19
Dagobert 273
Daniel (in the Lions' Den) 239
Darom 16, 61, 139, 209
David 58; 'Shield of' 75
Dead Sea Sect 6, 11
Decapolis 18
decemprimi 61, 100
defensoris civitatis 216, 247
delatio see denunciation
demosia see land-tax
denarius 102–3
denunciation 66, 100, 130, 142
Derekh Erets Zuta 68
deuterosis 250
Dhu-Nawas 253
Dhu-Yazan, Saif ibn 253
Diaspora 10, 13, 27–8, 62, 74, 76, 122,
  146–9, 193
diatagmas 129
dikion 69
R. Dimmi 105
Dio-Caesarea *see* Sepphoris
Diocletian 91, 96, 100, 101, 104, 106, 121,
  125, 127, 241
Dionysus Sabazius 3
disputes with Judaeo-Christians and Christians 144–5, 148, 169–71
ducenarius 128
Dumah (Rome) 67
dux 91–2, 108, 116, 127, 130, 132, 243
dyeing 22

earthquake 201, 209
east of the Jordan 106, 139; *see also* Decapolis
Easter (feast of) 165, 166, 249
Ebionites 139
economy 19–25, 221–3, 238
Edessa 258, 271, 272, 273
'Edom' ('Esau') = Rome 58, 70, 126, 129–32,
  171–2
Egypt 40, 221, 226, 267
'Ekron' = Caesarea 129
Elath (Akaba) *see* Aila
R. Eleazar 108, 133
R. Eleazar b. Abbina 172
R. Eleazar b. Harsom 99
R. Eleazar b. Hyrcanos 81, 143, 144
R. Eleazar b. Pedath 64, 82, 98, 106, 110, 118,
  130
R. Eleazar b. Shemua 106
R. Eleazar b. Simeon 23, 71
R. Eleazar (Eliezer) ha-Kappar 72, 145
Eleona 265
Eleutheropolis (Beth Gubrin) 109, 139, 220
Eliakim (Alcimus) 4
R. Eliezer b. Dama 140
R. Eliezer b. Yose the Galilean 15
R. Eliezer ha-Kappar *see* R. Eleazar ha-
  Kappar
Elijah, prophet 71, 80
Elisha, prophet 221

Elisha b. Abuyah (Aher) 23, 67, 72 n. 102, 80
Elvira, council of 153, 174
Emesa 127
emigration 25–9, 105, 124
Emmaus 78, 138
emperor 45, 66, 76, 77, 90, 91–3, 148
Enoch 144, 170
eparchoi 92; see also *hyparchoi*
Ephraim the Syrian 193, 201
epidemics 106–7
Epiphanius 167–8
Esau *see* Edom
Essenes 8, 11
estates *see* latifundia
Ethiopia 252–3
Eusebius 77, 139, 151, 160, 168, 194
Eustathius 271
Euthymius 221
Eutropius 227
Eutychius (Ibn Batriq) 163, 241, 267–8
excommunication 49, 60, 145
exilarch 58, 237
export, prohibition of 28–9, 109
Ezechiel b. Abba 71

famine 106
farmers, farming *see* peasants
fasting, prohibition of 165
feasts, dates of 62, 122, 165–6
Firmilianus 160
fiscus 93, 98
fiscus iudaicus 49
fishing, fishermen 22, 57
forced baptism 250, 254–5, 273
forced labour *see* angaria
Fronto 36
fruit-trees 21
funeral 57, 122

Gadara 138
Galilee 6, 13, 18–19, 21, 23–4, 29, 61, 106,
  131, 132–3, 240, 263, 271, 273
Gallienus 102, 107
Gallus Caesar 89, 174, 176–81
Gamliel I 221
Gamliel II 55–7, 58, 59, 72, 95, 96, 120, 142,
  143
Gamliel III 59–61, 62, 67, 96, 109, 119
Gamliel IV 120, 122
Gamliel VI 228
Garizim, Mount 242
Gaul 172
Gaza 189–90, 198, 220, 238, 240, 272, 274
Gedora 138
Gelasios 73
Genizeh 142
Georgius 254
Gerasa 238–9, 251
gerim see proselytism
German 59, 120, 126, 221
Gethsemane, church 265
Ginnosar 80
Giscala 22
Gladiator 105

glass industry 24
Gnostics 150
'God-fearing' 37, 39, 146, 147
Golan 21, 59, 122, 132, 272
Gophna 16, 51
Gothic 59, 120
governors 42–4, 48, 66, 77, 99, 165; *see also* consuls, *hegemones*
Greece 172
Greek 71–6; *see also* Hellenism
Gregory of Nazianzus 193, 201
Gush Halav *see* Giscala
gynecaeum 175

Habakkuk, prophet 221
haber 63, 100, 108, 124
Hadrian 12–14, 15, 23, 25, 36–7, 45, 46, 47, 50, 54, 56, 81, 83, 91
Haggadists *see* popular preachers
R. Haggai 121
Haifa 78
hairdressing, Greek fashion 72
Hakam 57, 60, 62, 122
Halamish 78
R. Hama 48
Hammath-Gader 240
R. Hanania b. Gamliel 81
R. Hanina 122, 143
R. Hanina b. Hama 44, 62, 70, 98, 103, 107, 120, 122
R. Hanina b. Pappa 123
R. Hanina b. Teradion 67
Hasidim 3–5
Hasmoneans 4–7
Hebrew 73
'Hebrews' 151
hegemones 66, 108
R. Helbo 82, 124
Helena 165
Heliogabalus 40, 42
'Hellenes' 162, 179, 198, 203; *see also* Hellenism
Hellenism 2–7, 8, 71–6, 186–7, 211
Henoticon 235, 247
Heracles 76
Heraclius 258, 273
hereditary professions 106, 118
'heretics' 247; *see also* Minim
Herod 7–10, 16
'Herodians' 8–9, 12, 64
Herodium 16, 51
Hesychius 227
high priest 2, 9, 11, 12, 65, 196
Hilarion 220
R. Hillel 169
Hillel II 167, 194
Hillel (Jullus), brother of Judah II 150
Hillel, the House of 12, 56, 58, 66, 196, 228
Himyar, Himyarites 252–3
hipparchoi 108
Hippus *see* Susitha
Hispania 172
R. Hiyya b. Abba (Rabba) the elder 21, 26, 48, 58, 70, 80, 81

R. Hiyya b. Abba the younger 105, 121, 122, 127, 209
holidays *see* feasts
Holy Trinity, dogma of 144, 170
Honorius 227
R. Hosheyahu 48, 128
Hosius 153
R. Huna b. Abin 124, 125, 166, 172
hunters 22
Husifah 240, 251
hyparchoi 130, 132
hypatikoi see consuls
Hyrcanus, John I 6
Hyrcanus, John II 6, 9, 10

iconoclasm 239
R. Iddi 170
idolatry, idols 10, 45, 47, 72, 125, 129, 139
Idumea 6
R. Ilai 101
images of human beings 72, 76, 239
Imma Shalom 143
immigration 25
industry 22, 175
inflation 102–4
inheritance tax 97
in hoc signo vinces 161
inn 95
inscriptions on tombstones 73
Irenaeus of Lugdunum 152
R. Isaac 23, 80, 82, 91, 106, 108, 123, 128
R. Isaac b. Joseph 105
Isaac, the Offering of 239
R. Ishmael b. Yose 48, 58, 71
Israel *see* Christians, = 'true Israel'
issar 106

R. Jacob b. Abin 99
'Jacob the Convert' 246, 254, 260, 267, 273
Jacob of Kefar Neburaya 119
Jacob of Kefar Sikhnin 143
Jaffa 7, 22, 38, 47, 73, 138
Jamnia *see* Yabneh
Japhet 73
R. Jeremiah 99, 101, 122, 124, 128, 167, 172
R. Jeremiah b. Abba 27
Jericho 27, 139, 240
Jerome 221–4, 227
Jerusalem (Aelia Capitolina) 12, 28, 50, 51, 79–81, 129–30, 132, 141, 143, 160, 163–4, 165, 179, 190, 192–7, 223, 224, 240, 263–9, 271–3, 275
Jesus 140, 141, 143, 144, 146, 150, 169, 170, 171, 192–3
Jezreel, Valley of 7, 59, 132, 180
John *see* Hyrcanus
John the Baptist 200 n. 54, 221
John Chrysostom 171, 173, 191, 201–3, 220, 222, 223, 227
R. Jonah 123, 181
R. Jonathan 48, 80, 122, 145
R. Jonathan b. Amram 110
R. Jonathan b. Eleazar 21, 70
Jonathan the Hasmonaean 4

Jordan, Jordan Valley 16, 18, 27, 59, 102, 240, 254, 267
Joseph 221
R. Joseph 169
Joseph, *comes* 167–9
R. Joshua b. Hanania 66, 81, 143
R. Joshua b. Karhah 66, 71
R. Joshua b. Levi 44, 48, 71, 73, 80, 122, 123, 140, 142
Jotaba 237, 253
Jovian 208, 209
Judaea 6, 15–18, 29, 106
Judaeo-Christians 51, 139–44
Judah *see* Aristobulus
R. Judah 21, 107
Judah I 26, 30, 39–41, 47, 57–60, 62, 63, 67–8, 70, 73, 96, 101, 103, 106, 108–10, 117, 119, 120, 122, 133
Judah II 58, 59, 109, 116, 118–20, 122, 128
Judah III 120–1, 167
Judah IV 122, 167
R. Judah b. Baba 54–5
R. Judah the baker 23
R. Judah b. Bathyra 25
R. Judah b. Ezechiel 124
R. Judah b. Ilai 65
R. Judah b. Levi 118
R. Judah, *morina* 60
R. Judah b. Shalom 170
R. Judah b. Simeon b. Pazzi 82, 165, 169, 172, 211
judaizare 153, 215
Judas Maccabaeus 4
Judges 118–19, 143
Julia Domna 40, 77
Julian, emperor 185–204
Julianus, Samaritan 243
Jupiter Capitolinus 49, 81, 200
jurisdiction, autonomous 48–9, 63–4, 118–19, 217–18, 222, 226, 227–8
Justin I 247
Justin II 254
Justin of Neapolis 140, 149, 152
Justinian 242, 243, 246–53
Justus 73
Justus, Samaritan 243
Juvenal 234

Kafra 101, 121
Kalendae 45
Kavad I 236
Kefar Gamala 221
Kefar Hanania 23, 24
Kefar Nahum *see* Capernaum
Kefar Neburaya 140
Kefar Otnay 36
Kefar Samma 140
Kefar Sikhnin 140, 143
Kefar Soganeh 24
kehillah (edah) kedoshah 80
Kitsyon 77
Kitya b. Shalom 83
'Kozebite' coins 28
Kratesis 45

landed property 29–30, 59
land-owners 21
land-tax (*demosia*) 95, 97, 98
Laodicaea, canons of 71, 78, 154
latifundia 21, 107
laws concerning the Jews 162–5, 174–6, 213–20, 236, 247–51
Leda 76
Legio (town) 36, 78, 138
legions 11–13, 36, 37, 92–3, 98, 118 n. 11
leiturgia 118
Leo, emperor 235, 237
Leontius 267
leshon ra'a see denunciation
'Letter to the Hebrews' 141
R. Levi 26, 92, 96, 98, 107, 116, 128, 131
R. Levi b. Hittah 74
lex Cornelia de veneficiis 45
Libanius 198, 225
linen 22, 59, 100
Livias 267
loipos 116
Lot's wife 27
ludarius 105
Lydda-Diospolis 16, 22, 47, 59, 61, 71, 78, 138, 178–80, 263

Macarius of Jerusalem 194
Maccabees 3–5, 9, 58; *see also* Hasmoneans
Machaerus 22
Magdiel 133
magicians 140
Magina 218
Mahalol 19
Maiumas 190
Malalas 242
R. Mana 122, 125, 181
Maon 240
Mar Zutra 237
Marcus Aurelius 39, 40, 102
Marcianus 242, 246
Marnas 190
Mary, garments of the Virgin 221
mas ha-kelila see crown-tax
R. Mattithiah b. Heresh 25
Mauricius, emperor 254, 258
Maximianupolis *see* Legio
Maximinus Thrax 91, 102
Mazaca (Caesarea) 126, 260
Media 172
Medusa 76
R. Meir 16, 23, 27, 57, 63, 67
Menahem 11
Menelaos 3
Meshummadim 142
Mesopotamia 38, 189, 199
Messianic movement 7, 12, 68–70, 130–2, 143, 169, 197–8, 260–1
Midrashim 104, 250, 261, 266
Mimus 105
minae 59
Minim 139–45, 153, 170
Minut 158
minyan 119

Mishnah 170
mission 147, 149–50, 153, 169
mixed marriages 154, 174, 214
Modestus of Jerusalem 269
money 30; *see also aureus, denarius*, inflation, *solidus*
monks 210, 220, 224, 236
Monophysites 234–6, 246–7, 259, 272
'Monothelism' 272
morina see R. Judah, morina
mosaic pavements (in synagogues) 238–9
Moserim 142
Moses 27, 55, 58, 145, 170; Seat of 75
mules 59
mystery religions 90, 150
myths, mythological 76

Naaran 78, 238, 239, 267
Nablus *see* Neapolis
R. Nahman 125, 169, 172
R. Nahum b. Simai 66
names, Jewish (Hebrew) 72, 73, 224
naphtha (petrol) 93
Narbata, district of 18
nasi 196; *see also* patriarch
R. Nathan 57
Naveh 78
'Nazarenes' 140
Nazareth 160, 168, 263, 271
Neapolis (Nablus) 41, 78, 243
neeman see haber
Negev 238
R. Nehemia 23
Nehemiah b. Hushiel 266, 269
Nehorai 122
neo-Platonic 187, 188
Nero 11, 102
Nestorius, Nestorians 246
Nicopolis *see* Emmaus
nidduy see excommunication
Niger, Pescennius 77, 92
Nisibis 38
Noah's Ark 239
Nonus 255
Notserim 142
numerus 93

Odenathus 91, 126
Og, King of Bashan 27
oil 23–4, 59, 109
olive groves 21, 23, 59
Onias, house of 2, 4
ordination 26, 55–7, 60, 61, 121–2
Oreine 16, 51
Orfitianus, Julius Commodus 43
Orient and Rome 39
Origen 49, 80, 139, 150–1
oxygarum 24, 59

Palestine 92, 124, 160, 161, 189, 220–1, 228;
see also Syria-Palaestina
pallium 73
Palmyre, Palmyrene 126, 131
Pamphylia 38

Paneas 101, 109, 190
Paregorios 73
parnas, parnasim 61, 101, 107, 121
parties 8–10, 64–71, 127–8, 166–7
Parthian, Parthians 37–8; *see also* Persians
Passover 249
patriarch (*nasi*), patriarchate 39–40, 47, 52–64, 68, 72–3, 76, 108–10, 114–23, 163, 167, 168, 191–7, 217, 225–9
'patriarchs, little', provincial 191, 216, 226, 228
Patricius 176–8
patrocinia 107
Paul, apostle 141, 146–7
peace 68–9
peacocks 239
peasants 20–1, 59, 74, 90, 105–6
'people of the land' *see am ha-arets*
Pella 141
Persia, Persians 1–2, 5, 65–6, 126, 176–8, 189, 192, 199, 213, 253, 257–74
Pharisees 5, 6, 8, 10, 12, 63
Pheroras 240
Philip the Arab 92
Phocas 254, 258, 261
Pilgrim of Bordeaux *see* Bordeaux Pilgrim
pilgrimages, pilgrims 79–81, 164, 222, 223
R. Pinhas b. Hama 121, 124, 164, 172, 209
R. Pinhas b. Yair 109
Piri-Shapur 189
pissim 97
pitkah 60
polemarchos 92
poll-tax 50, 95, 96, 97
polygamy 214
Pompey 6, 35
pontifex maximus 162, 186
population, number of 19, 132–3, 222, 241
postal service 94
pottery 24
poverty 104–6, 108
praefectus praetorio 195, 228
prayer 142–3; *see also Shema*
preachers, popular 72, 82, 119–20, 128–31
priests 2, 26, 57, 163, 198
privileges 10, 163
Proclus 181
Procopius of Caesarea 243
procurator ad capitularia Iudaeorum 49
procurators 10
proselytism 45, 81–3, 147–8, 150, 162, 171, 175, 214, 215, 267
Ptolemais *see* Acre
Ptolemies 2
Purim 218

Raba 58, 106, 165, 166
Rabbath-Moab 225
rabbinical students 26, 60. 61, 63, 110, 117
recruits 93, 129
Red Sea 251–3
relic of the cross *see* cross, relic of
relics 221
religio licita 45, 148, 162, 249

religious persecution 165–6, 190, 243, 250–1, 272
revolts, of the Jews 11–12, 36, 76–9, 173–4, 251, 254, 259; *see also* Bar Kokhba; Rome, wars against
revolts, of the Samaritans *see* Samaritans
rhetors 48
Romanus 251
Rome (city) 129, 146
Rome (empire) 6–7, 8–10, 33–51, 63, 64–71, 90–3, 108, 116, 125–32, 168–74; division of 211–12; wars against 11–12, 12–14, 141; *see also* Bar Kokhba; revolts, of the Jews
rosh ha-perek 237
Rufinus 191, 194, 201, 202
Rufus 73

Sabazius *see* Dionysus Sabazius
Sabbath 24, 30, 104–5, 181, 217
Sabbatical year 22, 95, 105, 108–9, 198
sacrifice 186–7, 188, 191–2, 266
Sadducees 5, 9
R. Safra 170
Samaria 132; *see also* Sebaste
Samaritans 41, 78, 179, 222, 250; revolts, of the 241–3, 251, 254
R. Samuel b. Abba 58
R. Samuel b. Isaac 124
R. Samuel b. Judah 105
R. Samuel ha-Katan 142
R. Samuel b. Nahman 96, 99, 130, 131
Samuel, prophet 221
sanctity of the Holy Land 26–7
Sanhedrin 12, 19, 48, 55–7, 60, 121, 180, 196, 228
santerim (watchmen) 107
Saturnalia 45
scholars (*talmide hakamim*) 62, 64, 110, 117–119
scribes (*soferim*) 2
sculptures 76
Scythopolis *see* Beth-Shean
Seat of Moses *see* Moses
Sebaeus 262, 273, 274
Sebaste 138, 190
sebomenoi see 'God-fearing'
Seleucids 2–4, 6
semikah see ordination
semissis 119
senatus consultum 50
Sennabris 181
Sepphoris 11, 18, 21, 22, 36, 38, 44, 46–7, 61, 99, 107, 126, 139, 168, 178–81
Septimius Severus 40, 41, 45–6, 47, 77–9, 91, 92, 102
Septuagint 148 and n. 35, 250
Sergius 272
Severus, Gaius Julius 43
Shahr-baraz 258, 265
Shapur I 126
Shapur II 176, 260
sheep-rearing 22, 28
Shefaram 19
Shekinah 80, 164

Shem 73
Shema 74, 272
Sheshbazzar 2
Shihin 24
ships 59
Shiroy 269
Shuthelah b. Ephraim 173
sicarii (*sikarikun*) 9, 29–30
Sidon 131
siege 93
Sigibert 273
signa 92
silver coins 102–3
R. Simeon 23
Simeon I 56
Simeon II 25, 56–7, 59–60, 67–8, 72, 119, 125
R. Simeon b. Abba 105, 107
Simeon of Beth Arsham 252
R. Simeon b. Eliezer 70
R. Simeon b. Halafta 68
Simeon the Hasmonaean 5
R. Simeon b. Judah 58, 60, 62, 103, 122
SimeonKamtra 80
Simeon b. Kozziba *see* Bar Kokhba
R. Simeon b. Lakish 26, 69, 70, 82, 92, 98, 105, 106, 107, 116, 118–19, 128
R. Simeon b. Pazzi 128
R. Simeon b. Yakim 23
R. Simeon b. Yohai 15, 26, 27, 48, 65, 71, 109, 128
R. Simlai 104
Simonias (Kh. Samuniya) 61
slaves 21, 162–3, 175, 228, 248
'small cattle' 28
soferim see scribes
soldiers' revolts 92–3
solidus 104
Solomon 170, 251; 'Seal of' 75
'Solomon's Stables' 201
Sophronius of Jerusalem 262
Sozomenus 191, 199
Stephen, proto-martyr 221
Stephanus 251
Stilicho 227
Stobi 62
stock of cattle 21
Strategius (of Mar Saba) 263
strategoi 47, 101, 130, 132
Susitha 78
Sykaminum 254
synagogues 25, 61, 64, 74–6, 141, 142 n. 15, 163, 195, 209–10, 212, 218–20, 225, 227–8, 238–40, 249–50, 251
Syria 25–6, 226
Syria-Palaestina 37, 42–3
Syrians 16

talit 73
Tamar 48
R. Tanhuma b. Abba 171
R. Tarfon 21, 139
taxes 49–50, 95–8, 116–18; collection of 98–102

Temple 1, 3–4, 10, 12, 141; rebuilding of
    191–204
Tertullian 51, 149
testes veritatis 150
Tetracomia 61
Thadun (Anthedon) 272
theatre 104–5
Theodora 247
Theodoret 58
Theodosius I 210–13
Theodosius II 212, 219, 227
Theophilus 254
Tiberias 22, 24, 38, 40, 46, 47, 61, 78, 92,
    98–9, 101, 104, 106, 117, 118, 125, 130,
    139, 168, 178–81, 187, 224, 248, 253, 260,
    271, 273
tironia see recruits
Tobiads 2
towns (cities) 10, 18–19, 47, 61, 77–8, 90,
    100–1
trade 23, 217, 222, 251
Trajan 13, 37, 38, 102
tremissis 119
tributum capitis see poll-tax
tributum solis see land-tax
Tsemah 109
tsumot see angaria
Tyre 22, 68, 127, 131, 267–8

Ulla 71
Uranius, Aurelius 92
Ursicinus 176–81
Usha 15, 22, 56
usurers 105

Vaballathus 126
Valens 209–10
Valentinian 209

veredarius 117
Vespasian 11, 49
villages, Jewish 16; Christian 139, 220
vine-scrolls 239
vivaria 22

Wailing Wall (Western Wall) 164
war damages 25–31
weaving 22, 59, 175, 179

Yabneh (Jamnia) 12, 16, 22, 55
R. Yannai 67, 69, 109
Yarmuk River 273
Yezdegerd 213
R. Yohanan (b. Napaha) 26, 27, 30, 44, 73,
    80, 82, 91, 94, 100, 101, 105, 106, 118, 122,
    124, 127, 128, 129, 130, 132, 133, 144
R. Yohanan the sandal-maker 15, 23
R. Yohanan b. Turta 66
R. Yohanan b. Zakkai 10, 56, 63, 65, 66, 141
R. Yose 122, 181
Yose of Beth Maon 120
R. Yose b. Halafta 15, 23, 47, 65, 68, 70, 71,
    80, 101, 121, 123
R. Yose b. Hanina 69, 101
R. Yose b. Kisma 66
R. Yudan 181, 198

Zealots 9–12, 13, 66, 79, 109, 171, 173, 198,
    242, 251
Zecharias (patriarch) 265–6
R. Zeira 94, 101, 119, 122, 124, 165, 172
zekenim ('elders') 121
Zeno, emperor 235, 242, 246
Zenobia 91, 126
Zerubbabel 2
Zerubbabel, The *Book of* 266, 268, 269
Zodiac 239